Advanced Research on Intelligent Building Construction and Management

Advanced Research on Intelligent Building Construction and Management

Guest Editors

Lin Liu
Taotao Shui
Chun Wang

MDPI

Basel • Beijing • Wuhan • Barcelona • Belgrade • Novi Sad • Cluj • Manchester

Guest Editors

Lin Liu
School of Civil and Transportation Engineering
Guangdong University of Technology
Guangzhou
China

Taotao Shui
School of Environment and Energy Engineering
Anhui Jianzhu University
Hefei
China

Chun Wang
School of Management
Chongqing University of Science and Technology
Chongqing
China

Editorial Office
MDPI AG
Grosspeteranlage 5
4052 Basel, Switzerland

This is a reprint of the Special Issue, published open access by the journal *Buildings* (ISSN 2075-5309), freely accessible at: https://www.mdpi.com/journal/buildings/special_issues/WJ6J742QA5.

For citation purposes, cite each article independently as indicated on the article page online and as indicated below:

Lastname, A.A.; Lastname, B.B. Article Title. *Journal Name* **Year**, *Volume Number*, Page Range.

ISBN 978-3-7258-7082-0 (Hbk)
ISBN 978-3-7258-7083-7 (PDF)
https://doi.org/10.3390/books978-3-7258-7083-7

Contents

About the Editors

Lin Liu

Lin Liu is an Associate Professor and a master's supervisor at the School of Civil and Transportation Engineering, Guangdong University of Technology, China. She obtained her B.S., M.S., and Ph.D. degrees from Harbin Institute of Technology. She has been dedicated to urban climate research since 2013, conducting in-depth investigations into fine-scale numerical simulation of urban climate multi-physics, formation mechanisms of spatiotemporal distributions of thermal environments and pollutants, and coupling effects of urban climate on energy consumption and carbon emissions. Her work provides a scientific basis and technical support for the multi-objective synergistic governance of urban cooling, energy conservation, and carbon reduction. She is the project leader of more than 10 research projects and has published more than 70 academic papers in international journals such as *Building and Environment*, *Urban Climate*, *Applied Energy*, etc.

Taotao Shui

Taotao Shui, Ph.D., is an Associate Professor and doctoral supervisor at the School of Environment and Energy Engineering, Anhui Jianzhu University. He also serves as the Deputy Director of the Department of Building Environment and Thermal Engineering and the Deputy Director of the Key Laboratory of Low-Carbon Energy and Artificial Environment at Anhui Jianzhu University. His research primarily focuses on urban climate prediction and assessment techniques, numerical simulation, and application of machine learning algorithms in building environments. He is the project leader of more than 10 research projects and has published more than 20 academic papers in international journals such as *Building and Environment*, *Urban Climate*, and *Applied Thermal Engineering*, etc.

Chun Wang

Chun Wang, Ph.D., is a master's supervisor and lecturer in the School of Management at Chongqing University of Science and Technology. From 2011, he was a member of the Youth Committee of Hunan Engineering Management Society, where he was mainly engaged in research in the fields of architectural digitization and digital protection of historical and cultural heritage. He has published nearly 10 papers in authoritative journals such as *Engineering, Construction and Architectural Management*, *Buildings*, and *Energy for Sustainable Development* and 1 monograph with a national publishing house. He has also authorized 1 invention patent, hosted 3 provincial and ministerial level projects, and has been responsible for over 10 horizontal projects with a total budget exceeding 1 million yuan.

buildings

MDPI

Article

Analysis of Progressive Collapse Resistance in Precast Concrete Frame with a Novel Connection Method

Qinghu Xu [1,2,*], Junjie Qian [1], Yu Zhang [1], Liping Tang [1,2], Dawei Man [1,2], Xuezhi Zhen [1] and Tingting Han [1,2]

1 School of Civil Engineering, Anhui Jianzhu University, Hefei 230009, China
2 BIM Engineering Center of Anhui Province, Hefei 230051, China
* Correspondence: qinghx@ahjzu.edu.cn

Abstract: The configuration of beam–column joints in precast concrete (PC) building structures varies widely, and different connection methods significantly affect the progressive collapse resistance of the structure. This study investigates the progressive collapse resistance of an innovative beam–column connection node frame. Finite element models of four-story, two-span space frame structures made of reinforced concrete (RC) and PC were developed using ANSYS 14.0/LS-DYNA R5.x software, employing nonlinear dynamic and static analysis to examine structural collapse behavior under bottom middle or corner column damage. Numerical results indicate that following the failure of the middle or corner column due to explosion loading, the vertical displacement and collapse rate of the PC structure with the novel connection method are less than those of the RC structure during collapse progression. Furthermore, upon removal of the middle or corner column, the residual load-carrying capacity of the PC structure with the innovative connection increased by 7% and 3.7%, respectively, compared to the RC structure. This suggests that PC structures with this type of connection demonstrate superior performance in resisting progressive collapse, offering valuable insights for future engineering applications.

Keywords: precast concrete; numerical modeling; collapsed settlement; structural analysis

1. Introduction

Structures are often subjected to damage and destruction due to accidental loads caused by factors such as explosions, fires, and impacts [1]. In cases where the building is unable to withstand such loads, these events may result in local or partial damage to the structure's substructure. In some cases, this collapse can extend beyond the initial damage, resulting in large-scale destruction disproportionate to the initial impact. This phenomenon is commonly known as progressive collapse [2]. Due to the catastrophic consequences of building collapses, there is an increasing global emphasis on addressing the issue of progressive collapse. The General Services Administration (GSA) [3] and the Department of Defense (DoD) [4] have introduced comprehensive directives for structural design.

Scholars have conducted extensive research in recent years on the resistance of reinforced concrete structures to progressive collapse [5–10]. Fedorova et al. [11] dis-cussed the use of indirect reinforcement as a method of protection in reinforced concrete structures and numerically analyzed a two-span continuous beam, which showed the effectiveness of reinforcement in protecting the structural system from progressive collapse. To investigate the effect of structural redundancy on reinforced concrete frame structures' resistance to continuous collapse, Ameri et al. [12] analyzed three reinforced concrete frame models with different levels of redundancy by nonlinear dynamic methods, and the results showed that increasing the redundancy improves the resistance of reinforced concrete frame structures to continuous collapse. Due to the growing focus on low-carbon environmental protection, precast buildings have become widely adopted. As a result, researchers have also begun to focus on the progressive collapse resistance of precast structures [13–18]. Kang et al. [19]

conducted experimental investigations on four distinct types of precast concrete frames, aiming to delve into the progressive collapse resistance exhibited by frames featuring discontinuous steel reinforcement. Feng et al. [20] conducted four static loading tests and two dynamic loading tests to investigate the progressive collapse resistance of conventional precast concrete frames. The test results showed that the connection details and beam reinforcement ratio had a significant effect on the progressive collapse resistance.

Due to the high cost and lengthy duration of experiments, scholars often utilize a combination of experimental and numerical simulation approaches when studying such phenomena [21,22]. To enhance the robustness against progressive collapse in precast buildings, El-sanadedy [23] numerically investigated 11 sets of half-scale beam–column combinations with newly developed precast moment connections using LS-DYNA software. The conclusions of the study highlight that the adoption of innovative connection techniques can significantly reduce the risk of progressive collapse in precast concrete structures. Zhou et al. [24] designed two half-scale reinforced concrete and precast concrete moment substructures to evaluate the asymptotic collapse performance in the presence of sudden loss in the column. Numerical simulations using ABAQUS 2020 finite element software were analyzed and found to be in good agreement with the experimental results.

In conclusion, the progressive collapse of precast concrete substructures or planar frames has been studied more frequently, while the collapse resistance of monolithic structures has been studied less. Therefore, this article analyzes the monolithic frame of the structure, which greatly compensates for the shortcomings of the previous research. At the same time, a new method of connection is proposed, and exploration and research are carried out with regard to the progressive collapse resistance of precast concrete with this new type of connection. These studies provide a reference for future scholars to study the progressive collapse resistance of monolithic frame structures and provide new ideas for the design of new nodes in precast concrete structures.

2. Substructure Finite Element Model Verification

This paper focuses on the joints described in reference [25] as the subject of investigation. The schematic diagram of the splicing node and the site photograph of the substructure concrete pouring are shown in figures 2-3 and 2-4, respectively, as cited in reference [25]. This assembled structure comprises five components characterized by three precast column segments with cantilever beams and two precast beam segments. The longitudinal reinforcement in the joint is bent at a 90-degree angle and subsequently securely welded to the steel connector. The steel connector consists of an end steel plate and four spliced steel plates arranged in a two-row, two-column configuration. High-strength bolts are used to connect each precast segment. The spliced joint area of the precast beam–column segment has a length of 200 mm. Once the assembly is complete, the concrete is poured to create a solid structure.

2.1. *Selection and Establishment of Finite Element Model*

The reinforced concrete component S1 and precast concrete component SS-2 from reference [25] are chosen as the basis for model verification. The cross-section and cross-section reinforcement of the precast concrete members are the same as those of the reinforced concrete members, and only the difference in the connection node settings is considered to compare the differences between the two types of members. The column section has a side length of 200 mm, while the beam section measures 200 mm × 130 mm. The columns are constructed with 16 mm HRB400 longitudinal bars, while the beams utilize 12 mm HRB400 longitudinal bars. The spacing of the encrypted area of the hoop reinforcement of the component is taken as 50 mm, and the spacing of the non-encrypted area is taken as 100 mm. For reinforced concrete component S1, the encrypted area of the beams is within a length of 550 mm from the nodes of the columns, and the encrypted area of the columns is within the failing columns and within a length of 450 mm from the top of the columns of the side columns as a starting point; for precast concrete component SS-2, the encrypted area of the beams is within the cantilevered beams in the prefabricated column segments. For precast concrete component SS-2, the encryption interval for beams is the portion of the cantilever beam in the prefabricated column section. Substructure models for both reinforced concrete and precast concrete are developed, and their numerical simulation results are compared with experimental tests to evaluate the reliability of the models. The concrete frame substructure is modeled in isolation without considering the slip between reinforcement and concrete, and the model mesh sizes are 50 mm, 25 mm, and 20 mm. The member dimensions and the section dimensions are shown in figures 2–5 of reference [25], and the finite element model is shown in Figures 1 and 2.

(a) (b)

Figure 1. Finite element model of the substructure: (**a**) Reinforced concrete substructure frame; (**b**) precast concrete substructure frame.

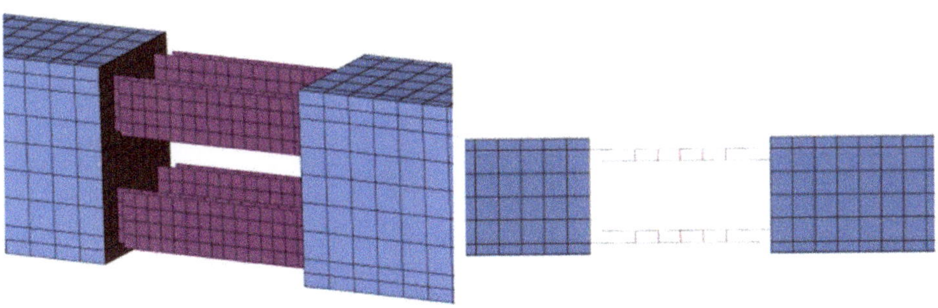

Figure 2. Finite element schematic of beam–column joint.

2.1.1. Material Model

The finite element model of concrete utilizes the SOLID164 solid element, with the material model being 072R3 material (*MAT_CONCRETE_DAMAGE_REL3) in LS-DYNA. The finite element model of reinforcement and bolts adopts the BEAM161 beam cell, with the material model being *MAT_PLASTIC_KINEMATIC. The connection section steel and column foot steel plate are modeled using the SHELL163 shell unit. The connection section steel adopts the *MAT_PLASTIC_KINEMATIC material model, while the column foot steel plate adopts the *MAT_ELASTIC material model.

2.1.2. Boundary Conditions and Loads

The model enforces omnidirectional displacement constraints on the joints of the column base steel plates on both sides. The left and right beam ends are simulated using the COMBI165 spring element and the MASS166 mass element. The *MAT_SPRING_ELASTIC keyword is employed to represent the lateral displacement constraints in the test. The keyword *BOUNDARY_PRESCRIBED_MOTION_RIGID_LOCAL (Disp) is utilized in combination with the *DEFINE_CURVE keyword to apply displacement to the failed column.

2.2. Test Validation

According to the test program in the literature [25], perforated steel plates are welded at the bottom of column A and column C, and the components are fixed by high-tensile bolts. The pre-buried high-strength screws at both ends of the component beam structure and the steel plates arranged at the top of Column A and Column C are connected to the A-frame, which is bolted to the steel beams, and all the steel beams are fixed by ground anchors. Hydraulic jacks are arranged at the top of columns A and C. The force applied to the jacks reacts on the top of the side columns. The loading action of the frame is realized by counterweights arranged on the span of the beams. The bottom of the center column is provided with a temporary steel support, which is connected to the steel beam by means of a pivot. The sudden failure of the center column is realized by hitting the steel support at the bottom of the center column with an external force so that it leaves the bottom of the center column quickly.

2.3. Comparative Analysis of the Results

This paper selects the S1 reinforced concrete structural model for comparative verification of the first group and the SS-2 precast concrete structure model for comparative verification of the second group. Figure 3 presents the load–displacement curves and experimental outcomes for the S1 and SS-2 finite element analyses.

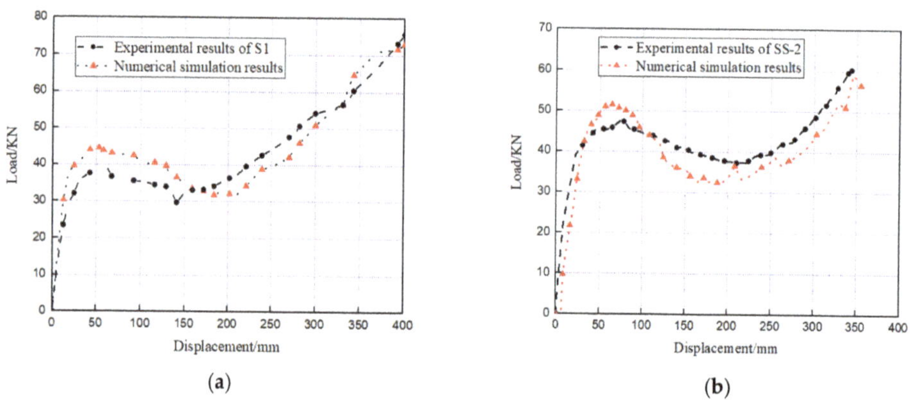

Figure 3. Load–displacement curve of specimen test and simulation results: (**a**) S1; (**b**) SS-2.

The first load peak of specimen S1 is 40 KN, while the finite element simulation result is 44.2 KN, resulting in an error of 10.5%. The initial load peak of the SS-2 specimen is 47.8 KN, whereas the finite element simulation result is 51.9 KN, resulting in an error of 8.58%. The load–displacement curve trends of the two simulation sets exhibit a close resemblance, confirming the accuracy of the finite element model developed in this study. Building upon this foundation, a spatial frame structure is established to analyze the performance of progressive collapse resistance.

3. Analysis of Precast Concrete Space Frame Structure Based on Direct Dynamic Method

3.1. Finite Element Model

In accordance with the code for the design of concrete structures [26] and the code for seismic design of buildings [27], a four-story, two-span concrete frame structure is designed using PKPM V5.2.3 software. The structure consists of one span in the x-direction and two spans in the y-direction, with a column spacing of 4 m and a floor height of 3 m. The cross-sectional dimensions of the columns used are 400 mm × 400 mm and the beams are 350 mm high and 250 mm wide. The novel connections in the article are present at the highlighted locations in the model of the precast frame structure. Figure 4 shows the models of the reinforced concrete and precast concrete frame structure.

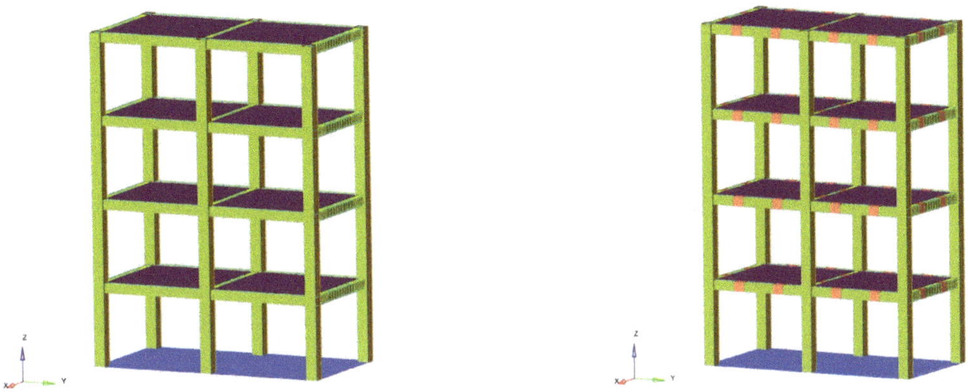

(a) (b)

Figure 4. The models of the frame structure: (**a**) Reinforced concrete frame; (**b**) precast concrete frame.

3.1.1. Basic Parameters

The structure consists of one span in the x-direction and two spans in the y-direction, with a column spacing of 4 m and a floor height of 3 m. The column sections have dimensions of 400 mm × 400 mm and are reinforced with eight HRB400 steel bars with a diameter of 22 mm. The beam sections measure 350 mm × 250 mm and are reinforced with six HRB400 steel bars with a diameter of 20 mm. The column stirrups are placed within a 500 mm range from the end of the columns, while the beam stirrups are placed within an 800 mm range near the column nodes. The stirrups consist of HRB335 steel bars with a diameter of 10 mm, and the spacing between them is 100 mm. Figure 5 shows the dimensions and reinforcement of the structure.

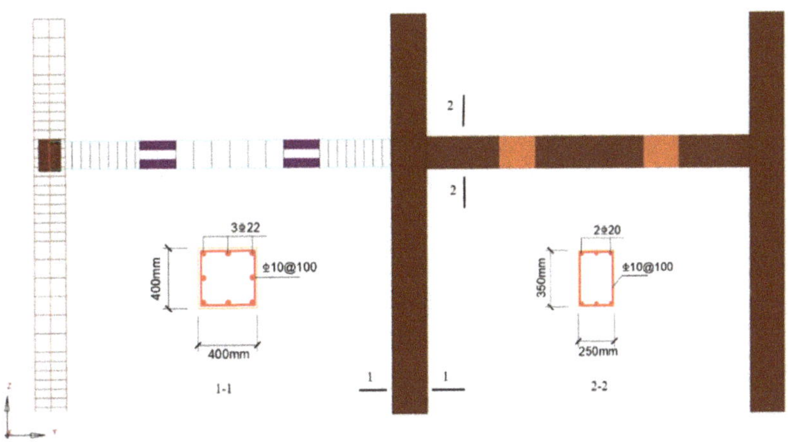

Figure 5. The dimensions and reinforcement of the structure.

3.1.2. Material Parameters

The damping of the material is considered to be Rayleigh damping and the damping ratio is taken as 0.05.

For the concrete material model, the concrete material model No. 072R3 (*MAT_CONCRETE _DAMAGE_REL3) from LSDYNA [28] is selected, which is to be used in conjunction with the equation of state, where the concrete pressure–volume–strain relationship is defined by means of the defined equation of state 8 (*EOS_TABULATED_COMPACTION). COMPACTION). The material parameters of the concrete are shown in Tables 1 and 2 [25]. Cracking and spalling failure occurs when the concrete reaches a certain level of deformation, and the failure of the concrete unit is controlled by defining the maximum strain in the keyword *MAT_ADD_EROSION.

Table 1. Precast concrete material model parameters.

Variable	MID	RO	PR	A0	RSIZE	UCF	LCRATE
Magnitude	1	0.0024	0.2	−40	0.03937	145	723

Note: MID is the material model number; RO is the density of the material in g/mm^3; PR is the Poisson's ratio of the material; A0 is the compressive strength of the concrete in MPa; RSIZE is the converted value between units of mm and inches; UCF is the converted value between units of MPa and psi; and LCRATE is the strain rate curve of the concrete.

Table 2. Post-cast concrete material model parameters.

Variable	MID	RO	PR	A0	RSIZE	UCF	LCRATE
Magnitude	2	0.0024	0.2	−45	0.03937	145	723

Note: MID is the material model number; RO is the density of the material in g/mm^3; PR is the Poisson's ratio of the material; A0 is the compressive strength of the concrete in MPa; RSIZE is the converted value between units of mm and inches; UCF is the converted value between units of MPa and psi; and LCRATE is the strain rate curve of the concrete.

The BEAM161 beam cell was chosen for the rebar finite element model cell, which is commonly used to simulate the strain produced by the rebar. The material model is *MAT_PLASTIC_KINEMATIC, which can be used to describe the isotropic hardening and hardening plasticity model, and the strain rate effect of the material can also be considered. The specific parameters are listed in Table 3.

Table 3. Reinforcement material model parameters.

Variable	MID	RO	E	PR	SRC	SRP	FS
Magnitude	3	0.00785	2.1×10^5	0.3	40	5	0.12

Note: MID is the model number of the material; RO is the density of the material in g/mm^3; E is the Young's modulus in MPa; PR is the Poisson's ratio of the material; SRC and SRP are the strain rate parameters; FS is the failure strain.

*MAT_PLASTIC_KINEMATIC was selected for the material model of the connecting steel and *MAT_ELASTIC was selected for the material model of the steel plate at the foot of the column. The steel plate of the column foot was set to the elastic state.

BEAM161 unit was selected for the finite element modeling of the bolt, whereas *MAT_PLASTIC_KINEMATIC was selected for material modeling.

3.1.3. Background and Model Parameters

Over the past few decades, there has been a proliferation of both man-made and accidental explosions. Explosions can damage structural components and may lead to disproportionate building collapse. For example, in the 1968 partial collapse of Ronan Point tower in England, a gas explosion on the 18th floor led to a cascade of failures that destroyed the entire corner of the building [29]. Protecting civil buildings from blast loads has become a popular research topic.

Columns, as key load-bearing members of a building, play a major role in the process of blasting loads. The article only uses the column as the member of the blast load scenario that carries the blast pressure.

To control material failure under explosive loads, the effective plastic strain and volume tensile strain are taken into account, following the approach presented by Xu et al. [30]. In the numerical simulation, the primary criterion for implementing the erosion algorithm is that the principal tensile strain reaches 0.01. The reasonable values for the two erosion criteria were determined based on the studies by Shi et al. [31] and Kim et al. [32]. Based on the numerical results, the erosion principal strain criterion and shear strain criterion have limits of 0.15 and 0.9, respectively. The explosion load is applied to the surface of the structure in the x-axis direction using the LOAD_BLAST_ENHANCED command in LS-DYNA. Based on the TNT equivalent and the distance from the target position, the dynamic load on the surface of the unit is automatically generated using the BLE method to simulate the impact of the explosion. Figure 6 illustrates the blast points located within the first 3 m of the middle and corner columns.

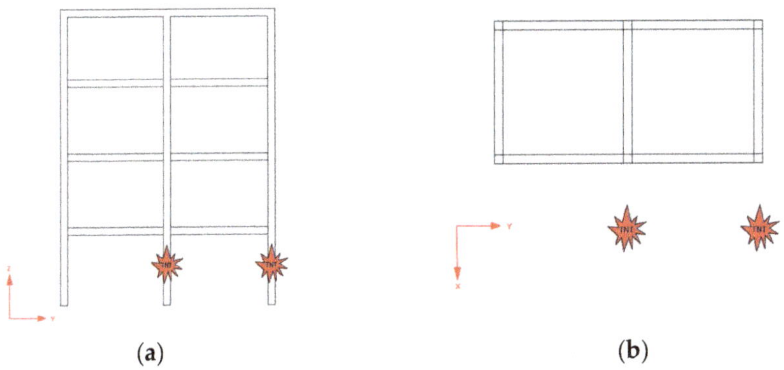

Figure 6. The location of the blast points: (**a**) Y-Z plane; (**b**) X-Y plane.

In this paper, the frame structure is subjected to the corresponding constant and live loads prior to the application of an explosive load at t = 100 ms. Various quantities of explosives are considered to induce initial damage to the selected column and minimal initial damage to the adjacent column within the range of proportional distances from 0.42 $m \cdot kg^{-1/3}$ to 0.73 $m \cdot kg^{-1/3}$. To minimize the damage to the adjacent column elements, a proportional distance of 0.48 $m \cdot kg^{-1/3}$ is selected to mitigate the extent of structural collapse.

3.2. Simulation Results under Blasting Load

3.2.1. Analysis of Bottom-Middle Column Damage

Figures 7 and 8 illustrate the state of the frame at 300 ms and 700 ms, respectively. When the blast shock wave reaches the structural columns, the central column at the bottom level is subjected to the blast impact, subsequently initiating structural deformation. This deformation is characterized by significant plastic strains observed at the first- and second-level center columns, as well as the beam–column nodes at each level. Upon the failure of the critical columns, the superstructure of the ground floor center column undergoes a downward displacement, while plastic strain propagates from the beam–column nodes to the mid-span of the beams and the middle of the floor slabs. At 700 ms, the beams on each floor of the reinforced concrete (RC) structure exhibit pronounced bending deformation. In contrast, the precast concrete (PC) structure displays varying degrees of bending at the beam nodal splices due to the different connection methods employed for the precast beams.

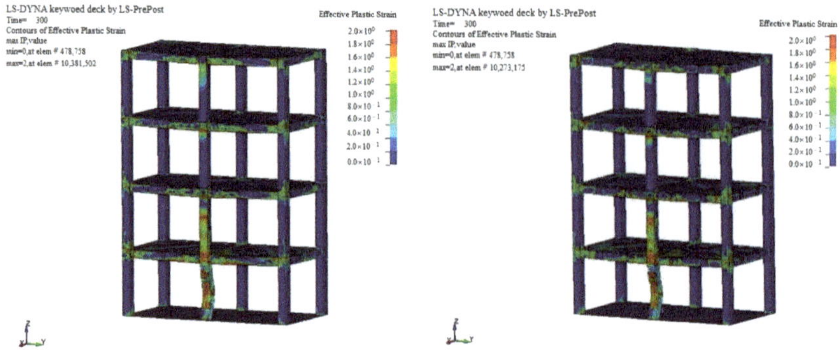

(a) (b)

Figure 7. The structural response of a building at 300 ms following damage to the middle column: (**a**) RC structure; (**b**) PC structure.

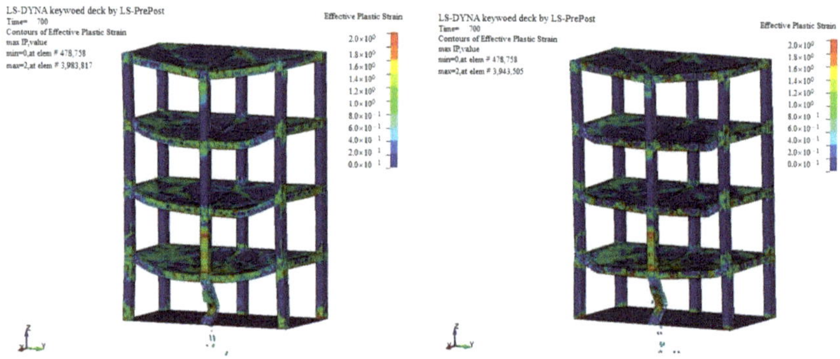

(a) (b)

Figure 8. The structural response of a building at 700 ms when the middle column is damaged: (**a**) RC structure; (**b**) PC structure.

Figure 9 presents the displacement–time curves in the z-direction for the fourth-floor vertices of the structures during the damage of the middle column. The curves reveal that at 100 ms, the vertical displacement of the reinforced concrete is −0.43 mm, while the precast concrete measures −0.37 mm. Upon the application of the blast load at 100 ms, the failure of the critical column triggers a downward collapse of the entire structure. Since the structure has not yet entirely lost its bearing capacity, the difference in vertical displacement between the two structures is not substantial. After 320 ms, as structural deformation and collapse progress, the disparity in vertical displacement between the reinforced concrete and precast concrete structures widens. At 400 ms, the vertical displacement of the reinforced concrete reaches −153.25 mm, while that of the precast concrete reaches displacement of −144.78 mm; at 500 ms, the vertical displacement of the reinforced concrete reaches −265.31 mm, while the displacement of the precast concrete reaches −220.22 mm; at 600 ms, the vertical displacement of the reinforced concrete reaches −458.46 mm, while that of the precast concrete reaches −342.53 mm; at 700 ms, the vertical displacement of the reinforced concrete reaches −744.29 mm, while that of the precast concrete reaches −539.36 mm. At 750 ms, the vertical displacement of the reinforced concrete reaches −921.61 mm, while that of the precast concrete reaches −671.54 mm. This indicates that the precast concrete created using this particular connection method exhibits greater collapse resistance compared to reinforced concrete.

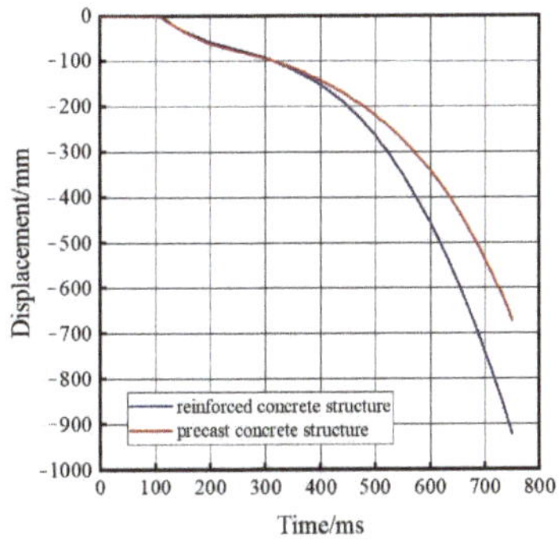

Figure 9. The displacement–time curves in the z-direction for the fourth-floor vertices of the structures during the damage of the middle column.

Figure 10 presents the velocity–time curve in the z-direction for the vertices of the middle column on the first floor. From the figure, it is evident that upon application of the blast load to the key column at 100 ms, the vertical velocity of the node at the top of the column experiences a rapid increase immediately after the impact damage. Subsequently, the node velocity briefly decreases due to the stiffness of the structure itself and the influence of the beams. Furthermore, as the damaged bottom column loses its supporting effect on the superstructure, the adjacent span of the damaged column becomes unstable and begins to displace downwards. The velocity of the node in the z-direction begins to rise. During the initial stage of collapse, the nodal velocities of both the reinforced and precast concrete are similar. However, as the collapse progresses, the nodal velocities of the reinforced concrete exhibit a greater acceleration compared to the precast concrete.

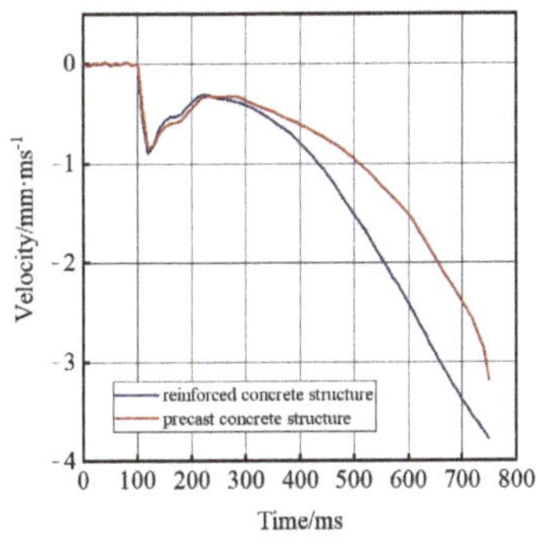

Figure 10. The velocity–time curve in the z-direction for the vertices of the middle column on the first floor.

To investigate the collapse behavior of the structure in the x-direction, the midpoint of the middle column on the second floor is selected for analysis. Figure 11 shows the velocity–time curve in the x-direction at the midpoint of the middle column on the second floor. As observed in the figure, at 100 ms, the blast load is gradually applied to the key column of the structure. Subsequently, the x-directional velocity of the node experiences a rapid increase within a short time period after the first-story middle column is damaged by the impact, followed by impact-induced damage to the bottom column from the x-direction. However, the nodal velocity returns to 0 since the tensile structural member in the x-direction remains intact, preventing structural collapse. As the support from the superstructure is lost due to the damage sustained by the bottom column, the structure collapses inwards, and the x-directional velocity of the node begins to increase. From the figure, it is evident that during the initial stage of collapse, the nodal velocities of both reinforced and precast concrete are similar. However, as the collapse progresses, the nodal velocities of reinforced concrete exhibit faster development compared to precast concrete.

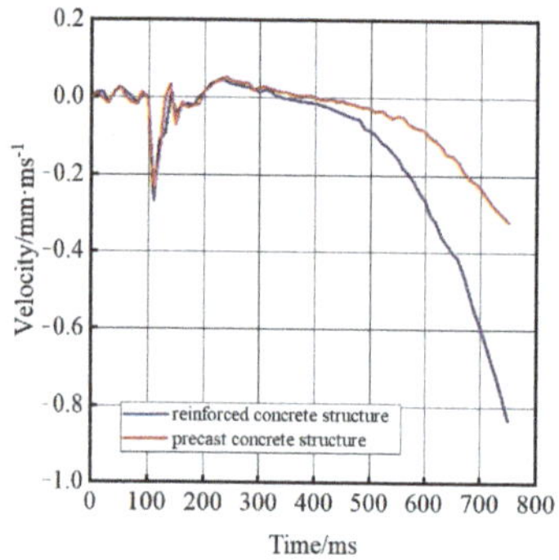

Figure 11. The velocity–time curve in the x-direction at the midpoint of the middle column on the second floor.

3.2.2. Analysis of Bottom-Corner Column Damage

Figures 12 and 13 show the states of the frame at 300 ms and 700 ms, respectively. From the figures, it is evident that once the blast shock wave reaches the structural columns, the bottom corner column absorbs the blast impact, initiating structural deformation. This deformation is characterized by larger plastic strains observed at the corner columns of the first and second floors, as well as at the nodes of the beams and columns on each floor. As the key columns fail, the superstructure of the ground floor corner column undergoes a downward displacement. By 700 ms, severe bending deformation is observed in the beams on each floor of the reinforced concrete (RC) structure, resulting in a complete collapse of the structure.

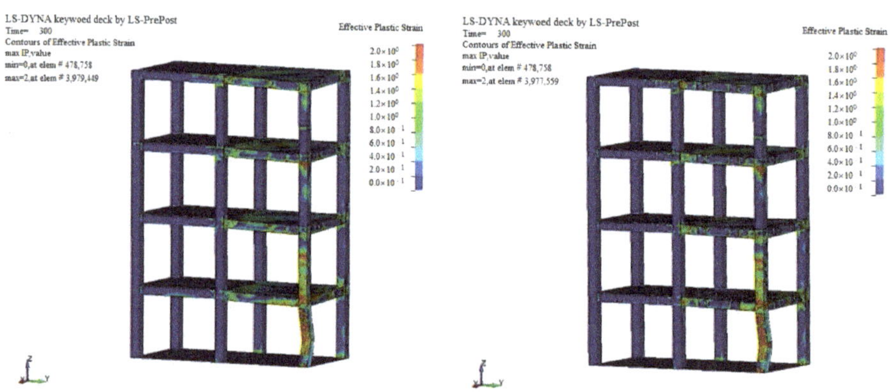

(**a**) (**b**)

Figure 12. The structural response of a building at 300 ms when the corner column is damaged: (**a**) RC structure; (**b**) PC structure.

Figure 14 presents the displacement–time curves in the z-direction for the fourth-floor vertices of the structures during the damage to the corner column. As observed in the figure, when the blast load is applied at 100 ms and the key column fails, resulting in the downward collapse of the structure, the vertical displacement of the reinforced concrete is greater than that of the precast concrete. However, before 200 ms, the vertical displacement gap between the two structures is not significant, as the structure has not yet fully lost its load-carrying capacity. As the structural deformation and collapse progress, the vertical displacement of the reinforced concrete exceeds that of the precast concrete. At 400 ms, the vertical displacement of the reinforced concrete reaches −231.78 mm, while that of the precast concrete reaches −166.25 mm; at 500 ms, the vertical displacement of the reinforced concrete reaches −415.43 mm, while that of the precast concrete reaches −317.22 mm; at 600 ms, the vertical displacement of the reinforced concrete reaches −740.76 mm, while that of the precast concrete reaches −594.52 mm; at 700 ms, the vertical displacement of the reinforced concrete reaches −1240.33 mm, while that of the precast concrete reaches −1040.28 mm. By 750 ms, the vertical displacement of the reinforced concrete reaches −1537.77 mm, while that of the precast concrete reaches −1316.55 mm. The precast concrete, created with this specific connection method, exhibits stronger collapse resistance compared to reinforced concrete when the corner columns are damaged.

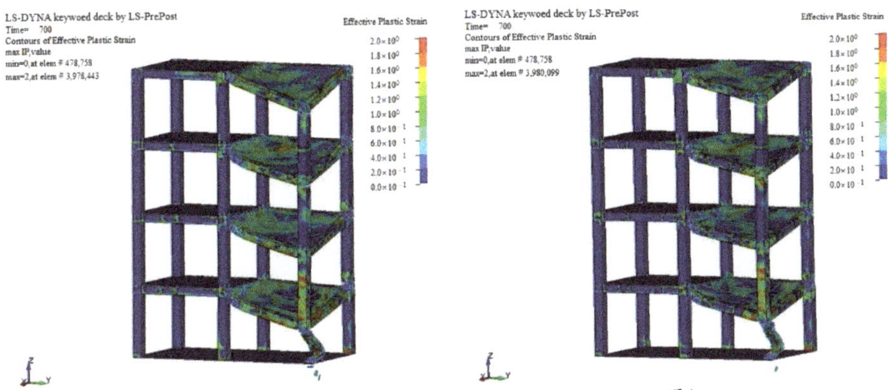

(a) (b)

Figure 13. The structural response of a building at 700 ms when the corner column is damaged: (**a**) RC structure; (**b**) PC structure.

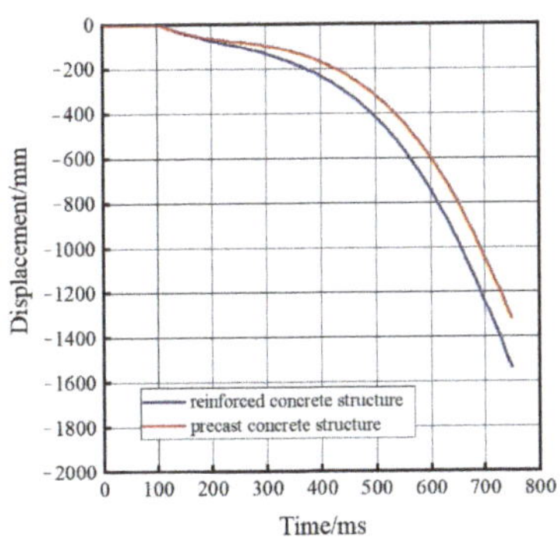

Figure 14. The displacement–time curves in the z-direction for the fourth-floor vertices of the structures during the damage of the corner column.

Figure 15 shows the velocity–time curve in the z-direction for the vertices of the corner column on the first floor. From the figure, it is evident that at 100 ms, the blast load is gradually applied to the key column of the structure. Consequently, the vertical velocity of the node at the top of the column undergoes a rapid increase within a short time period as a result of the impact damage. Afterwards, the node velocity experiences a temporary decrease caused by the inherent stiffness of the structure and the influence of the beam. When damage occurs to the bottom column, its ability to support the superstructure weakens, leading to instability in the adjacent span and subsequent downward displacement. The velocity of the node in the z-direction begins to rise. During the initial stage of collapse, the nodal velocities of both reinforced and precast concrete are similar. However, as the collapse progresses, the collapse velocity of the reinforced concrete becomes faster.

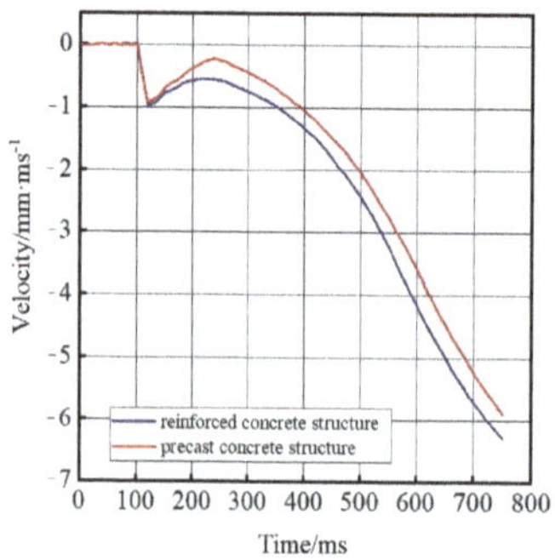

Figure 15. The velocity–time curve in the z-direction for the vertices of the corner column on the first floor.

To investigate the collapse behavior of the structure in the x-direction, the midpoint of the corner column on the second floor is selected for analysis. Figure 16 shows the velocity–time curve in the x-direction at the midpoint of the corner column on the second floor. As observed in the figure, at 100 ms, the blasting load is gradually applied to the key column of the structure. Subsequently, the x-directional velocity of the node experiences a rapid increase within a short time period following the impact damage of the corner column on the first floor and the impact force from the x-direction of the bottom column. However, the node velocity returns to 0, since the tensile structural member in the x-direction remains intact, preventing structural collapse. As the support provided by the bottom column is lost, the structure of the adjacent span cannot maintain stability and begins to displace downward, resulting in inward tipping of the structure. Concurrently, the x-directional velocity of the node initiates development. From the figure, it is evident that during the early stage of collapse, the nodal velocities of both reinforced and precast concrete are similar. However, as the collapse progresses, the nodal velocities of the reinforced concrete develop faster than those of the precast concrete.

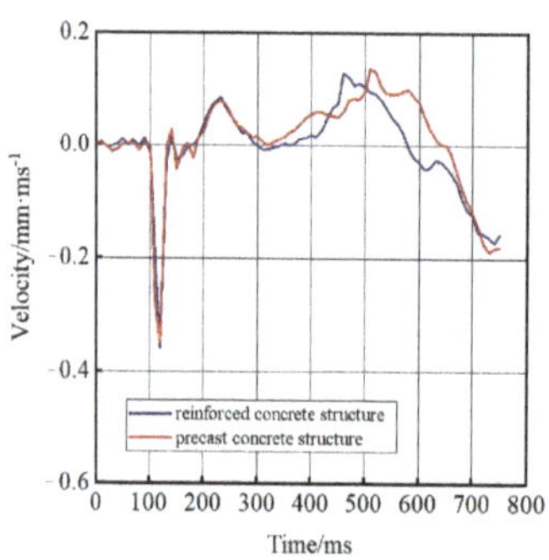

Figure 16. The velocity–time curve in the x-direction at the midpoint of the corner column on the second floor.

4. Pushdown Analysis

In nonlinear static Pushdown analysis using the damaged span loading mode [33], it is essential to apply increasing vertical loads to the damaged span structure, which will eventually lead to its collapse. In the load application process, the load coefficient is defined as the ratio of the vertical bearing capacity produced by the structure to the vertical bearing capacity of the initial design. This relationship is represented by Equation (1).

$$\alpha = \frac{P_t}{P_0} \tag{1}$$

where α represents the load coefficient, P_t represents to the vertical bearing capacity of the structure, and P_0 represents the vertical bearing capacity of the initial design of the structure. P_0 refers to the collapse analysis load combination in DOD [4] specification.

During the assessment of the frame beam's bearing capacity, the ultimate deformation of the beam is considered to be the failure criterion for the beam member. As per the requirements outlined in DoD [4] and the current progressive collapse resistance code, failure occurs when the vertical displacement of the column end reaches one-fifth of the beam span. In the LS-DYNA simulated loading process, the structure is deemed to have experienced progressive collapse when the vertical displacement of the lower end of the column reaches 800 mm.

Figures 17 and 18 represent structural models where columns have been removed from various positions. The Pushdown analysis is conducted on the residual structure after the removal of the middle column in the reinforced concrete (RC) structure and the corner column in the precast concrete (PC) structure. This analysis aims to compare the relative load–displacement relationships of the different structures.

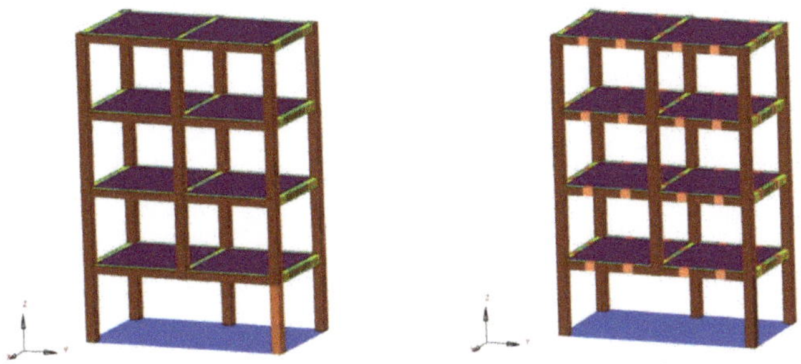

(**a**) (**b**)

Figure 17. Structural model of the bottom middle column removal: (**a**) Reinforced concrete structure model; (**b**) precast concrete structure model.

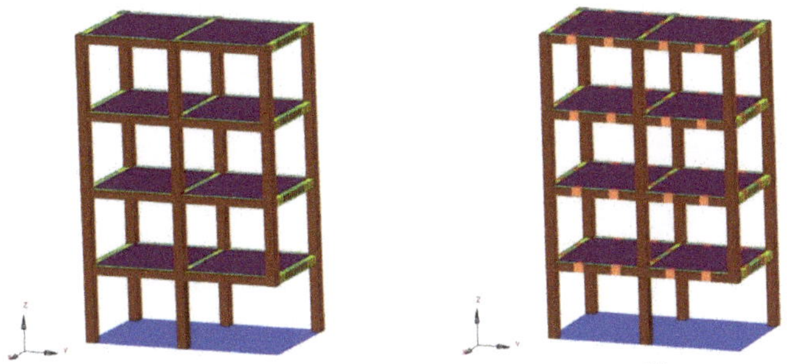

(**a**) (**b**)

Figure 18. Structural model of the bottom corner column removal: (**a**) Reinforced concrete structure model; (**b**) precast concrete structure model.

4.1. Analysis of the Results of Removing the Bottom Middle Column

Figure 19 presents the relative load–displacement curves derived from Pushdown analysis performed on the remaining structures subsequent to the removal of middle columns in both reinforced concrete and precast concrete structures. The Pushdown curves reveal a notable augmentation in the structural bearing capacity during the initial elastic phase as the vertical displacement of the frame progresses. However, as the structure transitions into the plastic phase, the structural bearing capacity increases only marginally, even as the vertical displacement rapidly increases. The relative load coefficients (P_t/P_0) for the vertical displacement of the failed column at 800 mm are 2.58 and 2.76 for the reinforced concrete and precast concrete structures, respectively. This suggests that the vertical ultimate load capacity of the remaining structure after column failure can reach 2.58 g and 2.76 g, where g = 1.2 G + 0.5 L. Furthermore, the precast joint with this specific connection method enhances the relative load capacity of the remaining structures by 7% in the event of middle column failure. This finding highlights the fact that the structure incorporating this type of precast concrete frame possesses sufficient redundancy and load-bearing capacity to contain the unbalanced load stemming from the initial failure of the middle column, thus averting the progressive collapse of the entire structure.

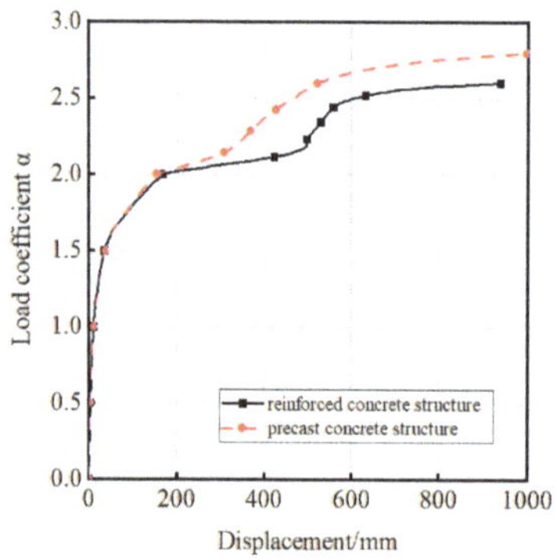

Figure 19. The relative load–displacement curve of the remaining structure with middle columns removed.

4.2. Analysis of the Results of Removing the Bottom Corner Column

Figure 20 shows the relative load–displacement curves derived from Pushdown analysis performed on the remaining structures subsequent to the removal of corner columns. The curve reveals that when the corner column of the structures fails, the corresponding relative load coefficient (P_t/P_0) for a vertical displacement of 800 mm is 2.16 and 2.24, respectively. Additionally, the precast joint utilizing this particular connection method enhances the relative load capacity of the remaining structures by 3.7%.

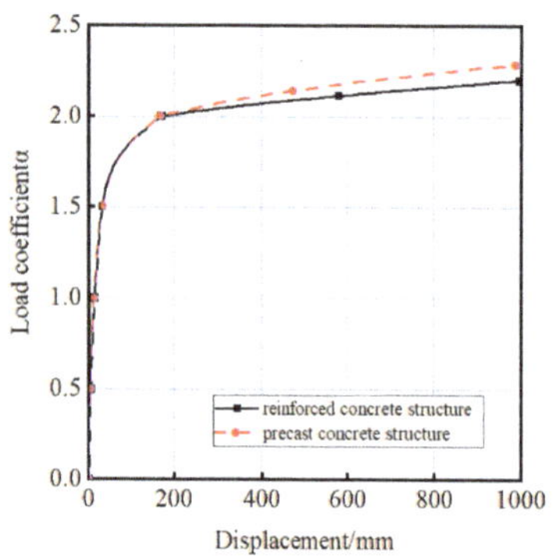

Figure 20. The relative load–displacement curve of the remaining structure with corner columns removed.

5. Conclusions

This paper focuses on a novel type of precast concrete frame structure. A four-story two-span spatial frame is constructed to investigate the impact of precast joints on the collapse resistance of the structure. The study, after a rigorous examination of the data and thorough analysis of the results, has yielded several crucial conclusions.

During the nonlinear dynamic analysis, the reinforced concrete structure experiences a maximum vertical displacement of −921.61 mm at 750 ms when the middle column fails. In contrast, the precast concrete structure demonstrates a vertical displacement of −671.54 mm under the same circumstances. Furthermore, in the absence of the corner column, the reinforced concrete structure experiences a maximum vertical displacement of −1537.77 mm, while that of the precast concrete structure reaches −1316.55 mm. Comparing these results with those of the reinforced concrete structure, it is evident that the remaining structural bearing capacity is weaker in the event of corner column failure. Consequently, attention must be given to the design of corner columns in building structures. With the failure of the critical columns, the superstructure of the corner column at the ground level experienced downward displacement. This reveals the vulnerability of critical elements of the structure to load and the effect on the stability of the overall structure.

By conducting Pushdown analysis and comparing the relative load–displacement curves of the precast concrete frame and reinforced concrete structures, it is observed that the utilization of precast nodes increases the relative load capacity of the remaining structure by 7% and 3.7% when the middle column and the corner column fail, respectively.

A comparison and analysis are conducted under nonlinear dynamic and static conditions after the key columns in various positions are removed. In the elastic stage, the structure exhibits greater integrity and collapse resistance. However, as the structure transitions into the plastic stage, the collapse and failure mechanisms progress at a faster rate. Numerical results demonstrate that the precast concrete building, which employs this novel connection method, exhibits improved resistance to progressive collapse. These findings hold significant value for engineering applications, offering valuable insights for future engineering design.

Author Contributions: Conceptualization, Funding acquisition and data curation, Q.X. Writing—original draft and writing—review & editing, J.Q.; Software and validation, Y.Z.; Visualization and project administration, L.T.; Formal analysis and supervision, D.M.; Investigation and methodology, X.Z.; Visualization and project administration, T.H. All authors have read and agreed to the published version of the manuscript.

Funding: This study was financially supported by BIM Engineering Center of Anhui Province (AHBIM2021ZR02 and AHBIM20202ZR) and the Project of Science and Technology Plan of Department of Housing and Urban–Rural Development of Anhui Province (2023-YF127).

Data Availability Statement: Available by authors.

Conflicts of Interest: The authors declare no conflicts of interest.

References

1. Ellingwood, B.R. Mitigating risk from abnormal loads and progressive collapse. *J. Perform. Constr. Facil.* **2006**, *20*, 315–323. [CrossRef]
2. Osteraas, J.D. Murrah building bombing revisited: A qualitative assessment of blast damage and collapse patterns. *J. Perform. Constr. Facil.* **2006**, *20*, 330–335. [CrossRef]
3. United States General Services Administration. *Progressive Collapse Analysis and Design Guidelines for New Federal Office Buildings and Major Modernization Projects*; United States General Services Administration: Washington, DC, USA, 2016.
4. Department of Defense. *Design of Buildings to Resist Progressive Collapse Unified Facilities Criteria (UFC): 4-023-16*; Department of Defense: Washington, DC, USA, 2016.
5. Kiakojouri, F.; De Biagi, V.; Marchelli, M.; Chiaia, B. A conceptual note on the definition of initial failure in progressive collapse scenarios. *Structures* **2024**, *60*, 105921. [CrossRef]
6. Pang, B.; Wang, F.; Yang, J.; Zhang, W.; Huang, X.-H.; Azim, I. Evaluation on the progressive collapse resistance of infilled reinforced concrete frames based on numerical and semi-analytical methods. *Eng. Struct.* **2022**, *267*, 114684. [CrossRef]

7. Kiakojouri, F.; De Biagi, V.; Chiaia, B.; Sheidaii, M.R. Strengthening and retrofitting techniques to mitigate progressive collapse: A critical review and future research agenda. *Eng. Struct.* **2022**, *262*, 114274. [CrossRef]
8. Azim, I.; Yang, J.; Bhatta, S.; Wang, F.; Liu, Q.-F. Factors influencing the progressive collapse resistance of RC frame structures. *J. Build. Eng.* **2020**, *27*, 100986. [CrossRef]
9. Pham, A.T.; Tan, K.H.; Yu, J. Numerical investigations on static and dynamic responses of reinforced concrete sub-assemblages under progressive collapse. *Eng. Struct.* **2017**, *149*, 2–20. [CrossRef]
10. Ma, F.H.; Gilbert, B.P.; Guan, H.; Xue, H.; Lu, X.; Li, Y. Experimental study on the progressive collapse behaviour of RC flat plate substructures subjected to corner column removal scenarios. *Eng. Struct.* **2019**, *180*, 728–741. [CrossRef]
11. Fedorova, N.V.; Phan, D.Q.; Korenkov, P.A. Indirect reinforcement of reinforced concrete elements as a means of protecting a constructive system from a progressive collapse. *IOP Conf. Ser. Mater. Sci. Eng.* **2020**, *753*, 032032. [CrossRef]
12. Ameri, M.R.; Massumi, A.; Masoomi, H. Effect of structural redundancy on progressive collapse resistance enhancement in RC frame structures. *J. Perform. Constr. Facil.* **2019**, *33*, 04018092. [CrossRef]
13. Quiel, S.E.; Naito, C.J.; Fallon, C.T. A non-emulative moment connection for progressive collapse resistance in precast concrete building frames. *Eng. Struct.* **2019**, *179*, 174–188. [CrossRef]
14. Alshaikh, I.M.H.; Abadel, A.A.; Alrubaidi, M. Precast RC structures' progressive collapse resistance: Current knowledge and future requirements. *Structures* **2022**, *37*, 338–352. [CrossRef]
15. Alanani, M.; Ehab, M.; Salem, H. Progressive collapse assessment of precast prestressed reinforced concrete beams using applied element method. *Case Stud. Constr. Mater.* **2020**, *13*, e00457. [CrossRef]
16. Qian, K.; Liang, S.L.; Fu, F.; Fang, Q. Progressive collapse resistance of precast concrete beam-column sub-assemblages with high-performance dry connections. *Eng. Struct.* **2019**, *198*, 109552. [CrossRef]
17. Li, Z.X.; Liu, H.K.; Shi, Y.C.; Ding, Y.; Zhao, B. Experimental investigation on progressive collapse performance of prestressed precast concrete frames with dry joints. *Eng. Struct.* **2021**, *246*, 113071. [CrossRef]
18. Nimse, R.B.; Joshi, D.D.; Patel, P.V. Behavior of wet precast beam column connections under progressive collapse scenario: An experimental study. *Int. J. Adv. Struct. Eng. (IJASE)* **2014**, *6*, 149–159. [CrossRef]
19. Kang, S.B.; Tan, K.H. Progressive collapse resistance of precast concrete frames with discontinuous reinforcement in the joint. *J. Struct. Eng.* **2017**, *143*, 04017090. [CrossRef]
20. Feng, F.F.; Hwang, H.J.; Yi, W.J. Static and dynamic loading tests for precast concrete moment frames under progressive collapse. *Eng. Struct.* **2020**, *213*, 110612. [CrossRef]
21. Wang, F.L.; Yang, J.; Nyunn, S.; Azim, I. Effect of concrete infill walls on the progressive collapse performance of precast concrete framed substructures. *J. Build. Eng.* **2020**, *32*, 101461. [CrossRef]
22. Feng, D.C.; Wang, Z.; Wu, G. Progressive collapse performance analysis of precast reinforced concrete structures. *Struct. Des. Tall Spec. Build.* **2019**, *28*, e1588. [CrossRef]
23. Elsanadedy, H.M. New moment-resisting beam-column joints to increase progressive collapse resistance of precast concrete buildings. *J. Build. Eng.* **2021**, *44*, 102884. [CrossRef]
24. Zhou, Y.; Hu, X.; Pei, Y.L.; Hwang, H.-J.; Chen, T.; Yi, W.; Deng, L. Dynamic load test on progressive collapse resistance of fully assembled precast concrete frame structures. *Eng. Struct.* **2020**, *214*, 110675. [CrossRef]
25. Xie, Y.K. Research on Collapse Performance of Prefabricated Concrete Structure. Master's Thesis, Guangxi University, Nanning, China, 2020.
26. *GB 50010-2010*; Code for Design of Concrete Structures. Ministry of Housing and Urban-Rural Development of the People's Republic of China: Beijing, China, 2010.
27. *GB 50011-2010*; Code for Seismic Design Of Buildings. Ministry of Housing and Urban-Rural Development of the People's Republic of China: Beijing, China, 2010.
28. Livemore Software Technology Corporation. *LS-DYNA Keyword User's Manual*; Livemore Software Technology Corporation: California, CA, USA, 2003.
29. Griffiths, H.; Pugsley, A.; Saunders, O.A. *Report of the Inquiry into the Collapse of Flats at Ronan Point, Canning Town: Presented to the Minister of Housing and Local Government*; HM Stationery Office: Richmond, UK, 1968.
30. Xu, K.; Lu, Y. Numerical simulation study of spallation in reinforced concrete plates subjected to blast loading. *Comput. Struct.* **2006**, *84*, 431–438. [CrossRef]
31. Shi, Y.C.; Li, Z.X.; Hao, H. A new method for progressive collapse analysis of RC frames under blast loading. *Eng. Struct.* **2010**, *32*, 1691–1703. [CrossRef]
32. Kim, H.S.; Ahn, H.S.; Ahn, J.G. Erosion criteria for the blast analysis of reinforcement concrete members. *J. Archit. Inst. Korea Struct. Constr.* **2014**, *30*, 21–28. [CrossRef]
33. Khandelwal, K.; El-Tawil, S. Pushdown resistance as a measure of robustness in progressive collapse analysis. *Eng. Struct.* **2011**, *33*, 2653–2661. [CrossRef]

buildings

MDPI

Article

Adaptability Analysis of Integrated Project Delivery Method in Large- and Medium-Sized Engineering Projects: A FAHP-Based Modeling Solution

Huiyu He [1], Xiwei Gan [2], Lin Liu [2,*] and Xing Zhang [1]

1 Shenzhen General Integrated Transportation and Municipal Engineering Design & Research Institute Co., Ltd., Shenzhen 518003, China; huiyu_he@163.com (H.H.); 18027662716@163.com (X.Z.)

2 School of Civil and Transportation Engineering, Guangdong University of Technology, Guangzhou 510006, China; 2112309180@mail2.gdut.edu.cn

* Correspondence: liulin@gdut.edu.cn

Abstract: With the emerging large- and medium-sized engineering projects, prominent project delivery methods make sense in terms of cost, risk, management, and schedule. Among these, the Integrated Project Delivery (IPD) method stands out due to its adaptability for growing scale and complexity projects. This study compares the IPD method with other methods, emphasizing its benefits in large- and medium-sized projects and introducing the Fuzzy Analytic Hierarchy Process (FAHP) model to analyze IPD's adaptability quantitatively. By conducting a matrix calculation of eighteen second-level indicators, this study derived weight values for four first-level indicators: Cost control, Risk control, Management control, and Schedule control. These first-level indicators were then used to formulate the total evaluation index calculation. Based on this foundation, we verified the calculations using a case study in Fujian. Implementing the IPD method led to a lower cost than the Owner's Representative method and a one-year schedule acceleration. The FAHP model introduced in this study offers a novel and objective approach for adaptability analysis of the IPD method in large- and medium-sized engineering projects, coupling decision theory into project management.

Keywords: adaptability analysis; grade evaluation; integrated project delivery; project management; selection decision

1. Introduction

Project management has been discussed a lot since the 1950s and is widely used in multiple industries like petroleum, chemical, medicine, architecture, and other sectors [1–4]. Various project delivery methods are applied during the field implementation of engineering projects, some well executed and others not. An inappropriate project delivery method may result in a series of problems, including an unreasonable progress schedule, project cost overruns, and reduced execution efficiency [5,6], aggravating the risks taken by the owner and management company and complicating their responsibilities. Therefore, selecting appropriate project delivery methods in specific engineering projects is crucial to effective project implementation.

Accompanied by rapid urbanization and economic development, several project delivery methods are developed and applied in a wide range of engineering projects. Among them, several standard project delivery methods, like the Design–Bid–Build (DBB), Design–Build (DB), Construction Manager at Risk (CM at Risk), and Build–Operate–Transfer (BOT), are widely used in traditional projects [7–10]. With the increasing investment scale and project complexity in international engineering projects, typical delivery methods of Engineering Procurement Construction (EPC), Owner's Representative (OR), Owner's Construction Management (OCM), Public–Private Partnerships (PPP), and other delivery methods came into being [11–14]. Especially with the deepening cooperation between domestic and foreign enterprises and the continuous expansion of industrial scale, engineering projects also tend to become larger [15]. Especially in China, large- and medium-sized engineering projects have grown markedly over the past two decades.

Due to the characteristics of significant investment, long cycle, high complexity, and complex coordination in large- and medium-sized engineering projects, the Integrated Project Delivery (IPD) method has gradually been known and applied in recent years [16]. However, existing studies were more likely to use the IPD method mechanically, which lacked systematic discussion and comparison with other project delivery methods. As a newly integrated and emerging project delivery method, whether to select the IPD and how to apply the IPD in large- and medium-sized engineering projects are key subjective decision issues, especially under specific engineering project circumstances. The decision to select the IPD method usually depends on multiple factors, such as project scale, technical difficulty, project team membership, owner participation, etc. [17]. Therefore, the adaptability analysis of the IPD method in large- and medium-sized engineering projects deserves a deep inspection.

The relevant literature has focused on studying the performance and benefits of the IPD method in engineering projects [18]. However, an important aspect that has been overlooked is the adaptability analysis of the IPD method in these projects. Whether to utilize the IPD method becomes crucial, and the decision theory plays an important role in providing a quantitative index to account for the varying importance of factors influencing each project. However, there is a knowledge gap surrounding the limited use of decision theory in evaluating the adaptability of the IPD method in large- and medium-sized engineering projects. In this research, the Fuzzy Analytic Hierarchy Process (FAHP) [19] model is employed to comprehensively analyze and evaluate the adaptability of the IPD method by considering various aspects in large- and medium-sized engineering projects. The FAHP model could contribute to project policymakers' evaluation of the suitability of adopting the IPD method in large- and medium-sized engineering projects. This study aims to introduce a modeling solution to guide the adaptability analysis of the IPD method.

The remainder of this paper is structured as follows: Section 2 describes a research review of the IPD method by consulting the existing literature to make clear the research status and its application fields, and a detailed comparison between IPD and other typical project delivery methods is conducted through characteristic analysis. Section 3 applies the FAHP model based on the factors affecting large- and medium-sized engineering projects as indicators, clarifying the interpretation of each indicator, its calculation process, and the significance of its weight scale. Section 4 establishes the weight matrix through the scoring results of experts in various fields in the industry and establishes a model for calculating the weights. By applying the FAHP model to an engineering project case, the adaptability of the IPD method was evaluated, resulting in notable advantages. Section 5 summarizes the conclusions of the article and describes the innovations and contributions of the article to the adaptability analysis of the IPD method.

2. Development of the IPD Method

2.1. Research Trends of Project Management

Before illustrating the research status of IPD, a bibliometric analysis of information on project management in the literature was conducted to display the related research trends. First, a general search on the project management category from the Elsevier ScienceDirect journal database was carried out, considering the twenty years from 2000 to the end of 2022. As shown in Figure 1, a total of 26,684 related articles were retrieved. Figure 1a shows the annual number of articles related to project management. There has been a significant increase in the number of annual published articles in the last two decades, which indicates accelerated growth in project management-related research, discussion, and application.

Figure 1b shows the classified statistics of different subject fields of this literature. Among these subject fields, themes on "environmental science" occupy the maximum quantity with more than 6500 articles, followed by "engineering". There is also a substantial amount of literature covering several fields of "social sciences", "medicine and dentistry", and "agriculture and biological sciences".

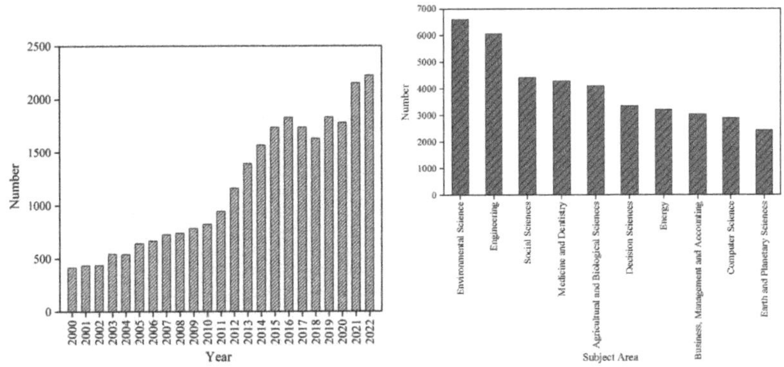

(**a**) (**b**)

Figure 1. Literature analysis of annual publications related to project management (database: Elsevier ScienceDirect journal). (**a**) The annual number of articles related to project management. (**b**) The classified statistics of different subject fields.

Second, considering the background of the dramatic development in engineering projects in China, a literature analysis on project management-related publications in China is conducted by searching the Chinese National Knowledge Infrastructure (CNKI) in the past two decades. As shown in Figure 2a, a total of 45,647 articles were retrieved, and the annual amount of literature about project management rose sharply from under 100 in 2000 to over 3000 in 2014. The yearly publication amount will maintain at about 3000 over the next five years. However, after 2020, the amount of literature declined significantly due to the COVID-19 pandemic [20]. Figure 2b also displays the number distribution of ten different main keywords related to project management. It can be seen that although several keywords covering "Risk management" and "Construction engineering" have more than 1000 publications, the keyword "project management" still occupies the majority, more than 70 percent. These search results reveal that topics on project management research stay relatively conservative in the particular project management field from these studies. Then, a further classification of these studies by subjects is displayed. As shown in Figure 2c, the subject of "architectural science and engineering" accounts for the highest proportion, followed by "industrial economics", "macroeconomic management and sustainable development", "business economics", and "computer software and computer applications". These subjects share more than 60 percent of the total project management-related studies.

It can be seen from these project management-related studies that project management knowledge has been widely used worldwide in recent years, covering multiple research fields of environmental science, engineering, social sciences, et al. Especially in developing countries accompanied by rapid industrial development, project management research has been well applied in actual engineering projects covering a wide range of fields in urbanization and urban infrastructure forums. During the implementation process of an engineering project, a reasonable project delivery method is usually considered as the suppressed premise of high-quality project completion on time or ahead of schedule.

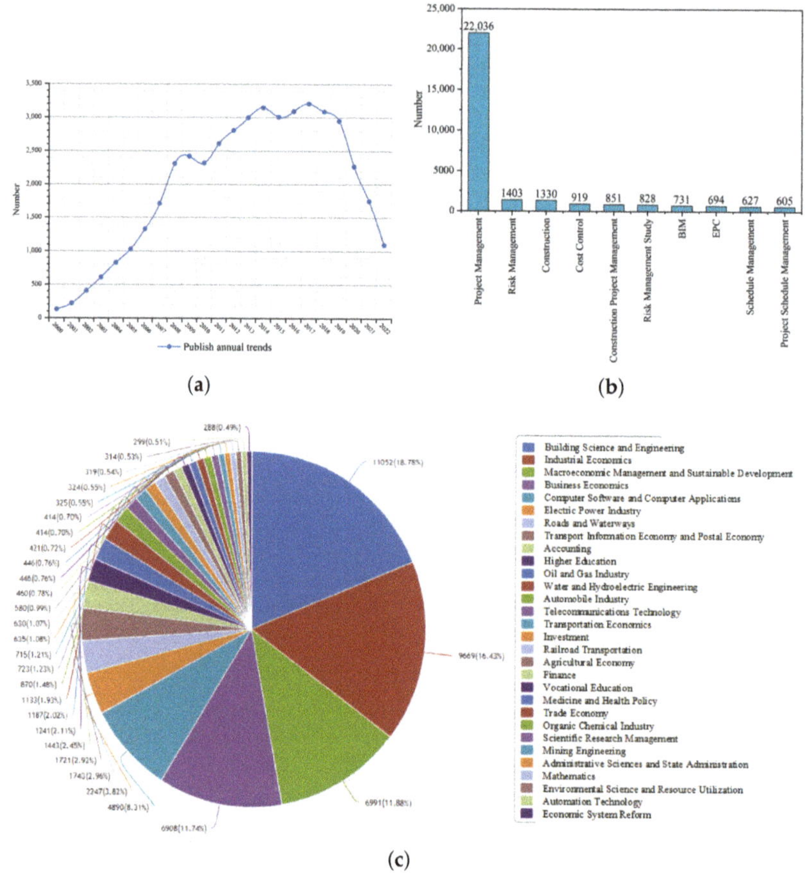

Figure 2. Literature analysis on project management-related publications in China from 2000 to the end of 2022. (database: China National Knowledge Infrastructure). (**a**) Annual amount variations of literature. (**b**) Distribution of major topics published in each literature (**c**) Project management statistics by subject area of literature published.

2.2. Development of the IPD Method

2.2.1. Introduction of the IPD Method

Emerging project delivery methods in engineering projects have attracted increasing attention in the international engineering fields [21]. With continuous progress in science, technology, social economy, and international financial service systems, more requirements of higher construction levels and the management ability of international contractors are put forward to deal with the larger investment scale of international engineering projects and greater complexity of international engineering projects [22,23]. The selection basis of one particular project delivery method is usually determined by several factors, including the project owner's capacity and level of involvement, the degree of participation of the project management or construction engineering company, and the scope of their services. These factors collectively dictate the organizational and implementation approach for project management. This research aims to conduct a comparative analysis of several commonly used methods: Engineering Procurement Construction (EPC), Owner's Construction Management (OCM), Owner's Representative (OR), and the Integrated Project Delivery (IPD) method.

- The EPC method.

The Engineering Procurement Construction (EPC) method is a globally recognized management approach that integrates design, procurement, and construction [12]. In this method, the owner must complete the pre-project work by themselves or entrust experts to complete the project, then select the general contractor through public bidding. In the process of project construction, the general engineering contractor is entrusted by the owner to undertake all or most of the work of the project's design, procurement, and construction within the scope of the contract. The owner's representative oversees project budgeting and completion acceptance, among other responsibilities. The EPC general contractor must also manage various risks, including design uncertainties, environmental changes, unexpected circumstances, and challenges.

Generally, the owner's contract is with the general contractor on only one side of the project, who then subcontracts the design, procurement, and construction. The three segments of engineering subcontracting can be composed in various combinations. The EPC method can be flexible depending on the project's size and the owner's requirements. And it is widely used worldwide [24], where all parties are familiar with the procedures involved. However, with this method, the owner lacks the project management personnel to serve it directly, and the investment in the early stage is high. When there is a significant change in the project, it is easy to cause more claims, and if there is a dispute between the design unit and the construction subcontractor, the owner's interests are often jeopardized [25].

- The OCM method.

The Owner's Construction Management (OCM) method refers to the owner-led approach to project management. In this method, the owner establishes a project management department within a matrix system that takes on the responsibility of project construction on behalf of the owner [26,27]. This department is solely accountable for organizing and implementing the construction project. In the OCM method, a temporary function is established under the owner, primarily staffed by permanent employees in key management positions. In contrast, secondary staff members are usually seconded or recruited temporarily. Presently, numerous small- to medium-sized projects adopt the OCM method, particularly those with relatively simple requirements and modest investments.

Under the OCM method, project management on the owner's side becomes more involved, and tasks are decentralized. The owner must allocate significant human and material resources to ensure effective project control and meet quality, cost, and schedule requirements. On the other hand, the OCM method also imposes high demands on the owner's professional and managerial capabilities. The owner's ability to build upon and apply previous construction experience, the freedom to select supervisors for project oversight, control over design requirements, and complete decision-making power regarding project implementation. Nevertheless, suppose the owner lacks adequate management personnel or the necessary management experience to meet project management standards. In that case, the achievement of project goals cannot be assured, potentially resulting in project failure and investment loss.

- The OR method.

The Owner's Representative (OR) method is a project delivery method in which the owner hires a professional project management company to manage and provide services on behalf of the owner for the whole process or several stages of the organization and implementation of the project [26]. Project management companies with OR qualifications have a strong technical force, complete professional configuration, rich experience in engineering management, mature project management systems and mechanisms, and integrated project management software platforms. As a result, they have increasingly become the primary providers of project management service outsourcing.

OR contractors typically begin with the owner's investment planning, conducting project planning, organization, and interface coordination on behalf of the owner. They also effectively oversee the project's schedule, quality, cost, and other critical elements throughout the construction process, including project design, construction, and acceptance, to achieve the desired objectives [28]. With the OR method, the owner needs to retain a smaller workforce to manage the project and make decisions on critical issues, thus allowing the owner to focus more on their core business. However, this approach also results in limited owner involvement, restricted change rights, and potential coordination challenges. The primary risk for the owner lies in selecting a reputable project management company [13].

- The IPD method.

Due to the characteristics of significant investment, long cycle, high complexity, and complex coordination in large- and medium-sized engineering projects, the Integrated Project Delivery (IPD) method has gradually become known and applied in recent years. It has been created to fit the requirements of the international engineering field in particular [29,30]. IPD is an integrated system that combines organizational personnel, project management processes, engineering and construction connections, and management objectives. This integration ensures a streamlined and consistent approach to project implementation [31]. The IPD method involves the implementation of multifaceted agreements encompassing a collaborative team comprising architects, engineers, and construction experts representing diverse organizations [32].

In recent years, large-scale engineering construction projects have come to the fore in the context of rapid urbanization. These projects have a large amount of investment and a long construction period with vital time nodes and many personnel and organizations, making their management very difficult. Other entities usually carry out the different phases of project implementation, often forming separate management processes. It is prone to problems such as fragmentation of functional relationships, lack of communication, and inconsistent objectives. According to the characteristics of these large construction projects, the IPD method has begun to be accepted with more prominent features in the application of engineering practice and has been widely adopted in these specific construction fields.

2.2.2. Benefits of the IPD Method Compared to Other Methods

To be precise, the IPD method is a fusion of several OCM and OR and EPC methods. It integrates the strengths of each method and complements the weaknesses and shortcomings of each delivery method [17]. Each participating unit combines the team strengths of each party to cooperate and manage together, avoiding the contradiction of traditional project delivery [33]. Integration management integrates the original independent project processes and elements together, which is conducive to the standardization and integrity of large-scale project design and construction [34].

The IPD method involves the establishment of a collaborative project management department by the owner, engineering project management company, and other involved parties, according to a cooperation agreement. This collaborative entity jointly manages the entire project process. This integration encompasses the integration of organizational structure and staffing. In addition, this method facilitates the integration of various project management process systems and the targeted interests of all parties involved in the project [?]. Owners can leverage the expertise of project management contractors and benefit from their skilled professional knowledge and project management experience. This allows for a rational redistribution of integration within the project organization, enabling the utilization of the contractor's expertise while maintaining owner control.

Compared to other delivery methods, IPD excels in mobilizing and complementing the technical expertise and project delivery experience of team members, maximizing the use of project resources [36]. Owners can focus on their core competencies by delegating project management responsibilities to contractors and transferring most project management tasks. This approach addresses owner workforce constraints and maximizes resource utilization, resulting in significant value adds to the project. Additionally, the owner's management system, experience, and tools are enhanced through this process, establishing a stronger foundation for future projects.

By adopting the IPD method, integrated teams are formed to create a new type of "partnership" in which participants work together based on mutual respect and resource sharing. It enables unified decision-making and the hierarchical management of projects, which dramatically improves the efficiency and management level of project management during the construction period. The operational mechanism of IPD is characterized by integrated management. The method particularly highlights the synergy between individual members of the organization and organizational goals in the management concept so that the members can better achieve cooperation. The IPD method enhances the owner's participation and decision-making power in project management, resulting in project outputs that align with the owner's expectations and requirements. In collaborative cooperation, the owner's participants can also acquire advanced project management systematic knowledge, and their management capabilities can improve.

2.2.3. Integration of IPD and Other Methods

In complex and challenging large-scale petrochemical projects, such as those involving large oil fields and long-distance pipelines, the owner's management and technical capabilities alone may not be sufficient to handle all aspects of the project [37], from the initial definition phase to the management of EPC contractors during implementation [38]. To address this issue, many oil companies have successfully adopted the OR and EPC method, which involves introducing an OR management company to compensate for the owner's lack of expertise. However, this method has its limitations. Firstly, the widely used "Cost and Fee" billing method of OR can lead to high contracting costs because OR management companies sometimes prioritize their interests at the expense of project schedules and costs. Secondly, the owner may lack effective control over the construction process when using this method, resulting in inefficiency.

To overcome these drawbacks, the IPD and EPC project delivery method has been proposed [39]. This method inherits the advantages of the OR method's management specialization while addressing its shortcomings. It is a new method that expands and extends the "Owner and OR and EPC" method, fundamentally different from the newer IPD method. The IPD and EPC method aims to balance practical management specialization and maintaining control over the construction process, offering a more efficient and cost-effective approach to project management in complex petrochemical projects.

2.2.4. Research Necessity of the IPD Method in Engineering Projects

According to existing research, the organization structure of the IPD method has reached a stable state. The strengths and weaknesses of this method have been identified, and an academic consensus has been reached [40]. The IPD method leverages the abilities of both the owner and the consultant to enhance project efficiency [41]. It also enables the owner to control and supervise the project effectively throughout the process [42]. Additionally, it facilitates the owner's development of competent management personnel. Several characteristic analyses prove that integrating IPD and EPC and other methods usually exhibits remarkable advantages in actual projects.

However, emphasis on the scientific selection of project delivery methods through advanced, precise, and rational assessment methods is insufficient. The lack of a clear delineation of rights and responsibilities among parties involved in the IPD method may result in project inefficiencies [43]. Currently, it is still difficult to quantitatively judge the applicability and adaptability of these management methods. Advanced solutions addressing the adaptability analysis of the IPD method in large- and medium-sized engineering projects are rarely discussed in detail. Therefore, a reasonable advanced decision-making method should be conducted to illustrate the adaptability analysis of the IPD method in specific engineering.

3. Modeling Methods

Given the distinctive features of the IPD method and the specific requirements of medium and large-sized engineering projects, a systematic and objective evaluation model is essential for assessing the adaptability of the IPD method for such projects. In this research, the widely recognized decision theory model, the Fuzzy Analytic Hierarchy Process (FAHP) [19], is employed to comprehensively analyze and assess the IPD adaptability by considering various aspects of considerations in these medium and large-sized projects. The study outlines a set of computational equations to quantitatively measure the IPD method's adaptability, as discussed below.

3.1. FAHP-Based Evaluation Indicators

3.1.1. A Brief Description of FAHP Theory

Among the various decision-making methods, the Analytic Hierarchy Process (AHP) [44,45] is preferred by many contractors for its ability to effectively blend qualitative and quantitative aspects in addressing diverse evaluation factors and its system flexibility. The AHP method conducts quantitative analysis based on qualitative analysis, facilitating a more cohesive integration of the two. Additionally, it offers a systematic approach to problem analysis, aiding in scientific management and rational decision-making. The AHP method initiates qualitative and quantitative analysis by breaking down the decision problem elements into distinct levels of objectives, criteria, and scenarios, thereby mathematizing and systematizing the analyst's thought process. The AHP method identifies key decision factors through decomposition and synthesis, assigns weights based on their interrelationships, and establishes an analytical structural model to determine the optimal solution.

However, the AHP method has limitations. It can only select the best option from the original choices and may not generate entirely new and improved alternatives [46]. Furthermore, it may prioritize a suboptimal option over others, and inconsistencies in judgment matrices may complicate the decision-making process, requiring multiple adjustments to achieve consistency.

To overcome these limitations, the FAHP model emerges as a practical solution for multi-objective evaluation and decision-making problems with optimal ranking [47]. Differing from the AHP method, FAHP categorizes indicators, uses fuzzy mathematical tools [48] to determine indicator weights, and employs the fuzzy comprehensive judgment method for thorough evaluation. By establishing relationships between factors, creating a judgment matrix, and calculating relative indicator weights, FAHP effectively addresses bias in systematic scoring, enhancing the realism and accuracy of evaluation processes and outcomes [49].

3.1.2. FAHP-Based Indicators

Indicators affecting the decision-making for choosing the IPD method are first focused on during the quantitative adaptability evaluation. Four dimensions of cost, risk, management, and schedule are usually recognized as critical indicators that could significantly influence successful project implementation and management [50,51]. The IPD method is designed to ensure effective control of infrastructure projects in terms of these four aspects to achieve project objectives. These interconnected indicators require integrated consideration and balance to ensure comprehensive project control. Thorough evaluation of these indicators when selecting an IPD method can assist the project management team in achieving project objectives and ensure smooth project implementation and management. Therefore, drawing from a review of the pertinent literature and insights gained from large- and medium-sized engineering projects, "Cost control", "Risk control", "Management control", and "Schedule control" are identified and utilized as four first-level indicators. These indicators are considered crucial aspects that influence project construction.

In the FAHP model, the bottom level is the sub-criteria level, which contains all the elements to be sorted; the middle level is the criterion level, which governs the lower elements and is also governed by the upper elements to determine the criterion for the sorting of the elements; and the highest level, which has only one element, is called the target level [52]. The highest level is the score for IPD method selection, denoted as P_{IPD}, which is a quantitative indicator of whether to select the IPD method in an engineering project during the decision process.

- *Cost control.*

Cost control is a crucial process in project management, encompassing budgeting, monitoring, and adjusting project costs throughout the project lifecycle. This involves comparing actual costs to estimated costs, identifying discrepancies, and preparing forecasts to ensure the rational allocation of project resources and maintain cost control. Development cost (DC), purchase cost (PCC), production cost (PDC), and selling cost (SC) are key factors influencing the overall project cost control.

DC encompasses expenses related to real estate sales, including the fees for ancillary facilities, environmental landscaping, and external pipeline networks. PCC comprises materials and procurement-related other expenditures. PDC refers to the expenses incurred by the production unit for manufacturing products or providing labor services, serving as a crucial indicator of the enterprise's technical and management capabilities. SC includes the production expenses of sold products, labor costs for services provided, and other business-related sales expenses.

By effectively managing development, purchase, production, and selling costs, project teams can optimize cost control measures and enhance project performance.

- *Risk control.*

Risk control encompasses the measures and strategies employed by managers and risk controllers to mitigate potential risks and minimize associated losses, aiming to reduce the likelihood of risk events and prevent unmanageable losses. It involves identifying existing or potential risks during the risk identification process and analyzing their impact on project construction based on their likelihood of occurrence and severity of loss. In the project construction process, the occurrence of a risk event can impact various project attributes, including schedule, quality, cost, and personnel, leading to Schedule Risk (SR), Quality Risk (QR), People Risk (PR), and Cost Risk (CR).

SR pertains to potential schedule disruptions in the project, which can result in project delays. SR involves the possibility of quality issues such as requirement changes, design flaws, or inadequate testing. PR arises from uncertainties and potential risks within an enterprise or organization stemming from human behavior and quality. CR encompasses the probability and severity of foreseeable hazardous situations, comprehensively assessing the risks and consequences associated with cost-increasing scenarios.

- *Management control.*

Management control involves effectively organizing, planning, and coordinating resources to achieve specific objectives in practical work and establishing routine working procedures and management systems. Its purpose is to enable the strategy to be implemented to achieve the organization's goals. This encompasses Quality Management (QM), Investment Management (IM), Human Resources Management (HRM), Health, Safety, and Environment Management (HSEM), and Communication Management (CM).

QM encompasses all management activities to define quality programs and implement them through quality system processes. IM involves the comprehensive management of tasks throughout the investment project development cycle to achieve investment objectives using project management principles. HRM consists of formulating human resource policies and corresponding management activities within an enterprise. HSEM is a comprehensive system focusing on health, safety, and environmental considerations [53]. CM is vital for organizational success, as effective communication is integral to management. By understanding customer needs, integrating resources, and delivering quality products and services, organizations can create value for customers and generate wealth for the enterprise and society.

- *Schedule control.*

Schedule control in engineering refers to the process of monitoring and adjusting the progress of a project to ensure that it can be completed on time according to plan. It is combined with the process of time and the need for deadlines. It is mainly used to control whether the production or engineering progress is completed on schedule and whether the operations can relate to each other in time. According to the project development and construction process, it is divided into five progress nodes: Initiation Phase (IP), Exploration Phase (EP), Construction Phase (CP), Acceptance Phase (AP), and Operation and Maintenance Phase (OMP).

IP puts a predetermined project into the formal implementation stage, which contains the basic information of the project's goal, plan, time and cost, etc., and is an indispensable step in the realization process of the project. EP includes engineering surveys, engineering geology, and hydrogeology investigations, which are a series of comprehensive evaluations conducted to find out the natural conditions of the project's construction site. CP is a critical stage of capital construction. It is essential that construction activities adhere to the engineering design, construction organization design, and acceptance specifications to guarantee timely completion and high-quality outcomes. AP refers to the acceptance of quality assurance information, quality control information, and physical appearance of the unit work, as well as the acceptance phase of physical safety function sampling. OMP is the process by which the deliverables of a project are put into production or operation to produce benefits on an ongoing basis. Figure 3 illustrates the correlation between the eighteen sub-criteria levels and the four criterion levels, as well as their association with the target level.

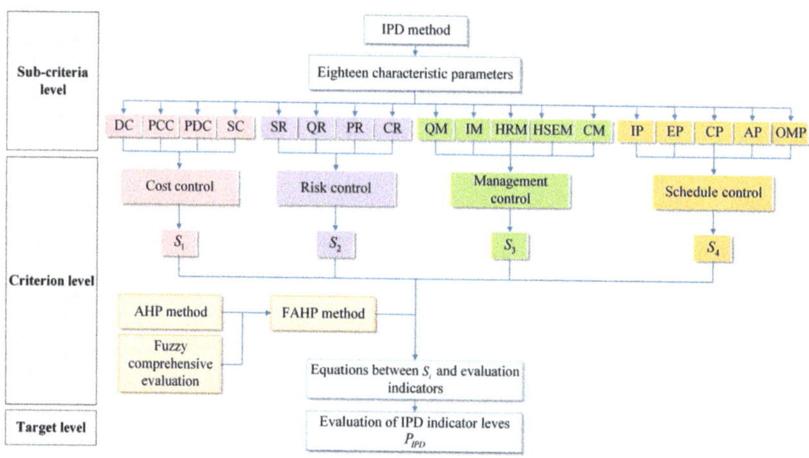

Figure 3. Hierarchy analysis indicators of the IPD method.

3.2. FAHP-Based Modeling Process

The FAHP method converts the qualitative assessment of the system into a quantitative evaluation based on an Intuitionistic Fuzzy Set (IFS) [48], which represents the degree of agreement or disagreement of decision-makers towards the indicator. As shown in Figure 4, S_1 represents the indicator of Cost control; S_2 displays the indicator expressing Risk control; S_3 is the indicator describing Management control; S_4 is the indicator reflecting Schedule control. Each S has its corresponding secondary indicator, and the number of these basic characteristic parameters of its S varies with different considerations. For S_1 and S_2, there are four basic characteristic parameters with the j value of 4, while S_3 and S_4 cover five characteristic parameters and the j takes the value of 5.

Some basic calculation steps applied in this manuscript are shown as follows.

Step 1 (Definitions): We consider that S_k $(k = 1, 2, 3, 4)$ represents the integrated spatial factors. Let $X = \{x_1, x_2, x_3, \ldots, x_n\}$ be a finite set of alternatives, in which x_i $(i = 1, 2, \ldots, n)$ means the sub-factors of the corresponding S_k. Then, ω means the underlying subjective priority weight, which belongs to a vector $\omega = (\omega_1, \omega_2, \omega_n)$ with $\omega_i > 0$ $(i = 1, 2, \ldots, n)$, and $\sum_{i=1}^{n} \omega_i = 1$. Then, let a matrix $A = (a_{ij})_{n \times n}$, where a_{ij} is the intensity of preference of x_i over x_j measured using the 0.1 to 0.9 scales and satisfies the reciprocal conditions $0 < a_{ij} < 1$ and $a_{ij} + a_{ji} = 1$. a_{ij} indicates the degree that the alternative x_i is preferred to x_j, and the case $a_{ij} = 0.5$ indicates that there is indifference regarding the alternatives x_i and x_j.

Step 2 (Weight calculation): We consider the matrix $A = (a_{ij})_{n \times n}$ as a fuzzy complementary judgment matrix. Then, summing the data according to matrix row, we obtain $r_i = \sum_{k=1}^{n} a_{ik}$, $i = 1, 2, \ldots, n$. Then, after mathematical transformation we obtain $r_{ij} = (r_i - r_j)/a + 0.5$. Let $a = 2(n-1)$; then, we obtain $r_{ij} = \frac{(r_i - r_j)}{2(n-1)} + 0.5$. Thus, $R = (r_{ij})_{n \times n}$ is a fuzzy complementary judgment matrix. Then, with the normalizing rank aggregation, we apply the matrix R to the n-dimensional vector $\omega = (\omega_1, \omega_2, \ldots, \omega_n)$ and obtain the calculation formula $\omega_i = \frac{\sum_{i=1}^{n} a_{ij} + \frac{n}{2} - 1}{n(n-1)}$.

Step 3 (Consistency check): If $A = (a_{ij})_{n \times n}$ and $B = (b_{ij})_{n \times n}$ are both fuzzy complementary judgement matrixes, then $CI(A, B) \frac{1}{n^2} \sum_{i=1}^{n} \sum_{j=1}^{n} |a_{ij} - b_{ij}|$ is the compatibility indicator of A and B. Then, if we consider $W = (W_1, W_2, \ldots, W_n)^{\Gamma}$ as the weight vector of $A = (a_{ij})_{n \times n}$, then $\omega_{ij} = \omega_i - \omega_j + 0.5$ and then, $CI(A, W) \frac{1}{n^2} \sum_{i=1}^{n} \sum_{j=1}^{n} |a_{ij} - \omega_{ij}|$ is the compatibility indicator of $A = (a_{ij})_{n \times n}$. If $CI(A, W) < \partial$ (where ∂ represents the attitude of the decision-maker and is usually set as 0.1), we consider the matrix $A = (a_{ij})_{n \times n}$ to be consistently acceptable and then calculate the weight values.

Step 4 (Hierarchy sort): We singly sort the $W = (W_1, W_2, \ldots, W_n)^{\Gamma}$, and obtain the relative weight of an element on a given layer compared to a related element on the previous layer. Then, we perform hierarchical total ordering and calculate the ranking weights of the relative importance of all elements with respect to the target layer, a process that starts at the highest layer and proceeds layer by layer to the lowest layer. For example, S_1 includes n risky determinates $X = \{x_1, x_2, x_3, \ldots, x_n\}$, and its weight proportional to S_1 separately is $a = \{a_1, a_2, a_3, \ldots, a_n\}$. And the next level of the A_1, which includes m parameters, designed to $B = \{B_1, B_2, B_3, \ldots, B_m\}$. The weight proportional of the B to A_1 is b = $\{b_{j1}, b_{j2}, b_{j3}, \ldots, b_{jm}\}$. Then, we consider the $b_j = \sum_{k=1}^{m} a_k b_{kj}$, $(j = 1, 2, \ldots, m)$. The weights of the remaining layers are also calculated layer by layer in this way, until the bottom layer, we can obtain the weight order of all factors relative to the top layer, which is the target layer, and we can realize the importance order of all factors.

Following the steps outlined in the FAHP model, we derive the mathematical equations necessary to compute the final decision evaluation value. The detailed calculation steps are shown in Figure 4.

3.3. Decision-Making Score Evaluation Method

The selection of comprehensive evaluation indexes for deciding the IPD method is established based on a thorough consideration of engineering projects. This process involves an extensive selection of indexes related to Cost control, Risk control, Management control, and Schedule control. The comprehensive evaluation of the IPD method includes many qualitative indexes, making it challenging to define the boundaries of relative opposites. The FAHP provides a powerful aid in transforming qualitative indicators into quantitative indicators; relative concepts such as high and low project costs and fast and slow project schedules can be accurately quantified.

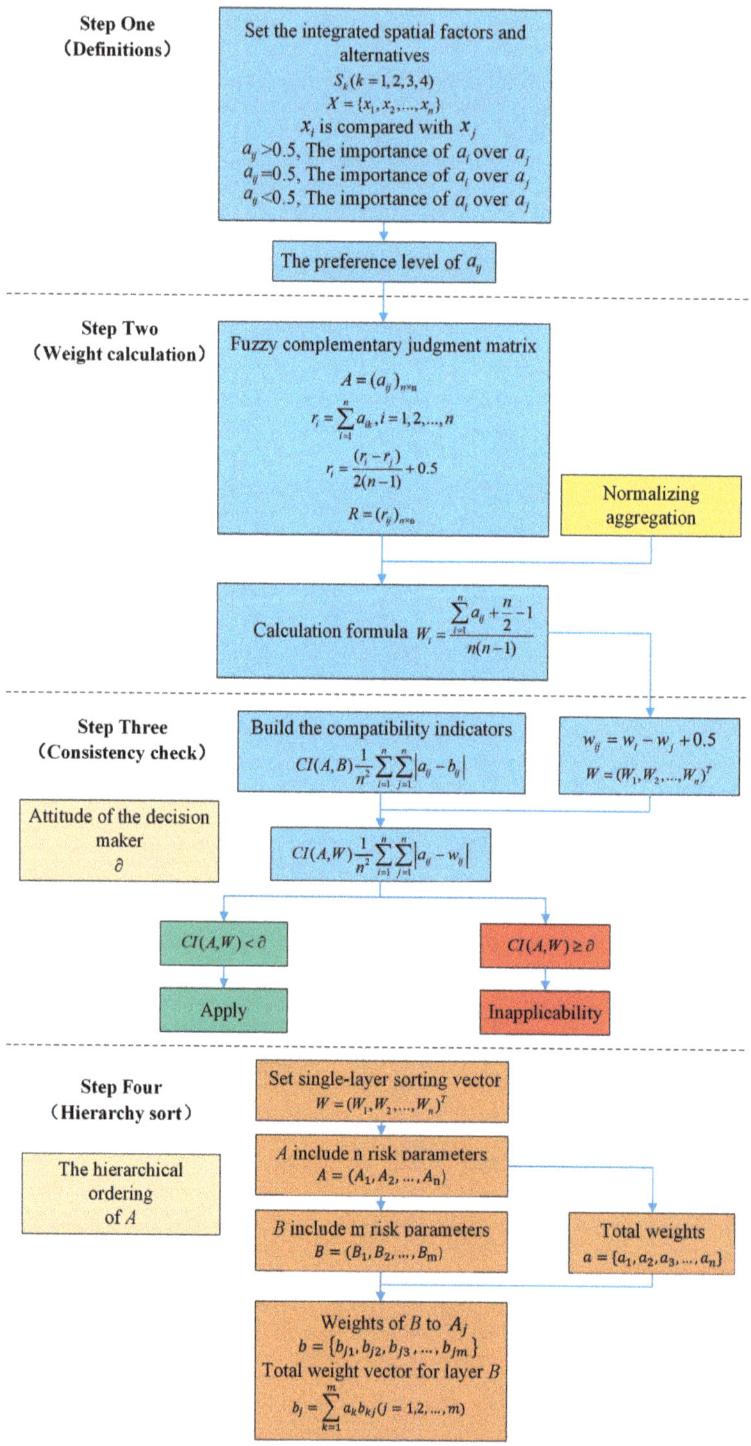

Figure 4. FAHP model calculation steps.

In the FAHP model, a_{ij} represents the importance of one criterion relative to another. The value of a_{ij}, ranging from 0.1 to 0.9 in increments of 0.1, is determined based on experts' judgments using the Saaty 1–9 scale [54]. A lower a_{ij} value indicates less importance attached to the indicator than others at the same level. By comparing each indicator with others at the same level, an evaluation matrix is constructed to calculate the weight value of each indicator. This process helps determine the significance of different indicators in the evaluation of the IPD method.

As shown in Table 1, the expert scoring table is utilized to create the evaluation matrix, encompassing the assessment of four first-level indicators and eighteen second-level indicators. Experts can methodically compare element weights using this table, drawing on their engineering expertise to establish a comprehensive weight matrix. A value of 0.5 serves as the threshold: values above 0.5 signify the column elements' higher significance compared to the row elements. The greater the deviation from 0.5, the greater the importance, and conversely.

Determining the rating levels in the sub-indicators using expert scoring allows further calculation of the scores for each S_i, resulting in a rating score for the IPD method. The method's indicator level evaluation, which must meet the basic level requirements for most indicators to qualify, uses a value greater than or equal to 3 as the basis for selection. As shown in Figure 5, four S_i scales are illustrated, where a position further to the right on the scale indicates better adaptation of the IPD method to the metric. In comparison, a position towards the left suggests poorer adaptation.

Among these indicators, Cost control utilizes cost as a control measure. A score exceeding 3 in engineering signifies that employing the IPD method can effectively reduce project costs, leading to cost savings. Similarly, a score above 3 in Risk control indicates that the IPD method can mitigate or minimize the likelihood of risk events and their associated losses. Manage control involves the managerial influence on organizational members to align with the organization's strategy. A score exceeding 3 indicates the effective utilization of the IPD method in this aspect. Schedule control involves employing systematic methods to meet scheduling objectives in harmony with quality, cost, and safety goals. A score above 3 of Schedule control suggests that the IPD method can expedite project scheduling, thereby reducing duration and enhancing efficiency while aligning with quality, cost, and safety objectives.

In general, using the FAHP model to evaluate each index of the IPD method, the evaluation function model of IPD method selection is established through weight assignment and calculation, which provides a calculation basis and practical tool for the optimal delivery method scheme of engineering projects.

Table 1. Expert scoring table.

Target Level		**Criterion Level**			
		Cost control	Process control	Management control	Schedule control
P_{IPD}	Cost control	0.5			
	Risk control		0.5		
	Management control			0.5	
	Schedule control				0.5
Criterion Level		**Sub-Criteria Level**			
		DC	PCC	PDC	SC
Cost control	DC	0.5			
	PCC		0.5		
	PDC			0.5	
	SC				0.5

Table 1. *Cont.*

Criterion Level		Sub-Criteria Level				
		SR	QR	PR	CR	
Risk control	SR	0.5				
	QR		0.5			
	PR			0.5		
	CR				0.5	
		QM	IM	HRM	HSEM	CM
Management control	QM	0.5				
	IM		0.5			
	HRM			0.5		
	HSEM				0.5	
	CM					0.5
		IP	EP	CP	AP	OMP
Schedule control	IP	0.5				
	EP		0.5			
	CP			0.5		
	AP				0.5	
	OMP					0.5

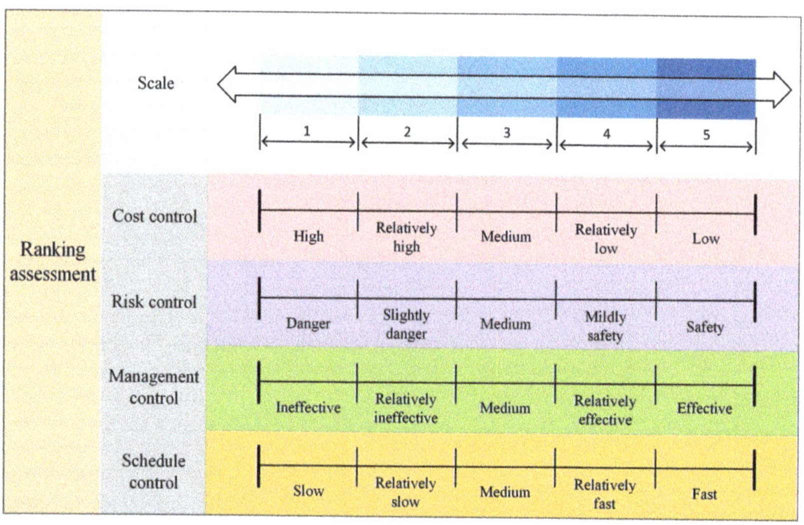

Figure 5. Indicator evaluation scale.

4. Results and Case Application

4.1. Mathematical Expressions for IPD Adaptability

Based on the fuzzy hierarchical analysis, the final model expression of the IPD is as follows.

$$P_{IPD} = \omega_c \times S_1 + \omega_r \times S_2 + \omega_m \times S_3 + \omega_s \times S_4 \quad (1)$$

where, P_{IPD} represents the evaluation values of the IPD method. ω_c denotes the weight assigned to Cost control, with S_1 representing the corresponding indicators. Similarly, ω_r indicates the weight for Risk control, with S_2 as the associated indicators. The weight for Management controls is denoted by ω_m, with S_3 representing the Management control indicators. Additionally, ω_s signifies the weight allocated to Schedule control, with S_4

representing the Schedule control indicators. The S also contains subsidiary evaluation indicators $S = \{S_1, S_2, S_3, S_4\}$, which expression is as follows for example.

$$S_i = \omega_1 \times V_1 + \omega_2 \times V_2 + \omega_3 \times V_3 + \omega_4 \times V_4 \quad (2)$$

According to the FAHP model described above, screening of appropriate experts is necessary. This study used the F-test to calculate the number of experts with an effect size of 0.25 (α = 0.05, 1 − β = 0.8), quantifying a significant difference between groups [55]. G*Power 3.0.10 software was used to calculate the sample size. During the calculation, the number of measurements was five, denoting the maximum limit of secondary indicators, and with the number of measurements was four, each consisting of four measures. After calculation, the required sample size was determined as 30, as shown in Appendix A. Therefore, more than thirty experts participated in the questionnaire, covering a wide professional range, including engineers, managers, and academics in related fields across the whole of China. In this way, the calculation results can be applied to relevant large- and medium-sized engineering projects in different regions. Each expert provided ratings for the weight matrix based on Table 1 in the questionnaire, and the average scores from all experts were computed to determine the weight assigned to each indicator in the evaluation process.

The first level indicator of Cost control according to the questionnaire can be obtained as a judgment matrix:

$$\begin{bmatrix} 0.50 & 0.15 & 0.30 & 0.25 \\ 0.85 & 0.50 & 0.15 & 0.30 \\ 0.70 & 0.85 & 0.50 & 0.15 \\ 0.75 & 0.70 & 0.85 & 0.50 \end{bmatrix} \quad (3)$$

It can be calculated according to the weighting formula:

$$\omega_1 = \frac{\sum_{i=1}^{n} a_{1_{ij}} + \frac{n}{2} - 1}{n(n-1)} = 0.267 \quad (4)$$

$$\omega_2 = \frac{\sum_{i=1}^{n} a_{2_{ij}} + \frac{n}{2} - 1}{n(n-1)} = 0.233 \quad (5)$$

$$\omega_3 = \frac{\sum_{i=1}^{n} a_{3_{ij}} + \frac{n}{2} - 1}{n(n-1)} = 0.317 \quad (6)$$

$$\omega_4 = \frac{\sum_{i=1}^{n} a_{4_{ij}} + \frac{n}{2} - 1}{n(n-1)} = 0.183 \quad (7)$$

The first-level indicator of the Cost control calculation equation is

$$S_1 = 0.267 \times v_{dc} + 0.233 \times v_{pcc} + 0.317 \times v_{pdc} + 0.183 \times v_{sc} \quad (8)$$

The first-level indicator of the Risk control calculation equation is

$$\begin{bmatrix} 0.50 & 0.15 & 0.25 & 0.35 \\ 0.85 & 0.50 & 0.15 & 0.25 \\ 0.75 & 0.85 & 0.50 & 0.15 \\ 0.65 & 0.75 & 0.85 & 0.50 \end{bmatrix} \quad (9)$$

$$\omega_1 = \frac{\sum_{i=1}^{n} a_{1_{ij}} + \frac{n}{2} - 1}{n(n-1)} = 0.271 \quad (10)$$

$$\omega_2 = \frac{\sum_{i=1}^{n} a_{2_{ij}} + \frac{n}{2} - 1}{n(n-1)} = 0.229 \quad (11)$$

$$\omega_3 = \frac{\sum_{i=1}^{n} a_{3_{ij}} + \frac{n}{2} - 1}{n(n-1)} = 0.188 \quad (12)$$

$$\omega_4 = \frac{\sum_{i=1}^{n} a_{4_{ij}} + \frac{n}{2} - 1}{n(n-1)} = 0.312 \tag{13}$$

The first-level indicator of the Risk control calculation equation is

$$S_2 = 0.271 \times v_{sr} + 0.229 \times v_{qr} + 0.188 \times v_{pr} + 0.312 \times v_{cr} \tag{14}$$

The first-level indicator of the Management control calculation equation is

$$\begin{bmatrix} 0.50 & 0.10 & 0.15 & 0.20 & 0.35 \\ 0.90 & 0.50 & 0.10 & 0.15 & 0.20 \\ 0.85 & 0.90 & 0.50 & 0.10 & 0.15 \\ 0.80 & 0.85 & 0.90 & 0.50 & 0.10 \\ 0.65 & 0.80 & 0.85 & 0.90 & 0.50 \end{bmatrix} \tag{15}$$

$$\omega_1 = \frac{\sum_{i=1}^{n} a_{1_{ij}} + \frac{n}{2} - 1}{n(n-1)} = 0.260 \tag{16}$$

$$\omega_2 = \frac{\sum_{i=1}^{n} a_{2_{ij}} + \frac{n}{2} - 1}{n(n-1)} = 0.233 \tag{17}$$

$$\omega_3 = \frac{\sum_{i=1}^{n} a_{3_{ij}} + \frac{n}{2} - 1}{n(n-1)} = 0.167 \tag{18}$$

$$\omega_4 = \frac{\sum_{i=1}^{n} a_{4_{ij}} + \frac{n}{2} - 1}{n(n-1)} = 0.200 \tag{19}$$

$$\omega_5 = \frac{\sum_{i=1}^{n} a_{5_{ij}} + \frac{n}{2} - 1}{n(n-1)} = 0.140 \tag{20}$$

The first-level indicator of the Management control calculation equation is

$$S_3 = 0.260 \times v_{qm} + 0.233 \times v_{im} + 0.167 \times v_{hrm} + 0.200 \times v_{HSEm} + 0.140 \times v_{cm} \tag{21}$$

The first-level indicator of the Schedule control calculation equation is

$$\begin{bmatrix} 0.50 & 0.05 & 0.15 & 0.30 & 0.35 \\ 0.95 & 0.50 & 0.05 & 0.15 & 0.30 \\ 0.85 & 0.95 & 0.50 & 0.05 & 0.15 \\ 0.70 & 0.85 & 0.95 & 0.50 & 0.05 \\ 0.65 & 0.70 & 0.85 & 0.95 & 0.50 \end{bmatrix} \tag{22}$$

$$\omega_1 = \frac{\sum_{i=1}^{n} a_{1_{ij}} + \frac{n}{2} - 1}{n(n-1)} = 0.173 \tag{23}$$

$$\omega_2 = \frac{\sum_{i=1}^{n} a_{2_{ij}} + \frac{n}{2} - 1}{n(n-1)} = 0.227 \tag{24}$$

$$\omega_3 = \frac{\sum_{i=1}^{n} a_{3_{ij}} + \frac{n}{2} - 1}{n(n-1)} = 0.257 \tag{25}$$

$$\omega_4 = \frac{\sum_{i=1}^{n} a_{4_{ij}} + \frac{n}{2} - 1}{n(n-1)} = 0.143 \tag{26}$$

$$\omega_5 = \frac{\sum_{i=1}^{n} a_{5_{ij}} + \frac{n}{2} - 1}{n(n-1)} = 0.200 \tag{27}$$

The first-level indicator of the Schedule control calculation equation is

$$S_4 = 0.173 \times v_{\text{ip}} + 0.227 \times v_{\text{ep}} + 0.257 \times v_{cp} + 0.143 \times v_{ap} + 0.200 \times v_{omp} \tag{28}$$

where, $v_{\mathbf{dc}}$ is development cost, $v_{\mathbf{pcc}}$ is purchase cost, $v_{\mathbf{pdc}}$ is production cost, $v_{\mathbf{sc}}$ is selling cost; $v_{\mathbf{sr}}$ is schedule risk, $v_{\mathbf{qr}}$ is quality risk, $v_{\mathbf{psr}}$ is people risk, $v_{\mathbf{cr}}$ is cost risk; $v_{\mathbf{qm}}$ is quality management, $v_{\mathbf{im}}$ is investment management, $v_{\mathbf{hrm}}$ is human resources management, $v_{\mathbf{HSEm}}$ is HSE management, $v_{\mathbf{cm}}$ is communication management; $v_{\mathbf{ip}}$ is initiation phase,

$v_{\mathbf{ep}}$ is exploration phase, $v_{\mathbf{cp}}$ is construction phase, $v_{\mathbf{ap}}$ is the acceptance phase, $v_{\mathbf{omp}}$ is the operation and maintenance phase.

The final evaluation model expression is

$$P_{IPD} = 0.273 \times S_1 + 0.228 \times S_2 + 0.189 \times S_3 + 0.310 \times S_4 \tag{29}$$

Based on the evaluation ratings, sub-indicators can be used to calculate the IPD values under multiple sampling S_1, S_2, S_3, and S_4 combinations. The $P_{\mathbf{IPD}}$ magnitude can be calculated based on the final evaluation model expression. The model's indicator level evaluation, which needs to meet the requirements of the base plane for most indicators to be qualified, takes a value greater than or equal to 3 as the basis for selection. The IPD method is applicable to a specific project when the calculated $\boldsymbol{P}$ score for that project is greater than or equal to 3. As shown in Figure 6, it illustrates the calculation of the coefficient matrix for the IPD method using the FAHP model.

The results indicate a clear hierarchy of the importance of various indicators within the IPD method. In Cost control, PDC occupies the majority proportion, followed by DC, PCC, and SC. This prioritization underscores the emphasis on investing in production costs, particularly construction materials, over selling costs. In Risk control, CR takes up a more excellent reweighting ratio, reflecting a focus on mitigating financial risks to ensure project cash flow remains unimpeded. While risks related to personnel, such as construction-related injuries, bear a lower weight, they are not to be disregarded.

Management control sees QM as the most critical indicator, followed by IM, HSEM, HRM, and finally CM. It may demonstrate a commitment to ensuring high-quality project outcomes. Progress control highlights the importance of CP in managing construction phase timelines, with AP carrying less weight due to its position at the project's conclusion. In the final evaluation model expression, Schedule control reigns supreme, followed by Cost control, Risk control, and finally Management control. It aligns with the IPD method's emphasis on optimizing economic benefits through efficient project cycles and cost reductions.

4.2. *Case Application*

4.2.1. Description of the Case Project

A case project in Fujian, China, has been selected to express the IPD application. The case project is a significant collaboration between the multiple cooperative institutions [56]. This project aims to establish an oil refining capacity of 8 million tons per year, along with an ethylene production capacity of 800,000 tons per year, encompassing 18 process units and associated infrastructure. Initially, the project adopted the OR method, engaging a consortium of two international oil companies through a public tender. The International Engineering Company was also involved in the EPC contracting for the ethylene and Integrated Gasification Combined Cycle (IGCC) plants.

As the project progressed, various issues and discrepancies within the management model became apparent. Divergent corporate cultures and interests among the OR parties led to conceptual differences, resulting in sluggish project advancement. Moreover, discrepancies between the construction standards of foreign companies and those in Chinese projects significantly impeded project development. Financially, the project experienced substantial cost overruns, with the OR construction exceeding the budget by RMB 4.5 billion. The management fees and implementation costs associated with the OR method were exorbitant, with project management expenses reaching RMB 400 million. One of the oil companies quoted RMB 1.8 billion for the ethylene plant, while another RMB 200 million was paid for the IGCC plant. In terms of scheduling, the project faced significant delays. Under the OR method, completion was estimated to take fifty months, with an additional ten months required for operational readiness.

Evaluation subjects	Intergrated indicators	Sub-indication	Pair-wise comparison					Weighting indicator	Overall weighting indicators
P_{IPD}	S_1	DC	0.50	0.15	0.30	0.25		0.267	0.273
		PCC	0.85	0.50	0.15	0.30		0.233	
		PDC	0.70	0.85	0.50	0.15		0.317	
		SC	0.75	0.70	0.85	0.50		0.183	
	S_2	SR	0.50	0.15	0.25	0.35		0.271	0.228
		QR	0.85	0.50	0.15	0.25		0.229	
		PR	0.75	0.85	0.50	0.15		0.188	
		CR	0.65	0.75	0.85	0.50		0.312	
	S_3	QM	0.50	0.10	0.15	0.20	0.35	0.260	0.189
		IM	0.90	0.50	0.10	0.15	0.20	0.233	
		HRM	0.85	0.90	0.50	0.10	0.15	0.167	
		HSEM	0.80	0.85	0.90	0.50	0.10	0.200	
		CM	0.65	0.80	0.85	0.90	0.50	0.140	
	S_4	IP	0.50	0.05	0.15	0.30	0.35	0.173	0.310
		EP	0.95	0.50	0.05	0.15	0.30	0.227	
		CP	0.85	0.95	0.50	0.05	0.15	0.257	
		AP	0.70	0.85	0.95	0.50	0.05	0.143	
		OMP	0.65	0.70	0.85	0.95	0.50	0.200	

- The IPD evaluation mode expression:

$$P_{IPD} = 0.273 \times S_1 + 0.228 \times S_2 + 0.189 \times S_3 + 0.310 \times S_4$$

- The first-level indicator of Cost control calculation equation:

$$S_1 = 0.267 \times v_{dc} + 0.233 \times v_{pcc} + 0.317 \times v_{pdc} + 0.183 \times v_{sc}$$

- The first-level indicator of Risk control calculation equation:

$$S_2 = 0.271 \times v_{sr} + 0.229 \times v_{qr} + 0.188 \times v_{pr} + 0.312 \times v_{cr}$$

- The first-level indicator of Management control calculation equation:

$$S_3 = 0.260 \times v_{qm} + 0.233 \times v_{im} + 0.167 \times v_{hrm} + 0.200 \times v_{HSEm} + 0.140 \times v_{cm}$$

- The first-level indicator of Schedule control calculation equation:

$$S_4 = 0.173 \times v_{ip} + 0.227 \times v_{ep} + 0.257 \times v_{cp} + 0.143 \times v_{ap} + 0.200 \times v_{oms}$$

Figure 6. FAHP model calculation matrix.

4.2.2. Application of the IPD Method

To address the OR method's deficiencies, the project requires a dynamic and efficient management approach to enhance performance in management, cost, and scheduling aspects. Based on the research, the IPD method may effectively address these shortcomings. This study used the FAHP model to evaluate the adaptability of the IPD method to the primary conditions. First, the weighting calculation, determining the coefficient matrix V and S using the FAHP model, was determined through a ranking assessment conducted by the expert group. As shown in Table 2, the scores for S_1, S_2, S_3, S_4 are 3.60, 3.71, 3.10, and 3.37, respectively. The final value of P_{IPD} is 3.46, exceeding the threshold of 3, with each Si also assigning over 3. According to the evaluation threshold definition, the IPD method is well-suited for the project.

Table 2. Weighting calculation using the FAHP model.

Indicators	Weighting Calculation	Scale
S_1	$S_1 = 0.267 \times 3 + 0.233 \times 5 + 0.317 \times 4 + 0.183 \times 2$	3.60
S_2	$S_2 = 0.271 \times 4 + 0.229 \times 3 + 0.188 \times 2 + 0.312 \times 5$	3.71
S_3	$S_3 = 0.260 \times 3 + 0.229 \times 4 + 0.167 \times 3 + 0.200 \times 1 + 0.140 \times 5$	3.10
S_4	$S_4 = 0.173 \times 1 + 0.227 \times 5 + 0.257 \times 4 + 0.143 \times 3 + 0.200 \times 3$	3.37
P_{IPD}	$P_{IPD} = 0.273 \times 3.60 + 0.228 \times 3.71 + 0.189 \times 3.10 + 0.310 \times 3.37$	3.46

4.2.3. Comprehensive Benefit Analysis between the IPD Method and OR Method

The project staff actually applied the IPD method. After establishing infrastructure management expertise and on-site realities, a comprehensive management strategy for each project phase and process was considered based on the IPD method. This approach standardized management protocols and systems, streamlined workflows, and boosted functional department efficiency. In terms of personnel management, the IPD method differs from the OR method by aligning managers with shared cultural philosophies and objectives, fostering collaborative efforts towards common goals through contractual obligations and administrative cooperation. Notably, the owner's oversight in the IPD method is more robust, enabling proactive leadership and decisive involvement in critical project milestones. Implementing the IPD method resulted in significant project advancements, reducing project duration by twelve months compared to the OR method and enhancing project operational efficiency. In terms of cost, the IPD method achieved substantial savings, including RMB 400 million in management expenses, RMB 1.3 billion in imported material procurement costs, and a total project investment reduction of RMB 4.5 billion compared to the OR method, yielding considerable cost efficiencies.

The successful application of this project management approach has not only expedited project delivery but also equipped the engineering construction management team with valuable experience, laying a solid foundation for cultivating skilled and proficient project management. The whole set of methods can be appropriately extended to evaluate other large- and medium-sized engineering projects, facilitating effective control of the four aspects of cost, risk, management, and schedule.

4.3. Limitations and Future Directions

4.3.1. Contributions

This study addresses the needs of large- and medium-sized engineering projects both domestically and internationally in project management, with a specific focus on the adaptability of integrated project delivery methods. Decision-making suggestions for large- and medium-sized project delivery methods are provided based on decision-theoretic parsing schemes. The results of this study are highly relevant to the project reality, offering valuable insights for management teams to effectively select delivery methods that align with project requirements such as cost, risk, management, and schedule. From a scientific research perspective, the FAHP model is innovatively applied in the decision-making process for delivery methods of large- and medium-sized projects. By establishing a weight calculation equation to construct the FAHP model, this study addresses the common challenges faced by various large- and medium-sized projects in selecting delivery methods.

4.3.2. Limitations

This paper derives the weighting formula for evaluating the applicability of IPD using the FAHP model. This study only focused on the classical FAHP model to conduct the adaptability analysis of the specific IPD method. However, in the decision theory field, numerous brilliant evaluation methods may better evaluate the adaptability analysis of different engineering management methods. When applied to managing different projects, there is a lack of detailed discussion of the advantages and disadvantages of varying decision theory models. Furthermore, in this study, the FAHP scoring results were mainly applied to one single petrochemical case project without exploring its potential in other domains, lacking a broader application across multiple cases.

4.3.3. Future Directions

Based on the current research findings, several future works can be immediately undertaken. First, while the IPD method was initially tailored for construction projects, we seek to explore its applicability across a broader spectrum of project types, including logistics management. Second, to tackle the issue of inadequate communication with engineers, we plan to develop an evaluation tool incorporating the FAHP model for automated assessment of the IPD method's efficacy, streamlining the evaluation process for engineering projects. Last but not least, we aspire to gather additional real-world engineering cases to enhance our utilization of the FAHP model, thereby refining model precision and accuracy.

It is important to mention that the choice of experts can be customized based on different factors, such as the specific characteristics and needs of the project, as well as its unique environmental features. Professionals working across various regions and projects can create evaluation models that take into account local nuances, thereby improving the precision of the model. In addition, by increasing the number of experts and expanding into more areas in the near future, the reliability of the associated weight coefficients can be enhanced.

5. Conclusions

In large- and medium-sized engineering projects, the IPD method is favored for its excellent coordination and control characteristics. Currently, studies place more emphasis on the economic benefits brought by the IPD method, remaining in the absence of comprehensive research on the adaptability analysis of IPD. This study applies an evaluation model for analyzing IPD adaptability; weighting equations are obtained and applied in engineering projects with positive results.

Compared to the EPC, OCM, and OR methods, the IPD method combines organizational personnel, project management processes, engineering and construction connections, and management objectives. This integration ensures a streamlined and consistent approach to project implementation. Each participating unit combines the team strengths of each party to cooperate and manage together, avoiding the contradiction of traditional project management. Integration management integrates the original independent project processes and elements, which is conducive to the standardization and integrity of large-scale project design and construction.

This study conducted a matrix calculation using eighteen second-level indicators to derive weight values for four first-level indicators: Cost control, Risk control, Management control, and Schedule control. These first-level indicators were then used to formulate the total evaluation index calculation. By assigning quantitative values based on the importance of each index, the FAHP model calculated the first-level index S_i and the total index P_{IPD}. Values exceeding 3 indicate the utilization of the IPD method in the project. The model can provide a basis for decision analysis in the case of large- and medium-sized engineering projects considering multiple aspects of the situation.

More than thirty large- and medium-sized project experts, including engineers, managers, and academics, participated in the questionnaire that resulted in the weighting matrix formula. In a practical case study of oil engineering in Fujian, the FAHP model was employed to assess the applicability of IPD. The calculated values for the four first-level indexes S_1, S_2, S_3, S_4 were 3.60, 3.71, 3.10, and 3.37, resulting in a final P_{IPD} value of 3.46, all exceeding 3, indicating a high suitability for the IPD method. By implementing IPD, the project achieved significant cost savings of RMB 4.5 billion and accelerated the schedule by 12 months.

It should be noted that the evaluation results of this study are mainly applied to a petrochemical case project, and there is a lack of practical application in other large- and medium-sized engineering case studies. In the future, the research will expand the application scope of the FAHP model, increase the number of experts, and broaden their areas of expertise to enhance the model's accuracy. As a whole, this paper contributes a novel and objective approach to the adaptability analysis of the IPD method in large- and medium-sized engineering projects by coupling decision theory into project management.

Author Contributions: Conceptualization, H.H.; methodology, L.L.; validation, L.L.; investigation, X.G. and X.Z.; resources, X.Z.; data curation, X.G.; writing—original draft preparation, X.G.; writing—review and editing, L.L.; visualization, X.G.; supervision, H.H.; project administration, H.H.; funding acquisition, L.L. All authors have read and agreed to the published version of the manuscript.

Funding: This work was kindly supported by the financial support (Research on Application of project management method in Municipal Transportation Industry grant number 23HK0121) from Shenzhen General Integrated Transportation and Municipal Engineering Design & Research Institute, Co., Ltd.

Data Availability Statement: The original contributions presented in the study are included in the article, further inquiries can be directed to the corresponding author.

Acknowledgments: The authors would like to thank all the members involved in this project for their help in developing this article. The authors declare that generative AI and AI-assisted technologies were not used in the writing process in this paper.

Conflicts of Interest: Authors Huiyu He and Xing Zhang were employed by the company Shenzhen General Integrated Transportation and Municipal Engineering Design & Research Institute Co., Ltd. The authors declare that the research was conducted in the absence of any commercial or financial relationships that could be construed as a potential conflict of interest. The authors declare that this study received funding from Shenzhen General Integrated Transportation and Municipal Engineering Design & Research Institute Co., Ltd. The funder was not involved in the study design, collection, analysis, interpretation of data, the writing of this article or the decision to submit it for publication.

Abbreviations

The following abbreviations are used in this manuscript:

IPD	Integrated Project Delivery
FAHP	Fuzzy Analytic Hierarchy Process
DBB	Design–Bid–Build
DB	Design–Build
CM at Risk	Construction Manager at Risk
BOT	Build–Operate–Transfer
EPC	Engineering Procurement Construction
OR	Owner's Representative
OCM	Owner's Construction Management
PPP	Public–Private Partnerships
AHP	Analytic Hierarchy Process
DC	Development Cost
PCC	Purchase Cost
PDC	Production Cost
SC	Selling Cost
SR	Schedule Risk
QR	Quality Risk

PR	People Risk
CR	Cost Risk
QM	Quality Management
IM	Investment Management
HRM	Human Resources Management
HSEM	Health, Safety, and Environment Management
CM	Communication Management
IP	Initiation Phase
EP	Exploration Phase
CP	Construction Phase
AP	Acceptance Phase
OMP	Operation and Maintenance Phase

Appendix A

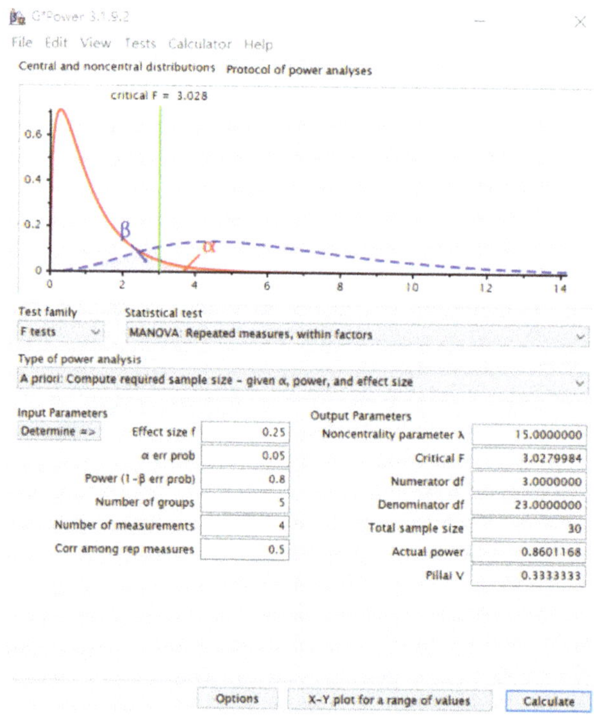

Figure A1. The F-test result in the G*Power 3.0.10.

References

1. Locatelli, G.; Ika, L.; Drouin, N.; Müller, R.; Huemann, M.; Söderlund, J.; Geraldi, J.; Clegg, S. A Manifesto for project management research. *Eur. Manag. Rev.* **2023**, *20*, 3–17. [CrossRef]
2. Guo, K.; Zhang, L. Multi-objective optimization for improved project management: Current status and future directions. *Autom. Constr.* **2022**, *139*, 104256. [CrossRef]
3. Kadenic, M.D.; Tambo, T. Resilience of operating models: Exploring the potential of agile project management as enabler. *Int. J. Manag. Proj. Bus.* **2023**, *16*, 521–542. [CrossRef]
4. Pan, Y.; Zhang, L. A BIM-data mining integrated digital twin framework for advanced project management. *Autom. Constr.* **2021**, *124*, 103564. [CrossRef]
5. Mavi, R.K.; Standing, C. Critical success factors of sustainable project management in construction: A fuzzy DEMATEL-ANP approach. *J. Clean. Prod.* **2018**, *194*, 751–765. [CrossRef]
6. Müller, R. Exploring the future of research in project management. *Rev. Gestão Proj.* **2023**, *14*, 14–26. [CrossRef]
7. Hallowell, M.; Toole, T.M. Contemporary Design-Bid-Build Model. *J. Constr. Eng. Manag.* **2009**, *135*, 540–549. [CrossRef]

8. Chen, Y.; Zhu, X.; Zhang, N. *Comparison of Project Objectives and Critical Factors between DBB and DB in China*; IEEE: Piscataway, NJ, USA, 2009; Volume 12, pp. 583–587. [CrossRef]
9. Carpenter, N.; Bausman, D.C. Project Delivery Method Performance for Public School Construction: Design-Bid-Build versus CM at Risk. *J. Constr. Eng. Manag.* **2016**, *142*, 05016009. [CrossRef]
10. Huang, Y.L.; Pi, C.C. Real-Option Valuation of Build-Operate-Transfer Infrastructure Projects under Performance Bonding. *J. Constr. Eng. Manag.* **2014**, *140*, 04013068. [CrossRef]
11. Sholeh, M.N.; Fauziyah, S. Current state mapping of the supply chain in engineering procurement construction (EPC) project: A case study. *MATEC Web Conf.* **2018**, *195*, 06015. [CrossRef]
12. Shen, Z.; Zhao, J.; Guo, M. Evaluating the Engineering-Procurement-Construction Approach and Whole Process Engineering Consulting Mode in Construction Projects. *Iran. J. Sci. Technol. Trans. Civ. Eng.* **2023**, *47*, 2533–2547. [CrossRef]
13. Abe, R.; Saito, Y.; Shide, K. Research on each actor's awareness of procurement methods involving contractors and consultants in the design phase: Based on interviews with persons in charge. *Jpn. Archit. Rev.* **2023**, *6*, e12384. [CrossRef]
14. Vasilenko, M.A.; Drozdov, N.A.; Tagiltseva, J.A.; Kuzina, E.L.; Kuzina, M.A. *Systematic Approach and Advanced Marketing in Public-Private Partnerships*; IEEE: Piscataway, NJ, USA, 2017; Volume 9, pp. 27–31. [CrossRef]
15. Santolini, M.; Ellinas, C.; Nicolaides, C. Uncovering the fragility of large-scale engineering projects. *EPJ Data Sci.* **2021**, *10*, 36. [CrossRef]
16. Jadidoleslami, S.; Saghatforoush, E.; Heravi, A.; Preece, C. A practical framework to facilitate constructability implementation using the integrated project delivery approach: A case study. *Int. J. Constr. Manag.* **2022**, *22*, 1225–1239. [CrossRef]
17. Trach, R.; Polonski, M.; Hrytsiuk, P. Modelling of Efficiency Evaluation of Traditional Project Delivery Methods and Integrated Project Delivery (IPD). *IOP Conf. Ser. Mater. Sci. Eng.* **2019**, *471*, 112043. [CrossRef]
18. Choi, J.; Yun, S.; Leite, F.; Mulva, S.P. Team Integration and Owner Satisfaction: Comparing Integrated Project Delivery with Construction Management at Risk in Health Care Projects. *J. Manag. Eng.* **2019**, *35*. [CrossRef]
19. Demirel, T.; Çetin Demirel, N.; Kahraman, C. Fuzzy Analytic Hierarchy Process and its Application. In *Fuzzy Multi-Criteria Decision Making*; Springer: Boston, MA, USA, 2008; pp. 53–83. [CrossRef]
20. Chih, Y.Y.; Hsiao, C.Y.L.; Zolghadr, A.; Naderpajouh, N. Resilience of Organizations in the Construction Industry in the Face of COVID-19 Disturbances: Dynamic Capabilities Perspective. *J. Manag. Eng.* **2022**, *38*, 04022002. [CrossRef]
21. Bypaneni, S.P.K.; Tran, D.Q. Empirical Identification and Evaluation of Risk in Highway Project Delivery Methods. *J. Manag. Eng.* **2018**, *34*. [CrossRef]
22. Koolwijk, J.S.J.; van Oel, C.J.; Wamelink, J.W.F.; Vrijhoef, R. Collaboration and Integration in Project-Based Supply Chains in the Construction Industry. *J. Manag. Eng.* **2018**, *34*, 04018001. [CrossRef]
23. Han, J.; Lee, S.H.; Kim, J.K. A process integrated engineering knowledge acquisition and management model for a project based manufacturing. *Int. J. Precis. Eng. Manuf.* **2017**, *18*, 175–185. [CrossRef]
24. Kabirifar, K.; Mojtahedi, M. The impact of Engineering, Procurement and Construction (EPC) Phases on Project Performance: A Case of Large-scale Residential Construction Project. *Buildings* **2019**, *9*, 15. [CrossRef]
25. Wang, Q.; Wang, J. Research on Key Risk Factors and Risk Transmission Path of Procurement in International Engineering Procurement Construction Project. *Buildings* **2022**, *12*, 534. [CrossRef]
26. Institute, P.M. *Construction Extension to the PMBOK Guide*; Project Management Institute, Inc.: Newtown Square, PA, USA, 2016.
27. Council, F.F. *Federal Facilities Council Technical Report, Number 149: Reducing Construction Costs: Uses of Best Dispute Resolution Practices by Project Owners: Proceedings Report*; National Academies Press: Washington, DC, USA, 2007.
28. Forcael, E.; Rodríguez, C.; Vargas, S.; Álvarez, P.; Ponce, L. Role of the Owner's Representative Within the Construction Industry: Case Study of Chile. *Iran. J. Sci. Technol. Trans. Civ. Eng.* **2020**, *44*, 197–208. [CrossRef]
29. Mesa, H.A.; Molenaar, K.R.; Alarcón, L.F. Exploring performance of the integrated project delivery process on complex building projects. *Int. J. Proj. Manag.* **2016**, *34*, 1089–1101. [CrossRef]
30. Sherif, M.; Abotaleb, I.; Alqahtani, F.K. Application of Integrated Project Delivery (IPD) in the Middle East: Implementation and Challenges. *Buildings* **2022**, *12*, 467. [CrossRef]
31. Kahvandi, Z.; Melhado, S.; Viana, M.L. Solutions to Overcome Integrated Project Delivery Implementation Barriers: A Meta-Synthesis Approach. *J. Constr. Dev. Ctries* **2023**, *28*, 63–89. [CrossRef]
32. Hall, D.M.; Scott, W.R. Early Stages in the Institutionalization of Integrated Project Delivery. *Proj. Manag. J.* **2019**, *50*, 128–143. [CrossRef]
33. Barutha, P.J.; Jeong, H.D.; Gransberg, D.D.; Touran, A. Evaluation of the Impact of Collaboration and Integration on Performance of Industrial Projects. *J. Manag. Eng.* **2021**, *37*, 04021037. [CrossRef]
34. Salleh, R.M.; Mustaffa, N.E.; Rahiman, N.A.; Ariffin, H.L.T.; Othman, N. The Propensity of Building Information Modelling and Integrated Project Delivery in Building Construction Project. *Int. J. Built Environ. Sustain.* **2019**, *6*, 83–90. [CrossRef]
35. Jünger, H.C.; Hofmann, A.; Schneebecke, J.; Scharpf, S.; Auch, N. Die Erweiterung der Integrierten Projektabwicklung auf den Lebenszyklusansatz/The expansion of Integrated Project Delivery to the life cycle approach. *Bauingenieur* **2022**, *97*, 298–305. [CrossRef]
36. Mesa, H.A.; Molenaar, K.R.; Alarcón, L.F. Comparative analysis between integrated project delivery and lean project delivery. *Int. J. Proj. Manag.* **2019**, *37*, 395–409. [CrossRef]

37. Dzhusupova, R.; Bosch, J.; Olsson, H.H. *Challenges in Developing and Deploying AI in the Engineering, Procurement and Construction Industry*; IEEE: Piscataway, NJ, USA, 2022; Volume 6, pp. 1070–1075. [CrossRef]
38. Sangroungrai, S.; Sukchareonpong, P.; Witchakul, S. *Engineering, Procurement and Construction (EPC) Project Management for Reducing Cost and Time: A Case Study of Petrochemical Plant*; IEEE: Piscataway, NJ, USA, 2018; Volume 5, pp. 402–406. [CrossRef]
39. Pishdad-Bozorgi, P.; Austin, R.; Garza, J.M.D.L. Flash Track Practices Distilled via Structured Interviews from EPC Projects. *Am. Soc. Civ. Eng.* **2016**, *5*, 168–178. [CrossRef]
40. Kahvandi, Z.; Saghatforoush, E.; ZareRavasan, A.; Viana, M.L. A Review and Classification of Integrated Project Delivery Implementation Enablers. *J. Constr. Dev. Ctries* **2020**, *25*, 219–236. [CrossRef]
41. Ling, F.Y.Y.; Teo, P.X.; Li, S.; Zhang, Z.; Ma, Q. Adoption of Integrated Project Delivery Practices for Superior Project Performance. *J. Leg. Aff. Disput. Resolut. Eng. Constr.* **2020**, *12*, 05020014. [CrossRef]
42. Zhang, Y.; Hu, H. Utilization of a cognitive task analysis for integrated project delivery application: Case study of constructing a campus underground parking facility. *Cogn. Syst. Res.* **2018**, *52*, 579–590. [CrossRef]
43. Ashcraft, H. Transforming project delivery: Integrated project delivery. *Oxf. Rev. Econ. Policy* **2022**, *38*, 369–384. [CrossRef]
44. Saaty, R. The analytic hierarchy process—What it is and how it is used. *Math. Model.* **1987**, *9*, 161–176. [CrossRef]
45. Saaty, T. The negotiation and resolution of the conflict in South Africa: The AHP. *ORiON* **2003**, *4*. [CrossRef]
46. Huang, G.; Sun, S.; Zhang, D. Safety Evaluation of Construction Based on the Improved AHP-Grey Model. *Wirel. Pers. Commun.* **2018**, *103*, 209–219. [CrossRef]
47. Lyu, H.M.; Sun, W.J.; Shen, S.L.; Zhou, A.N. Risk Assessment Using a New Consulting Process in Fuzzy AHP. *J. Constr. Eng. Manag.* **2020**, *146*, 04019112. [CrossRef]
48. Saaty, T.L.; Tran, L.T. Fuzzy Judgments and Fuzzy Sets. *Int. J. Strateg. Decis. Sci.* **2010**, *1*, 23–40. [CrossRef]
49. Zhang, X.L.; Wang, L.H. *Choosing an Appropriate Construction Project Delivery Method Using FAHP in China*; IEEE: Piscataway, NJ, USA, 2009; Volume 10, pp. 78–82. [CrossRef]
50. Kerzner, H. *Project Management: A Systems Approach to Planning, Scheduling, and Controlling*, 12th ed.; John Wiley & Sons, Inc.: Hoboken, NJ, USA, 2017.
51. Sears, S.K. *Construction Project Management: A Practical Guide to Field Construction Management*, 6th ed.; Wiley: Hoboken, NJ, USA, 2015.
52. Liu, L.; Lin, Y.; Xiao, Y.; Xue, P.; Shi, L.; Chen, X.; Liu, J. Quantitative effects of urban spatial characteristics on outdoor thermal comfort based on the LCZ scheme. *Build. Environ.* **2018**, *143*, 443–460. [CrossRef]
53. Benson, C.; Obasi, I.C.; Akinwande, D.V.; Ile, C. The impact of interventions on health, safety and environment in the process industry. *Heliyon* **2024**, *10*, e23604. [CrossRef] [PubMed]
54. Saaty, T.L. Correction to: Some mathematical concepts of the analytic hierarchy process. *Behaviormetrika* **2021**, *48*, 193–194. [CrossRef]
55. Hand, D.J. Statistical Concepts: A Second Course, Fourth Edition by Richard G. Lomax, Debbie L. Hahs-Vaughn. *Int. Stat. Rev.* **2012**, *80*, 491. [CrossRef]
56. Song, D. Analysis and Discussion on Management Modes of Large-scale Petrochemical Engineering Projects. *Pet. Petrochem. Today* **2018**, *26*, 48–52. [CrossRef]

buildings

MDPI

Article

Numerical Analysis of Dynamic Characteristics of an Asymmetric Tri-Stable Piezoelectric Energy Harvester under Random Vibrations in Building Structures

Dawei Man [1,2], Qingnan Hu [1], Qinghu Xu [1,2], Liping Tang [1,2], Dong Chen [1,2], Ziqing Yuan [3,*] and Tingting Han [2]

1 School of Civil Engineering, Anhui Jianzhu University, Hefei 230601, China; mandawei@ahjzu.edu.cn (D.M.); huqingnan@stu.ahjzu.edu.cn (Q.H.); qinghx@ahjzu.edu.cn (Q.X.); tangliping2018@ahjzu.edu.cn (L.T.); chendong@ahjzu.edu.cn (D.C.)
2 BIM Engineering Center of Anhui Province, Hefei 230601, China; hantingting@ahjzu.edu.cn
3 School of Civil and Hydraulic Engineering, Hefei University of Technology, Hefei 230009, China
* Correspondence: yuanziqing@mail.hfut.edu.cn

Abstract: This study presents a novel design for a tri-stable piezoelectric vibration energy harvester with an asymmetric structure, which is enhanced with an elastic base (TPVEH + EB), meticulously designed to enhance energy extraction from irregular vibrations in architectural structures. The cornerstone of this design is the asymmetric tri-stable piezoelectric cantilever beam, distinctively arranged within a U-shaped block and fortified with an elastic foundation. A carefully positioned spring (kf)-mass (Mf) system between the U-shaped block and the beam's fixed end significantly boosts the vertical displacement of the beam during oscillations. Utilizing Lagrange's equations, we formulated a dynamic model for the asymmetric TPVEH + EB, examining the effects of potential well asymmetry, the stiffness of the elastic base and spring-mass system, the mass of the spring-mass system, and the tip magnet mass on the system's nonlinear dynamic responses. Our results demonstrate that the asymmetric TPVEH + EB significantly enhances energy harvesting from low-amplitude random vibrations (1.5 g), with the output voltage of the asymmetric TPVEH + EB increasing by 30% and the output power by 25%. Extensive numerical and theoretical analyses verify that the asymmetric TPVEH + EB provides a highly efficient solution for scenarios typically hindered by low energy conversion rates. Its reliable performance under varied and unpredictable excitation conditions highlights its excellence in advanced energy harvesting applications. The improvements detailed in this research underscore the potential of the asymmetric TPVEH + EB to boost energy harvesting efficiency, particularly in powering wireless sensor nodes for structural health monitoring in buildings. By overcoming the limitations of traditional harvesters, the asymmetric TPVEH + EB ensures enhanced efficiency and reliability, making it an ideal solution for a wide range of practical applications in diverse environmental conditions within buildings.

Keywords: asymmetric tri-stable; dynamic amplifier; random excitation; energy conversion efficiency; nonlinear dynamics

1. Introduction

Currently, utilizing structural health monitoring (SHM) systems to detect structural damage, assess performance, and make proactive operational and maintenance decisions has become an effective approach to ensuring the safe operation of building structures. A large number of wireless sensor nodes in SHM systems require a continuous and stable power supply. However, traditional chemical batteries are toxic and have limited lifespans, making it challenging and costly to replace batteries for widely distributed wireless sensor nodes, not to mention the difficulties in disposing of used batteries. Therefore, providing a clean and sustainable power source for wireless sensor nodes in SHM systems to ensure long-term real-time monitoring of building health is a critical technological issue in the field of building disaster prevention [1–3]. Harvesting environmental vibrational energy and storing it is an eco-friendly and highly efficient mechanism for energy collection. This approach can be widely applied to various building structures and can operate effectively even in extreme environments. Piezoelectric vibration energy harvesters (PVEHs) are distinguished within the array of energy harvesting technologies, attracting significant interest for their high energy density, straightforward design, easy implementation, and excellent expandability [4–6].

The fundamental principle behind piezoelectric energy harvesting involves the use of piezoelectric materials, such as lead zirconate titanate (PZT) or polyvinylidene fluoride (PVDF), which generate electric charge when subjected to mechanical deformation. These materials can be configured in different structures, such as cantilever beams or membrane structures, to maximize the energy conversion efficiency [7]. Recent advancements have led to the development of multi-stable and nonlinear energy harvesters that can operate efficiently over a broader range of frequencies and at lower levels of excitation [8]. These innovations are crucial for applications in structural health monitoring, where the energy requirements are met through harvesting ambient vibrations. Traditional PVEHs only generate a strong amplitude response when their resonance frequency aligns perfectly with that of ambient vibrations. However, this alignment is rare in most practical situations, leading to inefficient energy conversion due to limited output power and a narrow frequency range. Addressing this challenge, researchers have explored the concept of magnet-induced nonlinearity, including bi-stability [9–11], tri-stability [12–14], and various forms of multi-stability [15–17], to expand the operational frequency range and enhance performance at minimal base excitations. For instance, Zhou et al. [18] introduced a tri-stable PVEH (TPVEH) with lower energy barriers than its bi-stable counterpart (BPVEH), showcasing superior energy harvesting from vibrations. Further, Zhou et al. [19] demonstrated the potential of dynamic-stable PVEHs in capturing energy from fluid flow, noting a decreased airflow speed threshold for high voltage generation. Mei et al. [20] deployed a quad-stable PVEH in a rotating setting, achieving variable potential wells that lower energy barriers and increase conversion efficiency. Nonetheless, the common issue among these innovations is the symmetrical potential energy wells with high barriers, making transitions from intra-well to inter-well orbits challenging, especially under weak excitations.

Recently, efforts have been made to incorporate asymmetrical or adjustable potential functions into harvesters, aiming at barrier reduction and efficiency enhancement. Yang et al. [21] and Li et al. [22] developed a broad-spectrum BPVEH employing a movable magnet for easier snap-through transitions. Zhou and Zou [23] delved into the dynamic advantages of an asymmetric TPVEH in boosting energy collection. Cai [24] examined the dynamic behavior of an asymmetric TPVEH integrated with an AC-DC conversion circuit. Through Monte Carlo simulation, Li and Zhou [25] assessed the probabilistic dynamics of an asymmetric TPVEH. Additionally, Ma et al. [26] applied the Melnikov method to study the energy-capturing capabilities of an asymmetric TPVEH. Targeting efficient low-amplitude vibration energy harvesting across a wide-frequency spectrum, Wang et al. [27,28] investigated the synergy of an elastic base (EB) within a coupled elastic system, focusing on enhancing BPVEH and TPVEH setups for low-frequency energy capture. This approach, as our prior work [29] also highlights, involves a TPVEH equipped with a dynamic amplifier for optimized low-orbit vibration energy harvesting. While strides have been made, the understanding of asymmetric TPVEH dynamics with an elastic base under stochastic excitation remains incomplete. A thorough grasp of the nonlinear dynamics in such systems, particularly with a dynamic amplifier under random stimulation, is crucial for further improving energy harvesting efficacy and its practical deployment.

Previous research has explored various methods to enhance the performance of PVEHs, including the introduction of bi-stable and tri-stable configurations to broaden the operational frequency range and improve energy harvesting efficiency. Despite these advancements, symmetrical potential wells in these configurations often result in high energy barriers, making it difficult for the system to transition between states, especially under weak excitations. This research proposes an asymmetric TPVEH that overcomes these challenges by integrating an elastic base (EB) and a spring-mass mechanism, resulting in asymmetric potential wells. This design significantly lowers the energy barriers, facilitating easier transitions between states and enhancing energy harvesting efficiency under low-frequency random vibrations. The TPVEH + EB is intended to power wireless sensor nodes in structural health monitoring systems installed on buildings, as illustrated in Figure 1. We performed both theoretical analyses and numerical simulations to assess the device's performance under random excitations experienced by building structures. The results reveal that the asymmetric TPVEH + EB facilitates inter-well motions more readily and produces higher output voltages compared to its symmetric counterpart, even under weak random excitations. Our findings demonstrate that the proposed asymmetric TPVEH + EB significantly enhances energy harvesting efficiency, making it particularly suitable for powering wireless sensor nodes in structural health monitoring systems. This advancement ensures a continuous and reliable power supply, overcoming the limitations of traditional energy sources and improving the long-term, real-time monitoring of building health.

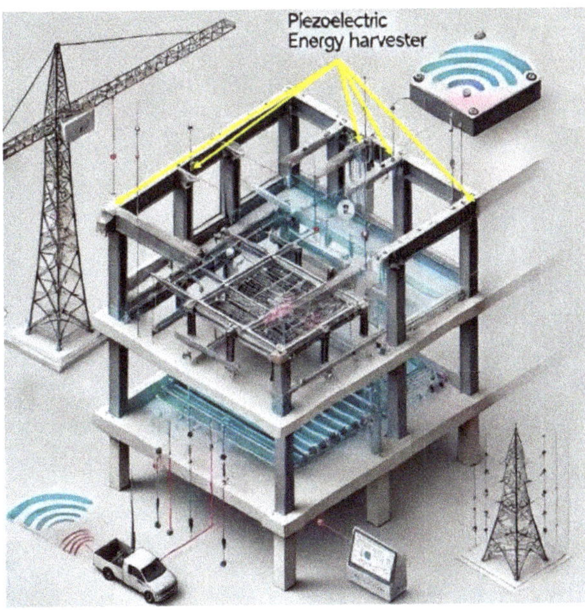

Figure 1. Schematic diagram of the piezoelectric energy harvester arrangement in the structural health monitoring system of a building.

Compared to the previous research, which focused on symmetrical tri-stable PVEHs, this study introduces several key innovations: (1). The design of the TPVEH + EB, with its asymmetric configuration, enhances energy capture from low-amplitude vibrations by lowering the barriers of the potential wells. (2). The inclusion of an elastic base and a strategically placed spring-mass system amplifies the vertical displacement of the beam, further improving energy conversion efficiency. (3). The detailed numerical and theoretical analyses presented in this study provide a comprehensive understanding of the nonlinear dynamics of the asymmetric TPVEH + EB under random excitations, highlighting its superior performance in practical applications.

2. Structural Layout and Dynamic Modeling of the Asymmetric TPVEH + EB

Figure 2 depicts the structural layout of the proposed asymmetric TPVEH + EB. This model features a pair of piezoelectric layers bonded to both sides of a cantilever beam's metal layer, which is of length l. A tip magnet is fastened at the beam's free end, with two external magnets asymmetrically positioned on the U-shaped block. The term d_h represents the horizontal separation between the tip magnet and the external magnets, while d_{v1} and d_{v2} indicate the respective vertical distances. Define o' as the point where the horizontal projection from the tip magnet intersects the line joining the external magnets, o as the midpoint of this line, and d_0 as the distance from o to o'. EB, consisting of a spring and U-shaped block, is strategically positioned between the asymmetric TPVEH and the elastic base. The mass M_f, situated at the constrained end of the beam, connects to both the beam and the U-shaped block via a vertical spring k_f, which enhances the vertical movement of the beam.

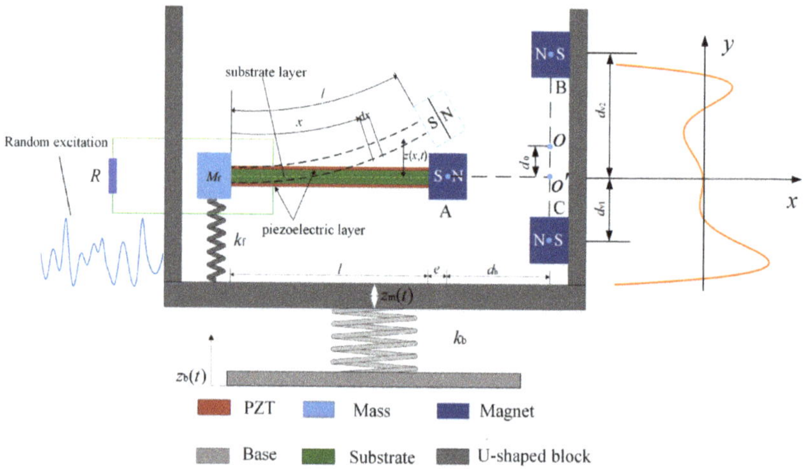

Figure 2. Configuration of the asymmetric TPVEH + EB [30].

Figure 2 illustrates the transverse displacements $z(x,t)$ at position x during the beam's vibration. The transverse displacements of the EB are denoted by $z_b(t)$, and the transverse displacements of the U-shaped block are represented by $z_m(t)$. The tip magnet's eccentricity is indicated by e. The primary interactions between the substrate and piezoelectric layers are detailed below:

$$\left.\begin{array}{l} T_1^s = Y_s S_1^s \\ T_1^p = Y_p(S_1^p - d_{31}E_3) \\ D_3 = d_{31}T_1 + \varepsilon_{33}^T E_3 \end{array}\right\} \tag{1}$$

Here, the subscript/superscript s refers to parameters related to the substrate layer, while the subscript/superscript p refers to those associated with the piezoelectric layer. The subscripts 1 and 3 denote the x and y directions, respectively. T, S, and Y represent stress, strain, and Young's modulus, respectively. $E_3 = -V(t)/(2t_p)$ signifies the electrical displacement, where $V(t)$ indicates voltage. d_{31} is the piezoelectric constant, and ε_{33}^T denotes the dielectric constant. The relationship between displacement and strain within the beam is expressed by the equation $S_1^s = S_1^p = -yw''$, with y representing the distance from the beam's neutral axis to any position within its cross-section.

The Lagrange equation governing the dynamics of asymmetric TPVEH + EB is presented below:

$$\int_{t_1}^{t_2} [\delta(T_K + W_P + U_g - U_e - U_m - U_d) + \delta W]dt = 0 \tag{2}$$

where T_k, W_p, U_g, U_e, U_m, and U_d represent the kinetic energy, electrical energy, gravitational potential energy, strain energy, magnetic potential energy, and elastic potential energy, respectively.

Based on the geometric relationship depicted in Figure 2, the kinetic energy of the asymmetric TPVEH + EB is mathematically formulated as follows:

$$\begin{aligned} T_{\mathrm{k}} = \frac{1}{2}\int_0^l m(\dot{z}+\dot{z}_{\mathrm{m}}(t))^2\mathrm{d}x + \frac{1}{2}M_{\mathrm{t}}\left(\dot{z}(l,t)+e\dot{z}'(l,t)+\dot{z}_{\mathrm{m}}(t)\right)^2 \\ +\frac{1}{2}J\dot{z}'(l,t)^2 + \frac{1}{2}M_{\mathrm{f}}(\dot{z}(0,t)+\dot{z}_{\mathrm{m}}(t))^2 + \frac{1}{2}M_{\mathrm{m}}\dot{z}_{\mathrm{m}}(t)^2 \end{aligned} \tag{3}$$

where J denotes the moment of inertia of the tip magnet.

The strain energy of the asymmetric TPVEH + EB is mathematically expressed as follows:

$$U_{\mathrm{e}} = \frac{1}{2}\int_0^l \left[YIz''^2 - Y_{\mathrm{P}}bd_{31}\left(h+\frac{t_{\mathrm{p}}}{2}\right)Z(t)z''\right]\mathrm{d}x \tag{4}$$

where $YI = \frac{2}{3}\left[Y_{\mathrm{s}}bh^3 + Y_{\mathrm{p}}b\left(3h^2t_{\mathrm{p}} + 3ht_{\mathrm{p}}^2 + t_{\mathrm{p}}^3\right)\right]$ denotes the stiffness of the beam.

The gravitational potential energy of the asymmetric TPVEH + EB is given by:

$$U_{\mathrm{g}} = mg\int_0^l (z+z_{\mathrm{m}}(t))\mathrm{d}x + M_{\mathrm{t}}g(z(l,t)+z_{\mathrm{m}}(t)) + M_{\mathrm{f}}g(z(0,t)+z_{\mathrm{m}}(t)) \tag{5}$$

The elastic potential energy of the EB is defined as:

$$U_{\mathrm{d}} = \frac{1}{2}k_{\mathrm{f}}z(0,t)^2 + \frac{1}{2}k_{\mathrm{b}}z_{\mathrm{m}}^2 \tag{6}$$

The formula detailing electrical energy is as follows:

$$W_{\mathrm{P}} = \frac{1}{2}Y_{\mathrm{P}}bd_{31}(\mathrm{h}+\frac{t_{\mathrm{p}}}{2})V(t)\int_0^l z''\mathrm{d}x + bl\varepsilon_{33}^{S}\frac{V(t)^2}{4t_{\mathrm{p}}} \tag{7}$$

where $\varepsilon_{33}^{s} = \varepsilon_{33}^{T} - d_{31}^2Y_{\mathrm{p}}$.

Employing Galerkin's method, $z(x,t)$ can be represented as:

$$z(x,t) = \sum_{r=1}^{n}\phi_{\mathrm{r}}(x)X_{\mathrm{r}}(t) \tag{8}$$

where $\phi_{\mathrm{r}}(x)$ denotes the rth order mode shape function of the beam and $X_{\mathrm{r}}(t)$ represents the generalized coordinates of the beam. The orthogonality condition is established as:

$$\begin{aligned} &\int_0^l \phi_{\mathrm{s}}(x)m\phi_{\mathrm{r}}(x)\mathrm{d}x + \phi_{\mathrm{s}}(l)M_{\mathrm{t}}\phi_{\mathrm{r}}(l) + \phi_{\mathrm{s}}(l)M_{\mathrm{t}}e\phi_{\mathrm{r}}'(l) \\ &+\phi_{\mathrm{s}}(0)M_{\mathrm{f}}\phi_{\mathrm{r}}(0) + \phi_{\mathrm{s}}'(l)(J+M_{\mathrm{t}}e^2)\phi_{\mathrm{s}}'(l) \\ &+\phi_{\mathrm{s}}'(l)M_{\mathrm{t}}e\phi_{\mathrm{r}}(l) = \delta_{\mathrm{rs}} \end{aligned} \tag{9}$$

$$\int_0^l \frac{\mathrm{d}^2\phi_{\mathrm{s}}(x)}{\mathrm{d}x^2}YI\frac{\mathrm{d}^2\phi_{\mathrm{r}}(x)}{\mathrm{d}x^2}dx + \phi_{\mathrm{s}}(0)k_{\mathrm{f}}\phi_{\mathrm{r}}(0) = \omega_{\mathrm{r}}^2\delta_{\mathrm{rs}} \tag{10}$$

where δ_{rs} denotes the Kronecker delta function. The intrinsic frequency of the undamped vibration of the beam is $\omega_{\mathrm{r}} = \lambda_{\mathrm{r}}^2\sqrt{YI/(ml^4})$ and λ_{r} is the eigenvalue. λ_{r} and the mode functionare computed as described in the referenced literature [31].

Based on the authors' earlier research, the formula for magnetic potential energy, taking into account only first-order modes of the tip magnet, is presented as follows:

$$\begin{aligned} U_{\mathrm{m}} = k_0 + k_1X_1 - \tfrac{1}{2}k_2X_1^2 + \tfrac{1}{3}k_3X_1^3 + \tfrac{1}{4}k_4X_1^4 + \tfrac{1}{5}k_5X_1^5 + \\ \tfrac{1}{6}k_6X_1^6 + o(X_1^7) \end{aligned} \tag{11}$$

where $k_0 = \frac{kq_1}{D_1^{\frac{5}{2}}} + \frac{kq_2}{D_2^{\frac{5}{2}}}$, $k_1 = \frac{k}{D_1^{\frac{5}{2}}}(5q_1q_3/D_1 + q_5) - \frac{k}{D_2^{\frac{5}{2}}}(5q_2q_4/D_2 + q_6)$,
$k_2 = -\frac{2k}{D_1^{\frac{5}{2}}}(q_1q_7 + 5q_3q_5/D_1 + q_9) - \frac{2k}{D_2^{\frac{5}{2}}}(q_2q_8 + 5q_4q_6/D_2 + q_{10})$,
$k_3 = \frac{3k}{D_1^{\frac{5}{2}}}(q_1q_{11} + 5q_3q_9/D_1 + q_5q_7 + q_{13}) - \frac{3k}{D_2^{\frac{5}{2}}}(q_2q_{12} + 5q_4q_{10}/D_2 + q_6q_8 + q_{14})$,
$k_4 = \frac{4k}{D_1^{\frac{5}{2}}}(q_1q_{15} + 5q_3q_{13}/D_1 + q_5q_{11} + q_7q_9 + q_{17}) + \frac{4k}{D_2^{\frac{5}{2}}}(q_2q_{16} + 5q_4q_{14}/D_2 + q_6q_{12} + q_8q_{10} + q_{18})$,
$k_5 = \frac{5k}{D_1^{\frac{5}{2}}}(q_1q_{19} + 5q_3q_{17}/D_1 + q_5q_{15} + q_9q_{11} + q_7q_{13} + q_{21})$
$-\frac{5k}{D_2^{\frac{5}{2}}}(q_2q_{20} + 5q_4q_{18}/D_2 + q_6q_{16} + q_{10}q_{12} + q_8q_{14} + q_{22})$,
$k_6 = \frac{6k}{D_1^{\frac{5}{2}}}(q_1q_{23} + 6q_3q_{21}/D_1 + q_5q_{19} + q_7q_{17} + q_9q_{15} + q_{11}q_{13} + q_{25})$
$+\frac{6k}{D_2^{\frac{5}{2}}}(q_2q_{24} + 6q_4q_{22}/D_2 + q_6q_{20} + q_8q_{18} + q_{10}q_{16} + q_{12}q_{14} + q_{26})$.

The detailed expressions for the k and $q_{1\ldots26}$ are detailed in the Appendix A.

Upon substituting Equation (8) into Equation (2), then into Lagrange's variational equation, we obtain:

$$\begin{cases} \frac{\mathrm{d}}{\mathrm{d}t}\left(\frac{\partial L}{\partial \dot{z}_{\mathrm{m}}}\right) - \frac{\partial L}{\partial z_{\mathrm{m}}} + \frac{\partial W}{\partial z_{\mathrm{m}}} = 0 \\ \frac{\mathrm{d}}{\mathrm{d}t}\left(\frac{\partial L}{\partial \dot{X}_1}\right) - \frac{\partial L}{\partial X_1} + \frac{\partial W}{\partial X_1} = F(t) \\ \frac{\mathrm{d}}{\mathrm{d}t}\left(\frac{\partial L}{\partial \dot{V}}\right) - \frac{\partial L}{\partial V} + \frac{\partial W}{\partial V} = Q(t) \end{cases} \tag{12}$$

where $F(t) = -2\xi_1\omega_1\dot{X}_1(t)$ represents the generalized dissipative force of the asymmetric TPVEH + EB, ω_1 represents the first-order natural frequency, ξ_1 is the damping ratio of the system, and $Q(t)$ signifies the generalized charge. Then, the electromechanical coupled motion equations for the ATPVEH + EB are derived using Equation (12), as demonstrated.

$$\begin{cases} M_0\ddot{X}_1(t) + M_1\ddot{z}_{\mathrm{m}}(t) + k_{\mathrm{b}}z_{\mathrm{m}} = -M_1\ddot{z}_{\mathrm{b}}(t) \\ \ddot{X}_1(t) + 2\xi_1\omega_1\dot{X}_1(t) + {\omega_1}^2X_1(t) + g_0 + k_1 - k_2X_1(t) \\ +k_3X_1(t)^2 + k_4X_1(t)^3 + k_5X_1(t)^4 + k_6X_1(t)^5 - \theta_1V(t) \\ +M_0\ddot{z}_{\mathrm{m}}(t) = -M_0\ddot{z}_{\mathrm{b}}(t) \\ C_{\mathrm{P}}\dot{V}(t) + \frac{V(t)}{R} + \theta_1\dot{X}_1(t) = 0 \end{cases} \tag{13}$$

where $M_0 = m\int_o^l \phi_1(x)\mathrm{d}x + M_{\mathrm{t}}\phi_1(l) + M_{\mathrm{t}}e\phi'_1(l) + M_{\mathrm{f}}\phi_1(0)$, $M_1 = ml + M_{\mathrm{t}} + M_{\mathrm{f}} + M_{\mathrm{m}}$, $g_0 = mg + M_{\mathrm{t}}g\phi_1(l) + M_{\mathrm{f}}g\phi_1(0)$ ${\omega_1}^2 = YI\int_0^l \phi_1''(x)^2\mathrm{d}x + k_{\mathrm{f}}\phi_1(0)^2$,
$\theta_1 = Y_{\mathrm{p}}bd_{31}\left(h + \frac{t_{\mathrm{p}}}{2}\right)\int_0^l \phi_1''(x)\mathrm{d}x$, $C_{\mathrm{p}} = \frac{bl\varepsilon_{33}^S}{2t_{\mathrm{p}}}$.

Several dimensionless parameters are introduced, namely, $x = X_1/l$, $\bar{z}_{\mathrm{m}} = z_{\mathrm{m}}/l$, $\bar{z}_{\mathrm{b}} = z_{\mathrm{b}}/l$, $\overline{V} = VC_{\mathrm{p}}/(l\theta_1)$ and $\tau = \omega_1 t$. Then, the following expression can be obtained:

$$\begin{cases} M_0\ddot{x} + M_1\ddot{\bar{z}}_{\mathrm{m}} + K_{\mathrm{b}}\bar{z}_{\mathrm{m}} = -M_1\ddot{\bar{z}}_{\mathrm{b}} \\ \ddot{x} + 2\xi_1\dot{x} + (1 - K_2)x + G_0 + K_1 + K_3x^2 + K_4x^3 + K_5x^4 + K_6x^5 \\ -\Theta\overline{V} + M_0\ddot{\bar{z}}_{\mathrm{m}} = -M_0\ddot{\bar{z}}_{\mathrm{b}} \\ \dot{\overline{V}} + \alpha\overline{V} + \dot{x} = 0 \end{cases} \tag{14}$$

where $K_{\mathrm{b}} = \frac{k_{\mathrm{b}}}{{\omega_1}^2}$, $K_1 = \frac{k_1}{{\omega_1}^2 l}$, $K_2 = \frac{k_2}{{\omega_1}^2}$, $K_3 = \frac{k_3 l}{{\omega_1}^2}$, $K_4 = \frac{k_4 l^2}{{\omega_1}^2}$, $K_5 = \frac{k_4 l^3}{{\omega_1}^2}$, $K_6 = \frac{k_4 l^4}{{\omega_1}^2}$, $G_0 = \frac{g_0}{{\omega_1}^2 l}$,
$\Theta = \frac{{\theta_1}^2}{C_{\mathrm{p}}{\omega_1}^2}$, $\alpha = \frac{1}{C_{\mathrm{p}}R\omega_1}$.

Let $\varepsilon_{\mathrm{R}} = \sqrt{f/\Delta t}\cdot\mathrm{normrnd}(1, N)$, where f is the strength of the random excitation, Δt represents the time interval, and normrnd(1,N) denotes N random numbers following a normal distribution. When the base excitation is modeled as a Gaussian white noise process, i.e., $\varepsilon_{\mathrm{R}} = -M_0\ddot{\bar{z}}_{\mathrm{b}}$, the dimensionless dynamical equation of the asymmetric TPVEH + EB system under random excitation is expressed as follows:

$$\begin{cases} M_0\ddot{x} + M_1\ddot{\overline{z}}_\mathrm{m} + K_\mathrm{b}\overline{z}_\mathrm{m} = \frac{M_1}{M_0}\varepsilon_\mathrm{R} \\ \ddot{x} + 2\xi_1\dot{x} + (1-K_2)x + G_0 + K_1 + K_3x^2 + K_4x^3 + K_5x^4 + K_6x^5 \\ -\Theta\overline{V} + M_0\ddot{\overline{z}}_\mathrm{m} = \varepsilon_\mathrm{R} \\ \dot{\overline{V}} + \alpha\overline{V} + \dot{x} = 0 \end{cases} \tag{15}$$

Let $z_1 = x, z_2 = \dot{x}, z_3 = \overline{z}_\mathrm{m}, z_4 = \dot{\overline{z}}_\mathrm{m}, z_5 = \overline{V}$. Equation (15) is transformed into a state space form:

$$\begin{bmatrix} \dot{x} \\ \ddot{x} \\ \dot{\overline{z}}_\mathrm{m} \\ \ddot{\overline{z}}_\mathrm{m} \\ \dot{\overline{V}} \end{bmatrix} = \begin{bmatrix} z_2 \\ \frac{M_0K_\mathrm{b}z_3 - 2\xi_1M_1z_2 + (1-K_2)M_1z_1 + M_1(G_0+K_1) + M_1K_3{z_1}^2 + M_1K_4{z_1}^3 + M_1K_5{z_1}^4 + M_1K_6{z_1}^5 - \Theta z_5}{M_1 - {M_0}^2} \\ z_4 \\ \frac{-K_\mathrm{b}z_3 + 2\xi_1M_0z_2 + (1-K_2)M_0z_1 + M_0(G_0+K_1) + M_0K_3{z_1}^2 + M_0K_4{z_1}^3 + M_0K_5{z_1}^4 + M_0K_6{z_1}^5 - \Theta z_5}{M_1 - {M_0}^2} - \frac{\varepsilon_\mathrm{R}}{M_0} \\ -\alpha z_5 - z_2 \end{bmatrix} \tag{16}$$

The electrical power value of the asymmetric TPVEH + EB is defined as follows [32]:

$$P = \sqrt{\frac{1}{\tau}\int_0^\tau {p^\mathrm{ins}}^2 \mathrm{d}\tau} \tag{17}$$

where p^ins is the instantaneous power at an instant of time τ and p^ins is defined as $p^\mathrm{ins} = \overline{V}^2/R$.

The RMS voltage can be expressed by the following formula:

$$\overline{V}_\mathrm{rms} = \sqrt{\frac{1}{\tau}\int_0^\tau \overline{V}^2 \mathrm{d}\tau} \tag{18}$$

3. Dynamic Performance Analysis

In this section, we numerically investigate the potential well asymmetry, the stiffness of the elastic base and spring-mass system, the mass of the spring-mass system, and tip magnet mass on the dynamic characteristics of the asymmetric TPVEH + EB by using MATLABR2021b software's ode45 solver. The piezoelectric material PZT-5H was chosen due to its high piezoelectric coefficients, mechanical robustness, and ability to generate significant electric charge under mechanical stress. These characteristics are crucial for maximizing energy harvesting efficiency, especially in environments with varying and low-frequency vibrations, which are typical in structural health monitoring applications. The geometric and material parameters of the asymmetric TPVEH + EB are listed in Table 1.

When $d_0 = 0$, the two external magnets are symmetrically arranged, resulting in a symmetric potential well for the system's tri-stable potential energy function. Conversely, when $d_0 \neq 0$, the two external magnets are arranged asymmetrically, leading to an asymmetric potential well in the system's tri-stable potential energy function. Figure 3 illustrates the RMS voltages of the TPVEH + EB system under varying random excitation intensities and different d_0 values. A comparative analysis of the RMS voltages indicates that the asymmetric tri-stable system exhibits significantly enhanced capability in harvesting vibrational energy compared to the symmetric tri-stable system. Figure 4 presents the electrical power outputs harvested by the symmetric and asymmetric tri-stable systems under different random excitation intensities. The results clearly demonstrate that the asymmetric tri-stable system achieves significantly higher electrical power output than the symmetric tri-stable system. This performance disparity highlights the superior energy conversion efficiency of the asymmetric TPVEH + EB system. This performance disparity is attributed to the asymmetric potential energy wells, which have lower potential differences and more unstable characteristics compared to their symmetric counterparts, thereby enhancing energy harvesting performance. In both cases, the system reaches its maximum power at around $f = 0.0055$, which falls within the commonly encountered low-level excitation intensity range in building structures, facilitating the collection of vibrational energy from the structure.

Table 1. The geometric and material parameters of the asymmetric TPVEH + EB.

Parameters	Symbol	Value
Mass of the tip magnet	M_t	14 g
Mass of the beam's restricted end	M_f	28 g
Length of the beam	l	75 mm
Width of the beam	b	20 mm
Thickness of the substrate layer	h_s	0.2 mm
Thickness of the piezoelectric layer	t_p	0.2 mm
Young's modulus of the substrate layer	Y_s	70 GPa
Density of the substrate layer	ρ_s	2700 kg/m^3
Density of the piezoelectric layer	ρ_p	7750 kg/m^3
Volume of the magnetic	V_A V_B V_C	1.0×10^{-6} m^{-3}
Damping ratio	ξ_1	0.01
Young's modulus of the piezoelectric layer	Y_P	60.98 GPa
Piezoelectric strain constant	d_{31}	-1.71×10^{-10} C/N
Stiffness of the base spring	k_b	8000 N/m
Stiffness of the vertical spring	k_f	50,000 N/m
Piezoelectric dielectric constant	ε_{33}^s	-1.33×10^{-8} F/m
Resistance	R	300 kΩ

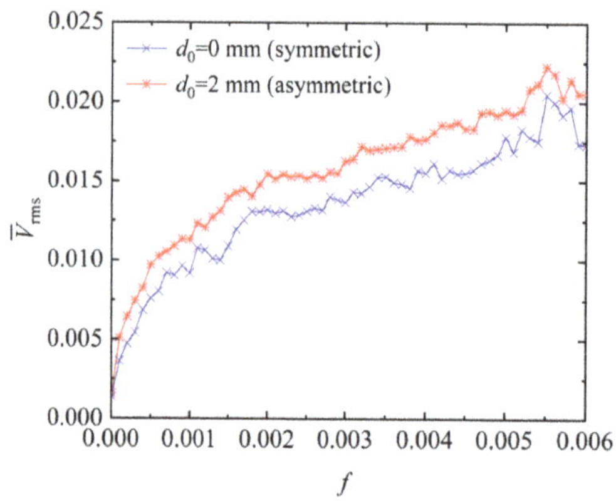

Figure 3. RMS voltages of TPVEH + EB for different d_0.

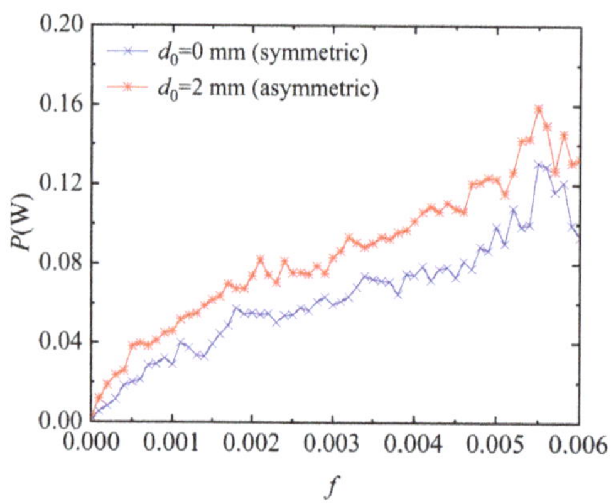

Figure 4. Power response of TPVEH + EB for different d_0.

Figures 5–7 display the displacement and output voltage time histories, along with phase diagrams, for the asymmetric TPVEH + EB (d_0 = 2 mm) and symmetric TPVEH + EB (d_0 = 0 mm) at random excitation intensities of f = 0.00001, f = 0.0001 and f = 0.0003, respectively, in order to represent the commonly encountered low-level excitations in building structures. As shown in Figure 5, at f = 0.00001, the symmetric TPVEH + EB (d_0 = 0 mm) system exhibits minor intra-well oscillations, resulting in a very small output voltage, whereas the asymmetric TPVEH + EB (d_0 = 2 mm) system undergoes chaotic motion, generating a large but unstable output voltage. As shown in Figure 6, increasing the random excitation intensity to f = 0.0001 allows both the asymmetric TPVEH + EB (d_0 = 2 mm) and symmetric TPVEH + EB (d_0 = 0 mm) systems to achieve barrier-crossing motions, with oscillations between potential wells, and the asymmetry of the potential wells and the nature of the random vibrations lead to the asymmetry of the displacement signals. Consequently, both configurations generate substantial output voltages. However, the symmetric TPVEH + EB (d_0 = 0 mm) experiences fewer frequent transitions between potential wells, resulting in a relatively lower output voltage. In contrast, the asymmetric TPVEH + EB (d_0 = 2 mm) exhibits frequent transitions between wells, thus producing a significantly higher voltage. Figure 7 illustrates that as the random excitation intensity increases to f = 0.0003, both the asymmetric TPVEH + EB (d_0 = 2 mm) and symmetric TPVEH + EB (d_0 = 0 mm) systems enter inter-well motion, with the asymmetric TPVEH + EB (d_0 = 2 mm) producing a higher output voltage. From the above observations, it is evident that the asymmetric TPVEH + EB is more suitable for energy harvesting at low rotational speeds.

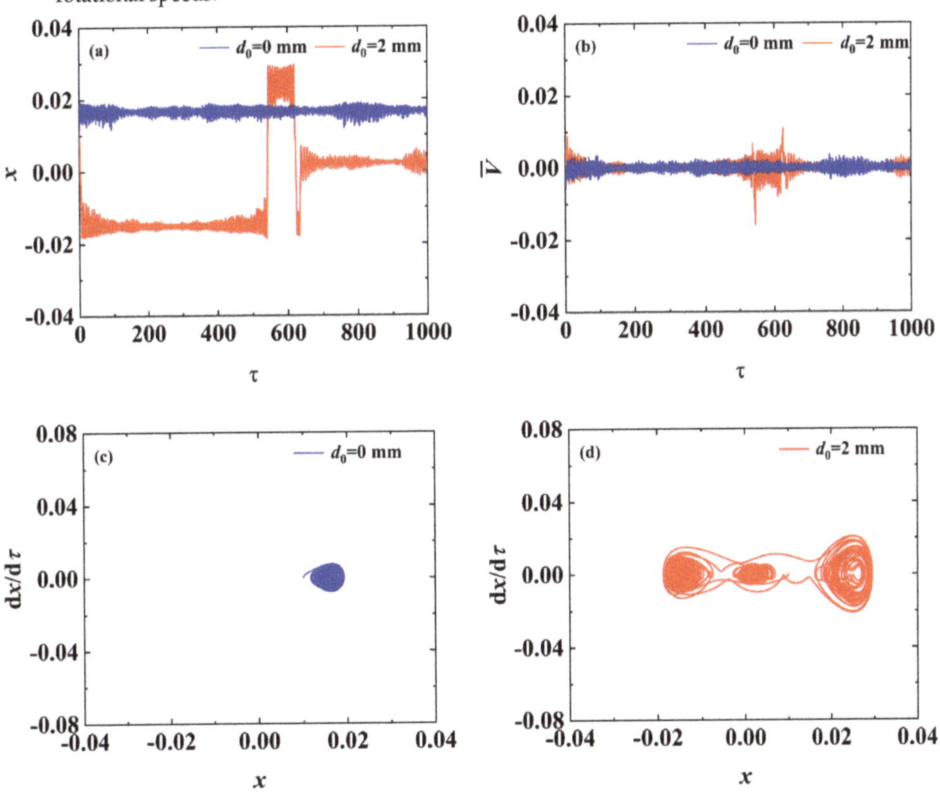

Figure 5. Responses of TPVEH + EB for f = 0.00001: (**a**) displacement (d_0 = 0 mm, d_0 = 2 mm), (**b**) voltage (d_0 = 0 mm, d_0 = 2 mm), (**c**) phase portrait (d_0 = 0 mm), (**d**) phase portrait (d_0 = 2 mm).

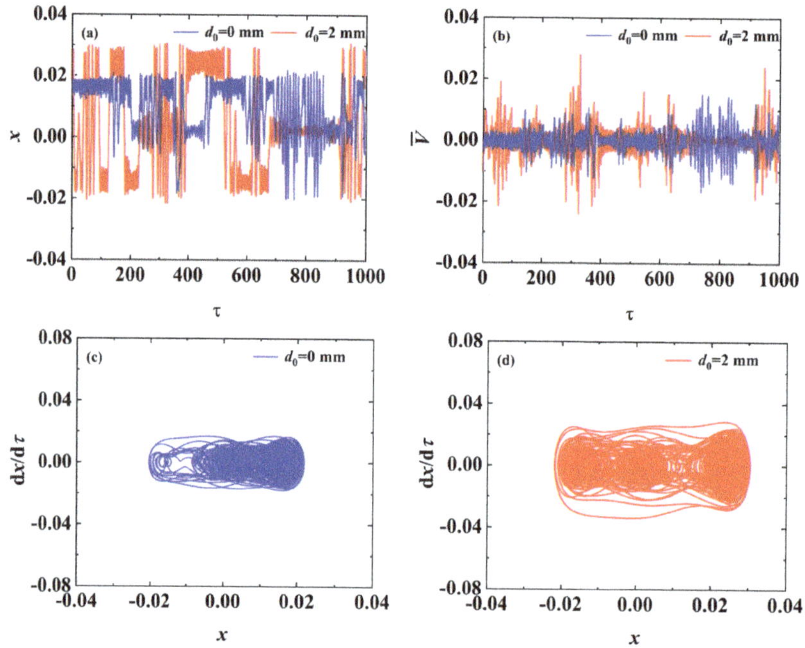

Figure 6. Responses of TPVEH + EB for f = 0.0001: (**a**) displacement (d_0 = 0 mm, d_0 = 2 mm), (**b**) voltage (d_0 = 0 mm, d_0 = 2 mm), (**c**) phase portrait (d_0 = 0 mm), (**d**) phase portrait (d_0 = 2 mm).

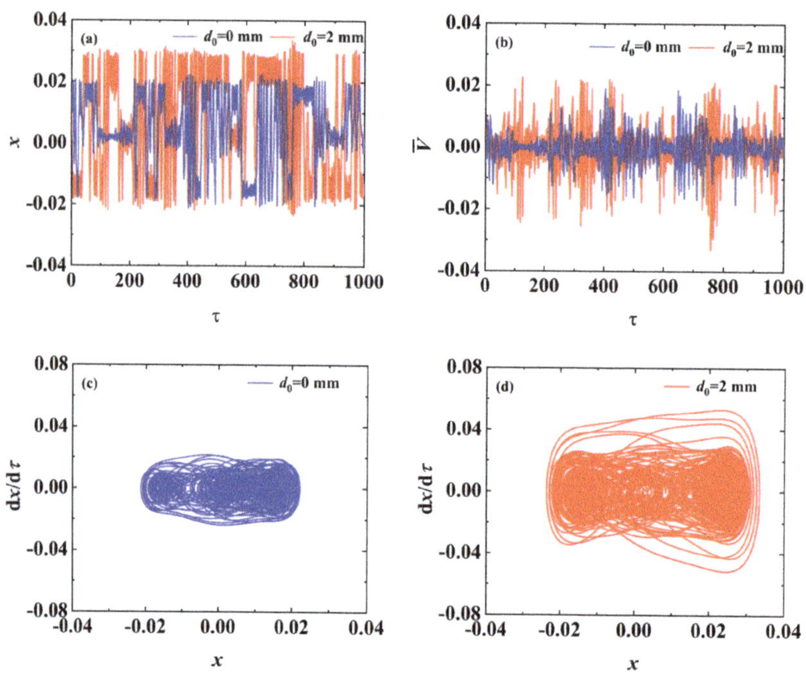

Figure 7. Responses of TPVEH + EB for f = 0.0003: (**a**) displacement (d_0 = 0 mm, d_0 = 2 mm), (**b**) voltage (d_0 = 0 mm, d_0 = 2 mm), (**c**) phase portrait (d_0 = 0 mm), (**d**) phase portrait (d_0 = 2 mm).

Figures 8–10 respectively present the displacement, output voltage time histories, and phase diagrams of the asymmetric TPVEH + EB (d_0 = 2 mm) under three base spring stiffnesses (k_b = 8000 N/m, k_b = 15,000 N/m, k_b = 25,000 N/m) at f = 0.0001. The choice of the stiffness values for the vertical springs is based on our previous experience from studies on simplified excitation and rotational excitation piezoelectric energy harvesters, aiming to optimize the dynamic response of the system [27]. The figures clearly show that when k_b = 8000 N/m, the asymmetric TPVEH + EB begins to overcome the barrier constraints and exhibits small-amplitude inter-well motion, resulting in a relatively lower output voltage. As k_b increases to 15,000 N/m, the asymmetric TPVEH + EB undergoes frequent transitions between potential wells, generating a significantly higher output voltage. However, with a further increase in k_b to 25,000 N/m, the asymmetric TPVEH + EB returns to less frequent inter-well transitions, resulting in a lower output voltage.

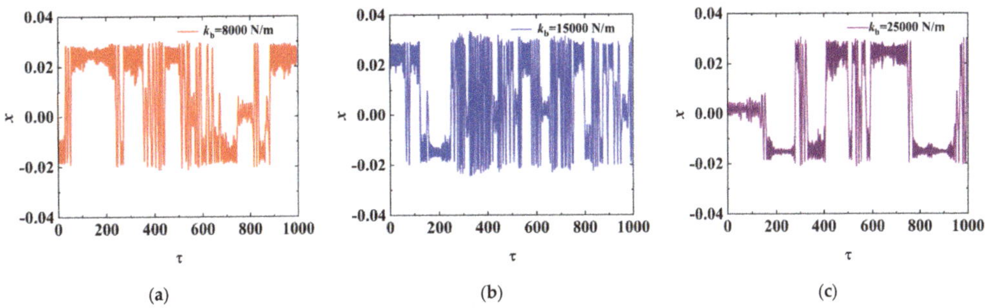

Figure 8. Displacement time–history diagram of asymmetric TPVEH + EB for d_0 = 2 mm when (**a**) k_b = 8000 N/m, (**b**) k_b = 15,000 N/m, (**c**) k_b = 25,000 N/m.

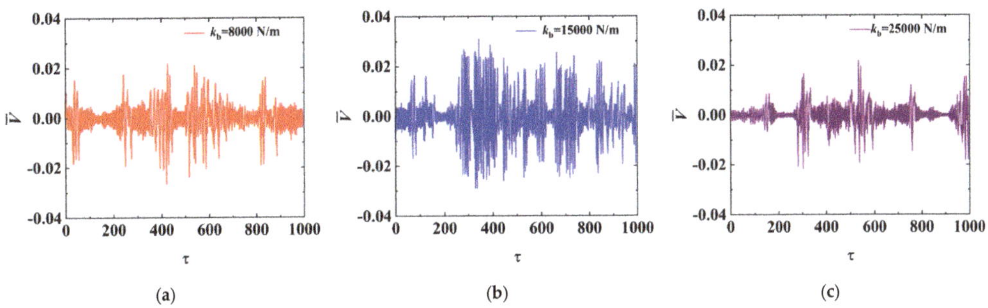

Figure 9. Voltage time–history diagram of asymmetric TPVEH + EB for d_0 = 2 mm when (**a**) k_b = 8000 N/m, (**b**) k_b = 15,000 N/m, (**c**) k_b = 25,000 N/m.

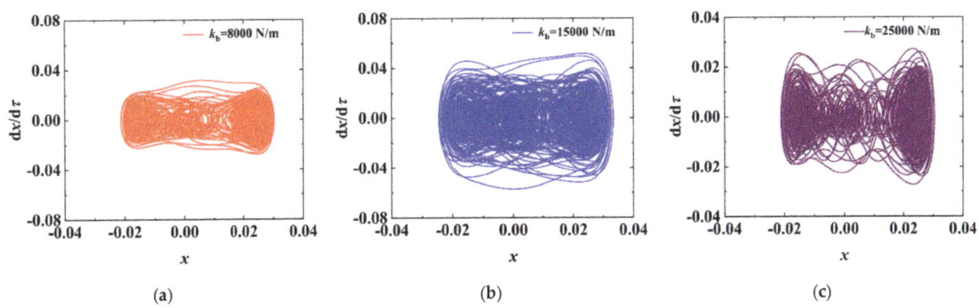

Figure 10. Phase portrait of asymmetric TPVEH + EB for d_0 = 2 mm when (**a**) k_b = 8000 N/m, (**b**) k_b = 15,000 N/m, (**c**) k_b = 25,000 N/m.

Figures 11–13 illustrate the displacement, output voltage time histories, and phase diagrams of the asymmetric TPVEH + EB (d_0 = 2 mm) under three different vertical spring stiffnesses (k_f = 45,000 N/m, k_f = 90,000 N/m, k_f = 150,000 N/m). The figures indicate that when k_f = 45,000 N/m, the asymmetric TPVEH + EB undergoes chaotic motion, resulting in a smaller and unstable output voltage. As k_f increases to 90,000 N/m, the asymmetric TPVEH + EB begins to exhibit large-amplitude inter-well motion, generating a significantly higher output voltage. With a further increase in k_f to 150,000 N, although the asymmetric TPVEH + EB can still perform inter-well motion, the frequency of transitions between potential wells decreases, leading to a reduction in output voltage. To summarize, under a constant intensity of random excitation, an appropriate increase in both k_b and k_f can help the asymmetric TPVEH + EB to more easily achieve large-amplitude inter-well motions. However, when k_b and k_f surpass certain thresholds, further increasing these parameters no longer enhances the system's output voltage amplitude.

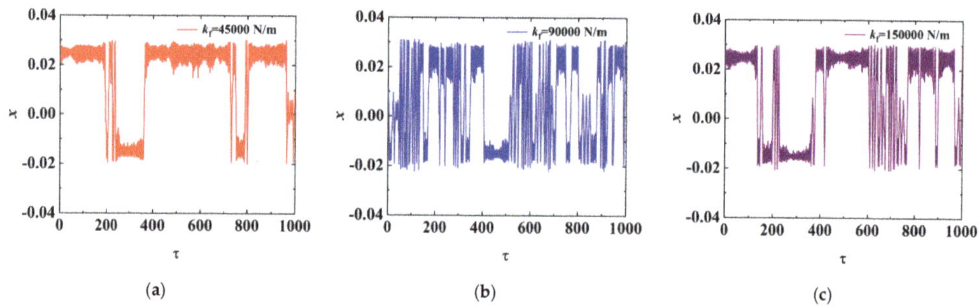

Figure 11. Displacement time–history diagram of asymmetric TPVEH + EB for d_0 = 2 mm when (**a**) k_f = 45,000 N/m, (**b**) k_f = 90,000 N/m, (**c**) k_f = 150,000 N/m.

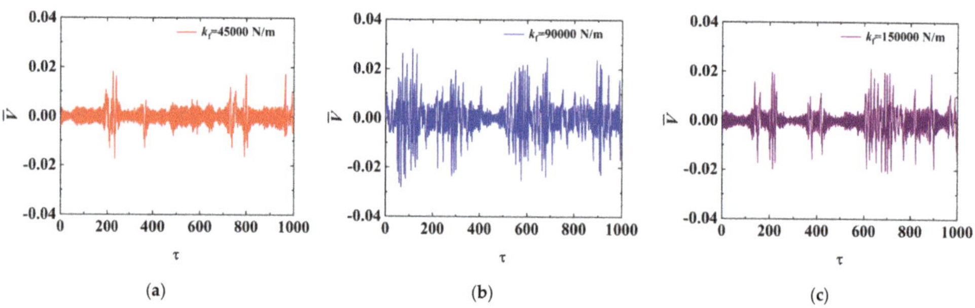

Figure 12. Voltage time–history diagram of asymmetric TPVEH + EB for d_0 = 2 mm when (**a**) k_f = 45,000 N/m, (**b**) k_f = 90,000 N/m, (**c**) k_f = 150,000 N/m.

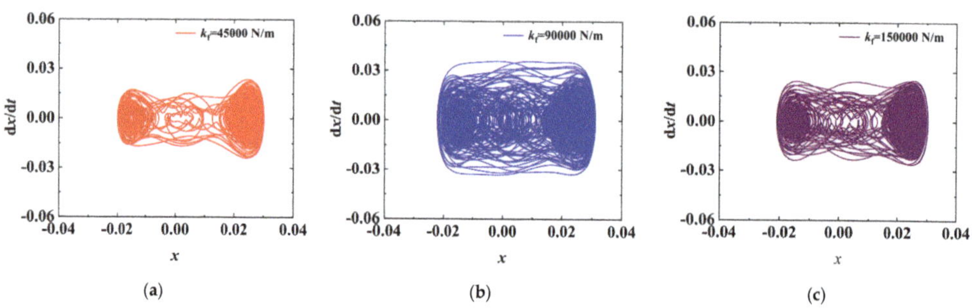

Figure 13. Phase portrait of asymmetric TPVEH + EB for d_0 = 2 mm when (**a**) k_f = 45,000 N/m, (**b**) k_f = 90,000 N/m, (**c**) k_f = 150,000 N/m.

Figure 14 depicts the RMS power of the asymmetric TPVEH + EB (d_0 = 2 mm) subjected to different levels of random excitation intensity for various tip magnet masses (M_t) while the spring-mass system mass (M_f) is fixed at 42 g. The data unequivocally demonstrate that increasing the mass of the tip magnet significantly enhances the energy conversion efficiency of the asymmetric TPVEH + EB. Moreover, as illustrated in Figure 15, increasing the mass of the spring-mass system (M_f) to 60 g reveals through comparative analysis that the asymmetric TPVEH + EB system with M_t = 15 g exhibits significantly superior energy conversion efficiency compared to the system with M_t = 10 g. These findings suggest that strategic adjustments to the mass of the tip magnet and the spring-mass system are crucial for maximizing the efficiency of piezoelectric energy harvesting systems, providing valuable insights for their design and optimization in mitigating random vibrations in building structures.

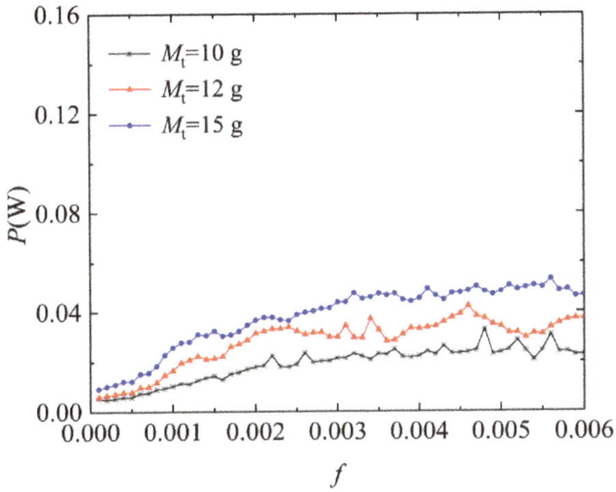

Figure 14. RMS power of asymmetric TPVEH + EB for different values of m_t when d_0 = 2 mm and M_f = 42 g.

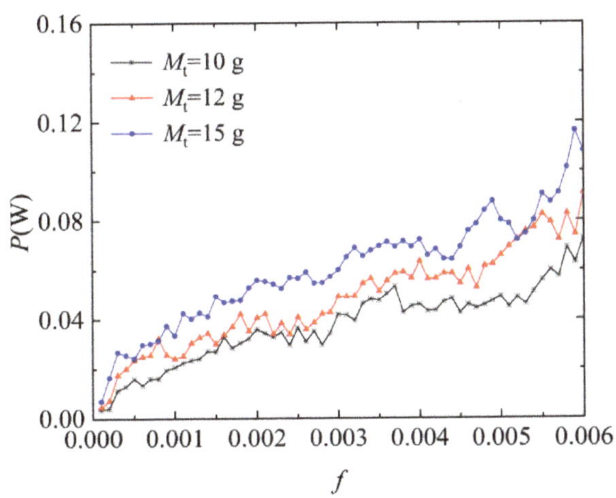

Figure 15. RMS power of asymmetric TPVEH + EB for different values of m_t when d_0 = 2 mm and M_f = 60 g.

To evaluate the cost-effectiveness of the proposed system, we used the Levelized Cost of Energy (LCOE) metric. LCOE is calculated as the ratio of the total costs (including capital, operational, and maintenance costs) to the total energy output over the system's lifetime. The LCOE for the asymmetric TPVEH + EB system was found to be $0.15 per kWh, compared to $0.20 per kWh for traditional symmetric systems. This reduction in LCOE indicates that despite the higher initial costs associated with the more complex design of the asymmetric TPVEH + EB, the overall cost per unit of energy harvested is lower due to the improved energy conversion efficiency. The initial capital costs for the asymmetric TPVEH + EB system are approximately 20% higher than those of symmetric systems, primarily due to the additional components such as the elastic base and the spring-mass system. However, the increased energy output and longer operational lifespan result in a more favorable LCOE, demonstrating the cost-effectiveness of the proposed design.

4. Conclusions

The theoretical and numerical investigation of the nonlinear dynamics of an asymmetric TPVEH + EB is performed in this study. The asymmetric TPVEH + EB comprises a tri-stable piezoelectric cantilever beam connected to a vertical magnet-spring system, with an elastic base installed at the bottom of the cantilever beam. This system exhibits significant energy-harvesting advantages under random excitations in building structures. The installation of the asymmetric TPVEH + EB device requires initial structural modifications to accommodate the elastic base and the spring-mass system. This can be integrated during the construction phase or retrofitted into existing structures with minimal disruption. The modular design of the device allows for flexibility in installation, making it adaptable to different building configurations. The main conclusions of this study are summarized as follows:

Compared to the conventional symmetric TPVEH + EB, the asymmetric TPVEH + EB shows a marked enhancement in output power and its ability to transition between potential wells under low-frequency random excitations.

Under random excitation conditions, the output voltage of the asymmetric TPVEH + EB initially increases and then decreases as the stiffness of the elastic base and the vertical spring increases. This suggests the existence of an optimal stiffness for both the elastic base and the vertical spring that maximizes the output voltage under random excitations.

Altering the mass of the beam's fixed-end dynamic magnifier and the tip magnet significantly impacts the system's output power. By optimally adjusting the masses of these two components, the energy conversion efficiency of the asymmetric TPVEH + EB under random excitation can be markedly improved.

By harnessing ambient vibrations and converting them into usable electrical energy, the TPVEH + EB device promotes sustainable energy practices. The reduction in battery usage for sensor nodes also minimizes environmental waste, aligning with green building initiatives.

The proposed asymmetric TPVEH + EB offers significant performance improvements over traditional symmetric TPVEHs and competitive advantages over electromagnetic and electrostatic harvesters in specific scenarios. Its cost-effectiveness, particularly in terms of LCOE and long-term operational savings, makes it a viable solution for a wide range of applications. Our results indicate the potential for enhanced energy harvesting efficiency with specific configurations, which could be beneficial for powering wireless sensor nodes in structural health monitoring systems. However, efficiently managing the harvested energy and integrating it with existing power systems for wireless sensor nodes or other applications were not extensively covered in this study. Future research should address the development of effective power management systems to maximize the usability of the harvested energy.

Author Contributions: Writing—original draft, Q.H.; Writing—review & editing, D.M., Q.X., L.T., D.C., Z.Y. and T.H. All authors have read and agreed to the published version of the manuscript.

Funding: This research was funded by the Anhui Provincial University Provincial Natural Science Research Project-Key Project (2022AH050240), the Doctoral Startup Foundation of Anhui Jianzhu

University (2020QDZ07), the Anhui Provincial Natural Science Foundation (2108085MA28), the Mechanical Properties Research of FRP Connectors in Fabricated Concrete Sandwich Insulation Wall Panels after Fire (KJ2021A0608), the Anhui Provincial Course Ideological and Political Demonstration Course (2022kcsz060).

Data Availability Statement: The original contributions presented in the study are included in the article, further inquiries can be directed to the corresponding authors.

Conflicts of Interest: The authors declare no conflict of interest.

Appendix A

$$\kappa = \mu M_A V_A M_B V_B / 4\pi = \mu M_A V_A M_C V_C / 4\pi, D_1 = d_h{}^2 + d_{v1}{}^2, D_2 = d_h{}^2 + d_{v2}{}^2, r_1 = e\phi_1'(l) + \phi_1(l),$$
$$r_2 = d_h e\phi_{11}'(l)^2 + e^2\phi_1'(l)^2 + 2e\phi_1(l)\phi_1'(l) + \phi_1(l)^2, q_1 = 2d_h{}^2 - d_{v1}{}^2, q_3 = d_{v1}r_1, q_5 = 2d_{v1}r_1 + 3d_h d_{v1}\phi_1'(l),$$
$$q_7 = -(5/2)r_2/D_1 + (35/2)d_{v1}{}^2 r_1{}^2/D_1{}^2, q_9 = -0.5(2d_h{}^2 - d_{v1}{}^2)\phi_1'(l)^2 - r_3,$$
$$q_{11} = -(5/2)d_{v1}e\phi_1'(l)^3/D_1 - (35/2)d_{v1}r_1 \cdot (d_{v1}e\phi_1'(l)^2 + r_1{}^2)/D_1{}^2 + (105/2)\cdot d_{v1}{}^3 r_1{}^3/D_1{}^3,$$
$$q_{13} = -0.5(2d_{v1}r_1 + 3d_h d_{v1}\phi_{11}'(l))\phi_1'(l)^2 + 0.5ed_{v1}\phi_1'(l)^3,$$
$$\begin{aligned} q_{15} = {} & (5/2)((3/4)(ed_h\phi_1'(l)^4 + e^2\phi_1'(l)^4) + e\phi_1(l)\phi_1'(l)^3)/D_1 - ((35/2)d_{v1}{}^2 r_1 e\phi_1'(l)^3 + \\ & (35/8)r_2{}^2/D_1{}^2 - (315/4)d_{v1}{}^2 r_1{}^2 r_2/D_1{}^3 + (1155/8)d_{v1}{}^4 r_1^4/D_1{}^4, \end{aligned}$$
$$\begin{aligned} q_{17} = {} & (3/8)(2d_h^2 - d_{vl}^2)\phi_1'(l)^4 - 0.5(-r_1^2 + 2ed_h\phi_1'(l)^2 - 3d_h r_1\phi_1'(l))\phi_1'(l)^2 + r_1 e\phi' - (3/2)d_h e\phi_1'(l)^4 + \\ & 0.5e^2\phi_1'(l)^4 - (3/2)(-d_h e\phi_1'(l)^3 + r_1 e\phi_1'(l)^2)\phi_1'(l), \end{aligned}$$
$$\begin{aligned} q_{19} = {} & (15/8)d_{v1}e\phi_1'(l)^5/D_1 + ((35/2)d_{v1}r_1((3/4)d_h e\phi_1'(l)^4 + (3/4)e\phi_1'(l)^3 r_1) + (35/4)r_2 d_{v1}e\phi_1'(l)^3)/D_1^2 - \\ & (105/4)(r_1^2 d_{v1}^3 e\phi_1'(l)^3 + d_{v1}r_1)r_2^2 + (3/256)(-4480 r_1 e d_{v1}^2\phi_1'(l)^3 + 1120 d_{v1}r_1 r_2^2/D_1^3 - (1155/4)d_{v1}^3 r_1^3 r_2/D_1^4 + \\ & (3003/8)d_{v1}^5 r_1^5/D_1^5, \end{aligned}$$
$$q_{21} = (3/8)(2d_{v1}r_1 + 3d_h d_{v1}\phi_1'(l))\phi_1'(l)^4 - (5/8)d_{v1}e\phi_1'(l)^5,$$
$$\begin{aligned} q_{23} = {} & (-5/2)((5/8)e\phi_1'(l)^6(d_h + e) + (3/4)e\phi_1(l)\phi_1'(l)^5)/D_1 + ((1/8)d_{v1}{}^2 e\phi_1'(l)^5 r_1 + (35/4)r_2((-3/4)(d_h + e) - \\ & e\phi_1(l)\phi_1'(l)^3))/D_1^2 + ((105/4)d_{v1}{}^2 r_1(r_1(-3/4)e\phi_1'(l)^4(d_h + e) - e\phi_1(l)\phi_{11}'(l)^3)) + e\phi_{11}'(l)^3 r_2)/D_1^3 + d_{v1}{}^2 r_1{}^2 \cdot \\ & ((105/2)((3/4)e\phi_{11}'(l)^4(d_h + e) + e\phi_1(l)\phi_{11}'(l)^3) - (1155/16)d_{v1}{}^2 e\phi_{11}'(l)^3 r_1 + (3465/32)r_2^2 - (105/16)r_2^3)/ \\ & D_1^4 + ((3465/32)d_{v1}{}^2(r_1{}^2(-2d_{v1}{}^2 e\phi_{11}'(l)^3 + r_2^2) - (10515/16)d_{v1}{}^4 r_1{}^4 r_2)/D_1^5 + (10515/16)d_{v1}{}^6 r_1/D_1{}^6, \end{aligned}$$
$$q_{25} = -(1/8)r_1\phi_{11}'(l)^4(3\phi_1(l) + 9d_h\phi_{11}'(l) - 5e\phi_{11}'(l)) - (1/4)e\phi_{11}'(l)^6(d_h + 2e)$$

By replacing D_1 with D_2 and d_{v1} with d_{v2} in the above $q_{i=1,3,5,7,\cdots,25}$, we get $q_{i=2,4,6,8,\cdots,26}$.

References

1. Zhang, Z.; Xiang, H.; Tang, L. Modeling, analysis and comparison of four charging interface circuits for piezoelectric energy harvesting. *Mech. Syst. Signal Process.* **2021**, *152*, 107476. [CrossRef]
2. Wei, X.; Yi, Z.; Li, W.; Zhao, L.; Zhang, W. Energy harvesting fueling the revival of self-powered unmanned aerial vehicles. *Energy Convers. Manag.* **2023**, *283*, 116863. [CrossRef]
3. Ma, X.; Zhou, S. A review of flow-induced vibration energy harvesters. *Energy Convers. Manag.* **2023**, *283*, 115223. [CrossRef]
4. Cao, Y.; Yang, J.; Yang, D. A magnetic excitation enhanced energy harvester with combined beam for rotational motion. *Sens. Actuators A Phys.* **2023**, *360*, 114569. [CrossRef]
5. Cao, Y.; Yang, J.; Yang, D. Performance investigation and parameter identification of inverse variable cross-section energy harvester. *Int. J. Mech. Sci.* **2023**, *248*, 108204. [CrossRef]
6. Chen, R.W.; Long, R.; Xia, H.K.; Yuan, X.W.; Liu, X.J. Energy harvesting performance of a dandelion-like multi-directional pie-zoelectric vibration energy harvester. *Sens. Actuators Phys.-A* **2015**, *230*, 1–8. [CrossRef]
7. Montanini, R.; Quattrocchi, A. Experimental characterization of cantilever-type piezoelectric generator operating at resonance for vibration energy harvesting. *AIP Conf. Proc.* **2016**, *1740*, 060003.
8. Yao, F.; Meng, W.; Zhao, J.; Yin, H. Cantilever Beam Based Piezoelectric Energy Harvester. *Int. J. Smart Sens. Intell. Syst.* **2015**, *8*, 2018–2041.
9. Alhadidi, A.H.; Daqaq, M.F. A broadband bi-stable flow energy harvester based on the wake-galloping phenomenon. *Appl. Phys. Lett.* **2016**, *109*, 033904. [CrossRef]
10. Wang, W.; Cao, J.; Bowen, C.R.; Inman, D.J.; Lin, J. Performance enhancement of nonlinear asymmetric bistable energy harvesting from harmonic, random and human motion excitations. *Appl. Phys. Lett.* **2018**, *112*, 213903. [CrossRef]
11. Xing, J.; Fang, S.; Fu, X.; Liao, W.-H. A rotational hybrid energy harvester utilizing bistability for low-frequency applications: Modelling and experimental validation. *Int. J. Mech. Sci.* **2022**, *222*, 107235. [CrossRef]
12. Yang, T.; Cao, Q. Dynamics and performance evaluation of a novel tristable hybrid energy harvester for ultra-low level vibration resources. *Int. J. Mech. Sci.* **2019**, *156*, 123–136. [CrossRef]
13. Panyam, M.; Daqaq, M.F. Characterizing the effective bandwidth of tri-stable energy harvesters. *J. Sound Vib.* **2017**, *386*, 336–358. [CrossRef]
14. Kumar, K.A.; Ali, S.F.; Arockiarajan, A. Magneto-elastic oscillator: Modeling and analysis with nonlinear magnetic interaction. *J. Sound Vib.* **2017**, *393*, 265–284. [CrossRef]

15. Zhou, Z.; Qin, W.; Zhu, P. A broadband quad-stable energy harvester and its advantages over bi-stable harvester: Simulation and experiment verification. *Mech. Syst. Signal Process.* **2017**, *84*, 158–168. [CrossRef]
16. Zhou, Z.; Qin, W.; Zhu, P.; Du, W.; Deng, W.; Pan, J. Scavenging wind energy by a dynamic-stable flutter energy harvester with rectangular wing. *Appl. Phys. Lett.* **2019**, *114*, 243902. [CrossRef]
17. Fu, H.; Jiang, J.; Hu, S.; Rao, J.; Theodossiades, S. A multi-stable ultra-low frequency energy harvester using a nonlinear pendulum and piezoelectric transduction for self-powered sensing. *Mech. Syst. Signal Process.* **2023**, *189*, 110034. [CrossRef]
18. Zhou, S.; Cao, J.; Erturk, A.; Lin, J. Enhanced broadband piezoelectric energy harvesting using rotatable magnets. *Appl. Phys. Lett.* **2013**, *102*, 173901. [CrossRef]
19. Zhou, Z.; Qin, W.; Du, W.; Zhu, P.; Liu, Q. Improving energy harvesting from random excitation by nonlinear flexible bi-stable energy harvester with a variable potential energy function. *Mech. Syst. Signal Process.* **2019**, *115*, 162–172. [CrossRef]
20. Mei, X.; Zhou, S.; Yang, Z.; Kaizuka, T.; Nakano, K. Enhancing energy harvesting in low-frequency rotational motion by a quad-stable energy harvester with time-varying potential wells. *Mech. Syst. Signal Process.* **2021**, *148*, 107167. [CrossRef]
21. Yang, W.; Towfighian, S. A hybrid nonlinear vibration energy harvester. *Mech. Syst. Signal Process.* **2017**, *90*, 317–333. [CrossRef]
22. Li, X.; Li, Z.; Huang, H.; Wu, Z.; Huang, Z.; Mao, H.; Cao, Y. Broadband spring-connected bi-stable piezoelectric vibration energy harvester with variable potential barrier. *Results Phys.* **2020**, *18*, 103173. [CrossRef]
23. Zhou, S.; Zou, L. Nonlinear dynamic analysis of asymmetric tristable energy harvester for enhanced energy harvesting. *Commun. Nonlinear Sci. Numer. Simul.* **2018**, *61*, 271–284. [CrossRef]
24. Cai, W.; Harne, R.L. Characterization of challenges in asymmetric nonlinear vibration energy harvesters subjected to realistic excitation. *J. Sound Vib.* **2020**, *482*, 115460. [CrossRef]
25. Li, Y.; Zhou, S. Probability analysis of asymmetric tristable energy harvesters. *AIP Adv.* **2018**, *8*, 125212. [CrossRef]
26. Ma, X.; Li, H.; Zhou, S.; Yang, Z.; Litak, G. Characterizing nonlinear characteristics of asymmetric tristable energy harvesters. *Mech. Syst. Signal Process.* **2022**, *168*, 108612. [CrossRef]
27. Wang, G.; Liao, W.-H.; Yang, B.; Wang, X.; Xu, W.; Li, X. Dynamic and energetic characteristics of a bistable piezoelectric vibration energy harvester with an elastic magnifier. *Mech. Syst. Signal Process.* **2018**, *105*, 427–446. [CrossRef]
28. Wang, G.; Ju, Y.; Liao, W.-H.; Zhao, Z.; Li, Y.; Tan, J. A hybrid piezoelectric device combining a tri-stable energy harvester with an elastic base for low-orbit vibration energy harvesting enhancement. *Smart Mater. Struct.* **2021**, *30*, 075028. [CrossRef]
29. Man, D.; Jiang, B.; Xu, Q.; Tang, L.; Zhang, Y.; Xu, G.; Han, T. Enhancing low-orbit vibration energy harvesting by a tri-stable piezoelectric energy harvester with an innovative dynamic amplifier. *AIP Adv.* **2024**, *14*, 045210. [CrossRef]
30. Man, D.; Hu, Q.; Jiang, B.; Zhang, Y.; Tang, L.; Xu, Q.; Chen, D.; Chen, L. A novel asymmetric tri-stable piezoelectric vibration energy harvester for low-orbit vibration energy harvesting enhancement. *AIP Adv.* **2024**, *14*, 065223. [CrossRef]
31. Tang, L.; Wang, J. Modeling and analysis of cantilever piezoelectric energy harvester with a new-type dynamic magnifier. *Acta Mech.* **2018**, *229*, 4643–4662. [CrossRef]
32. De Paula, A.S.; Inman, D.J.; Savi, M.A. Energy harvesting in a nonlinear piezomagneticoelastic beam subjected to random excitation. *Mech. Syst. Signal Process.* **2015**, *54*, 405–416. [CrossRef]

buildings

MDPI

Article

Research on Arrangement of Measuring Points for Modal Identification of Spatial Grid Structures

Chunjuan Zhou [1,2], Jinzhi Wu [1], Guojun Sun [1,*], Jie Hu [1], Qize Xu [1], Yang Li [1] and Mingliang Liu [2]

[1] College of Architectural and Civil Engineering, Beijing University of Technology, Beijing 100124, China; harvestzhou@163.com (C.Z.); kongjian@bjut.edu.cn (J.W.); hujie0403@163.com (J.H.); xuqize5316@163.com (Q.X.); 13848465181@163.com (Y.L.)

[2] Shaanxi Architecture Science Research Institute Co., Ltd., Xi'an 710082, China; liumingliang-35@163.com

* Correspondence: sunguojun@bjut.edu.cn

Abstract: In structural health monitoring, because the number of sensors used is far lower than the number of degrees of freedom of the structure being monitored, the optimization problem of the location and number of sensors in the structures is becoming more and more prominent. However, spatial grid structures are complex and diverse, and their dynamic characteristics are complex. It is difficult to accurately measure their vibration information. Therefore, an appropriate optimization method must be used to determine the optimal positioning of sensor placement. Aiming at the problem that spatial grid structures have many degrees of freedom and the fact that it is difficult to obtain complete vibration information, this paper analyzed the typical EI method, MKE method, and EI-MKE method in the arrangement of the measuring points, and it was verified that the EI method was more suitable for the vibration detection of spatial grid structures through the example of a plane truss and spatial grid structures. Measuring points under the assumption of structural damage were explored, and it was proposed that there might have been a stable number of measuring points that could cover the possible vibration mode changes in the structures. At the same time, combined with the three-level improved Guyan recursive technique, in order to obtain better complete modal parameters, the influence of the number of measuring points on the complete vibration mode information was studied. It was concluded that MAC_d was better than MAC_n as the quantitative target.

Keywords: spatial grid structures; layout of measuring points; vibration mode expansion; modal identification

1. Introduction

As a kind of large-span structures, spatial grid structures have the characteristics of a complex form and a huge volume. It is impossible and unnecessary to obtain the response data of the structures through a large number of sensors [1–3]. The early optimal arrangement of sensors was based on the establishment of the finite element model of the structures and the arrangement of sensors based on experience. This method is more practical, but it can only be used for structures with fewer degrees of freedom. In the optimization of the number and location of sensors for complex and multi-node structures, it is very difficult to optimize the number and location of sensors only by experience, which makes it difficult to meet the requirements. Therefore, it is of great significance for the effective operation of whole-health monitoring systems to study and determine the optimal arrangement positions and reasonable number of sensors.

The optimal placement of sensors first needs to determine the objective function, and the principle is to obtain as much structural information as possible. One class of methods aims at the linear independence of the target mode [4,5]. For example, Kammer [6] proposed the effective independence method (EI) in 1991. The basic idea of the algorithm is to construct an idempotent matrix so that the measured points are linearly independent and orthogonal to each other as much as possible. Lim [7], combined with the eigensystem realization method, carried out sensor placement with the minimum condition number of the Hankel matrix. Wu et al. [8] proposed a sensor placement method based on a two-step method from the two aspects of the number and location of the sensors. Bao [9] studied the optimal placement of sensors for arched roofs and trussed roofs. Based on the EI method, the optimal placement criteria or general rules of the sensors are given. The other method of determining the objective function is to consider the arrangement of the measuring points from the perspective of energy. The modal kinetic energy method [10] (MKE) is used to arrange the measuring points with the maximum kinetic energy of the target mode. Gomes [11] determined the optimal sensor placement of dynamic systems from the perspective of parameter identification based on Fisher's information matrix from the perspective of obtaining structural information. In addition, the MinMAC method aims to minimize the maximum element value of the off-diagonal element of the modal assurance criterion matrix to select the sensor position in order to maximize the angle between the measured modal shape vectors. Considering the advantages and disadvantages of the EI method and the MKE method, Liu et al. [12] proposed an improved optimal sensor placement method, namely, the effective independence–modal kinetic energy method (EI-MKE). Li Dongsheng et al. [13] deeply analyzed the relationship between the MKE method, EI method, MinMAC method, modal matrix method, and other methods, and they revealed their differences and connections. The example showed that there were no two methods to determine the sensor position that were exactly the same. Zhang et al. [14] proposed a data-driven OSP strategy that achieves structural damage detection based on vibration sensors by precisely reconstructing modal shapes using only a few sensors that are incorporated into an SHM system. Zhan et al. [15] determined the optimal (and worst) locations for AE source localization in sensor clusters with unknown material properties of isotropic plates through a Bayesian optimal sensor placement strategy. Xu et al. [16] utilized convolutional neural networks for an ensemble-based data assimilation optimal sensor placement method. Guo et al. [17] proposed a new performance-based sensor optimization configuration method based on the proposed indicators of modal observability and damage detectability and introduced an OSP method for a single-line radar.

Damage identification is an important part of structural health monitoring [18,19]. In practical engineering, due to the limitation of the number of sensors and the measurement conditions, only limited measuring points can be monitored to obtain incomplete low-order vibration modes [20–23]. Some scholars have studied the application of model order expansion in damage identification. Xiao Feng et al. [24] studied a damage identification stiffness separation method for large spatial truss structures based on static response. Xiao Feng et al. [25] proposed a damage identification method for slender beam frame structures. Liu et al. [26] proposed a direct expansion method for mode expansion by using a composite vector composed of the measured value of the main degree of freedom and the estimated value of the slave degree of freedom, and they used the MAC method to evaluate the expansion results. Brincker et al. [27] used the SEREP method to expand the vibration mode of the plate numerical model after smoothing the measured vibration mode. These methods achieve the expansion of modal shapes by solving the transfer matrix and rely too much on the finite element analysis mode rather than the actual engineering state. Zhao et al. [28] used the SEREP method to expand the mode shape, established a linear system of equations for the damage coefficient, and used the Moore–Penrose generalized inverse to solve the equations. On the basis of the dynamic condensation method, Mousavi et al. [29] iteratively modified the damage coefficient and the model condensation matrix using only the translational degrees of freedom of the first mode of vibration for damage identification, but they still needed to measure more degrees of freedom. Aiming at the problem of limited measuring points and test noise in damage identification, Yang et al. [30] used a parametric dynamic condensation method to expand the vibration mode. Civalek et al. [31] used the DSC-HDQ method to solve the geometric nonlinear dynamic problem of a rectangular plate on an elastic foundation.

Based on the above analysis, it can be seen that in the process of modal parameter identification of large-span spatial structures with complex shapes, numerous nodes, and dense frequency, on the basis of the difference between the actual state of the structures and the theoretical model, the location of the sensors, the number and order of the selected modes, and the number of layouts still need to be further studied. At the same time, the application of modal order expansion in spatial grid structures, especially how to effectively link it with the arrangement of the measuring points in its inverse process and check whether the arrangement of the measuring points in the structures is reasonable, is still rare. In this paper, aiming at the problem that spatial grid structures have many degrees of freedom and it is difficult to obtain complete vibration information, a method of measuring a point arrangement that is suitable for spatial grid structures is verified and analyzed by an example. Combined with the three-stage improved Guyan recursive technique, the influence of the number of measuring points on obtaining the complete vibration mode information is studied. The suggestion that the measuring point can be preset before the dynamic detection of the spatial grid structures is put forward.

2. Applicability Analysis of Measuring Point Arrangement Method

The traditional measuring point optimization algorithm is essentially a process of finding the optimal solution. According to the defined objective function, the iterative optimization is carried out by using the different matrices formed. As shown in Table 1, the different measuring point arrangement methods proposed by different scholars essentially change the objective function of the optimization process and then search in the solution domain according to different objective functions. The search order is divided into three processes: gradual deletion, direct acquisition, and gradual accumulation. The suboptimal solution found by iteration is close to the optimal solution, which can usually meet the requirements of measuring point arrangement.

Table 1. The objective function of different measuring point arrangement methods.

Measuring Point Arrangement Method	Effective Independence Method (EI)	Modal Assurance Criterion (MAC)	Modal Kinetic Energy (MKE)	Covariance Matrix (VM)
Objective function	The estimation of the model coordinate estimation error covariance is the smallest.	The maximum element of the non-diagonal element of the MAC matrix is the smallest.	The kinetic energy of the modal degree of freedom is the largest.	The linear unbiased estimation error of the modal matrix is the smallest.
Target	The contribution to the target mode is the largest.	The spatial intersection angle of the modal vector of the measuring point is the largest.	The signal-to-noise ratio is the maximum	The ability to obtain the vibration mode and the signal strength are the largest.

The above measuring point algorithm has been widely used in engineering [32,33]. From the existing research, the contribution of the measuring point to the mode and the energy of the measuring point are the two factors that have the greatest influence on the structure; the EI method can efficiently select the degree of freedom that contributes a lot to the target mode shape; the MKE method improves the signal-to-noise ratio of the measuring point with the goal of degree-of-freedom energy. Therefore, this paper chooses the EI, MKE, and EI-MKE methods, three representative methods, to study the applicability of measuring point arrangement in spatial grid structures.

2.1. Principle of Measuring Point Arrangement Method

2.1.1. Effective Independence Method (EI) [34,35]

The EI method constructs the effective independence matrix E by solving the characteristic equation of Fisher's information matrix:

$$E = \Phi\left(\Phi^T\Phi\right)^{-1}\Phi^T \tag{1}$$

In the Equation (1), E is an idempotent matrix, whose diagonal elements satisfy $0 \leq E_{ii} \leq 1$, and the ith element represents the contribution of the ith degree of freedom to the rank of matrix E. If E_{ii} is close to 0, the degree of freedom contributes less to the linear independence of the target mode and should be removed; if E_{ii} is close to 1, the degree of freedom contributes more to the linear independence of the target mode and should be retained.

The starting point of constructing matrices by the EI method is that the vectors used to construct them are orthogonal. If the constructed vectors are not orthogonal, the orthogonal and cross orthogonal tests used in the derivation of EI method will cause large errors. For the orthogonal vibration mode $\Phi = \Phi_x\ \Phi_y\ \Phi_z$, the orthogonal test should be conducted:

$$\beta = \left[\Phi_x\Phi_y\Phi_z\right]^T\left[\Phi_x\Phi_y\Phi_z\right] = \Phi_x\Phi_x + \Phi_y\Phi_y + \Phi_z\Phi_z \tag{2}$$

Because the vibration mode is orthogonal, that is, β= 0, and considering the spatial structure, it is impossible to satisfy the three directional components of the structural mode, that is, $\Phi_x\Phi_x = 0$, $\Phi_y\Phi_y = 0$, $\Phi_z\Phi_z = 0$.

Thus, E represents the effective independent distribution of the set of candidate sensor positions, and the elements on the diagonal of E represent the linearly independent contribution of the corresponding sensor candidate points to the modal matrix. After the matrix E is obtained, the priority order of each candidate point is sorted according to the diagonal element size after the matrix E is obtained. The iterative algorithm is used to eliminate the smallest measurement point of the corresponding diagonal element each time, and the next iteration is then carried out until the required number of measurement points is reached. Through this iterative algorithm, the linear independence of the modal matrix is preserved as much as possible, that is, the characteristics of the original structure are preserved.

2.1.2. Modal Assurance Criterion (MAC) [36]

The modal confidence factor MAC is a good tool to evaluate the intersection angle of modal vectors. It can reflect the correlation between two spatial vectors, and its calculation formula is as follows:

$$MAC_{ij} = \frac{\left(\Phi_i{}^T\Phi_j\right)^2}{\left(\Phi_i{}^T\Phi_j\right)\left(\Phi_i{}^T\Phi_j\right)} \tag{3}$$

In the Equation (3), Φ_i and Φ_j are mode vectors of order i and j, respectively.

MAC_{ij} is located between 0 and 1, where 0 means that the two vectors are orthogonal, and 1 means that the two vectors are completely related. Therefore, the larger the non-diagonal elements of the MAC, the greater the correlation of the vectors, and the worse the independence of the modes of each order. The smaller the non-diagonal elements of the MAC, the better the independence of the modes of each order, and the better the characteristics of the original structure can be reflected. Generally, when the MAC is greater than 0.9, the two vectors are correlated, and the two vectors are indistinguishable. When it is less than 0.25, the two vectors are approximately considered orthogonal to each other.

2.1.3. Modal Kinetic Energy Method (MKE) [10]

The objective criterion of the MKE method is to find the set of measuring points so that the modal kinetic energy at the measuring points is the largest when the structure has the same number of measuring points. The modal kinetic energy expression is as follows:

$$MKE = \Phi^T M \Phi \tag{4}$$

In the Equation (4), M is the mass matrix obtained by the numerical modeling of the structure.

The contribution of the p-th degree of freedom to the kinetic energy of the q-th order mode is calculated as:

$$K_{pq} = \Phi_{pq} \sum_{s=1}^{n} M_{ps} \Phi_{sq} \tag{5}$$

The total contribution of the p-th degree of freedom to the kinetic energy of all target modes is given by:

$$K_p = \sum_{q=1}^{m} \Phi_{pq} \sum_{s=1}^{n} M_{ps} \Phi_{sq} \tag{6}$$

In the Equation (6), Φ_{pq} is the PTH element of the QTH mode; M_{ps} is the PTH row and s-th column element of the mass matrix M; and Φ_{sq} is the s-th element of the QTH mode. The optimum test point is determined based on the degree of freedom that contributes the most to the kinetic energy of a certain mode or the average kinetic energy of the target mode.

2.1.4. Covariance Matrix (VM) [37–39]

The covariance matrix method is based on the maximum information subset technique, which is used to solve the sensor optimization problem. Let matrix $Y = \{Y_s Y_p\} = [\Phi]^T$ be the modal matrix composed of the modal vectors of all feasible measuring points, and assume matrix $Y = \{Y_s Y_p\} = [\Phi]^T$, where Y_s is the modal mode of s observed measuring points, and Y_p is the modal mode of p unobserved measuring points, when Y_s is used to estimate Y_p linearly and without bias:

$$\hat{Y_p} = C_{pp} C_{ss}^{-1} Y_s \tag{7}$$

Among them, C_{ss} and C_{pp} are the diagonal submatrices of the matrix covariance matrix.

$$|cov(Y)| = \begin{vmatrix} C_{ss} & C_{sp} \\ C_{ps} & C_{pp} \end{vmatrix} = \begin{vmatrix} cov(Y_s) & C_{sp} \\ C_{ps} & cov(Y_p) \end{vmatrix} = |C_{ss}||D_{pp}| \tag{8}$$

where d is the estimated error

$$D_{pp} = cov\hat{Y_p}(-Y_p) = C_{pp} - C_{ps} C_{ss}^{-1} C_{sp} \tag{9}$$

Minimizing D_{pp} ensures an unbiased estimate of the mode displacement for unobserved measurement points using s sensors. As can be seen from Equation (9), this is equivalent to maximizing C_{ss}, that is, maximizing $|cov(Y_s)|$.

2.1.5. Effective Independence–Modal Kinetic Energy Method (EI-MKE)

EI-MKE method corrects EI method directly by multiplying the modal kinetic energy vector with the effective independent vector.

The EI method is directly revised by multiplying the modal kinetic energy vectors by the effective independent vectors.

$$EI_{MKE} = diag\left(\Phi\left(\Phi^T \Phi\right)^{-1} \Phi^T\right) \cdot diag\left(\Phi^T \Phi M\right) \tag{10}$$

2.2. Evaluation Criteria of Measuring Point Arrangement Results

Commonly used evaluations of test results include the energy, MAC, and determinant of Fisher's information matrix. This paper also evaluates the advantages and disadvantages of these three measuring point arrangement methods based on the energy angle, the orthogonality of the modal vector, and the determinant value of the Fisher information matrix. Due to the characteristics of the spatial bar structure, the extraction of the structural stiffness matrix and the mass matrix becomes easy to realize. Therefore, this paper proposes to improve the Guyan recursive technique and the complete modal MAC matrix of the theoretical modal expansion of the measuring point to evaluate the measurement point arrangement results.

2.2.1. Energy

The higher the energy of the candidate measuring points, the higher the signal-to-noise ratio that can be obtained in the test process, which is conducive to obtaining accurate structural parameters. The modal kinetic energy of the candidate measuring points is used to evaluate the arrangement of measuring points. The calculation of its value is the same as in Formula (3).

2.2.2. MAC

The MAC was originally proposed to detect structural damage and for damage location. It is now widely used in the correlation analysis of two curves. It is the most effective tool to judge the correlation between modes [1,2], especially test modes and theoretical modes.

$$MAC_{ij} = \frac{\left(\Phi_i{}^T\Phi_j\right)^2}{\left(\Phi_i{}^T\Phi_j\right)\left(\Phi_i{}^T\Phi_j\right)},\ j = 1,2,3,\ldots,m \tag{11}$$

According to Formula (4), the MAC matrix with the same number of output points is obtained. The diagonal elements represent the correlation between the two test curves, and the diagonal elements of the MAC matrix are represented by the MAC value. The higher the correlation between the two test curves, the closer the MAC value is to 1. The closer the MAC value of the two test curves is to 0, the more irrelevant the two test curves are. The MAC matrix of the feature vector formed by the candidate measuring points is used to evaluate the results of the measuring point arrangement. It is an index used to examine the advantages and disadvantages of the selected measuring points from the perspective of the linear independence of the modal vector. The smaller the off-diagonal element is, the larger the space vector intersection angle of the arranged measuring points.

2.2.3. The Determinant of Fisher's Information Matrix

$$F = lg\left(\frac{F_{select}}{F_{full}}\right) \tag{12}$$

According to the logarithm of the ratio of the determinant value of the Fisher information matrix at the selected measuring point position to the determinant value of the Fisher information matrix of the initial complete model, the information content of the selected measuring point containing the modal parameters is evaluated. The larger the F value, the more information about the structural modal parameters that is obtained.

2.2.4. Modal Expansion

The expansion process of the incomplete mode is based on the improved Guyan recursive technique. The principle is as follows:

The characteristic equation of an n-degree-of-freedom system is as follows:

$$Kx = \lambda Mx = f \tag{13}$$

According to the principal coordinate x_m and the vice coordinate x_s, the characteristic equation is divided into:

$$\begin{bmatrix} K_m & K_s \end{bmatrix} \begin{bmatrix} x_m \\ x_s \end{bmatrix} = \lambda \begin{bmatrix} M_m & M_s \end{bmatrix} \begin{bmatrix} x_m \\ x_s \end{bmatrix} \tag{14}$$

In the Equation (14), $K_m,\ M_m \in R^{N,m};\ K_s,\ M_s \in R^{N,s},\ m + s = N$

$$K_m = \begin{bmatrix} K_{mm} \\ K_{sm} \end{bmatrix},\ M_m = \begin{bmatrix} M_{mm} \\ M_{sm} \end{bmatrix},\ K_s = \begin{bmatrix} K_{ms} \\ K_{ss} \end{bmatrix},\ M_s = \begin{bmatrix} M_{ms} \\ M_{ss} \end{bmatrix} \tag{15}$$

Without considering the inertia force at the right end, the following is obtained:

$$\begin{bmatrix} K_m & K_s \end{bmatrix} \begin{bmatrix} x_m \\ x_s \end{bmatrix} = 0 \tag{16}$$

The coordinate transformation of the improved Guyan reduction is established from the above formula:

$$x_s = D_z x_m \tag{17}$$

$$D_z = -K_s^{+} K_m \tag{18}$$

$$Ks+ = (KsTKs) - 1KsT \tag{19}$$

Furthermore, the improved Guyan in reduced form is obtained.

$$x = \begin{bmatrix} I \\ D_z \end{bmatrix} x_m = T_z x_m \tag{20}$$

$$K_z = T_z^T K T_z = K_{mm} + K_{ms} D_z + D_z^T K_{sm} + D_z^T K_{ss} D_z \tag{21}$$

$$M_z = T_z^T M T_z = M_{mm} + M_{ms} D_z + D_z^T M_{sm} + D_z^T M_{ss} D_z \tag{22}$$

Using the above improved Guyanreduced solution to approximate the right-side inertial force of Formula (7), the k-order reduced matrix of the improved Guyan is obtained:

$$D^{(k)} = D_z + K_s^{+} (M_m + M_s D^{(k-1)}) [M^{(k-1)}]^{-1} K^{(k-1)} \tag{23}$$

$$K^{(k-1)} = K_{mm} + K_{ms} D^{(k-1)} + D^{(k-1)T} K_{sm} + D^{(k-1)T} K_{ss} \tag{24}$$

$$M^{(k-1)} = M_{mm} + M_{ms} D^{(k-1)} + D^{(k-1)T} M_{sm} + D^{(k-1)T} M_{ss} D^{(k-1)} \tag{25}$$

In the improved Guyan recursive technique, the retained principal coordinates are the degrees of freedom of the measuring points calculated by each measuring point algorithm. According to the obtained reduced matrix and the modes of the measuring points, the modal matrix of the whole structure is inversely deduced, and the MAC matrix of the calculated overall modal matrix and the theoretical modal matrix is calculated to evaluate the effectiveness of the measuring point arrangement. Practice shows that considering the calculation accuracy and calculation time, the three-stage improved Guyan recursive indentation technique can meet the requirements.

2.3. Research on Search Order of Algorithm

The plane truss structure shown in Figure 1 was established by using the finite element software Midas Gen 2024 v1.1. The chord length is 1.5 m, and the height is 1.2 m. The elastic modulus of the bar is 2.06×10^{11} N/m^2, the material density of the bar is 7.85×10^3 kg/m^3, the cross-sectional area is 3.96×10^{-4} m^2, and the additional mass of the joint is 1050 kg. The first six natural frequencies and vibration modes of the structure were calculated as shown in Figure 2.

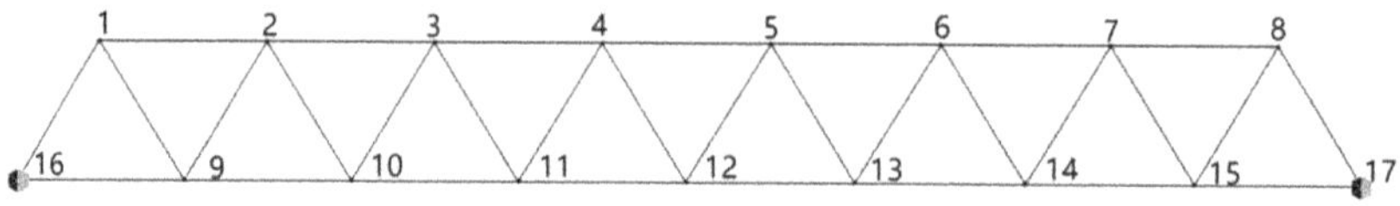

Figure 1. Midas Gen plane truss structure model.

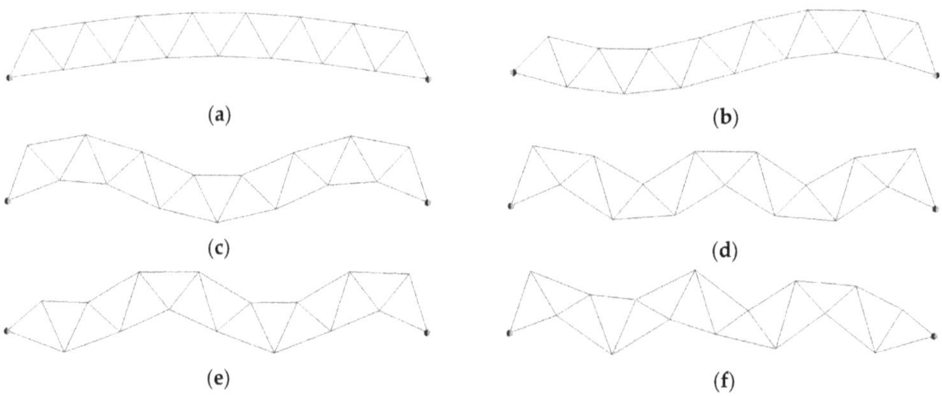

Figure 2. The first six modal frequencies and mode shapes of plane truss. (**a**) First mode of vibration (2.883 Hz); (**b**) Second-order vibration mode (6.981 Hz); (**c**) Third-order vibration mode (11.053 Hz); (**d**) Fourth-order vibration mode (13.386 Hz); (**e**) Fifth-order vibration mode (19.402 Hz); (**f**) Sixth-order vibration mode (21.025 Hz).

The targeting of the first six patterns and the selection of the six measuring points was achieved, and the layout schemes of the measuring points were provided according to three different search sequences: gradual deletion, direct acquisition, and gradual accumulation, as indicated in Table 2.

Table 2. Sensor placement using three methods.

Searching Sequence	EI	MKE	EI-MKE
Gradually deleted	1X 2Z 6X 7Z 11Z 13Z	2Z 5Z 7Z 9Z 13Z 15Z	2X 2Z 4Z 7X 7Z 13Z
Direct acquisition	2Z 7Z 11Z 13Z 9Z 15Z	2Z 5Z 7Z 9Z 13Z 15Z	2Z 7Z 13Z 9Z 15Z 5Z
Gradually accumulated	2Z 9Z 10Z 3Z 11Z 4Z	2Z 5Z 7Z 9Z 13Z 15Z	2Z 9Z 10Z 3Z 7Z 15Z

Four evaluation criteria were used to evaluate the layout of the measuring points, as shown in Figure 3. In order to avoid confusion, the maximum MAC of the off-diagonal element of the autocorrelation matrix of the measuring point is MAC_n. MAC_n characterizes the linear independence of the measuring point mode. The smaller the MAC_n, the better the orthogonality of the test mode and the better the anti-noise ability of the measuring point. The minimum diagonal element of the correlation matrix formed by the extended complete mode and the structural theoretical mode is MAC_d. MAC_d represents the correlation between the complete mode formed by the expansion of the measuring point and the complete mode information of the structure. The larger the MAC_d, the higher the correlation between the extended mode and the theoretical mode and the more complete the extended structural information.

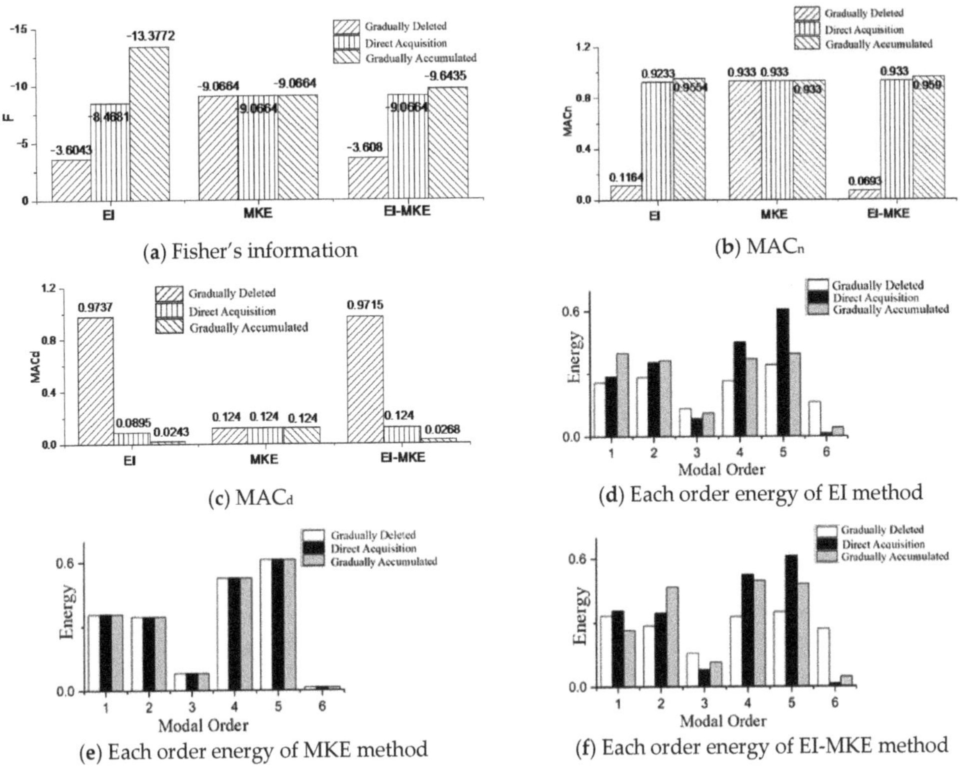

Figure 3. Sensor placement evaluation.

From the above results, the search order had no effect on the MKE method, and the results of the three search orders were the same. The search order had a great influence on the EI method and the EI-MKE method; as shown in Figure 3a, the obtained measurement points were gradually deleted, and the maximum Fisher information value was obtained; as shown in Figure 3b, the measured point modes obtained by gradually deleting had good orthogonality; and as shown in Figure 3c, after gradually deleting the obtained measuring points for complete modal expansion, the structural expansion mode had the greatest correlation with the theoretical mode. Therefore, the following algorithms in this paper were all based on the arrangement of the measuring points obtained by the gradual deletion process.

It can be seen from the results of the energy map shown in Figure 3d–f that the gradual deletion process, compared with the direct acquisition and gradual accumulation processes, obtained relatively less energy at the measuring point. However, it can be seen from the modal expansion results that as long as the vibration mode of the measuring point could be obtained, this lower energy did not affect the expansion of the incomplete mode of the structure into a complete mode. Therefore, the subsequent evaluation of the measuring point arrangement in this paper no longer considered the modal energy problem of the measuring points.

2.4. Algorithm Optimization

The three measuring point arrangement methods of the above plane truss example were evaluated, and the following conclusions were drawn:

(1) From the perspective of Fisher's determinant, the information of the measuring point arrangement obtained by the EI method was slightly higher than that obtained by the EI-MKE method, and the Fisher information obtained by the MKE algorithm was the least.

(2) From the perspective of MAC_n, the modal orthogonality of the measuring points obtained by the EI-MKE method was the best, followed by the EI method. The arrangement of the measuring points obtained by the MKE method and the non-diagonal elements of the MAC matrix reached more than 0.9, indicating that the orthogonality of the test mode was poor and that there was a cross mode.

(3) From the perspective of MAC_d, the extended mode obtained by the EI method had the best correlation with the theoretical mode of the structure, followed by the EI-MKE method. The minimum value of the extended mode MAC_d of the measuring point obtained by the MKE method reached within 0.2, indicating that the extended mode was almost orthogonal to the theoretical mode of the order and that the expansion result was poor.

Based on the above information, the MKE method was used to obtain the structural modal measurement points. Compared with the EI method and the EI-MKE method, there is a large lack of modal information, which is not suitable for the spatial grid structures when arranging the measurement points. The EI method and the EI-MKE method have their own advantages, so the application dimension of the algorithm should be expanded.

The structural dimension was expanded to three dimensions, and a 3 × 7 square pyramid grid structure model was established, as shown in Figure 4. The grid length was set as 1.5 m, the grid thickness was set as 1.2 m, and a fixed hinge support was set on the opposite side of the lower chord. The elastic modulus of the rod was set as 2.06×10^{11} N/m^2, the cross-sectional area of the upper and lower chords was set as 1.07×10^{-3} m^2, the cross-sectional area of the web member was set as 9.04×10^{-4} m^2, the material density of the rod was set as 7.85×10^3 Kg/m^3, and the added mass was set as 1700 Kg. The first six theoretical frequencies and modes of the structure were obtained by modal analysis, as shown in Figure 5.

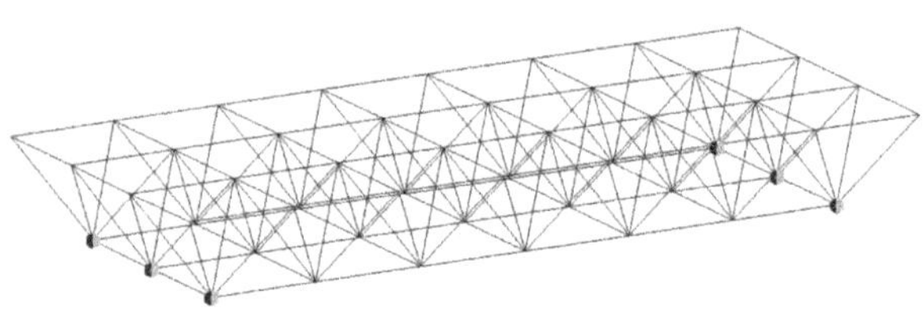

Figure 4. Midas Gen grid structure model.

Two algorithms (EI and EI-MKE) were applied. The first six modes and six measuring points were the targets. The node numbers of the grid structure are shown in Figure 6, and the arrangement results of the measuring points are shown in Table 3. Fisher's information, MAC_n, and MAC_d were used to evaluate the results of the measuring point arrangement, as shown in Figure 7.

Table 3. Sensor placement using EI and EI-MKE methods.

Measuring Point Arrangement Method	Measuring Point
EI	13Y 16Y 25Z 28Z 49Z 52Z
EI-MKE	21Y 25Z 28Z 49Z 50Z 52Z

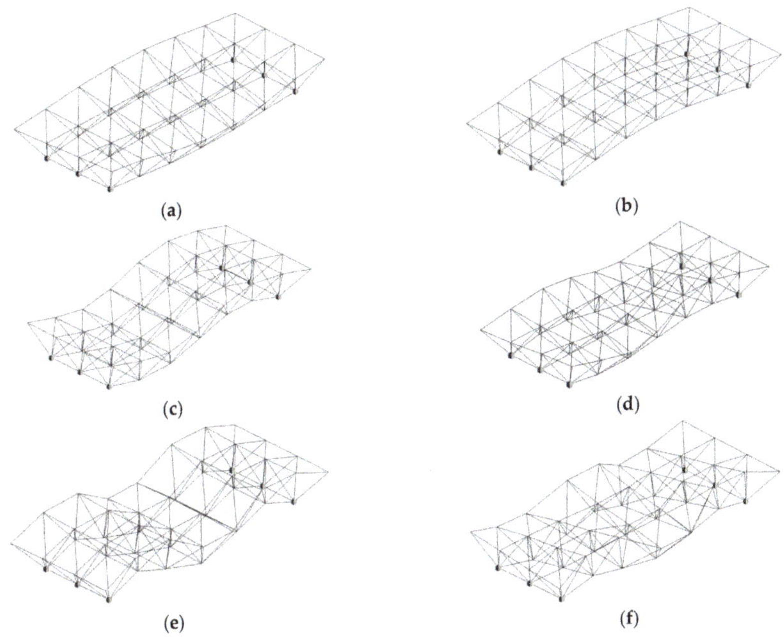

(a) (b) (c) (d) (e) (f)

Figure 5. The theoretical frequencies and vibration modes for the first six modes of the grid structure. (**a**) First mode of vibration (4.713 Hz); (**b**) Second mode of vibration (5.100 Hz); (**c**) Third mode of vibration (5.524 Hz); (**d**) Fourth mode of vibration (9.290 Hz); (**e**) Fifth mode of vibration (10.741 Hz); (**f**) Sixth mode of vibration (12.953 Hz).

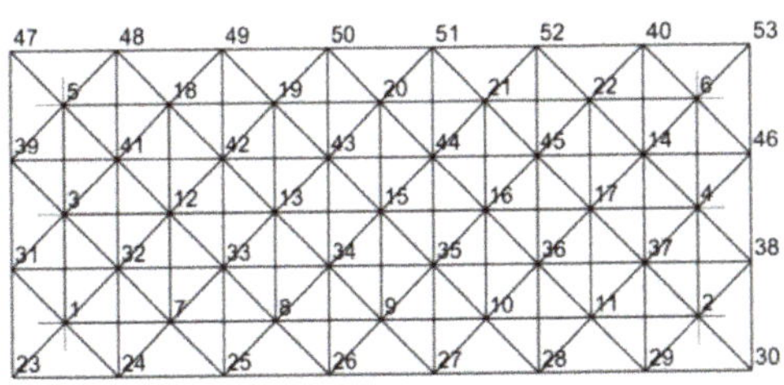

Figure 6. Node numbers of 3 × 7 grid structure.

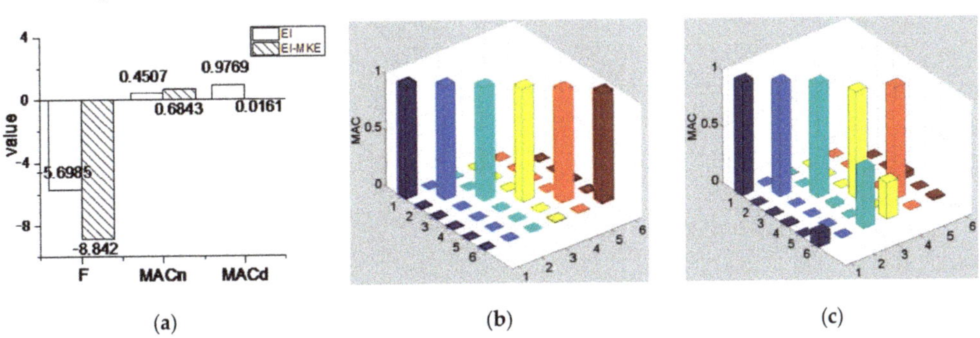

(a) (b) (c)

Figure 7. Sensor placement evaluation. (**a**) Evaluating indicator; (**b**) MAC of extended mode of EI method; (**c**) MAC of extended mode of EI-MKE method.

As shown in Figure 7, the extended mode MAC_d value was derived from the extended sixth-order mode. Although the EI-MKE method had good expansion results for the first five modes, the sixth-order MAC_d value was very small and almost orthogonal to the sixth-order theoretical mode, indicating that the EI-MKE method lost the sixth-order mode during the expansion process. The EI method was better than the EI-MKE method in terms of the amount of information at the measuring point, the orthogonality of the measuring point, and the integrity of the extended mode. Therefore, for a three-dimensional spatial grid structures, the EI method can obtain more measuring point arrangement information, which is more suitable for the measuring point arrangement of the spatial grid structures. The MAC matrix of the modal components in the three directions of the extended mode of the structure is the output, as shown in Figure 8.

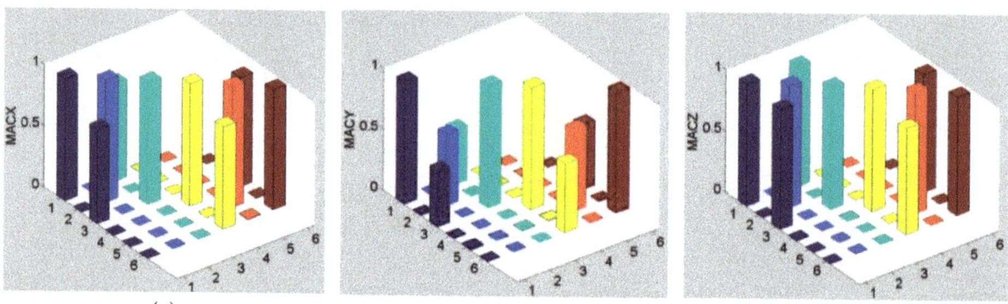

Figure 8. Mode expansion verification. (**a**) MACX; (**b**) MACY; (**c**) MACZ.

3. Arrangement of Structural Measuring Points with Damage

In order to verify whether the damaged structure still has a high correlation with the theoretical vibration mode of the original structure, this section performs a numerical simulation on the above grid example so that the number of structural members varies from zero damage to half damage, and the structural frequency and vibration mode are calculated. At the same time, the structural vibration mode and the MAC value of the original structure are calculated. Since the number of structural members in the example is 168, when the damage of the members reaches half, there may be too many damage combinations. For this reason, the concept of member sensitivity was introduced, and the single member damage was assumed to calculate the structural sensitivity coefficient. Then, in order to obtain the randomness of the structural vibration mode, random damage values of 0–10%, 20–30%, and 40–50% were imposed on the structural members. In the case of progressive damage of the rod, the MAC matrix of the first six orders of the damaged structure vibration mode and the theoretical vibration mode was calculated successively, and the MAC was counted as shown in Table 4.

Table 4. Damaged structure information statistics under different vibration mode member sensitivities.

Damage Situation	No.	Min(f)	Δf	MAC					
				>0.99	0.95–0.99	0.90–0.95	0.1–0.9	0.05–0.1	<0.05
0–10%	1	6.358	4.61%	168	0	0	0	0	0
	2	6.868	4.78%	168	0	0	0	0	0
	3	7.421	5.01%	168	0	0	0	0	0
	4	12.475	5.04%	168	0	0	0	0	0
	5	14.445	4.90%	168	0	0	0	0	0
	6	17.356	5.13%	168	0	0	0	0	0
20–30%	1	5.594	16.08%	115	50	3	0	0	0
	2	6.050	16.12%	67	101	0	0	0	0
	3	6.537	16.32%	77	63	26	2	0	0
	4	11.028	16.06%	154	14	0	0	0	0
	5	12.820	15.60%	115	53	0	0	0	0
	6	15.357	16.05%	152	16	0	0	0	0
40–50%	1	4.742	28.86%	63	55	17	33	0	0
	2	5.132	28.84%	17	28	66	48	1	8
	3	5.565	28.76%	72	12	21	63	0	0
	4	9.456	28.03%	68	100	0	0	0	0
	5	10.794	28.94%	26	78	54	10	0	0
	6	13.006	28.91%	27	119	22	0	0	0

For this space truss, as shown in Table 4, there was a positive correlation between the decrease in the structural frequency and the level of correlation of the structural vibration modes. In the range of a 5% decrease in the frequency, the structural vibration mode was highly consistent with the theoretical vibration mode. With the increase in the damage degree, such as with a decrease in frequency to about 28%, the vibration mode of each order of the grid structure deviated from the theoretical vibration mode of the undamaged structure to varying degrees, especially the third-order vibration mode, and the occurrence of MAC values below 0.9 happened 37.5% of the time.

The measurement point arrangement of the grid structure under undamaged and damaged conditions was carried out. The node number is shown in Figure 6, and the arrangement of the measuring points by the EI method is shown in Table 5. The theoretical distribution of the measuring points was the union distribution of 168 kinds of measuring points, which was obtained according to the damage order. MAC_n comes from the MAC matrix of the modal orthogonality check of the measuring points obtained by the non-destructive structural measuring points and the actual structural vibration mode displacement, which is the most unfavorable description in all the measuring points. MAC_d is derived from the MAC matrix of the extended modal correlation check of the measurement point arrangement corresponding to MAC_n.

It can be seen from Table 5 that after the occurrence of damage to the structure, the theoretical distribution of the measuring points changed, and as the damage increased, the orthogonality of the structural test mode became worse and worse, and the extended mode also showed a worse and worse correlation. However, the MAC values that characterized the modal orthogonality and the extended modal correlation of the measuring points were not much different from those of the undamaged structure. The number of combined measuring points could reflect the demand for measuring points of the first to sixth modes of the undamaged structures and damaged structures. In the case of damage within 10%, the number of merged elements was 18. With the increase in the damage degree, the number of merged measuring points changed to 20. According to the distribution of the measuring points generated by random damage, the change in the merging set was not large and basically remained stable. This shows that these degrees of freedom had the highest sensitivity to the first to sixth modes of the structure, and the structure had a basically stable distribution of measuring points. While the structural members were damaged and the vibration modes changed, the possibility of the measuring point distribution covering all the possible vibration modes could be basically guaranteed.

Table 5. Sensor placement information under different levels of damage.

Damage Quantity	No.	Theoretical Distribution of Measuring Points	MAC_n	MAC_d
0		13Y 16Y 25Z 28Z 49Z 52Z	0.4507	0.9769
0–10%	1	13Y 16Y 25Z 26Y 26Z 27Y 27Z 28Z 49Y 49Z 50Z 51Y 51Z 52Y 52Z	0.4552	0.9734
	2	13Y 16Y 25Z 26Y 26Z 27Y 27Z 28Y 28Z 49Y 49Z 50Y 50Z 51Z 52Z	0.4552	0.9749
	3	13Y 16Y 25Y 25Z 26Y 26Z 27Y 27Z 28Z 49Y 49Z 50Z 51Y 51Z 52Y 52Z	0.4547	0.9728
	4	13Y 16Y 25Y 25Z 26Y 26Z 27Y 27Z 28Y 28Z 49Y 49Z 50Y 50Z 51Y 51Z 52Y 52Z	0.4556	0.9740
	5	13Y 16Y 25Y 25Z 26Y 26Z 27Y 27Z 28Y 28Z 49Z 50Z 51Z 52Y 52Z	0.4574	0.9716
	6	13Y 16Y 25Z 26Y 26Z 27Y 27Z 28Y 28Z 49Y 49Z 50Y 50Z 51Y 51Z 52Y 52Z	0.4568	0.9729
Merge measuring points		13Y 16Y 25Y 25Z 26Y 26Z 27Y 27Z 28Y 28Z 49Y 49Z 50Y 50Z 51Y 51Z 52Y 52Z		
20–30%	1	10Y 13Y 16Y 25Y 25Z 26Z 27Y 27Z 28Y 28Z 49Y 49Z 50Y 50Z 51Y 51Z 52Z	0.4643	0.9646
	2	10Y 13Y 16Y 25Z 26Y 26Z 27Y 27Z 28Y 28Z 49Y 49Z 50Y 50Z 51Y 51Z 52Y 52Z	0.4652	0.9621
	3	10Y 13Y 16Y 25Y 25Z 26Y 26Z 27Y 27Z 28Y 28Z 49Y 49Z 50Y 50Z 51Y 51Z 52Y 52Z	0.4646	0.9640
	4	8Y 13Y 16Y 25Y 25Z 26Y 26Z 27Y 27Z 28Y 28Z 49Y 49Z 50Y 50Z 51Y 51Z 52Y 52Z	0.4648	0.9634
	5	8Y 13Y 16Y 25Y 25Z 26Y 26Z 27Y 27Z 28Y 28Z 49Y 49Z 50Y 50Z 51Z 52Y 52Z	0.4806	0.9389
	6	8Y 13Y 16Y 25Y 25Z 26Y 26Z 27Y 27Z 28Y 28Z 49Y 49Z 50Y 50Z 51Z 52Y 52Z	0.4694	0.9590
Merge measuring points		8Y 10Y 13Y 16Y 25Y 25Z 26Y 26Z 27Y 27Z 28Y 28Z 49Y 49Z 50Y 50Z 51Y 51Z 52Y 52Z		
40–50%	1	8Y 10Y 13Y 16Y 25Y 25Z 26Z 27Y 27Z 28Y 28Z 49Y 49Z 50Y 50Z 51Y 51Z 52Z	0.4689	0.9467
	2	10Y 13Y 16Y 25Z 26Y 26Z 27Y 27Z 28Y 28Z 49Y 49Z 50Z 51Y 51Z 52Z	0.4769	0.9448
	3	8Y 10Y 13Y 16Y 25Z 26Y 26Z 27Z 28Y 28Z 49Y 49Z 50Z 51Y 51Z 52Z	0.4688	0.9678
	4	8Y 10Y 13Y 16Y 25Y 25Z 26Y 26Z 27Z 28Y 28Z 49Y 49Z 50Y 50Z 51Z 52Z	0.4731	0.9124
	5	8Y 10Y 13Y 16Y 25Z 26Y 26Z 27Y 27Z 28Y 8Z 49Y 49Z 50Y 50Z 51Z 52Y 52Z	0.5114	0.8482
	6	8Y 10Y 13Y 16Y 25Y 25Z 26Y 26Z 27Y 27Z 28Y 28Z 49Y 49Z 50Z 51Z 52Y 52Z	0.4804	0.9345
Merge measuring points		8Y 10Y 13Y 16Y 25Y 25Z 26Y 26Z 27Y 27Z 28Y 28Z 49Y 49Z 50Y 50Z 51Y 51Z 52Y 52Z		

4. Study on the Number of Measuring Points

In order to ensure the spatial orthogonality of the test modes, many scholars use MAC_n to achieve a stable value as the upper limit of the number of measuring points, which lacks scientific basis. The modal expansion of the structure was carried out by using the three-stage improved Guyan recursive technique. It can be seen from Table 4 that within 10% damage, the real vibration mode of the structure had a good correlation with the theoretical vibration mode, and the MAC reached more than 0.99. Therefore, for the above grid example, the first six modes were the target modes, and the structural expansion mode was related to the theoretical vibration mode. The MAC reached 0.99 as the goal, and the change in the number of measuring points was studied compared with MAC_n, as shown in Figure 9.

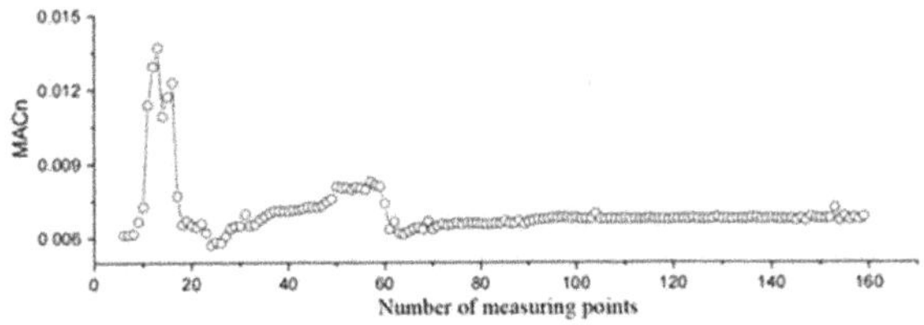

(**a**) MACn

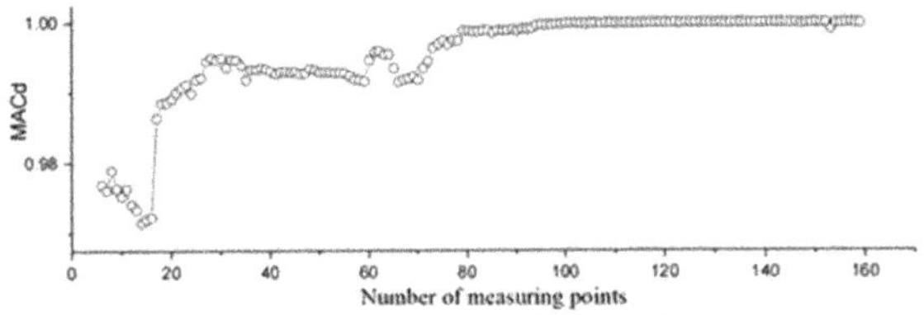

(**b**) MACd

Figure 9. Parameter change with increase in sensor number.

The orthogonality of the test modes is intended to prevent the crossing of the test modes, and if the modes of the measurement points are crossed, they can be tested. The arrangement of these points should aim to obtain as much structural information as possible; thus, MAC_d is considered superior to MAC_n as a numerical target. For this example, as shown in Figure 9, a minimum MAC_n value was reached when the number of measuring points reached 24; however, more than 60 measuring points were needed for the measuring point arrangement to achieve a stable state. Yet, when the number of measuring points was 24, the MAC_n value was found to be smaller than that of the sufficient number of measuring points until a stable and low MAC_n value was reached. Therefore, when the MAC_n value is taken as the condition, it is deemed the most economical and reasonable to select 24 measuring points. For MAC_d, when the number of measurement points reached 21, the correlation between the measured vibration mode and the theoretical vibration mode was greater than 0.99. Furthermore, the MAC_d value at 21 measurement points differed the least from the MAC_d value when the number of measurement points was sufficiently high for the MAC_d value to stabilize. Therefore, it is considered the most economically reasonable to use 21 measurement points when the MAC_d value is the criterion. From the perspective of the number of measurement points, the number of measurement points obtained with MAC_d as the target was found to be smaller than that with MAC_n as the target.

5. Conclusions

In this paper, through the verification of plane truss and grid structure examples, the problem of measuring point arrangement was studied. The main conclusions are as follows:

(1) The EI method, MKE method, and EI-MKE method, which have a great influence on the arrangement of the measuring points, were compared and analyzed. When the three methods were applied to the grid structure, the measuring points obtained by the gradually deleted search process had the greatest correlation between the structural extended mode and the theoretical mode. At the same time, it was concluded that the

EI method is the most suitable method for the arrangement of the measuring points in spatial grid structures.

(2) The effect of the search order on the MKE method was negligible, and the results for the three search orders were identical. However, the search order greatly influenced the EI method and the EI-MKE method. The MKE method was found to have significant missing modal information compared to the EI method and the EI-MKE method, making it unsuitable for measuring point layout in spatial grid structures. Both the EI method and the EI-MKE method have their own advantages. With reference to the extended MAC_d value of the sixth-order mode derived from the extended mode, it was observed that although the EI-MKE method yielded good expansion results for the first five order modes, the sixth-order MAC_d value was very small and was almost orthogonal to the sixth-order theoretical mode, indicating that the sixth-order mode is lost in the expansion process of the EI-MKE method. The EI method was found to be superior to the EI-MKE method in terms of measuring point information, measuring point orthogonality, and extended mode integrity. Therefore, the EI method can obtain more measuring point arrangement information for three-dimensional spatial grid structures and is considered more suitable for determining the measuring point arrangement of spatial grid structures.

(3) The numerical analysis of the grid was carried out, and the most unfavorable situation of structural damage was determined by the sensitivity method. The correlation of the structural modes under various damage conditions was compared. The statistical information shows that the structural frequency of the structure had a large loss under the different damage degrees, and the structural vibration mode and the vibration mode of the undamaged structure still maintained a good correlation. In particular, when the structural frequency decrease was less than 5%, the low-order vibration modes of the structure were still highly consistent with the theoretical vibration modes of the undamaged structure.

(4) It was found that with the increase in the damage amount, the MAC values of the modal orthogonality and extended modal correlation of the measuring points were less different from those of the undamaged structures. This shows that the structure had a basically stable distribution of measuring points that could basically cover the possibility of the measuring point distribution of all possible vibration modes.

(5) Combined with the three-level improved Guyan recursive technique, in order to obtain better complete modal parameters, the demand for the number of measuring points was studied, and it was concluded that the number target of MAC_d is better than that of MAC_n.

Author Contributions: Collection of data, Writing—Original Data, Methodology, C.Z.; Design of the study, Investigation, J.W.; Project administration, Writing—Review & Editing, G.S.; Writing—Review & Editing, Visualization, J.H.; Analyzed the data, Validation, Q.X.; Writing—Original Draft, Y.L.; Funding acquisition, Supervision, M.L. All authors have read and agreed to the published version of the manuscript.

Funding: The research was funded by the Key Research and Development Projects of Shanxi Province [2022LL-JB-13].

Data Availability Statement: The original contributions presented in the study are included in the article. For further inquiries, please contact the corresponding author.

Conflicts of Interest: Author Chunjuan Zhou and Mingliang Liu are employed by the Shaanxi Architecture Science Research Institute Co., Ltd. The remaining authors declare that the research was conducted in the absence of any commercial or financial relationships that could be construed as a potential conflict of interest.

References

1. Basu, B.; Bursi, O.S.; Casciati, F.; Casciati, S.; Del Grosso, A.E.; Domaneschi, M.; Faravelli, L.; Holnicki-Szulc, J.; Irschik, H.; Krommer, M.; et al. A European Association for the Control of Structures joint perspective. Recent studies in civil structural control across Europe. *Struct. Control Health Monit.* **2014**, *21*, 1414–1436. [CrossRef]
2. Chen, Y. Advances and prospects for optimal sensor placement of structural health monitoring. *J. Vib. Shock* **2015**, *45*, 1–9+52.
3. Yang, C.; Zheng, W.; Zhang, X. Optimal sensor placement for spatial lattice structure based on three-dimensional redundancy elimination model. *Appl. Math. Model.* **2018**, *66*, 576–591. [CrossRef]
4. Xiao, F.; Hulsey, J.L.; Balasubramanian, R. Fiber optic health monitoring and temperature behavior of bridge in cold region. *Struct. Control Health Monit.* **2017**, *24*, e2020. [CrossRef]
5. Xiao, F.; Hulsey, J.L.; Chen, G.S.; Xiang, Y. Optimal static strain sensor placement for truss bridges. *Int. J. Distrib. Sens. Netw.* **2017**, *13*, 1550147717707929. [CrossRef]
6. Kammer, D.C. Sensor placement for on orbit modal identification and correlation of large space structures. *J. Guid. Control Dyn.* **1991**, *14*, 251–259. [CrossRef]
7. Lim, T.W. Actuator/sensor placement for modal parameter identification of flexible structures. *Modal Anal. Int. J. Anal. Exp. Modal Anal.* **1993**, *8*, 1–13.
8. Wu, D.; Wu, Z.; Qin, X.; Yang, H. Optimal sensor placement based on two-step effective configuration method. *J. Xihua Univ. Nat. Sci.* **2008**, *27*, 48–51.
9. Hua, B. Study on sensor layout and damage identification of building cover in high speed railway station. *Build. Sci.* **2021**, *37*, 28–36.
10. Mei, H.; Lin, X. Damage Orientation Method Based on the Modal Kinetic Energy. *Appl. Mech. Mater.* **2012**, *256–259*, 1112–1116.
11. Gomes, G.F.; de Almeida, F.A.; da Silva Lopes Alexandrino, P.; da Cunha, S.S.; de Sousa, B.S.; Ancelotti, A.C. A multiobjective sensor placement optimization for SHM systems considering Fisher information matrix and mode shape interpolation. *Eng. Comput.* **2019**, *35*, 519–535. [CrossRef]
12. Liu, W.; Gao, W.; Liu, H. Theoretical Research on Two Improved Optimal Sensor Placement Methods. *Appl. Mech. Mater.* **2013**, *2544*, 1122–1129. [CrossRef]
13. Li, D.; Zhang, Y.; Ren, L.; Li, H. Sensor placement method and evaluation criteria in structural health monitoring. *Adv. Mech.* **2011**, *41*, 39–50.
14. Zhang, B.-Y.; Ni, Y.-Q. A data-driven sensor placement strategy for reconstruction of mode shapes by using recurrent Gaussian process regression. *Eng. Struct.* **2023**, *284*, 115998. [CrossRef]
15. Zhan, Z.; Fang, B.; Wan, S.; Bai, Y.; Hong, J.; Li, X. Application of a hybrid-driven framework based on sensor optimization placement for the thermal error prediction of the spindle-bearing system. *Precis. Eng.* **2024**, *89*, 174–189. [CrossRef]
16. Xu, Z.; Wang, S.; Zhang, X.L.; He, G. Optimal sensor placement for ensemble-based data assimilation using gradient-weighted class activation mapping. *J. Comput. Phys.* **2024**, *514*, 113224. [CrossRef]
17. Guo, X.; Zhang, J.; Zeng, Q.; Zhu, S.; Zong, S. Performance-based optimal sensor placement method for single-layer reticulated shells considering modal observability and damage identifiability. *Thin-Walled Struct.* **2023**, *188*, 110809. [CrossRef]
18. Xin, J.; Jiang, Y.; Wu, B.; Yang, S.X. Intelligent Bridge Health Monitoring and Assessment. *Buildings* **2023**, *13*, 1834. [CrossRef]
19. Deng, Z.; Huang, M.; Wan, N.; Zhang, J. The Current Development of Structural Health Monitoring for Bridges: A Review. *Buildings* **2023**, *13*, 1360. [CrossRef]
20. Sun, X.; Ou, J. Optimal sensor placement based on sensitivity of damage parameters. *J. Harbin Inst. Technol.* **2010**, *42*, 1530–1535.
21. Lin, J.; Xu, Y.; Zhan, S. Experimental investigation on multi-objective multi-type sensor optimal placement for structural damage detection. *Struct. Health Monit.* **2019**, *18*, 882–901. [CrossRef]
22. Cha, Y.J.; Agrawal, A.K.; Kim, Y.; Raich, A.M. Multi-objective genetic algorithms for cost-effective distributions of actuators and sensors in large structures. *Expert Syst. Appl.* **2012**, *39*, 7822–7833. [CrossRef]
23. Chang, M.; Pakzad, N.S. Optimal Sensor Placement for Modal Identification of Bridge Systems Considering Number of Sensing Nodes. *J. Bridge Eng.* **2014**, *19*, 04014019. [CrossRef]
24. Xiao, F.; Sun, H.; Mao, Y.; Chen, G.S. Damage identification of large-scale space truss structures based on stiffness separation method. In *Structures*; Elsevier: Amsterdam, The Netherlands, 2023; Volume 53.
25. Xiao, F.; Zhu, W.; Meng, X.; Chen, G.S. Parameter identification of frame structures by considering shear deformation. *Int. J. Distrib. Sens. Netw.* **2023**, *2023*, 6631716. [CrossRef]
26. Liu, F.; Guo, P.; Wang, C.; Dong, S. A direct mode shape expansion method. *Eng. Mech.* **2012**, *29*, 28–32.
27. Brincker, R.; Skafte, A.; López-Aenlle, M.; Sestieri, A.; D'Ambrogio, W.; Canteli, A. A local correspondence principle for mode shapes in structural dynamics. *Mech. Syst. Signal Process.* **2014**, *45*, 91–104. [CrossRef]
28. Zhao, J.; Zhang, L.; Xiang, B.; Wan, Y. A structural damage identification method under incomplete test data. *Chin. J. Appl. Mech.* **2010**, *27*, 670–673+845–846.
29. Mousavi, M.; Gandomi, H.A. A hybrid damage detection method using dynamic-reduction transformation matrix and modal force error. *Eng. Struct.* **2016**, *111*, 425–434. [CrossRef]
30. Yang, J.; Dong, C. Structural damage identification method based on incomplete modal information. *Chin. J. Comput. Mech.* **2019**, *36*, 290–296.

31. Civalek, Ö.; Öztürk, B.; Yavaş, A. Nonlinear transient dynamic response of clamped rectangular plates on two-parameter foundations by the algorithm of the singular convolution. *Int. J. Sci. Technol.* **2007**, *2*, 165–177.
32. Liu, B.; Yao, Y.; Ye, G. Study of optimal sensor placement for cable-stayed bridge. *Eng. Mech.* **2005**, *22*, 171–176.
33. Liu, G.; Yang, B.; Liu, Y.; Wong, S. Comparative analysis of three sensor placement optimization algorithms in tied arch bridge. *J. Vib. Shock* **2008**, *27*, 190–193.
34. Li, D.S.; Li, H.N.; Fritzen, C.P. The connection between effective independence and modal kinetic energy methods for sensor placement. *J. Sound Vib.* **2007**, *305*, 945–955. [CrossRef]
35. Zhan, J.Z.; Yu, L. An Effective Independence-Improved Modal Strain Energy Method for Optimal Sensor Placement of Bridge Structures. *Appl. Mech. Mater.* **2014**, *670*, 1252–1255. [CrossRef]
36. Desforges, M.J.; Cooper, J.E.; Wright, J.R. Mode tracking during flutter testing using the modal assurance criterion. *Proc. Inst. Mech. Eng. Part G: J. Aerosp. Eng.* **1996**, *210*, 27–37. [CrossRef]
37. Kuljus, K.; von Rosen, D. Rank covariance matrix estimation of a partially known covariance matrix. *J. Stat. Plan. Inference* **2008**, *138*, 3667–3673. [CrossRef]
38. Cui, W.; Zhang, X.; Liu, Y. Covariance matrix estimation from linearly-correlated Gaussian samples. *IEEE Trans. Signal Process.* **2019**, *67*, 2187–2195. [CrossRef]
39. Kim, S.H.; Cho, C. Effective independence in optimal sensor placement associated with general Fisher information involving full error covariance matrix. *Mech. Syst. Signal Process.* **2024**, *212*, 111263. [CrossRef]

buildings

MDPI

Article

Semantic Segmentation of Heavy Construction Equipment Based on Point Cloud Data

Suyeul Park and Seok Kim *

Department of Railroad Infrastructure Engineering, Korea National University of Transportation, Uiwang-si 16106, Republic of Korea; sypark@ut.ac.kr
* Correspondence: kimseok@ut.ac.kr; Tel.: +82-31-460-0567

Abstract: Most of the currently developed 3D point cloud data-based object recognition algorithms have been designed for small indoor objects, posing challenges when applied to large-scale 3D point cloud data in outdoor construction sites. To address this issue, this research selected four high-performance deep learning-based semantic segmentation algorithms for large-scale 3D point cloud data: Rand-LA-Net, KPConv Rigid, KPConv Deformable, and SCF-Net. These algorithms were trained and validated using 3D digital maps of earthwork sites to build semantic segmentation models, and their performance was tested and evaluated. The results of this research represent the first application of 3D semantic segmentation algorithms to large-scale 3D digital maps of earthwork sites. It was experimentally confirmed that object recognition technology can be implemented in the construction industry using 3D digital maps composed of large-scale 3D point cloud data.

Keywords: heavy construction equipment; semantic segmentation; 3D point cloud data; earthwork site; deep learning

1. Introduction

1.1. Research Background and Objectives

To address the challenge of low labor productivity in the construction industry, various initiatives have been suggested globally, including "regulatory innovation and enhanced transparency", "enhancing construction capabilities", "development of new construction materials", and "adoption of novel digital technologies" [1–10]. Recently, driven by advancements in artificial intelligence (AI), considerable research has focused on enhancing construction labor productivity through automation via machine learning and deep learning technologies [4,11–14].

In the construction industry, several AI-driven computer vision technologies have been employed to monitor safety and processes, as well as to assess concrete damage, primarily through the analysis of 2D images and videos [15,16]. Furthermore, recent research has focused on object recognition, which entails simultaneous identification and classification of various items and structures on construction sites. This involves utilizing 2D images and video data to ensure the proper usage of safety helmets and belts [17]; differentiating between construction personnel and the general public; identifying forklifts [18]; inspecting cracks in concrete structures, such as roads, buildings, and bridges; and assessing potentially hazardous situations [5,19–23].

While research on object recognition using 2D image data in the construction industry has been conducted with high object recognition rates and fast processing speeds, contributing to construction labor productivity, the utilization of 3D point cloud data is increasing. This is due to the growing need for accurate height values and 3D geometric information in recent research areas, such as terrain change detection and earthwork volume calculation using UAVs (Unmanned Aerial Vehicles) and UGVs (Unmanned Ground Vehicles), construction equipment location monitoring, autonomous driving path planning, and safe route securing [24–26]. Unlike 2D image data, 3D point cloud data includes Z-value information, ensuring the accuracy of 3D spatial location information. This makes it suitable for research requiring 3D geometric information, such as 3D digital map creation and utilization and robotics [11,27]. However, 3D point cloud data still requires continuous research to be utilized in various fields of the construction industry due to its larger file size, lower object recognition accuracy, and longer processing time compared to 2D data [28,29].

Studies on object recognition using 3D point cloud data in the construction industry are relatively limited compared with those using 2D image data. However, research in this area is gradually increasing, with several studies focusing on heavy construction equipment, which plays a crucial role in the entire construction process, affecting the construction quality, duration, manpower management, and safety. Therefore, research on object recognition for heavy construction equipment, development of machine guidance and machine control technologies, and use of unmanned heavy construction equipment is being actively conducted [12,22–24].

Object recognition studies for heavy construction equipment can be broadly categorized into those that use 2D image and 3D point cloud data. Studies utilizing 2D images of heavy construction equipment include those that generate image datasets, such as ImageNet [25] and the Alberta Construction Image Dataset (ACID) [26], as well as those focused on their classification [30]. In contrast, few studies have focused on the object recognition of heavy construction equipment using 3D point cloud data. There are relatively few studies on object classification and recognition for construction sites using 3D point cloud data, as the characteristics of such data are closely linked to the specific attributes of the data obtained from construction sites [8,31]. Generally, 2D image data is relatively lightweight and has uniformly arranged pixels, making it easier to handle. In contrast, 3D point clouds are unordered, are unstructured, and have irregular density, posing challenges for related research [32]. These characteristics of 3D point cloud data have made it difficult to apply deep learning and machine learning techniques compared to traditional 2D images [33]. Moreover, 3D point cloud data collected from earthwork sites are large-scale and high-density due to the irregular and extensive nature of construction sites, adding further complexity to related research. Construction sites are mostly located outdoors and are large-scale and irregular, resulting in 3D point cloud data with high density and large volume [31]. Therefore, due to these characteristics of 3D point cloud data from construction sites, it is challenging to apply machine learning and deep learning models originally developed for indoor environments. However, recent deep learning algorithms, such as PointNet [28], RandLA-Net [29], and KPConv [34], have exhibited remarkable object classification and semantic segmentation performance on large-scale datasets. Moreover, several large-scale 3D point cloud datasets, including Semantic3D [35], Paris-Lille-3D [36], and Toronto-3D [33], have also been published. Additionally, the development of 3D point cloud data libraries, such as the Point Cloud Library (PCL) [37], Open3D [38], and Point Data Abstraction Library (PDAL) [39], has facilitated deep learning research using extensive 3D point cloud data of construction sites.

In line with rapidly evolving technological advancements, this research addresses the question, "Is it possible to efficiently apply 3D semantic segmentation algorithms to large-scale 3D point cloud data in the form of 3D digital maps generated at earthwork sites?" To conduct this research, we first utilized the 3D-ConHE dataset (3D Point Clouds of Construction Heavy Equipment) [40] built from previous studies and 3D point cloud data from UAV-captured earthwork sites to construct a 3D digital map composed of large-scale 3D point cloud data of construction heavy equipment at earthwork sites. The constructed 3D digital map was then used to train and validate four semantic segmentation algorithms to create a 3D semantic segmentation model for construction heavy equipment. Subsequently, we tested and evaluated the performance of the 3D semantic segmentation model for the construction heavy equipment generated in this research. This research aimed to provide specific application directions for 3D deep learning technology using large-scale 3D point cloud data, which is increasingly utilized in the construction industry.

Through the results of this study, we propose a high-performance semantic segmentation algorithm based on 3D point cloud data, applicable to construction heavy equipment located on large-scale 3D digital maps of earthwork sites.

1.2. Research Scope and Methods

In this study, 14 digital maps comprising 3D point cloud data of road construction sites at the earthwork stage were created. Photogrammetry was conducted using UAVs at two road construction sites in Gwangju, Gyeonggi-do, and Jeungpyeong-gun, Chungcheongbuk-do, South Korea. Specifically, the maps exhibited various construction sections and topographical features. Before conducting 3D labeling, the 3D-ConHE dataset was integrated and aligned with the 3D digital maps. The integrated dataset comprised five types of primary heavy construction equipment commonly employed for earthwork: excavators, bulldozers, graders, dump trucks, and rollers. For 3D labeling, semantic segmentation labeling was performed based on 3D point cloud data by categorizing the integrated maps into three classes, resulting in 14 semantic segmentation datasets. These datasets were further divided into training and test sets and applied to the four semantic segmentation models to evaluate their performances.

First, a literature review was conducted to select the appropriate semantic segmentation algorithms, which were then trained and validated on semantic segmentation datasets comprising 3D point cloud data of heavy construction equipment. Subsequently, the models were tested on the test sets, and their performances were compared to determine the most efficient semantic segmentation algorithms for heavy construction equipment at outdoor construction sites. This paper is structured as follows. Section 1, the introduction, outlines the research background and objectives, scope, and methodology. Section 2 presents related works, analyzing major previous studies in line with the historical context. Section 3 covers the methodology used in this research, including the framework and performance measures for evaluating the semantic segmentation models. Section 4 details the data generation and construction of the semantic segmentation models. Section 5 focuses on testing and evaluating the performance of the constructed semantic segmentation models. Finally, Section 6 presents the conclusion.

2. Related Works

2.1. Object Recognition in the Construction Industry Using 2D Image Data

Several studies have aimed to conduct object recognition using 2D image data during both the construction and maintenance stages in the construction industry. Prior to the use of machine learning and deep learning in the construction industry, object recognition using genetic algorithms was employed in the field of architectural design. In the construction industry, genetic algorithms were mainly utilized for optimizing designs such as building floor plans, facade designs, and energy-efficient designs [41]. However, as the performance of machine learning and deep learning techniques has improved, these techniques are now more commonly used in the construction field than genetic algorithms. Next, to maintain bridges, Lee et al. (2018) conducted object detection to identify cracks and spalls in concrete bridge structures, which typically involve working at considerable heights [42]. The study used AlexNet, a deep learning-based artificial neural network, with 2D image data. Other studies have attempted to enhance safety management at construction sites by using 2D image data of collisions between heavy construction equipment and workers, as well as security camera footage, for object recognition [18,43]. Lee et al. (2022) developed an object detection model using data from security cameras installed at various sites to identify hazardous situations wherein workers collide with trucks or forklifts [43]. They achieved recognition accuracies of 88% and 92% for collisions between forklifts and workers in indoor and outdoor environments, respectively. Additionally, Jeong et al. (2021) developed an automatic recognition model for the autonomous operation of heavy construction equipment using computer vision technology [18]. They used footage from security cameras installed at construction sites for safety management to develop a Faster R-CNN model for identifying workers, signalmen, and forklifts through object detection technology [18]. They achieved an accuracy of 83.4% for detecting heavy construction equipment and workers, 84.2% for workers and signalmen, and 95.1% for heavy construction equipment and signalmen. As mentioned above, AI-driven object recognition models in construction have primarily employed 2D images or footage from security cameras for maintenance tasks, such as crack and spall detection in concrete structures, and safety management, such as recognizing and warning workers about collisions with heavy equipment at construction sites [15,27]. In addition to the construction field, recent research on 3D object detection for autonomous vehicles includes studies on Point RCNN. Point RCNN proposes a method that integrates image information with point cloud data, demonstrating excellent performance in object detection for autonomous vehicles [44].

Some studies have also conducted object recognition using 2D image data of heavy construction equipment at earthwork sites. Xiao et al. (2020) explored deep learning-based object detection and created the ACID for object classification [26]. This is a representative 2D image-based dataset of heavy construction equipment and comprises 100,000 labeled images for 10 types of heavy machinery: excavators, compactors, dozers, graders, dump trucks, concrete mixer trucks, wheel loaders, backhoe loaders, tower cranes, and mobile cranes [26]. It was used to train and test four image-based object recognition algorithms: region-based fully convolutional network (R-FCN)-ResNet101, Faster-RCNN-ResNet101, YOLO-v3, and inception-single shot multi-box detector (SSD), which achieved mean average precisions (mAPs) of 88.8%, 89.2%, 87.8%, and 83.0%, respectively. Moreover, YOLO-v3 exhibited the highest processing speed of 26.3 frames per second (fps) [26].

Arabi et al. (2019) conducted deep learning-based object detection using 2D images of heavy construction equipment by developing a MobileNet-SSD model for six types of heavy construction equipment: loaders, excavators, dump trucks, concrete-mixing trucks, rollers, and graders [45]. They used trained embedded systems, namely Jetson TX2 and Raspberry Pi 3B, for this construction equipment to reduce the processing time and enhance detection efficiency [45]. Thus, many studies have used databases such as ACID [26], AIM [45], ImageNet [25], and Microsoft COCO [46] that contain 2D images of heavy construction equipment. Among them, Xiao et al. (2020) [26] and Arabi et al. (2019) [45] created custom datasets comprising images of heavy construction equipment and selected 3D image-based object recognition algorithms that exhibited notable performance; they then trained and tested the models using these datasets. Therefore, these studies are academically significant for the application of object detection technology to the heavy construction equipment used at construction sites.

2.2. *Object Recognition in the Construction Industry Using 3D Point Cloud Data*

Most previous studies have employed 2D image and video data for object recognition during the construction and maintenance stages of construction projects. Although studies using 2D image data have been prevalent for some time, those on object recognition using 3D point cloud data emerged later but are steadily gaining traction. Most studies aimed at utilizing 3D point cloud data for the construction industry have concentrated on object classification of heavy equipment or structural elements, including walls, ceilings, doorways, and windows, or on semantic segmentation of bridges, railway tunnels, and temporary structures.

Xiong et al. (2013) classified building components, including walls, ceilings, floors, clutter, doorways, and windows, through a support vector machine (SVM), which is a widely used machine learning algorithm, to analyze point cloud data generated from building scans [47]. Kim et al. (2013) built 3D scan data for the construction site of a four-story concrete building; they classified the ground, second, third, and roof floors using an SVM classifier and compared the 3D scan data with a 4D building information model (BIM) for process management [48].

Subsequently, studies on semantic segmentation of construction sites have primarily targeted large-scale facilities, such as bridges and railway tunnels [24,49,50]. Kim et al.

(2020) employed a semantic segmentation algorithm based on point cloud data to analyze the components of road bridges, such as abutments, slabs, piers, and girders [24]. Additionally, Ryu et al. (2021) employed semantic segmentation techniques to analyze linings, drains, tracks, sleepers, and floors in railway tunnels [50], whereas Kim et al. (2022) created 3D point cloud data by scanning scaffolds at construction sites and applied semantic segmentation to generate a BIM model for scaffolds, using it for safety inspections [51].

Although various studies have focused on classification and segmentation using 3D point cloud data from construction sites, few have used these data for object detection. Current studies have mainly focused on applying object detection algorithms such as YOLO to 2D images of heavy construction equipment, construction personnel, and buildings [26,43,52]. The scarcity of object detection studies using 3D point cloud data in the construction industry is owed to the challenges posed by their large size, high density, and high levels of noise and occlusion [31], which make it difficult to apply object detection algorithms [47]. Therefore, further research is essential for developing object detection algorithms that can handle the large and highly dense point cloud data of construction sites.

Furthermore, Chen et al. [31] conducted a prominent object recognition study using 3D point cloud data of heavy construction equipment for classifying this equipment using machine learning. They developed a principal axes descriptor (PAD) and applied it to an SVM to classify five types of construction equipment: backhoe loaders, bulldozers, dump trucks, excavators, and front loaders. In a follow-up study, they developed an additional 3D descriptor alongside the PAD and employed machine learning to classify objects commonly found at construction sites, such as trailers, trucks, workers, excavators, and mobile cranes [53]. These studies are significant because they were the first to use 3D point cloud data for machine learning-based object classification of heavy construction equipment, whereas most prior research on classifying such equipment relied on 2D image data [31,53]. However, because they classified heavy construction equipment by converting AUTOCAD files into scanned files, it is challenging to apply their approach for semantic segmentation of large-scale 3D digital maps of earthwork sites created with advanced scanning devices, such as airborne laser scanning, mobile scanning technology, and terrestrial laser scanning (TLS). These studies were groundbreaking because they were the first to employ machine learning-based object classification techniques on 3D point cloud data of heavy construction equipment. Their significance lies in the application of cutting-edge technology in the construction industry, where CAD files of heavy construction equipment are transformed into 3D point cloud data files for use in an SVM. However, AI technology progressed rapidly in 2017 and 2018, coinciding with the publication of these studies. By 2023, when this study was conducted, numerous deep learning technologies with significantly enhanced performances had been developed. Therefore, this study successfully conducted semantic segmentation of heavy construction equipment using 3D point cloud data and the latest deep learning object recognition technologies.

2.3. Semantic Segmentation Based on Large-Scale 3D Point Cloud Data

Unlike the evolution of CNN-based object recognition methods, which primarily utilize 2D image data with uniform widths and heights, early research on 3D object recognition encountered several challenges, such as data loss. To address these challenges, PointNet, introduced in 2017, was the first deep learning-based object recognition algorithm designed to process 3D point cloud data [28]. PointNet utilizes properties unique to 3D point cloud data, such as permutation and transformation invariance, to address challenges such as non-uniform density, lack of structure, and unordered point cloud data in 3D object recognition tasks. In PointNet, permutation invariance is integrated into a deep neural network, ensuring that the index and its associated coordinate data remain consistent even when the indices of the 3D point cloud data are rearranged [54]. Transformation invariance is maintained using a transformation network (T-Net) that consolidates the reference coordinate axes into a unified perspective. This ensures that all text is observed from a consistent viewpoint regardless of the input data orientation [29]. These two fundamental principles of PointNet enable classification, partial segmentation, and semantic segmentation in object recognition tasks based on 3D point cloud data [28]. However, it allows processing a maximum of 2048 point clouds simultaneously, and its object recognition rate (mean intersection over union (mIoU)) is lower than that of 2D image-based object recognition methods [29,54].

Thus, although PointNet is groundbreaking because it facilitates object classification and semantic segmentation using 3D point cloud data, its limitation of processing a maximum of 2048 point clouds simultaneously renders it unsuitable for semantic segmentation using extensive 3D point cloud data from earthwork sites. Therefore, this study further reviewed recent research on the development of deep learning-based semantic segmentation algorithms using 3D point cloud data, specifically targeting urban areas. This is because deep learning-based semantic segmentation algorithms that utilize 3D point cloud data, particularly those aimed at urban areas, typically share similar characteristics with data obtained from large-scale earthwork sites. Among the latest deep learning-based semantic segmentation algorithms reviewed, we selected RandLA-Net [29], spatial contextual feature (SCF)-Net [55], and kernel point convolution (KPConv) [34]. They met the criteria for training and testing with the Semantic3D dataset employed in this study and using 3D point cloud datasets obtained through an UAV with properties similar to those of a static TLS. Accordingly, we conducted a literature review that focused on the features of these algorithms.

RandLA-Net is tailored to handle large-scale 3D point cloud data and exhibits remarkable performance, with the aim of addressing the constraints of PointNet that were prevalent at that time. The 3D scanning data of urban regions are large-scale 3D point cloud data that are unsuitable for applying object recognition technologies designed for indoor objects. RandLA-Net [29] offers various advantages, such as handling large-scale 3D point cloud data, processing significant amounts of data simultaneously, and improved accuracy and processing speed [54]. Moreover, it is suitable for semantic segmentation tasks involving datasets such as Semantic3D [35], SemanticKITTI [56], and Stanford 3D Indoor Scene Dataset (S3DIS) [57]. In an experiment using the Semantic3D dataset, which closely resembles the characteristics of the objects employed in this study, RandLA-Net achieved an mIoU of 77.4% and overall accuracy (OA) of 94.8%, indicating excellent performance for semantic segmentation tasks involving 3D point cloud data [29].

However, this algorithm has the drawback of long processing times owing to low GPU utilization during training and testing on the Semantic3D dataset. To address these limitations, SCF-Net was designed as a semantic segmentation algorithm for large-scale 3D point cloud data [55]. In a related study, the SCF-Net algorithm outperformed RandLA-Net in a semantic segmentation experiment using the Semantic3D dataset. Finally, KPConv is a semantic segmentation technique that utilizes the extensive 3D point cloud data employed in this study [34]. Unlike grid-based methods, such as VoxelNet [58], or multilayer perceptron (MLP)-based methods, such as PointNet, this algorithm is designed to be easily applicable to convolution without converting 3D point cloud data into 2D image data [28,34,58]. Thus, KPConv can be applied to large-scale 3D point cloud datasets such as Scannet, Semantic3D, S3DIS, or Paris-Lille-3D (PL3D). Additionally, rigid KPConv yielded a higher mIoU than deformable KPConv on the Semantic 3D dataset [34]. In this chapter, we conducted a literature review on large-scale 3D point cloud data-based semantic segmentation algorithms, examining the problems addressed by each algorithm over time. Among the various 3D point cloud data-based semantic segmentation algorithms reviewed in this research, the PointNet algorithm stands out. Unlike previous research and traditional semantic segmentation methods developed for small indoor objects, PointNet enabled the implementation of semantic segmentation technology using large-scale 3D point cloud data. This established PointNet as a pioneering approach in the field of large-scale 3D point cloud data-based semantic segmentation. Additionally, following the PointNet algorithm, newer methods such as RandLA-Net, SCF-Net, and KPConv algorithms have been developed. Our literature review confirms that these latest algorithms also make it possible to apply semantic segmentation technology to large-scale 3D digital maps of earthwork site point cloud data.

3. Methodology

3.1. Framework

This chapter proposes the framework, as illustrated in Figure 1, of a high-performance semantic segmentation algorithm based on 3D point cloud data for heavy construction equipment obtained from the 3D digital maps of earthwork sites. It is divided into four steps for efficient semantic segmentation of large-scale 3D point cloud data of earthwork sites.

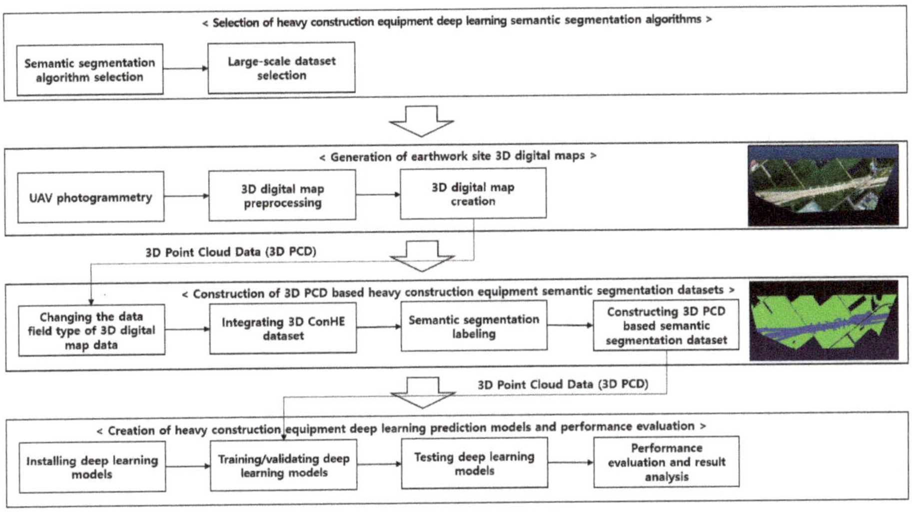

Figure 1. Semantic segmentation framework of this research.

First, in the "selection of deep learning-based semantic segmentation algorithms for heavy construction equipment" step, deep learning-based semantic segmentation algorithms suitable for large-scale 3D point cloud data of earthwork sites were reviewed and selected for object recognition. Large-scale 3D point cloud data in the form of 3D digital maps of earthwork sites are unsuitable for deep learning-based semantic segmentation algorithms developed for indoor environments. These methods are only applicable to algorithms developed for datasets collected from urban areas. Hence, applying them to high-performance semantic segmentation algorithms for 3D point cloud data is challenging. Therefore, we conducted a comprehensive literature review and preliminary testing to identify a high-performance semantic segmentation algorithm that is suitable for 3D digital maps of earthwork sites. We also examined customizable 3D point cloud data that can be applied to this algorithm. The relevant details are provided in Section 2.

Next, in the "generation of earthwork site 3D digital maps" step, photogrammetry was conducted using UAVs to collect topographic data from the sites. The collected data were then preprocessed to construct 3D digital maps of earthwork sites composed of 3D point cloud data. To achieve this, a road construction site that was undergoing earthwork was selected. Through UAV photogrammetry and data preprocessing, the data were converted into the 3D point cloud format, resulting in 14 3D digital maps of the earthwork sites. Subsequently, the 3D digital maps were postprocessed for "constructing 3D PCD-based heavy construction equipment semantic segmentation datasets". Additionally, the heavy construction equipment data from 3D-ConHE were integrated into the 3D digital maps and 3D labeled. These steps were crucial for creating a dataset comprising adequate heavy construction equipment data based on 3D point cloud data for training and testing the deep learning-based semantic segmentation models. This difficulty arises during the model training process using 3D digital maps of earthwork sites generated through UAV photogrammetry. The proposed data construction method addresses the problem of overfitting owing to insufficient training data. Finally, in the "creation of deep learning prediction models for heavy construction equipment and their performance evaluation" step, four semantic segmentation models based on 3D point cloud data were trained, validated, and tested on heavy construction equipment. Subsequently, the results were compared and analyzed to evaluate the model performances. The steps in the proposed semantic segmentation framework were structured chronologically.

3.2. Performance Metrics

We specifically selected the confusion matrix to evaluate the training effectiveness of the 3D semantic segmentation models employed in this study. Other metrics, such as OA, IoU, and mIoU, have been used to assess the performance of semantic segmentation models based on 3D point cloud data [29,33,34]. Equations (1)–(3) were used to compute the OA, IoU, and mIoU, respectively, to validate the semantic segmentation models trained in this study. True positives (TPs), true negatives (TNs), false positives (FPs), and false negatives (FNs) were defined based on the confusion matrix. Equation (3) represents the arithmetic mean, which is calculated by dividing the sum of the IoUs of multiple data points by the number of data points (N):

$$OA = \frac{\sum TP_n}{TP_n + FP_n + TN_n + FN_n} \tag{1}$$

$$IoU_n = \frac{TP_n}{TP_n + FP_n + FN_n} \tag{2}$$

$$mIoU_n = \frac{\sum IoU_n}{N} \tag{3}$$

4. Data Generation and Semantic Segmentation Model Construction

4.1. Generation of a 3D Digital Map of Earthwork Sites

4.1.1. UAV Photogrammetry of Earthwork Site and Data Preprocessing

The 3D point cloud data from two road construction sites were acquired via UAV photogrammetry using the DJI Phantom 4 RTK, which was connected to an RTK GNSS base station. The selected sites were close to Gwangju, Gyeonggi-do, and Jeungpyeong-gun, Chungcheongbuk-do, South Korea. Photogrammetry was performed at these sites on two separate occasions. Fourteen 3D digital maps encompassing the diverse topographical characteristics and types of heavy construction equipment employed at these sites were generated. Additionally, to ensure data consistency during the creation of 3D digital maps sites, UAV photogrammetry was conducted at an altitude of 100 m. However, owing to varying wind conditions, the UAV flew at altitudes ranging from 80 to 120 m wh. Additionally, the 2D images of the earthwork sites obtained through UAV photogrammetry were converted into 3D point cloud data via preprocessing, resulting in 14 3D digital maps in the LAS format. Finally, noise and outliers were removed from the maps using the open-source Cloudcompare software v2.12 alpha [64-bit] [59].

4.1.2. Changing the Format of 3D Digital Map Data

The 14 3D digital maps of the earthwork sites created in this study were converted into a dataset format suitable for training and testing before using them for the point cloud data-based semantic segmentation models. Thus, the Semantic3D dataset was selected, as its characteristics are similar to the dataset used in this study: large-scale and captured using stationary TLS. Consequently, the 3D digital maps were converted into the Semantic3D dataset format by converting their data fields into the [X, Y, Z, I, R, G, B] format. This process was conducted on a system comprising Windows 10 and Python 3.6.

This conversion process standardized the data field format of the 3D digital maps to match that of the Semantic3D dataset. Consequently, it allowed the application of the 3D point cloud data-based semantic segmentation algorithms selected for this study.

4.1.3. 3D-ConHE Dataset Integration and Custom Dataset Construction

After converting the 3D digital maps of the earthwork sites into the Semantic3D dataset format, the 3D point cloud data of heavy construction equipment from the 3D-ConHE dataset created in a previous study [40] were integrated into the 3D digital maps to generate a custom dataset. This was done because the 3D digital maps created in this study did not include sufficient data for the five types of heavy construction equipment, resulting in insufficient 3D point cloud data to adequately train the semantic segmentation models. To address this limitation, specific parts of the 3D-ConHE dataset were integrated into the construction section of the 3D digital maps. This process generated a custom dataset suitable for training and testing the semantic segmentation models. The same method was used to integrate 15 pieces of 3D-ConHE data into the 3D digital maps to create custom datasets comprising 14 files with a combined size of 5.046 GB and 145,584,227 points. Additionally, all the 3D digital files in the custom dataset had dimensions equal to or smaller than 600 × 500 × 90 m in width, length, and height, respectively. Each file was ≤500 MB and contained ≤15,000,000 points.

4.2. 3D Semantic Labeling

4.2.1. Labeling of Large-Scale 3D Point Cloud Data

The 15 custom datasets were subjected to 3D point cloud labeling. The Semantic Segmentation Editor is a common software Version 1.6.0 used to label semantic segmentation datasets of general 3D point cloud data [60] and is often employed in semantic segmentation or object detection tasks, particularly for autonomous vehicle data. However, the custom datasets created in this study were large-scale 3D digital maps containing 3D point cloud data obtained from earthwork sites, which differs from the typical smaller-scale 3D point cloud datasets of autonomous vehicles. Consequently, it could not be used for 3D labeling in this study. Instead, semantic segmentation labeling for the custom datasets was conducted using labeling software designed for TLS data.

To conduct labeling, three classes were defined to represent the diverse geographical characteristics of the earthwork sites: Class 1 (Ground), Class 2 (Non-ground), and Class 3 (Heavy Construction Equipment, HCE). Point clouds representing construction sections were labeled as "Ground" for Class 1, whereas those representing forests, roads, and fields were labeled as "Non-ground" for Class 2. Finally, the point clouds of all heavy construction equipment in 3D-ConHE were labeled "heavy construction equipment" for Class 3. Adequate training data were ensured by labeling all point clouds corresponding to the five types of heavy construction equipment as Class 3. This prevented overfitting during the training of the semantic segmentation models and facilitated stable training. Point clouds that did not fall into Classes 1, 2, or 3 were categorized as unlabeled points, denoted as Class 0. Following this, all 15 custom datasets were labeled and inspected to ensure the acquisition of high-quality labeled 3D point cloud data.

4.2.2. Creating a Heavy Construction Equipment Dataset Based on 3D Point Cloud Data

We conducted 3D point cloud data labeling to create 14 (10 for training, 4 for testing) heavy construction equipment datasets with 3D point cloud data suitable for training and testing the semantic segmentation algorithms. All data in these datasets were formatted in the TXT and LABELS format. The TXT data fields included the [X, Y, Z, I, R, G, and B] values corresponding to the Semantic3D dataset, whereas the LABELS data fields comprised the class value [C]. The 14 datasets had a combined file size of 5.046 GB and total point count of 145,584,227, representing the 3D digital maps generated from outdoor earthwork sites. All 3D digital files had dimensions of ≤600 m × 500 m × 90 m in width, length, and height, respectively.

4.3. Construction of Semantic Segmentation Models

4.3.1. Overview

In this study, the KPConv algorithm stood out due to its kernel point fully convolutional neural network (KP-FCNN) architecture, which is classified as rigid or deformable based on the kernel type used. To determine the most suitable version for earthwork sites, the algorithm was divided into rigid and deformable versions for the experiment. Accordingly, four algorithms were used for training, validation, and testing: RandLA-Net, KPConv Rigid, KPConv Deformable, and SCF-Net. It should be noted that all four algorithms were tested and validated simultaneously to develop semantic segmentation models for heavy construction equipment based on 3D point cloud data. Subsequently, they were subjected to sequential testing. The RandLA-Net and KPConv algorithms were implemented on a system comprising an Nvidia RTX 2080 Ti 11 GB GPU, whereas SCF-Net was implemented on one comprising an Nvidia GTX 1080 Ti 11 GB GPU.

4.3.2. Training and Validation

All four models were simultaneously trained and validated using a batch size of two, a maximum of 100 epochs, and a learning rate of 0.001. We used identical hyperparameters for all models to determine the most optimal model. For the experiment, 10 training datasets of 3D point cloud data of heavy construction equipment were used, comprising 110,591,765 points with a file size of 3.813 GB. In contrast to 2D image data-based object recognition algorithms, the models in this study were trained on the point clouds of each class rather than the number of files in the training data. Therefore, although the number of files in the training data may appear limited, the semantic segmentation models were trained on 10 datasets comprising 110,591,765 point clouds, thereby ensuring adequate training. The four models were trained for a single epoch. To assess their performance, their IoU, mIoU, and OA scores were evaluated at the end of each epoch. Subsequently, the models were trained for the maximum allowable number of epochs, and the best-performing model was selected to formulate the four semantic segmentation algorithms.

5. Results and Discussion

5.1. Test

The performance of the four semantic segmentation models trained on 3D point cloud data was evaluated using a batch size of two and step size of 100 on four test sets from the 3D point cloud datasets of heavy construction equipment. The test data had a combined size of 1.233 GB and comprised 34,992,462 point-clouds. Figure 2 illustrates Test Dataset 1 along with its ground truth-labeled version. In Figure 2b, Class 1 (Ground) is shown in blue, Class 2 (Non-ground) is shown in green, and Class 3 (Heavy Construction Equipment, HCE) is shown in red.

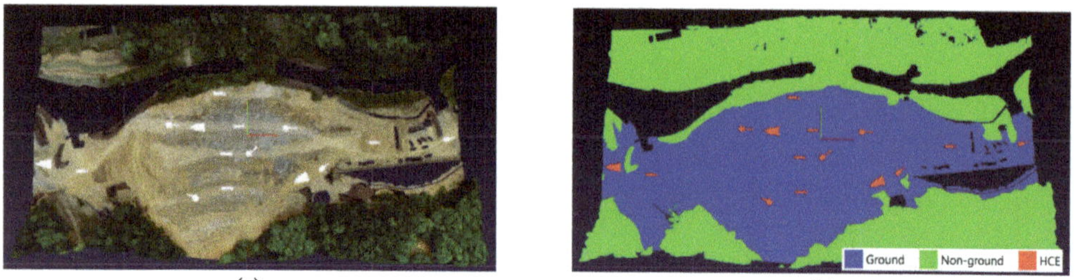

(a) (b)

Figure 2. Data used for testing the four semantic segmentation models: (**a**) Test Dataset 1 and (**b**) its ground truth labels.

5.2. Test Results and Discussions

In this section, the performance of each semantic segmentation model is compared and analyzed by consolidating the results of all four models. First, their prediction results for the four test datasets used in the experiment are visually compared.

Figure 3 shows a visual comparison of the results obtained for first test dataset. Evidently, RandLA-Net outperformed the other models for Class 1 (Ground) and Class 2 (Non-ground). Furthermore, for Class 3 (Heavy Construction Equipment), SCF-Net and RandLA-Net, which have the highest values for Test Dataset 1 in Table 1, exhibited similar results. In Figure 3, Class 1 (Ground) is shown in blue, Class 2 (Non-ground) is shown in green, and Class 3 (Heavy Construction Equipment, HCE) is shown in red.

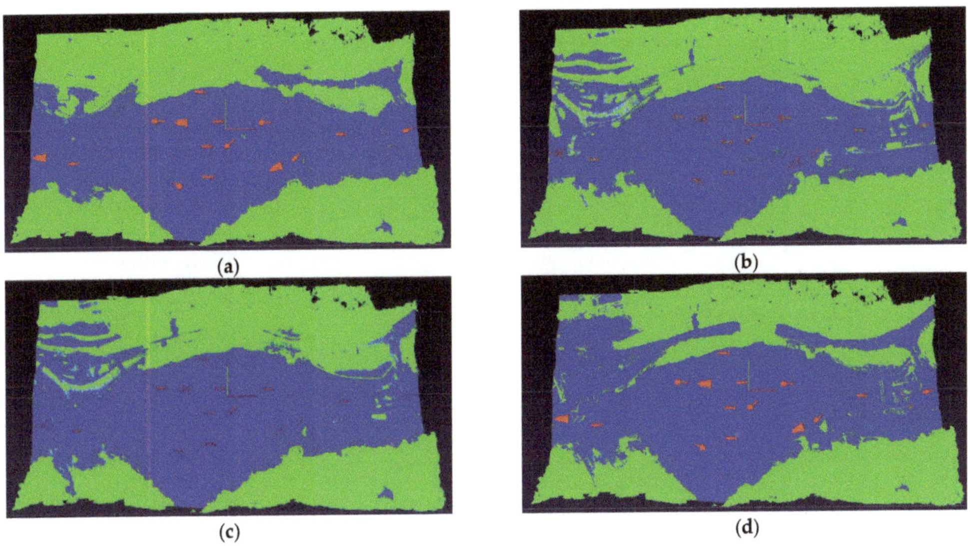

Figure 3. Semantic segmentation results of (**a**) RandLA-Net, (**b**) KPConv rigid, (**c**) KPConv deform, and (**d**) SCF-Net.

The mIoU, OA, and IoU values of the four trained semantic segmentation models for construction equipment for each class across the four test datasets are listed in Table 1. Additionally, it includes the mIoU, OA, and overall mIoU for each class across the four test datasets. Evidently, RandLA-Net achieved the highest overall mIoU of 79.8%, followed closely by SCF-Net at 78.1%. Moreover, RandLA-Net exhibited the highest OA of 84.4%, followed by KPConv Rigid and SCF-Net at 82.8%. In terms of the mIoU for each class, RandLA-Net achieved the highest value of 80.3% for Class 1 (Ground), whereas SCF-Net achieved the highest value of 86.4% for Class 2 (Non-ground). Finally, for Class 3 (Heavy Construction Equipment), SCF-Net achieved the best performance of 89.5%. The four test datasets were uniformly used to evaluate four semantic segmentation models. Among them, RandLA-Net exhibited superior performance in terms of mIoU, OA, and mIoU for Class 1 compared, whereas SCF-Net surpassed RandLA-Net in terms of the mIoU for Classes 2 and 3.

The tests of the four semantic segmentation models in this research showed mIoU ranging from 79.8% to 63.9% and overall accuracy ranging from 84.4% to 82.6%. Compared to the object recognition accuracy of 2D image data, which ranges from 88% to 96% as reviewed in related works [15,18,26,39–41,43,44], the results of this research are relatively lower. This indicates that the object recognition performance is related to the differences between 2D image-based object recognition algorithms and 3D point cloud data-based object recognition. For instance, the RandLA-Net algorithm selected in this study is known to have the best performance among currently developed 3D point cloud data-based semantic segmentation algorithms. However, according to related papers, it shows a performance of mIoU 77.4% and OA 94.8% when using the Semantic3D dataset, which is somewhat lower compared to 2D image-based object recognition. Various reasons may account for these results. According to PointNet [28], while 2D image data is composed of pixels of uniform size, 3D point cloud data is characterized by irregular density, unstructured nature, and lack of order among data points. These characteristics have delayed the development of related technologies. Therefore, 3D point cloud data-based object recognition is known to have relatively lower object recognition rates and higher error rates compared to 2D image-based object recognition. However, with the development of new 3D point cloud data-based semantic segmentation algorithms, such as OpenTrench3D [61], the object recognition rate is gradually increasing, and the error rate is decreasing. This trend is expected to narrow the performance gap between 2D image-based object recognition and 3D point cloud data-based object recognition over time.

Based on the results obtained from this research, we confirmed that although the accuracy is somewhat lower compared to 2D object recognition algorithms, 3D point cloud data-based semantic segmentation algorithms can be efficiently applied. These 3D point cloud data-based semantic segmentation algorithms are expected to become more applicable with improvements in object recognition rates [60]. Furthermore, the results of this research provide a direction for the application of deep learning technology based on large-scale 3D point cloud data, which is anticipated to increase in utility within the construction industry. This signifies the importance of the study's findings as foundational research in the related field.

Table 1. Test results of the four semantic segmentation models for heavy construction equipment.

Methods	Test Data	mIoU (%)	OA (%)	mIoU (%)		
			Accuracy (%)	IoU_{c1} (%)	IoU_{c2} (%)	IoU_{c3} (%)
RandLA-Net	**Total**	**79.8**	**84.4**	**80.3**	**82.6**	**76.6**
	1	71.4	73.9	71.6	68.3	74.3
	2	84.1	89.2	84.7	90.0	77.5
	3	82.9	84.6	81.4	83.4	83.4
	4	80.9	89.9	83.3	88.8	70.6
KPConv rigid	**Total**	**65.4**	**82.8**	**60.1**	**85.8**	**50.4**
	1	65.0	80.4	74.5	77.7	42.9
	2	67.4	82.9	73.5	83.2	45.5
	3	70.9	93.4	58.8	96.0	57.9
	4	58.4	74.7	33.8	86.2	55.4
KPConv deform	**Total**	**63.9**	**82.6**	**58.6**	**84.3**	**48.9**
	1	54.1	73.6	58.2	81.8	22.2
	2	68.9	82.7	72.0	83.6	52.0
	3	67.4	94.3	51.0	87.5	63.8
	4	65.0	79.9	53.3	84.4	57.4
SCF-Net	**Total**	**78.1**	**82.8**	**58.5**	**86.4**	**89.5**
	1	80.7	80.2	67.4	83.4	91.3
	2	78.3	81.4	68.0	82.4	84.6
	3	83.7	94.6	66.1	95.8	89.3
	4	69.7	74.9	32.5	83.8	92.8

6. Conclusions

With recent advancements in object recognition and preprocessing technologies based on 3D point cloud data, it has become possible to conduct research utilizing large-scale 3D point cloud data, which was previously difficult to apply. Consequently, various studies using 3D point cloud data have been conducted in the construction industry; however, research on object recognition targeting 3D digital maps of earthwork sites remains limited.

Therefore, this study selected a semantic segmentation algorithm suitable for large-scale 3D digital maps of earthwork sites from among various semantic segmentation algorithms based on large-scale 3D point cloud data and conducted research on semantic segmentation using this data. The methodology of this study involved first reviewing 3D point cloud data-based semantic segmentation algorithms targeting earthwork sites. Then, a 3D-ConHE dataset was installed on the 3D digital map of the earthwork site to construct a semantic segmentation dataset based on 3D point cloud data. Next, to build datasets for training, validation, and testing of the selected algorithms (RandLA-Net, KPConv rigid, KPConv deform, SCF-Net), labeling was conducted on the 3D digital map of the earthwork site with the 3D-ConHE dataset installed, resulting in the creation of a large and extensive semantic segmentation dataset consisting of 14 3D digital map forms of 3D point cloud data. The constructed 14 semantic segmentation datasets were then applied to the selected algorithms (RandLA-Net, KPConv rigid, KPConv deform, SCF-Net) to build a semantic segmentation training model for construction heavy equipment, and tests were conducted on the constructed model. The results of the construction heavy equipment semantic segmentation training model tested were quantified using performance evaluation metrics such as OA, IoU, and mIoU, and a performance evaluation was conducted to compare the performance of the four semantic segmentation models trained in this study.

According to the performance evaluation results of this study, RandLA-Net showed the highest mIoU at 79.8% among the total four models, as well as the highest OA at 84.4%. For each class mIoU, RandLA-Net showed the highest at 80.3% for Class 1 (Ground), while SCF-Net showed the highest at 86.4% for Class 2 (Non-ground). Lastly, SCF-Net showed the highest at 89.5% for Class 3 (Heavy Construction Equipment). These results indicate that RandLA-Net and SCF-Net algorithms perform well when applying 3D digital maps of earthwork sites composed of large-scale and extensive 3D point cloud data. The results of this study experimentally confirm the applicability of semantic segmentation techniques to 3D digital maps composed of large-scale and extensive 3D point cloud data, which have been known to be difficult to handle and require significant time and effort. This study's results contribute academically by being the first research on large-scale 3D semantic segmentation in the construction field using 3D digital maps of earthwork sites, thus facilitating subsequent research on various semantic segmentation applications. Moreover, this study proposed ways to enhance the utilization of 3D point cloud data generated at construction sites and improve the efficiency of AI research, serving as a foundational study for the increasing research on semantic segmentation of construction heavy equipment using large-scale 3D digital maps of earthwork sites. However, compared to 2D image-based object recognition research, the lower accuracy and applicability of 3D object recognition remain limitations of this study, requiring continuous research. Nevertheless, this study is expected to serve as a foundational study for technologies such as construction robot and UGV location tracking and safety assurance, leveraging the accurate depth and 3D geometric information characteristics of 3D point cloud data. The results of this study are expected to be utilized in various areas within the construction industry, such as terrain change detection, earthwork volume calculation, and terrain interpolation based on object recognition of 3D digital maps.

Author Contributions: Writing—original draft, S.P.; Writing—review & editing, S.K. All authors have read and agreed to the published version of the manuscript.

Funding: This research received no external funding.

Data Availability Statement: The original contributions presented in the study are included in the article, further inquiries can be directed to the corresponding authors.

Acknowledgments: This research was conducted with the support of the "National R&D Project for Smart Construction Technology (No. RS-2020-KA158708)" funded by the Korea Agency for Infrastructure Technology Advancement under the Ministry of Land, Infrastructure and Transport, and managed by the Korea Expressway Corporation.

Conflicts of Interest: The authors declare no conflict of interest.

References

1. Barbosa, F.; Mischke, J.; Parsons, M. Improving Construction Productivity. 2017. Available online: https://www.mckinsey.com/capabilities/operations/our-insights/improving-construction-productivity (accessed on 25 October 2023).
2. Durdyev, S.; Ismail, S. Offsite Manufacturing in the Construction Industry for Productivity Improvement. *Eng. Manag. J.* **2019**, *31*, 35–46. [CrossRef]
3. Jang, W.-S.; Skibniewski, M.J. Cost-Benefit Analysis of Embedded Sensor System for Construction Materials Tracking. *J. Constr. Eng. Manag.* **2009**, *135*, 378–386. [CrossRef]
4. Cai, S.; Ma, Z.; Skibniewski, M.J.; Bao, S. Construction Automation and Robotics for High-Rise Buildings over the Past Decades: A Comprehensive Review. *Adv. Eng. Inform.* **2019**, *42*, 100989. [CrossRef]
5. Hatami, M.; Flood, I.; Franz, B.; Zhang, X. State-of-the-Art Review on the Applicability of AI Methods to Automated Construction. In Proceedings of the Computing in Civil Engineering 2019: Data, Sensing, and Analytics, Atlanta, GA, USA, 17–19 June 2019; pp. 105–113.
6. Bamfo-Agyei, E.; Thwala, D.W.; Aigbavboa, C. Performance Improvement of Construction Workers to Achieve Better Productivity for Labour-Intensive Works. *Buildings* **2022**, *12*, 1593. [CrossRef]
7. Park, S.; Kim, S.; Seo, H. Study on Representative Parameters of Reverse Engineering for Maintenance of Ballasted Tracks. *Appl. Sci.* **2022**, *12*, 5973. [CrossRef]
8. Park, S.; Kim, S. Analysis of Overlap Ratio for Registration Accuracy Improvement of 3D Point Cloud Data at Construction Sites. *J. KIBIM* **2021**, *11*, 1–9.
9. Park, S.; Kim, S. Performance Evaluation of Denoising Algorithms for the 3D Construction Digital Map. *J. KIBIM* **2020**, *10*, 32–39.
10. Kim, Y.; Park, S.; Choi, Y.; Kim, S. Performance Verification of Integrated Module for Automatic Analysis of Digital Maps in Earthwork Sites. *J. Constr. Autom. Robot.* **2023**, *2*, 1–6. [CrossRef]
11. Kim, Y.-G.; Park, S.-Y.; Kim, S. Development of Framework for Digital Map Time Series Analysis of Earthwork Sites. *J. KIBIM* **2023**, *13*, 22–32. [CrossRef]
12. Choi, Y.; Park, S.; Kim, S. GCP-Based Automated Fine Alignment Method for Improving the Accuracy of Coordinate Information on UAV Point Cloud Data. *Sensors* **2022**, *22*, 8735. [CrossRef]
13. Choi, Y.; Park, S.; Kim, S. Development of Point Cloud Data-Denoising Technology for Earthwork Sites Using Encoder-Decoder Network. *KSCE J. Civ. Eng.* **2022**, *26*, 4380–4389. [CrossRef]
14. Li, X.; Yi, W.; Chi, H.L.; Wang, X.; Chan, A.P.C. A Critical Review of Virtual and Augmented Reality (VR/AR) Applications in Construction Safety. *Autom. Constr.* **2018**, *86*, 150–162. [CrossRef]
15. Mostafa, K.; Hegazy, T. Review of Image-Based Analysis and Applications in Construction. *Autom. Constr.* **2021**, *122*, 103516. [CrossRef]
16. Lasky, T.A.; Ravani, B. Sensor-Based Path Planning and Motion Control for a Robotic System for Roadway Crack Sealing. *IEEE Trans. Control Syst. Technol.* **2000**, *8*, 609–622. [CrossRef]
17. Li, H.; Lu, M.; Hsu, S.C.; Gray, M.; Huang, T. Proactive Behavior-Based Safety Management for Construction Safety Improvement. *Saf. Sci.* **2015**, *75*, 107–117. [CrossRef]
18. Jeong, I.; Kim, J.; Chi, S.; Roh, M.; Biggs, H. Solitary Work Detection of Heavy Equipment Using Computer Vision. *KSCE J. Civ. Environ. Eng. Res.* **2021**, *41*, 441–447.
19. Hsieh, Y.-A.; Tsai, Y.J. Machine Learning for Crack Detection: Review and Model Performance Comparison. *J. Comput. Civ. Eng.* **2020**, *34*, 04020038. [CrossRef]
20. Cha, Y.J.; Choi, W.; Büyüköztürk, O. Deep Learning-Based Crack Damage Detection Using Convolutional Neural Networks. *Comput. Civ. Infrastruct. Eng.* **2017**, *32*, 361–378. [CrossRef]
21. Ekanayake, B.; Wong, J.K.W.; Fini, A.A.F.; Smith, P. Computer Vision-Based Interior Construction Progress Monitoring: A Literature Review and Future Research Directions. *Autom. Constr.* **2021**, *127*, 103705. [CrossRef]
22. Dang, L.M.; Wang, H.; Li, Y.; Park, Y.; Oh, C.; Nguyen, T.N.; Moon, H. Automatic Tunnel Lining Crack Evaluation and Measurement Using Deep Learning. *Tunn. Undergr. Space Technol.* **2022**, *124*, 104472. [CrossRef]
23. Oh, K.; Yoo, M.; Jin, N.; Ko, J.; Seo, J.; Joo, H.; Ko, M. A Review of Deep Learning Applications for Railway Safety. *Appl. Sci.* **2022**, *12*, 572. [CrossRef]
24. Kim, H.; Kim, C. Deep-Learning-Based Classification of Point Clouds for Bridge Inspection. *Remote Sens.* **2020**, *12*, 3757. [CrossRef]
25. Fei-Fei, L.; Deng, J.; Li, K. ImageNet: Constructing a Large-Scale Image Database. *J. Vis.* **2010**, *9*, 1037. [CrossRef]
26. Xiao, B.; Kang, S.-C. Development of an Image Data Set of Construction Machines for Deep Learning Object Detection. *J. Comput. Civ. Eng.* **2021**, *35*, 05020005. [CrossRef]
27. Guo, Y.; Wang, H.; Hu, Q.; Liu, H.; Liu, L.; Bennamoun, M. Deep Learning for 3D Point Clouds: A Survey. *IEEE Trans. Pattern Anal. Mach. Intell.* **2021**, *43*, 4338–4364. [CrossRef]
28. Qi, C.R.; Yi, L.; Su, H.; Guibas, L.J. PointNet. In Proceedings of the 2016 Fourth International Conference on 3D Vision (3DV 2016), Stanford, CA, USA, 25–28 October 2016; pp. 601–610.

29. Hu, Q.; Yang, B.; Xie, L.; Rosa, S.; Guo, Y.; Wang, Z.; Trigoni, N.; Markham, A. Randla-Net: Efficient Semantic Segmentation of Large-Scale Point Clouds. In Proceedings of the 2020 IEEE/CVF Conference on Computer Vision and Pattern Recognition, Seattle, WA, USA, 13–19 June 2020; pp. 11105–11114. [CrossRef]
30. Kim, H.; Kim, H.; Hong, Y.W.; Byun, H. Detecting Construction Equipment Using a Region-Based Fully Convolutional Network and Transfer Learning. *J. Comput. Civ. Eng.* **2018**, *32*, 04017082. [CrossRef]
31. Chen, J.; Fang, Y.; Cho, Y.K.; Kim, C. Principal Axes Descriptor for Automated Construction-Equipment Classification from Point Clouds. *J. Comput. Civ. Eng.* **2017**, *31*, 04016058. [CrossRef]
32. Bello, S.A.; Yu, S.; Wang, C.; Adam, J.M.; Li, J. Review: Deep Learning on 3D Point Clouds. *Remote Sens.* **2020**, *12*, 1729. [CrossRef]
33. Tan, W.; Qin, N.; Ma, L.; Li, Y.; Du, J.; Cai, G.; Yang, K.; Li, J. Toronto-3D: A Large-Scale Mobile LiDAR Dataset for Semantic Segmentation of Urban Roadways2211. In Proceedings of the 2020 IEEE/CVF Conference on Computer Vision and Pattern Recognition Workshops, Seattle, WA, USA, 14–19 June 2020; pp. 797–806. [CrossRef]
34. Thomas, H.; Qi, C.R.; Deschaud, J.E.; Marcotegui, B.; Goulette, F.; Guibas, L. KPConv: Flexible and Deformable Convolution for Point Clouds. In Proceedings of the 2019 IEEE/CVF International Conference on Computer Vision, Seoul, Republic of Korea, 27 October–2 November 2019; pp. 6410–6419. [CrossRef]
35. Hackel, T.; Savinov, N.; Ladicky, L.; Wegner, J.D.; Schindler, K.; Pollefeys, M. Semantic3D.net: A new Large-scale Point Cloud Classification Benchmark. *arXiv* **2014**, arXiv:1704.03847. [CrossRef]
36. Roynard, X.; Deschaud, J.E.; Goulette, F. Paris-Lille-3D: A Large and High-Quality Ground-Truth Urban Point Cloud Dataset for Automatic Segmentation and Classification. *Int. J. Rob. Res.* **2018**, *37*, 545–557. [CrossRef]
37. Rusu, R.B.; Cousins, S. 3D Is Here: Point Cloud Library (PCL). In Proceedings of the 2011 IEEE International Conference on Robotics and Automation, Shanghai, China, 9–13 May 2011; pp. 1–4. [CrossRef]
38. Zhou, Q.-Y.; Park, J.; Koltun, V. Open3D: A Modern Library for 3D Data Processing. *arXiv*, 2018; arXiv:1801.09847.
39. Butler, H.; Chambers, B.; Hartzell, P.; Glennie, C. PDAL: An Open Source Library for the Processing and Analysis of Point Clouds. *Comput. Geosci.* **2021**, *148*, 104680. [CrossRef]
40. Park, S.; Kim, S. 3D Point Cloud Dataset of Heavy Construction Equipment. *Appl. Sci.* **2024**, *14*, 3599. [CrossRef]
41. Baduge, S.K.; Thilakarathna, S.; Perera, J.S.; Arashpour, M.; Sharafi, P.; Teodosio, B.; Shringi, A.; Mendis, P. Artificial Intelligence and Smart Vision for Building and Construction 4.0: Machine and Deep Learning Methods and Applications. *Autom. Constr.* **2022**, *141*, 104440. [CrossRef]
42. Lee, Y.I.; Kim, B.; Cho, S. Image-Based Spalling Detection of Concrete Structures Using Deep Learning. *J. Korea Concr. Inst.* **2018**, *30*, 91–99. [CrossRef]
43. Lee, T.; Kim, S.; Hwang, C.-H.; Jung, H. Worker Collision Safety Management System Using Object Detection. *J. Korea Inst. Inf. Commun. Eng.* **2022**, *26*, 1259–1265.
44. Hao, N. 3D Object Detection from Point Cloud Based on Deep Learning. *Wirel. Commun. Mob. Comput.* **2022**, *2022*, 6228797. [CrossRef]
45. Arabi, S.; Haghighat, A.; Sharma, A. A Deep Learning Based Solution for Construction Equipment Detection: From Development to Deployment. *arXiv* **2019**, arXiv:1904.09021.
46. Colleges, G.T.U.A.; Academy, O.; Academy, O.; Academy, O.; Science, A.C.; Technology, I.; Science, A.C. Microsoft COCO 2014. In Proceedings of the ECCV, Zurich, Switzerland, 5–12 September 2014; pp. 740–755.
47. Xiong, X.; Adan, A.; Akinci, B.; Huber, D. Automatic Creation of Semantically Rich 3D Building Models from Laser Scanner Data. *Autom. Constr.* **2013**, *31*, 325–337. [CrossRef]
48. Kim, C.; Kim, C.; Son, H. Automated Construction Progress Measurement Using a 4D Building Information Model and 3D Data. *Autom. Constr.* **2013**, *31*, 75–82. [CrossRef]
49. Lee, J.S.; Park, J.; Ryu, Y.M. Semantic Segmentation of Bridge Components Based on Hierarchical Point Cloud Model. *Autom. Constr.* **2021**, *130*, 103847. [CrossRef]
50. Ryu, Y.-M.; Kim, B.-K.; Park, J. Effect of Learning Data on the Semantic Segmentation of Railroad Tunnel Using Deep Learning. *J. Korean Geotech.* **2021**, *37*, 107–118.
51. Kim, J.; Chung, D.; Kim, Y.; Kim, H. Deep Learning-Based 3D Reconstruction of Scaffolds Using a Robot Dog. *Autom. Constr.* **2022**, *134*, 104092. [CrossRef]
52. Nath, N.D.; Behzadan, A.H. Deep Convolutional Networks for Construction Object Detection Under Different Visual Conditions. *Front. Built Environ.* **2020**, *6*, 97. [CrossRef]
53. Chen, J.; Fang, Y.; Cho, Y.K. Performance Evaluation of 3D Descriptors for Object Recognition in Construction Applications. *Autom. Constr.* **2018**, *86*, 44–52. [CrossRef]
54. Lee, D.-K.; Ji, S.-H.; Park, B.-Y. PointNet and RandLA-Net Algorithms for Object Detection Using 3D Point Clouds. *J. Soc. Nav. Archit. Korea* **2022**, *59*, 330–337. [CrossRef]
55. Fan, S.; Dong, Q.; Zhu, F.; Lv, Y.; Ye, P.; Wang, F.Y. SCF-Net: Learning Spatial Contextual Features for Large-Scale Point Cloud Segmentation. In Proceedings of the 2021 IEEE/CVF Conference on Computer Vision and Pattern Recognition, Nashville, TN, USA, 20–25 June 2021; pp. 14499–14508. [CrossRef]
56. Behley, J.; Garbade, M.; Milioto, A.; Quenzel, J.; Behnke, S.; Stachniss, C.; Gall, J. SemanticKITTI: A Dataset for Semantic Scene Understanding of LiDAR Sequences. In Proceedings of the 2019 IEEE/CVF International Conference on Computer Vision, Seoul, Republic of Korea, 27 October–2 November 2019; pp. 9296–9306. [CrossRef]

57. Thabet, A.; Alwassel, H.; Ghanem, B. Self-Supervised Learning of Local Features in 3D Point Clouds. In Proceedings of the 2020 IEEE/CVF Conference on Computer Vision and Pattern Recognition Workshops, Seattle, WA, USA, 14–19 June 2020; pp. 4048–4052. [CrossRef]
58. Zhou, Y.; Tuzel, O. VoxelNet: End-to-End Learning for Point Cloud Based 3D Object Detection. In Proceedings of the 2018 IEEE/CVF Conference on Computer Vision and Pattern Recognition, Salt Lake City, UT, USA, 18–23 June 2018; pp. 4490–4499. [CrossRef]
59. Girardeau-Montaut, D. CloudCompare. 2019. Available online: https://www.danielgm.net/cc/ (accessed on 10 November 2023).
60. Hitachi Automotive and Industry Laboratory Semantic-Segmentation-Editor. Available online: https://github.com/Hitachi-Automotive-And-Industry-Lab/semantic-segmentation-editor (accessed on 10 November 2023).
61. Hansen, L.H.; Jensen, S.B.; Philipsen, M.P.; Møgelmose, A.; Bodum, L.; Moeslund, T.B. OpenTrench3D: A Photogrammetric 3D Point Cloud Dataset for Semantic Segmentation of Underground Utilities. In Proceedings of the IEEE/CVF Conference on Computer Vision and Pattern Recognition (CVPR) Workshops 2024, Seattle, WA, USA, 17–21 June 2024; pp. 7646–7655.

buildings

MDPI

Article

Agile Construction Digital Twin Engineering

Philipp Zech [1,*], Alexandra Jäger [1], Larissa Schneiderbauer [2], Hans Exenberger [2], Georg Fröch [2] and Matthias Flora [2]

1 Department of Computer Science, University of Innsbruck, 6020 Innsbruck, Austria; alexandra.jaeger@uibk.ac.at
2 Unit of Construction Management and Tunnelling (iBT), University of Innsbruck, 6020 Innsbruck, Austria; larissa.schneiderbauer@uibk.ac.at (L.S.); hans.exenberger@uibk.ac.at (H.E.); georg.froech@uibk.ac.at (G.F.); matthias.flora@uibk.ac.at (M.F.)
* Correspondence: philipp.zech@uibk.ac.at

Abstract: Digital twins have attracted a lot of attention recently. However, the current manifestations are merely digital shadows, lacking means for bidirectional data exchange, which makes their use for assisting the construction of buildings much more difficult. We argue that this is due to the lack of a systematic process for developing a digital twin during a building's life cycle. We argue to look for a solution by combining agile engineering with IT change management to establish an agile, change-driven process for engineering digital twins. Such a process, of course, deserves a qualitative assessment of the engineering process and the resulting digital twin. In the future, it should be possible to obtain a digital twin from a BIM-based design process by applying IT change management in an agile manner. This should happen under maximum automation and life cycle orientation. Our proposal is motivated by several years of interdisciplinary collaboration between civil engineering and computer science and evaluated using the Technology Acceptance Model. While the TAM is not specifically designed for digital twin methodologies, its application here aims to assess perceived usefulness and ease of use of DT methodologies from the user's perspective, without addressing scalability concerns. This aims to provide actionable insights to guide the refinement of the process model, aligning it with user requirements and achieving its intended outcomes. Our evaluation confirms the proposed process's perceived usefulness and ease of use, with robust correlations indicating strong acceptance potential among stakeholders. These results highlight the feasibility of the proposed approach and its alignment with expectations in real-world applications.

Keywords: agile engineering; IT change management; digital twin engineering; building information modeling

1. Introduction

Despite already having been conceived two decades ago, digital twins (DTs; see Section 2.3), e.g., virtual replicas of cyber–physical systems (CPS; see Section 2.2), only started attracting widespread interest in recent years [1]. Current manifestations of DTs in the architecture, engineering, construction, and operator (AECO) domain mostly fall into the category of digital shadows lacking bidirectional connections with a building for remote control (see Figure 1) and describe ad hoc solutions, such as the early but ongoing integration of Building Information Modeling (BIM; see Section 2.2) and the Internet-of-Things (IoT) [2,3]. They aim to implement a specific, stakeholder-motivated use case rather than provide a holistic, digital replica of a physical asset customizable to stakeholders' use cases and available as early as the design phase of a building [1]. These ad hoc approaches exist on account of lacking a systematic process that allows for careful engineering of DTs, starting as early as the design phase. We argue, however, that the issue lies rather in the *engineering* aspects of such a process, as crafting a DT is mainly about *information integration and filtering relevant information*. As for DTs, these sources of information are as follows:

- **Static asset models** that subsume the plethora of system and engineering models (e.g., project information models), as well as related models describing a CPS (e.g., asset information models).
- **Dynamic asset models** comprise, among others, simulation models for behavior modeling and optimization, and machine learning models for informed decision-making.
- **Sensor, machine, and process** data from the actual CPS and its environment.

Following this line of thought, we claim that the successful engineering of a DT capitalizes on an engineering process's capacity to *integrate information from diverse and heterogeneous sources*. Therefore, pure forward (information) engineering fails in the long run because it is not designed to integrate feedback from the CPS, i.e., reflecting the CPS asset *as is instead of as planned or designed*, respectively. Beyond that, no CPS exists in the early phases. On the contrary, IT change management and agile engineering allow for the definition of a process scaffold for continuous, stakeholder-driven information integration, eventually yielding a DT.

IT change management (see Section 2.5) is a well-established IT service management discipline. The objective of change management is to ensure that standardized methods and procedures are used for efficient and prompt handling of all changes to control the IT infrastructure to minimize the number and impact of any related incidents upon service. Changes in the IT infrastructure may arise (i) reactively, in response to problems or externally imposed requirements, e.g., legislative changes, (ii) proactively, seeking improved efficiency and effectiveness, (iii) enabling or reflecting business initiatives, or (iv) from stakeholders. IT change management heavily relies on IT infrastructure modeling in combination with information integration from different physical sources in the physical IT infrastructure [4,5]. We thus conjecture that the application of IT change management for generating a DT is imperative to tackle the fundamental challenge of information integration.

Agile engineering (see Section 2.5) over the last two decades has emerged as an efficient process model in software engineering [6,7]. Specifically, agile engineering capitalizes on delivering a software system in small increments, thereby being completely driven by stakeholder and user requirements [6]. In addition, agile engineering employs rigid quality assurance to guarantee the deliverance of what is eventually expected by stakeholders and customers [6]. Considering the waterfall-like, rigid process structures that are currently employed in AECO [8,9], we argue that agile is a worthwhile alternative, as it allows for continuous reevaluation and revision of stakeholder and user requirements, thereby loosening AECO's rigid process structures [10].

In this article, we propose a novel engineering process for DTs in AECO motivated by well-established practices and techniques, as employed in agile engineering and IT change management, embedded in conventional design, construction, and operating BIM processes. This readily yields a process for iteratively building a DT by continuously integrating data sources from the CPS and its environment to keep it in synchronization with the virtual replica. Crucially, doing so yields two immediate benefits, viz. the change-anticipative nature of agile engineering provides the necessary leeway to **address** the unexpected, whereas change management provides the necessary procedure to **handle** the unexpected. In the early development phases, e.g., design and planning, many data sources may not be available, yet these can be mocked and replaced upon integrating the actual physical data source. Doing so allows the application of IT change management during the initial development phases and consequently tracks every change distinctively.

Eventually, the progress of the resulting process is driven by stakeholder requirements and accompanying use cases, therefore providing the necessary level of genericity to realize different stakeholders' use cases. Intriguingly, the resulting process naturally aligns with BIM, as BIM, by design, has a change-driven nature [11]. Finally, we discuss how to achieve a qualitative assessment of our proposed process by proposing a set of agile-inspired metrics [12]. This result is seminal as, so far, the AECO domain lacks quality metrics for processes. Observe that Succar's five BIM metrics are not applicable, as they are about assessing the performance of BIM and thus do not apply to the process level [13]. Our proposal is evaluated in an expert survey using a demonstrator and the Technology Acceptance Model (TAM) [14].

According to a recent study by Yilmaz et al., the construction industry is currently being substantially accelerated by the adoption of digital solutions [15]. Yet, many companies struggle to successfully conduct this digital transformation due to budget constraints and the complexity of the existing commercial, digital solutions [15]. Specifically, Yilmaz et al. mention unified change management as one of the top priorities in digitalizing the construction industry. Our proposal aims at delivering an approach to achieve unified change management by relying on existing, time-tested approaches.

Our contribution is structured as Design Science Research (DSR) [16] and delivers an artifact, e.g., our proposed process, to facilitate building DTs in AECO. Development of our artifact is initiated with the phase of requirements elicitation (see Section 4.1) and concludes with a single-case mechanism experiment (see Section 6.1). Our artifact is deployed as a treatment to the following design problem, expressed using the DSR template [17]:

Improve digital twin construction in AECO (context)
by developing an agile, change-driven process (artifact)
to deliver a context- and situation-aware method (requirements)
that delivers the construction digital twin (goal).

The remainder of our contribution is structured as follows. Section 2 introduces definitions of used relevant concepts, e.g., of CPSs, BIM, DTs, agile engineering, and IT change management. Following that, Section 3 presents the problem context on which our work is built. Next, Section 4 presents the main contribution of our article by proposing our novel, agile, change-driven process for the simplification of the processes for establishing a DT for engineers and architects. Section 5 then investigates the natural congruence of our proposed process with BIM. Section 6 evaluates our proposal using the TAM, positions our work with respect to related work, and discusses any threats to validity. We conclude in Section 7 with the current limitations of our work and an outlook.

2. Background and Definitions

Before discussing our manuscript's main ideas and contributions, relevant concepts must be defined. This section thus introduces definitions of CPSs, BIM, DTs, agile engineering, and IT change management to foster any subsequent discussions.

2.1. Cyber–Physical Systems

Cyber–physical systems (CPS) are a new breed of systems that integrate physical and computational capabilities and allow for a wide range of novel human–computer interactions [18]. The IoT, cloud computing, big data, and machine learning were some of the technological advancements that came together to form the concept of a CPS. These technologies are used by CPSs to build intelligent systems that can sense, process, and react to current events in real time [18]. CPSs are becoming more significant today as part of the ongoing digitalization of the manufacturing and construction industries, from smart homes and buildings to industrial automation and autonomous vehicles. They have the power to change how we work and live by enabling more effective, resilient, and sustainable systems [19]. As part of their interdisciplinary nature, CPSs pose unique challenges in terms of design, implementation, and operation, cf., modern, smart buildings [20]. These challenges include the need for real-time processing, reliability, and security. A CPS must be able to operate in dynamic environments and handle unexpected events without compromising safety or performance [21]. Successfully engineering a CPS thus requires specialized expertise in multiple domains, such as mechanical or construction engineering, electrical engineering, computer science, or control engineering.

2.2. Building Information Modeling

Building Information Modeling is a term that represents the digital transformation in the AECO sector and has gathered several definitions and interpretations in recent years [22–24]. In the internationally recognized standard ISO 19650-1 [25], Building Information Modeling is defined as the "*use of a shared digital representation of a built asset to facilitate design, construction and operation processes to form a reliable basis for decisions*". In other words, BIM refers to a fully integrated, collaborative process of modelling a digital building model. An important aspect regarding the definition of BIM is that it is not only about the purely geometric modeling of an asset, but that semantic information, such as material properties, specific characteristics for rooms and spaces, or information concerning cost and time, is of major importance for the description of a digital building model and thus constitutes Building Information Modeling.

Especially in the design phase, there are considerable differences to conventional processes. The integral and transparent collaboration of the disciplines is based on the generation of specialist models, which are referenced to each other so that a virtual replica of the asset is created even before the execution phase begins. The early detailing of building models enables the prevention of cost and schedule delays due to inadequate design quality.

In the field of building engineering or infrastructure engineering, this method offers the possibility of optimizing the life cycle performance of buildings in the early phases by means of various types of models and analyses.

2.3. Digital Twins

DTs, that is, virtual replicas of a CPS, e.g., an embedded system, a smart building, or a digital shopfloor, according to Grieves and Vickers [26] generally comprise three fundamental building blocks, viz. the following:

- The *virtual instance*, i.e., the assemblage of system, test, product, and simulation models, which together replicate the physical asset;
- The *product instance*, i.e., the built CPS;
- *Interchanged data and connections*, i.e., the digital thread, allowing for bidirectional communication between the virtual and product instance.

The assemblage of models to establish the virtual instance thereby epitomizes the central source of complexity in engineering a DT. Not only are these models heterogeneous in describing different aspects and stakeholder views, but more importantly, these models need to evolve alongside the physical asset to reflect it as is. As such, DTs typically manifest in three variants [27], as shown in Figure 1:

- **Digital model**: information exchange between the virtual and product instance is purely manual.
- **Digital shadow**: information exchange between the product and the virtual instance is automated.
- **Digital twin**: both directions of information exchange are automated.

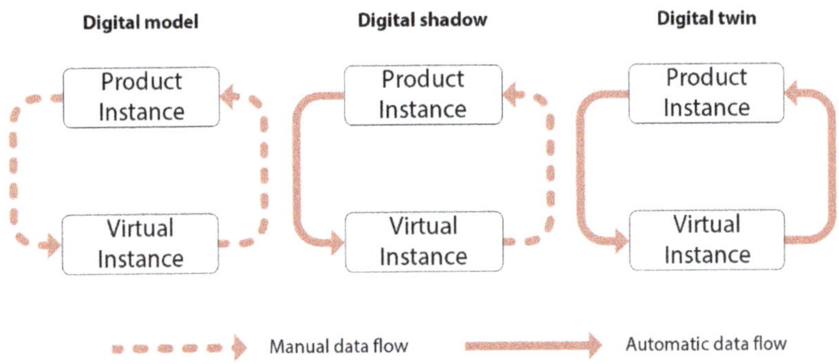

Figure 1. Manifestations of DTs [27].

Despite their concept having already been around for multiple decades [26], recent advances in the IoT, data analytics, and machine learning have ultimately made it possible to create more accurate and sophisticated models for being used in DTs. Regarding their resulting use to monitor, analyze, and optimize the performance of physical assets, predict failures, and simulate scenarios in a risk-free environment, DTs have the potential to revolutionize the way companies design, build, and operate physical assets and systems [28,29]. DTs are currently used across a wide range of industries, including manufacturing, energy, aerospace, healthcare, and more [30].

To illustrate this definition with an example from the construction sector, a digital model, as the first variant, might describe a building's HVAC system using only static data, such as its design specifications. A digital shadow could then build on this by displaying real-time sensor data, such as current temperatures and energy consumption, i.e., for monitoring purposes. In contrast, a digital twin would take this a step further by analyzing the real-time data alongside additional factors like weather forecasts, occupancy schedules, or energy demand. By integrating these inputs, the digital twin could automatically adjust HVAC settings to optimize energy efficiency, reduce costs, and maintain occupant comfort.

Boje et al. [31] extended the concept of DTs to the notion of a construction digital twin (CDT), which our work also addresses. The CDT is a virtual replica of a physical construction project that uses real-time data from sensors, construction management software, and other sources to simulate the behavior and performance of the project throughout its life cycle. Unlike manufacturing DTs, the CDT must account for the larger scale and intrinsically different dynamics of construction projects [31].

2.4. *Agile Engineering*

Since the early 2000s, the software engineering community has seen a tremendous change towards agile engineering to overcome issues often associated with plan-based development models by emphasizing continuous adaptation and customer collaboration [32,33]. In its essence, agile engineering postulates the introduction of short cycles, where each cycle focuses on a dedicated objective. After each cycle, the current state/progress of a project is evaluated, replanned if necessary, and execution continues with the next objective in line. At its core, agile describes a lightweight two-staged process that is repeated until all work is completed (see Figure 2). The first phase, i.e., requirements engineering, focuses on establishing the necessary requirements for the objective in the cycle. The second phase addresses the design and implementation of the objective, marking the end of the cycle. The SCRUM methodology [34] is one of the most established agile software engineering approaches. Agile engineering naturally anticipates change and goes hand in hand with metrics for assessing project progress and product quality after every cycle [12]. As for its benefits in faster time-to-market, higher quality software, and increased customer satisfaction, agile engineering has gained widespread acceptance nowadays, and has been systematically evaluated in several studies [35]. To fully deploy its benefits, agile engineering, however, demands constant communication and collaboration among all involved project stakeholders.

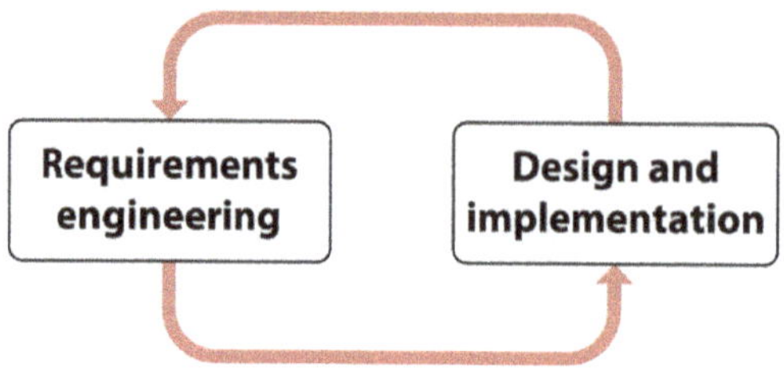

Figure 2. Agile engineering.

2.5. IT Change Management

IT change management describes a systematic procedure to manage changes to the IT infrastructures of an organization [36]. The systematic and structured management of such changes greatly reduces risk exposure as well as the severity of the impact and, consequently, operational disruptions. Most importantly, however, IT change management aims at facilitating the prolific implementation of a change at the first attempt. To successfully conduct such changes, change management heavily relies on well-defined process models, which define the necessary steps from recording the change to its evaluation, authorization, prioritization, planning, testing, implementation, documentation, and review [36]. The Information Technology Infrastructure Library (ITIL) defines an organizational framework and thus completely neglects the underlying technical infrastructure for implementing the framework. Nevertheless, a database-backed system for tracking changes in a dedicated format is beneficial.

Such process models may subsequently be implemented in change management tools. However, while software support may greatly ease the management of changes, at its heart, change management remains a process and is independent from any software solution. No specific input format, output format, or storage requirements need to be observed.

According to [36], a process for a typical change follows the model shown in Figure 3. Roughly speaking, to initialize a change, a request for change (RFC) containing relevant information regarding, e.g., initiator, trigger, and description is created and subsequently reviewed for feasibility. Such an RFC usually is motivated by either a necessary change or the addition of a feature, which eventually also boils down to a change that must be applied. If not rejected, the proposed change is assessed and evaluated, i.e., relevant resources are identified, and the impact of the change is elicited. After authorizing the change, given the RFC's evaluation and assessment, the change is implemented and finally reviewed. That is, stakeholder satisfaction and resource consumption are evaluated regarding the achievement of the change's objective. In synopsis, change management defines a framework, based on best practices, that aims at (i) minimizing risk and costs, (ii) optimizing efficiency and consistency, (iii) enhancing communication, (iv) alignment with operational strategies, and (v) reducing costs.

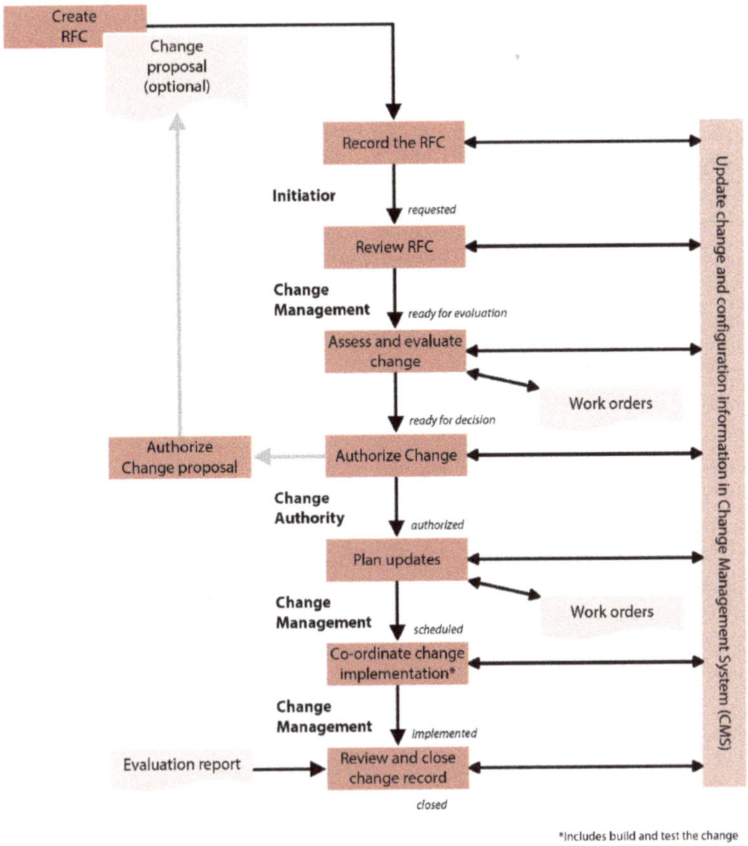

Figure 3. Process model for a typical change according to [36].

3. Problem Context

Typically, CDT requirements are defined based on dedicated use cases that emerge throughout the life cycle of a construction project. In addition, great care must be taken in defining the CDT's general functional requirements due to the extremely high friction of projects in the AECO industry. Even within a single project, the definition must account for the varying expectations of project stakeholders, technologies, and periods throughout the entire project life cycle. The CDT requirements must be consistently adapted as a project progresses, drawing parallels to agile processes [32].

In the following, we discuss two interdisciplinary research projects, viz. *BIM2BEM-Flow* and *TIM*, which establish the problem context of our work. Specifically, these projects target the establishment of DTs in the construction domain for the purpose of energy efficiency planning (BIM2BEM-Flow) and large-scale underground infrastructure management (TIM) using DTs.

Both BIM2BEM-Flow and TIM serve as foundational examples of how the unique challenges and opportunities in the construction domain can inform the development of a systematic and adaptive approach to CDT engineering. BIM2BEM-Flow highlights the critical role of data integration and life cycle orientation in supporting continuous energy efficiency improvements, a central objective that aligns closely with our proposed agile and change-driven methodology for CDT development. Similarly, TIM provides insights into the structured yet fragmented nature of large-scale infrastructure projects, where long implementation periods and complex stakeholder ecosystems demand a robust yet flexible process for CDT development. These projects not only highlight specific use cases but also demonstrate the broader challenges of aligning CDT development with life cycle dynamics, stakeholder needs, and technological evolution. By addressing these challenges, our research aims to provide a generalized, adaptable framework for engineering CDTs that builds upon the lessons learned from these interdisciplinary initiatives.

3.1. Use Cases in BIM2BEM-Flow

BIM2BEM-Flow is an interdisciplinary framework developed to bring BIM data into building energy modeling (BEM) environments, enabling continuous energy efficiency planning across all stages of a building's life cycle. BIM2BEM-Flow moves beyond BIM's traditional focus on design and coordination, embedding energy efficiency and sustainability as central goals in both the design and operational phases of a building. The framework is specifically tailored for complex workflows that require seamless data exchange between digital building models (BIM) and building physics tools for energy simulation, making it possible to incorporate energy insights dynamically as the project progresses.

The BIM2BEM-Flow framework supports a wide range of use cases, such as energy flow simulation, which allows project teams to evaluate energy demands and usage patterns in detail. It incorporates both natural and artificial lighting simulations, supporting informed lighting decisions to optimize both energy efficiency and occupant comfort. The system also enables robust building operation and maintenance workflows, leveraging data-rich BIM models to provide maintenance insights, extend asset life, and ensure energy systems perform as designed throughout a building's operational phase. BIM2BEM-Flow thus plays a critical role in integrating real-time performance data with energy models, bridging BIM's design-focused phase with ongoing energy performance monitoring.

In addition to monitoring, BIM2BEM-Flow supports continuous system optimization. By enabling real-time data integration for systems such as HVAC and lighting, it allows stakeholders to track energy usage, making adjustments as needed to meet or exceed predefined energy benchmarks. Additionally, the framework's data-driven approach supports proactive energy management, using data from various systems to identify optimization opportunities and ensure energy consumption remains aligned with project goals.

BIM2BEM-Flow is built to support interoperability through industry standards such as IFC and uses advanced meta-modeling techniques to automate data transformation processes, ensuring seamless collaboration between BIM and BEM tools. This interoperability empowers stakeholders across architecture, engineering, and facilities management to maintain energy efficiency without needing specialized knowledge of each tool's data formats. By defining data transformations and rules at the parameter level, BIM2BEM-Flow provides an adaptable framework for continuous energy performance improvement, ultimately supporting industry needs for sustainable, data-driven building operations.

3.2. Use Cases in Tunnel Information Modeling

Tunnel Information Modeling (TIM) is the specialized implementation of BIM in the tunneling industry and currently being driven forward intensively by industry and research. During this initial phase of BIM implementation, the focus of the industry strongly lies upon the design and construction phase, partly due to the long project implementation periods for big infrastructure projects like tunnels. As an example, Austrian infrastructure developers decided to establish general use cases for BIM in tunneling and came up with a list of 18 general BIM use cases [37]. These range from design or coordination, all the way to construction phase simulation or model-based billing. The operational phase is not yet included in these considerations, and therefore the last use case is the creation of an as-built model.

From the authors' experience from participating in various research and pilot projects for TIM, it can be said that the tunneling industry in general is predestined to work with BIM and a CDT. The very structured approach due to the usually huge project scope can very easily be aligned with the general approaches for BIM. The main limiting factors are the rather negative attitude towards digitalization of current management personnel, which can only be overcome by a generational change. Another limiting factor is the desire to work with fully developed structures, mature templates, and defined normative guidelines from the outset, as there can be no such practical developments without concrete project work.

As established earlier, BIM is only the preliminary stage for or a part of the digital twin. Many of the defined BIM use cases can be transferred to CDT use cases. Due to the high potential of CDT usage in the operational phase of a tunnel, these need to be added in the future. Siemens, for example, has created its own very specific DT for tunnels and defines, among other things, virtual initiation or the protection from threats as reasonable use cases [38].

3.3. Consolidated Use Cases

The discussions in Sections 3.1 and 3.2 outline the diverse use cases for which the CDT will ultimately be employed during its and the twin building's life cycle. Clearly, this is not an exhaustive list, and, depending on the nature of a construction project, new use cases may emerge over time. In our discussion, however, the two projects discussed in the preceding sections provide the empirical basis from which we derive our use cases and, consequently, the CDT's necessary requirements, as discussed in the following section. Table 1 is a summary of the aforementioned use cases.

Table 1. Consolidated use cases of discussed projects (Sections 3.1 and 3.2).

	Use Case	Empirical Basis
UC1	Asset system control	TIM
UC2	Energy flow and usage simulation	BIM2BEM-Flow, TIM
UC3	Physical asset life cycle management	TIM
UC4	Artificial and natural building lighting simulation	BIM2BEM-Flow, TIM
UC5	Building operation and maintenance	BIM2BEM-Flow, TIM
UC6	Building system monitoring (e.g., lighting, heating, and cooling)	BIM2BEM-Flow, TIM
UC7	Building operation optimization (e.g., energy consumption)	BIM2BEM-Flow, TIM
UC8	Construction site progress monitoring	TIM
UC9	Safety and hazard monitoring	TIM
UC10	Building visualization and product line engineering	BIM2BEM-Flow, TIM

4. Agile Construction Digital Twin Engineering

Engineering a CDT is a complex endeavor that encompasses the entire building life cycle. Eventually, however, prior to constructing it, it is necessary to infer the necessary requirements. In this work, we will not focus on the technical requirements of the CDT per se, but instead on the requirements for the underlying process as proposed in this work. We will therefore infer the necessary process requirements for our proposal below.

4.1. Requirements for the Construction Digital Twin

The CDT within the life cycle of a project can be divided into three distinct phases. The first phase is the phase of concept and design, during which no CPS exists. In this phase, the CDT is constructed, which aids the entire design process and serves as the foundation for the next phase. This is the construction phase, during which the CDT is utilized for supervising construction and must be adapted to all deviations resulting from differences between the planned and actual construction. The result is a constructed CDT that is identical to the CPS. After construction, the third phase consists of asset monitoring and operation. Few modifications will be made to the CDT's geometrical appearance and static properties, but its dynamic properties will be heavily utilized. In its concluding phase, the CDT serves two primary functions. First, the asset's dynamic properties enable its control via sensors and maintenance procedures. Second, the geometry and static properties serve as data storage for a variety of purposes, such as the history of each constructed element or as the premise for future adaptations.

Unlike a digital model (see Figure 1), which is already utilized in many projects employing the BIM method during the design phase, where it serves as the premise for the construction site, one of the essential requirements for a CDT is the incorporation of real-time data. During the design phase, this can include drafts and early simulations of the building. During the construction and operation phases, real-time data in the form of sensor and machine data become increasingly prevalent [14]. The bidirectional communication between the CDT and CPS unlocks new opportunities for enhancing processes or user convenience. An example would be a separate control for the HVAC system. Through the logical connection of intelligent systems and devices (such as sensors) to the CDT, energy flows are automatically monitored, analyzed, and regulated to achieve a perfectly balanced indoor climate.

With the integration of real-time data into the CDT, an enormous quantity of data are generated, which must be saved and systematically associated with CDT components. Filtering information is useful for comprehending and interpreting the data history in a meaningful manner. The use case, stakeholder, or project phase could be utilized to filter information. Currently, models are frequently reduced to the essential information at the start of a new phase, rather than retaining all information and filtering out the irrelevant information. In other words, the CDT should respond based on who is observing it, when they are observing it, and why they are observing it. Figure 4 summarizes the above discussion by visualizing the three phases of the CDT, which are subsequently defined more concisely.

4.1.1. CDT—Built as to Be Built—The Design Phase

As described earlier, no CPS exists in this phase, which makes it particularly interesting to define requirements for the CDT in the subsequent phases. The CDT in this phase must result from a collaborative work process akin to BIM and comprises all the sub-models from each design discipline as well as any mocked data. It is essential that each stakeholder, design office, and discipline has access to information on every sub-part of the CDT but can only edit and change the parts of the CDT in their responsibility. For all planning processes, the CDT is considered the single source of truth. The resulting requirements for the CDT in this phase are diverse. For example, the CDT must be able to handle the process of variant analysis. It should allow for quick and easy adjustments to find the best solution regarding the project's boundary conditions. These might dictate the best technical solution but can also regulate the costs or schedule for the project. In direct relation to this, the DT must be able to handle all kinds of design simulations. These might be a structural analysis, optimizations of energy efficiency, or construction process and progress simulations [31,39].

To sum up, in this phase, the DT is mostly required to, first of all, create itself, then optimize itself, and finally act as the basis for the certification of the to-be-built asset. The CDT in this phase delivers use cases UC2, UC4, and UC10 (cf. Table 1).

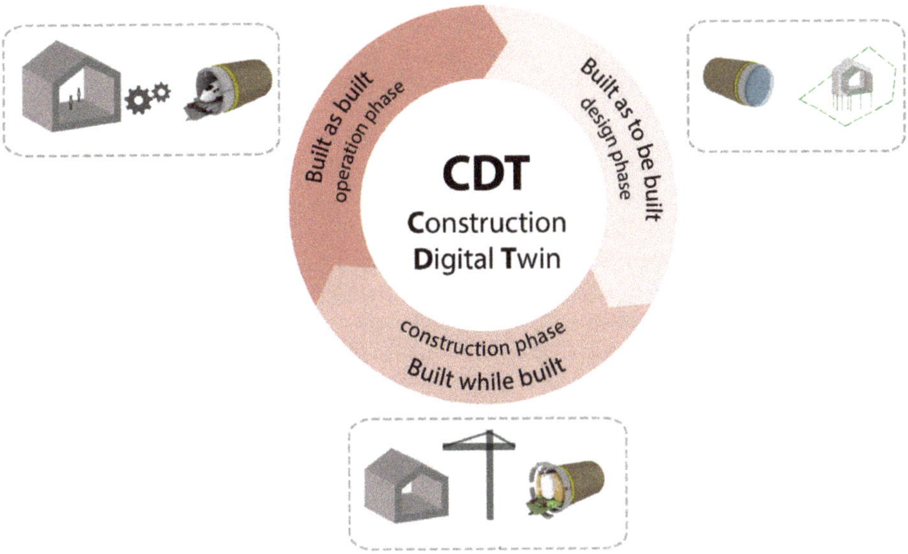

Figure 4. Three stages of the CDT.

4.1.2. CDT—Built While Built—The Construction Phase

The CDT performs an important role during the construction of the CPS. Since it already exists as intended, the CDT serves as the foundation for all construction planning. In this phase, the CDT must include not only temporary facilities, such as site equipment, but also structures required to construct the CPS, such as road diversions. During construction, the CDT must be modified to accommodate changes necessitated by deviations from the intended CPS. These modifications may be the consequence of impromptu decisions or an imprecise construction process. Therefore, the three most pertinent reasons are as follows. First, the DT must closely resemble the genuine CPS to meet all client requirements. Second, the CDT is a crucial instrument for bidding. Based on the CDT, the client will create the tendering documents and monitor all processes on it. Billing is the third and most essential reason. Using the CDT, the contractor typically invoices the client for actual costs, necessitating an exact replica of the CPS by the CDT. At the conclusion of the construction phase, the CDT must achieve two goals. The primary goal is to represent a knowledge base for all construction data. This could include knowing when a component was constructed, what materials were used, who constructed it, and even the weather at the time, to name a few examples. After construction is complete, the CDT must be transferred to facility management (FM) for computer-aided FM (CAFM). When a redevelopment or extension of the CPS is planned, or when a detrimental event occurs, design and construction information typically become relevant once again. The CDT in this phase delivers use cases UC3, UC8, and UC9 (cf. Table 1).

4.1.3. CDT—Built as Built—The Operation Phase

As indicated previously, the CDT for this phase should ideally be the result of the previous phase. During the phase of operation, the CDT is subject to a new set of requirements. One of the primary goals is to control the CPS using direct input signals and to collect data using sensors. From controlling the HVAC of a building to virtually stress-testing the CPS or controlling the railway signaling and movement of trains, this strategy could lead to useful outcomes. The second primary objective is facilities management and infrastructure upkeep, respectively. The CDT must permit the incorporation of CPS maintenance and repair procedures. Consequently, during the operation phase, the DT must react less to the geometric changes of the CPS and instead integrate all the data arriving directly from it. The CDT in this phase delivers use cases UC1, UC3, UC5, UC6, and UC7 (cf. Table 1).

4.2. Proposed Process

In Section 1, we argued that developing a DT is predominantly a matter of integrating information, as opposed to designing a (large-scale) system from scratch. This claim is firmly supported by the fact that a DT is typically co-designed with a CPS (such as an embedded system, a smart building, or a digital shopfloor). These CPSs are constructed according to well-established procedures [40,41]. These processes have a strong emphasis on engineering and are therefore not equipped to supervise the development of DTs. Pure forward engineering processes comprising engineering change management are intended to handle changes only after the release of a product, i.e., a completed structure (or portions thereof). Additionally, engineering change management is not optimized for information integration. A DT is typically constructed from existing information on and about the CPS (such as static information from models and dynamic information in the form of data available from and about the cyber–physical asset). This information must be integrated, correlated, and made available to stakeholders in accordance with their needs and use cases, thereby proving our primary point that generating a DT is about information integration. Alongside AECO's well-established engineering processes, IT change management provides a systematic approach to achieving this goal.

DTs are constructed based on the requirements of stakeholders and use cases. Consequently, a process that is agile and iterative (see Section 2) and is driven by stakeholder requirements and the use cases listed in Table 1 is a natural fit. Agile methods leverage the concept of delivering software systems in small increments that are driven by stakeholder needs and accompanied by rigorous quality assurance. Specifically, the agile manifesto proposes the four principles listed below [6]:

- *Individuals and interactions* over processes and tools (i.e., people drive the development process and not tools, so people take precedence).
- *Working software* over comprehensive documentation (i.e., shift the focus on the process outcomes and not the process itself).
- *Customer collaboration* over contract negotiation (i.e., customers are important not only for early requirement elicitation and final commissioning but throughout the whole development process).
- *Responding to change* over following a plan (i.e., deliver minimum viable increments that can immediately be evaluated and changed from iteration to iteration).

The agile manifesto promotes a shift away from rigid processes and planning toward a pervasive emphasis on the consumer and the to-be-created IT system. To facilitate close coordination based on tangible artifacts, early and continuous delivery of results to the client is one of the highest priorities. Changes to customer requirements are not rejected but rather viewed as a necessary course of action to produce a customer-value-generating project outcome. This is frequently referred to as *movable targets* [42]. In agile projects, the development of high-quality software is a top priority to make frequent technological changes conceivable. This includes a straightforward IT architecture and ongoing code quality assurance. In agile teams, social aspects such as effective communication, motivation, and personal accountability are also highly valued.

As described in Section 2, a CDT is subject to changing requirements. Agile engineering's change-anticipatory and iterative nature enables change response by default. However, agile methods were originally developed for software engineering and therefore do not fit CDT engineering seamlessly. In particular, the design and implementation tasks do not readily apply to the construction of a CDT, as no new artifacts are to be produced; rather, new information is to be integrated. In the case of the CDT, this will depend on the three phases, namely, in the first phase, information regarding building requirements will be integrated, in the second phase, information regarding the as-is manifestation of the CPS will be integrated, and in the third and final phase, information regarding the actual state of the CPS will be integrated (see Figure 3).

IT change management can be implemented as early as the design and planning phases to evaluate potential IT infrastructure manifestations. Eventually, a CDT becomes an IT infrastructure due to its combined need for hardware- and software-based components, resulting from its virtual replication of a CPS. This follows directly from Grieves and Vickers' earlier definition [26], in that a DT requires a digital representation, which is ultimately software-based, a physical counterpart, i.e., the hardware, and a middleware, i.e., software for exchanging data. Figure 5 depicts a generic change management process that makes it possible to realize a CDT in accordance with the requirements of its stakeholders in a step-by-step manner.

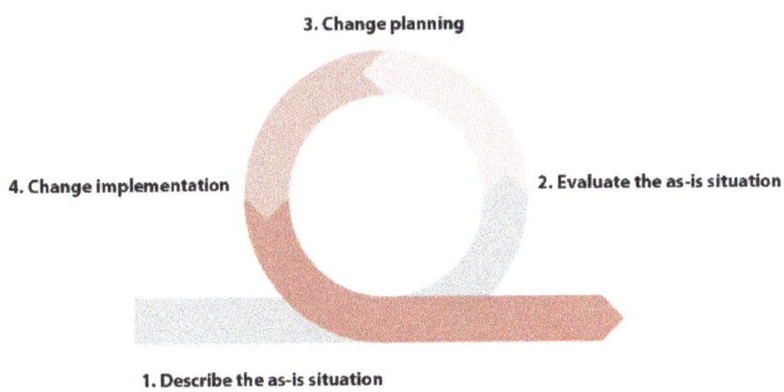

Figure 5. Generic change management process.

Figure 5 represents a simplified view of the detailed process depicted in Figure 3 by condensing multiple steps into one, such as *Create RFC*, *Record RFC*, and *Review RFC* condensing into *Describe the situation as is*. By embedding Figure 5's generic change management process within Figure 2's agile paradigm, the resulting combination of agile engineering and change management enables the development of Figure 6's extended, iterative agile process model for engineering DTs.

By beginning with stakeholder-motivated requirements engineering, the process depicted in Figure 6 is stakeholder-driven and ensures that stakeholders' requirements and use cases are satisfied upon completion of an iteration. In addition, by treating the CDT as an IT infrastructure, the requirements of stakeholders are translated into change requests that are systematically incorporated into the existing CDT in accordance with well-established procedures. Lastly, the agile nature of the process enables continuous alignment with stakeholder requirements and the delivery of these requirements with high quality. This procedure is easily applicable to all three phases of the CDT (see Figure 3). In addition to the benefits derived from the application of an agile methodology to the development of the CDT, change management offers the following advantages:

- *Improved communication*: by involving and informing team members and stakeholders about changes, communication throughout the entire project is enhanced.

- Reduced organizational friction and improved productivity: naturally, communication throughout the entire project is enhanced when team members and stakeholders are informed and included in the change process.
- Enhanced creativity and innovation: every change necessitates alternative/novel solutions, thereby fostering innovation and creativity among team members and stakeholders when exploring new problem-solving techniques.
- Improved decision-making: every change necessitates alternative/novel solutions, thereby fostering innovation and creativity among team members and stakeholders when exploring new problem-solving strategies.

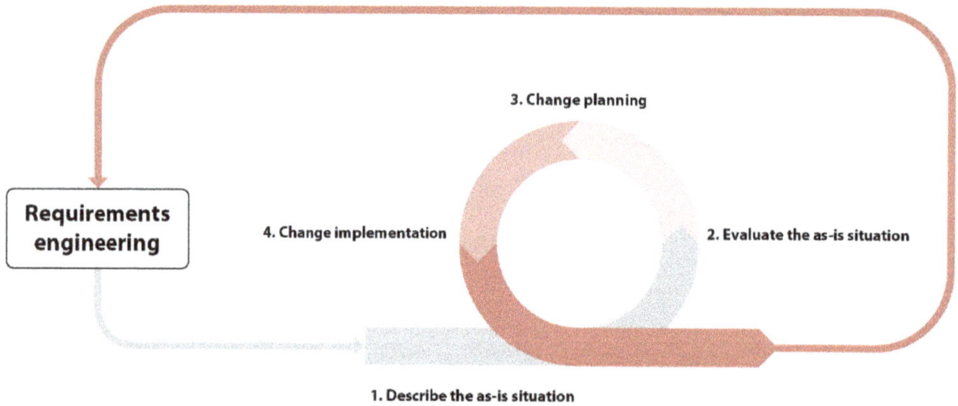

Figure 6. Agile, change-driven process model for engineering DTs.

4.3. Benefits of Proposal

The process proposed in Section 4 is based on well-established agile software engineering techniques [43,44]. Agile engineering's revisionist nature enables the identification of quick wins for stakeholders (see Section 4.3.1). In addition, process and product quality metrics of agile engineering merit additional research into their applicability and impact on CDT engineering, as discussed in Section 4.3.2.

4.3.1. Quick Wins for Stakeholders

As regards utilizing agile methods, quick wins, i.e., use cases with high strategic relevance and simple feasibility, can be easily identified to rapidly deliver value to customers/stakeholders (see Figure 7). Agile engineering's repeated requirements engineering during each iteration facilitates the identification of quick wins. Continuous and repeated consultation and evaluation of use case-related scenarios in each iteration yields a step-by-step strategy for constructing the CDT by realizing concrete, stakeholder-motivated scenarios that are progressively evaluated and quality-assured (see Section 4.3.2). Thus, the proper identification of quick wins permits the development of a minimum viable product (MVP) from the customer/stakeholder's perspective and enables the rapid delivery of a return on investment (ROI). As construction progresses on the CDT, all use cases are eventually addressed. Importantly, as the CDT's base grows, the use cases on the right side of Figure 7 become progressively simpler to implement.

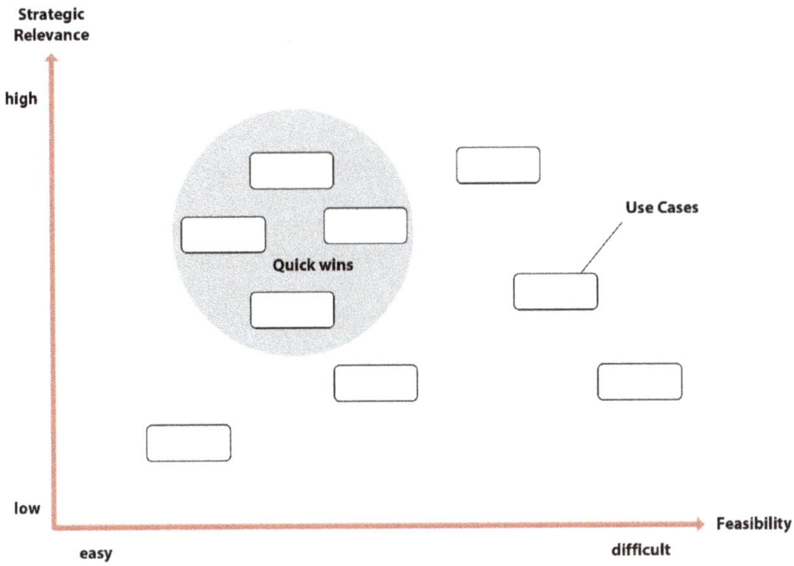

Figure 7. Identification of quick wins for customers and stakeholders.

4.3.2. Quality Metrics

The availability of metrics that provide insight into productivity throughout the various phases of a project's life cycle is an advantage of using an agile process. This helps to evaluate product quality and track team performance [12]. We cannot map all agile metrics to the AECO context due to the software development-related nature of agile metrics. In addition, not all selected metrics can be applied to every BIM use case, as should be evident from the context of the various use cases. Nonetheless, numerous metrics can be readily applied to the AECO context and contribute significantly to key quality criteria in the AECO domain [45]:

- Plannable processes;
- Transparent processes;
- Effective processes and groups;
- Situationally and contextually aware procedures;
- Resource-conscious procedures.

In the following, we illustrate how such metrics can be used not only for evaluating the CDT's quality (see Section "Measuring the Quality of the CDT") but also for team building (see Section "Measuring the Team Building the CDT"). All metrics that are part of the ensuing discussion are time-tested and have their roots in agile engineering [12].

Measuring the Quality of the CDT

Several agile engineering metrics are readily applicable to measuring the quality of the CDT. We contend that the following metrics can be mapped directly without additional effort or modification:

- *Mean time to repair* (MTTR) is used to track the time between detecting an issue in a product, triaging the issue, and determining and deploying a fix. In the context of the CDT, this refers to a missing or incorrectly configured information source. Importantly, MTTR typically induces a new change, resulting in additional lead and cycle time expenditures (see below).

- *Lead time* measures the time between the customer's first mention of a new feature and its eventual delivery to the end user. In the context of the CDT, this refers to the amount of time required for a change (the feature) to be deemed relevant and implemented. Importantly, lead time is a measure of long-term performance.
- *Cycle time*, unlike lead time, is a short-term measurement and a subset of lead time (see Figure 8). Importantly, it is the actual completion time a feature requires, i.e., from the time it is moved from defined to started/in-progress to complete. Cycle times are a direct measurement of the time required to complete a specific task, such as integrating a specific data source as part of implementing a change.
- *Mean time between failure* (MTBF) is used to monitor a product's availability and dependability. The greater the time between failures, such as a non-functioning twin (i.e., rather than displaying incorrect sensor values, it displays none), the more reliable the system.
- *Recidivism* is the measurement of tasks in reverse order. The recidivism rate increases if a task moves from planning to implementation, fails to meet the requirements, and then moves back to planning.

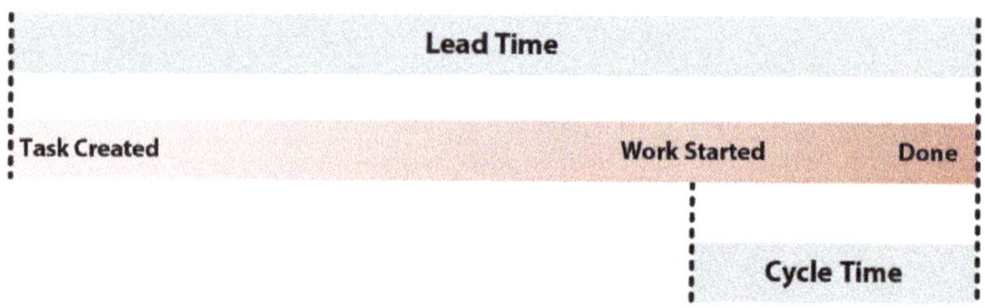

Figure 8. Relationship between lead time and cycle time.

Collectively, these metrics allow for the evaluation of the quality of both the process application and the final product. Despite the fact that this set of metrics is incomplete, it provides a fundamental foundation for assessing and measuring process and product quality in AECO.

Measuring the Team Building the CDT

In addition to measuring the quality of the process and the final product, agile methods place an even greater emphasis on measuring the development team. As is the case with technical quality metrics, agile methods also include a variety of team measurement metrics. As with technical quality metrics, however, not all team-related agile metrics are applicable to our proposed process. Again, we argue that the following metrics can be mapped without additional effort or adjustments:

- *Lead time* is not only a technical quality metric, but is also useful for measuring a team's efficiency by estimating the speed of the value chain, i.e., from change definition to delivery.
- Development time measures the completion time of a specific task after it has been specified and passed on to development. In the case of the CDT, this corresponds directly to change implementation, providing a valuable measure of the complexity of a task.
- Deploy frequency measures the frequency with which consumers/stakeholders receive updates.
- Good/failed deliveries assess the frequency with which customers/stakeholders receive a working product, i.e., a CDT that satisfies specified requirements.

- Total done determines the frequency with which a working product, i.e., a CDT that meets specified requirements, is delivered to customers/stakeholders.

As for team-based quality metrics, the above list is by no means exhaustive; rather, it is intended to demonstrate that agile methods can be used to evaluate not only process and product quality, but also a team's productivity and dedication. We claim that such measurement capacities are novel for the AECO domain and thus provide a valuable first step towards optimizing the construction of the CDT, and—if carried out thoroughly—also its accompanying CPS, i.e., the built asset. For such metrics to be effective and meet the aforesaid quality criteria, they must be utilized by the entire team, not just by a single individual. Additionally, metrics must be used in conjunction with other metrics, as each metric addresses only a particular aspect. Using them in tandem reveals the bigger and balanced picture of all project activities. Finally, metrics should be easily understandable and computable to provide meaningful insight and help in guiding day-to-day activities.

Table 2 summarizes these agile metrics, supported by descriptive examples from the AECO industry for each phase of the CDT that can readily be applied to our process in the AECO domain, as discussed next in Sections "Measuring the Quality of the CDT" and "Measuring the Team Building the CDT".

Table 2. Agile metrics for AECO combined with descriptive examples for each phase of the CDT.

		AECO Quality Criteria					**CDT Phase**		
		Plannable Processes	**Transparent Processes**	**Efficient Processes and Teams**	**Situation- and Context-Aware Processes**	**Resource-Aware Processes**	**Built as to Be Built**	**Built While Built**	**Built as Built**
Quality							Time...		
	Mean time to repair (MTTR)	X	X	X		X	... from discovery of a discipline-related collision to resolution	... to recognize and adapt deviations in the construction process from design to execution	... from the detection of an issue to its solution. Possible issue: sensor in the CDT does not track the data of the sensor in the CPS
							Time to implement a new requirement.		
	Lead time	X	X	X			Client-sourced (e.g., new facade system) or new requirements from a building law perspective	Adaptations due to deviating in situ geology	Changed conditions of use (e.g., changed lighting requirements)

Table 2. *Cont.*

		AECO Quality Criteria					**CDT Phase**		
		Plannable Processes	**Transparent Processes**	**Efficient Processes and Teams**	**Situation- and Context-Aware Processes**	**Resource-Aware Processes**	**Built as to Be Built**	**Built While Built**	**Built as Built**
Quality							Time from start to finish of a task.		
	Cycle time	X	X	X			Object designer incorporated new requirement of client	In case of critical event, processed immediately, equal to the lead time. For non-critical events, regular processing (lead time > cycle time)	Object planners and facility managers process new requirement due to changed conditions of use
	Mean time between failure (MTBF)	X	X		X	X	Failure (we define failure as the situation that occurs when a user does not perceive the expected result with respect to a request/ specification): integration of a submodel with supported format fails	Failure: registration of the last 5 tunnel segments in the CDT not possible	Failure: CDT falsely triggers fire alarm
							Rate of tasks having to be reperformed.		
	Recidivism		X	X	X		Submodel is rejected (e.g., by rule-based verification) because requirements are not met	Slab foundation is reduced to strip foundation and structural engineer not satisfied with design	Newly planned fixtures exceed capacity of the fuse

Table 2. *Cont.*

		AECO Quality Criteria					CDT Phase		
		Plannable Processes	**Transparent Processes**	**Efficient Processes and Teams**	**Situation- and Context-Aware Processes**	**Resource-Aware Processes**	**Built as to Be Built**	**Built While Built**	**Built as Built**
Team	**Lead time**						Time to implement a new requirement.		
			X	X	X		Implementation period for delivery of the modified facade system	Implementation period to deliver the adaptations through deviating in situ geologies	Implementation period of the delivery of the adapted CDT due to changed conditions of use
	Development time						Time to develop a new requirement.		
		X	X	X		X	Connection detail of the new facade system was specified, development-time subsumes the modeling of the detail	Time required for modeling of the changed in situ geology or time required for static calculation/ simulation of the new strip foundation	Fixing the link between the fire alarm system and CDT
	Deploy frequency						Number of delivered changes.		
				X			Number of deviation(s) from information delivery plan	Number of (partial) invoices extracted from CDT	Every new deployment (such as changing requirements, missing requirements, …)
	Good/failed deliveries						Number/ratio of good/failed changes.		
			X	X	X		Ratio of complete vs. incomplete data drops	Number of necessary deployments until the CDT reflects the CPS as is for subsequent invoice extraction	Ratio of rejecting/accepting the CDT in part of CAFM
	Total done						Number of finished tasks.		
		X		X		X	Number of solved issues from an issue tracking tool (e.g., BIMcollab)	Planned construction measures as well as differences between planned and executed (e.g., defects)	Total issues from an issue tracking tool (e.g., BIMcollab) in the operational phase

5. Alignment with BIM

Change management and agile engineering with BIM are congruent at this stage. In particular, the management aspect of BIM, which, among other things, defines the information requirements and how the information is delivered, is very similar to the change management and agile engineering methods described [25,46]. In all phases of an AECO project's life cycle, changes as such are the basis for all work, regardless of whether a classical or BIM approach is employed, because they are unavoidable. However, the BIM approach adds a significant collaborative element to the change-based working method. The combination of the two contributes to the proposed process model for agile, change-driven engineering of DTs (Figure 6). By stating that the CDT is the natural consequence of the proper implementation of BIM in construction projects [1,31], we complete the circle with the described congruence. In contrast, a properly constructed and utilized BIM can already represent a CDT, particularly during the design phase.

This congruence is prominently reflected in the BIM tools currently in use. Issue management tools, such as BIMCollab or Solibri, have made their way into standard BIM projects and assist in tracking all identified issues, which are merely another type of change. Similar to source code repositories in agile engineering [47], the use of common data environments (CDEs) strongly contributes to an agile work style. By establishing a single source of truth and near-real-time access to the most up-to-date models and project data in general, information-dependent parties can establish a collaborative and tightly integrated workflow. The resulting processes are consistent with agile engineering methodologies.

The necessity of the described process is most evident in the *built-as-built* CDT, which is one of the three phases of the CDT introduced in Section 3. An operating model for the CPS is required for this phase. This requirement exemplifies CAFM in that the proper operation and maintenance of a CPS, i.e., the built asset, cannot be carried out in the absence of a well-defined operating model. By incrementally and iteratively constructing the CDT in accordance with stakeholders, such as CAFM operators or residents, our requirements engineering process ultimately produces the required operating model. By taking into account all pertinent requirements pertaining to the operating model of a CPS and subsequently delivering the system by implementing the pertinent changes, the CDT directly reflects the operating model as required by respective stakeholders.

6. Evaluation and Discussion

The design, construction, and operation of a building or structure is an interaction of many processes, which together lead to a functioning building. To evaluate the hypotheses and the change management process outlined in Figure 6, a representative and common process within a BIM design process is taken into consideration.

6.1. Explaining Technology Use and Acceptance Using the TAM

The Technology Acceptance Model (TAM) is a commonly used theoretical framework for analyzing and predicting the acceptance and usage of information technology [14]. Originally proposed in the late 1980s, it has subsequently been worked upon by numerous scholars [48]. The TAM is useful for analyzing technology use and provides a structured approach to assessing user perception and decision-making for technology adoption. In our work, we employ a slightly modified version of the TAM proposed by Riemenschneider and Hardgrave [49], as shown in Figure 9. It includes the following components:

- **Training** (TRA) is a valuable exogenous variable in determining the use of novel technologies and directly influences both perceived usefulness and perceived ease of use.

- **Perceived ease of use** (EOU) assesses the extent to which users believe that using the technology or tool will be effortless and free from difficulties.
- **Perceived usefulness** (USF) focuses on whether users believe that the technology or tool will enhance their job performance or make their tasks more effective.
- **Use** (USE) represents the actual adoption and use of a technology or tool and is influenced by perceived ease of use and usefulness, respectively.

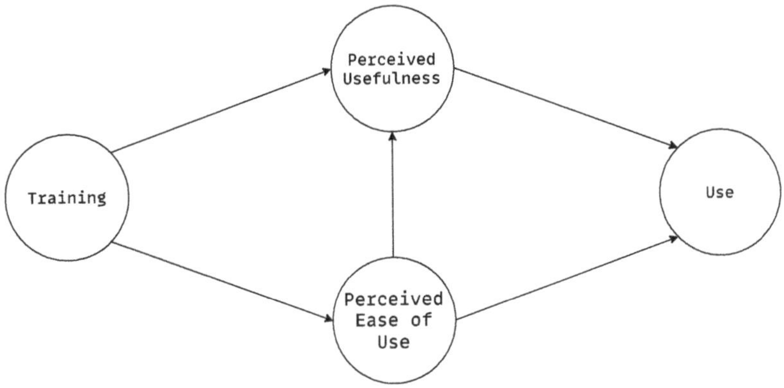

Figure 9. Technology Acceptance Model with the four constructs training, perceived usefulness, perceived ease of use, and use [49].

The TAM thus provides a systematic framework for evaluating user perceptions, attitudes, and intentions around technology adoption, making it essential for technology evaluation. This understanding can lead to changes, influence decision-making, and increase the possibility of successful technology deployment and use within an organization or user group [14,48].

6.2. Method

We created a user survey to be administered to our sample. The sample in this case comprises selected representatives from the construction domain with both academic and industrial backgrounds. After an online video demo of our proposed process model, we administered our survey to the 22 representatives, among them, BIM managers, software developers, project leads, and engineers. The average age of respondents is 38 years, with a reported average of 10 years of experience. Among the participants, there were 15 males and 7 females. The survey comprised the following question items:

- USE_1: Conceivable degree of utilization of the process;
- TRA_1: I understood the process from the instructions in the video;
- TRA_2: I already implement agile processes and already received special training;
- TRA_3: I will need appropriate training for the implementation of agile processes;
- USF_1: Using the process shown enables me to complete tasks more quickly;
- USF_2: Using the underlying process improves my work performance;
- USF_3: Using the underlying process increases my productivity;
- USF_4: Using the underlying process improves the quality of my work;
- USF_5: Using the underlying process makes my work easier;
- USF_6: The underlying process is useful for my work;
- USF_7: The underlying process is useful to me;
- USF_8: The advantages of using the underlying process outweigh the disadvantages;
- EOU_1: Learning the new process seems easy to me;
- EOU_2: I think the new process is clear and understandable;

- EOU_3: I find the new process flexible to use;
- EOU_4: It seems easy for me to use the new process skillfully;
- EOU_5: The new process is easy to use;
- EOU_6: The new process is not frustrating to use;
- EOU_7: Using the new process does not require much mental effort.

The Likert scale used for all question items (except for USE_1) consisted of seven points, with a rating of 1 representing "strongly disagree", a rating of 4 representing "neither agree nor disagree", and a rating of 7 representing "strongly agree". In case of USE_1, the scale consisted of four points, ranging from 1 representing "all the time" to 4 representing "rarely". Furthermore, demographic data, including age, gender, job role, and years of professional experience, were collected to describe the participants.

6.3. Model Evaluation

To thoroughly assess our suggested process model, we investigate the corresponding structural equation model [50]. Structural equation modeling (SEM) is a powerful tool for analyzing complex relationships, especially among latent variables. Two main approaches exist in SEM: covariance-based SEM (CB-SEM) and partial least squares SEM (PLS-SEM) [51]. PLS-SEM is beneficial in situations where the goal of the model is to predict and explain desired outcomes, such as technological acceptance [52]. The statistical programming language R version 4.2 was used together with the SEMinR package version 2.3 to analyze our instance of the TAM using the PLS-SEM technique [51,53].

6.3.1. Measurement Model Evaluation

Beginning with the dependability and accuracy evaluation of our reflective measurement, as per the approach outlined by Hair Jr. et al. [51], we investigate the reliability of each construct by (i) analyzing indicator loadings, (ii) evaluating the reliability of the measurement instrument by calculating composite reliability (ρ_c), Cronbach's alpha (ρ_T), and the reliability coefficient (ρ_A), (iii) assessing the convergent validity by calculating the average variance extracted (AVE), and (iv) verifying the discriminant validity by examining the Heterotrait–Monotrait (HTMT) ratios [51].

As to (i), all the loadings of the four constructs TRA, EOU, USF, and USE exhibit statistical significance at a confidence level of $CI_\alpha = 0.05$ or below. Furthermore, being above the threshold value of 0.708 [50], they suggest a sufficient level of indicator reliability [51]. Concerning (ii), all four constructs measured demonstrate internal consistency [50], with ρ_c, ρ_T, and ρ_A all surpassing 0.8 [50]. Moreover, with regard to (iii), it is important to mention that all the Average Variance Extracted (AVE) values are close to the threshold of 0.5 [54], indicating a substantial level of convergent validity for the measures of the four constructs [50]. Concerning (iv), all HTMT ratio values are below the cut-off threshold of 0.75 [54], indicating discriminant validity among the four constructs.

6.3.2. Structural Model Evaluation

After assessing both the reliability and validity of the four constructs TRA, EOU, USF, and USE, we now investigate the structural component of our model. Following Hair and Alamer's suggestions [54], we (i) examine the structural model for collinearity issues related to the variance inflation factor (VIF), (ii) assess the significance and relevance of the structural relationships by their path coefficients using model bootstrapping, and (iii) assess the explanatory capacity of the model using the determination coefficient (R^2) and the effect size (f^2).

Regarding (i), the VIF analysis shows that our model does not exhibit evidence of collinearity among the four constructs [50], as the greatest VIF values are below the threshold of 5 [51,54]. Regarding (ii), we assess the significance and the relevance of the structural model paths by bootstrapping the sampling distribution [55–57] to test the structural model's relationship coefficients for statistical significance at $CI_{\alpha} = 0.05$, as summarized in Figure 10. Finally, concerning (iii), the R^2 values (see Figure 10) for the endogenous constructs USF, EOU, and USE are located close to the moderate threshold of 0.5 [50]. This suggests that our model has a satisfactory ability to predict outcomes within the sample [51].

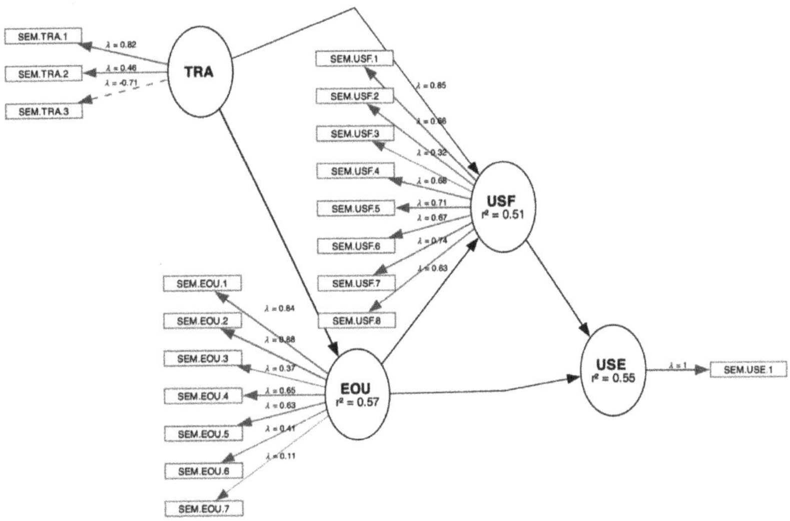

Figure 10. Bootstrapped model. Values in ovals denote the R^2 value of the construct; values in brackets indicate the 95% CI of the corresponding path. Asterisks indicate statistical significance at the 0.01 (***), 0.05 (**), and 0.1 (*) levels, respectively.

The measurement and structural model analysis results validate the TAM in our context, indicating that the constructs of USF and EOU consistently forecast the intention to utilize the process. These findings highlight the robustness of the links within the model and offer empirical validation for its internal consistency. The validated model indicates that user perceptions are precisely represented and that it may be reliably utilized to forecast technology acceptance in this context.

6.3.3. Interpretation of Results

The outcomes of the PLS-SEM analysis offer a distinct depiction of the interplay between various structures in the TAM, which impact the acceptance and use of the suggested technology. The model demonstrates that EOU has a substantial impact on the perception of USF, as evidenced by a robust path coefficient of 0.76. The significant level of influence emphasizes the necessity of developing the technology to be user-friendly, since the simplicity of use directly improves the perceived value and usefulness of the technology. Furthermore, the correlation between TRA and USF, with a path coefficient of 0.26, suggests that although TRA plays a significant role in determining real USF, it is not the sole contributing factor. The model proposes that several factors, such as user attitudes, external influences, and the implementation environment, have a substantial impact on the adoption of the technology in practice. The existence of a negative route coefficient (−0.28) between one of the components and USE indicates the possibility of resistance or obstacles that may discourage usage. These concerns could be linked to perceived barriers or complexities that users face. It is only reasonable that our plan is currently hindered by technological limitations, i.e., the availability of a supporting tooling infrastructure.

Nevertheless, our findings indicate that it would be beneficial to carry out additional research on the proposed process model after the necessary technology infrastructure has been established [10,58,59].

Implications

The analysis conclusions have significant consequences for stakeholders engaged in the development, implementation, and management of the proposed technology. The robust correlation between EOU and USE implies that to promote the acceptance and usage of a product or service, it is imperative to give utmost importance to enhancing the user experience. Streamlining user engagement and ensuring the technology is intuitive can greatly improve consumers' opinions of its USF, potentially resulting in increased adoption rates. The correlation between USF and USE suggests that merely making the technology beneficial is required but not enough to guarantee universal adoption. This highlights the necessity of adopting a comprehensive approach that considers elements such as user education, assistance mechanisms, resolving any possible apprehensions or misunderstandings that users might have, and the availability of a relevant tooling infrastructure. The probability of effective adoption increases when thorough support is provided and user concerns are addressed. The inverse correlation identified with USE serves as an indication that certain characteristics of a technology or its implementation may be causing difficulties for users. This may encompass intricacies in the functionality of the technology, insufficient support systems, or other obstacles that cause people to be reluctant in completely embracing the technology. It is crucial to identify and address these difficulties to enhance the technology's overall adoption and ensure that it fulfills the demands and expectations of its intended users. Evidently, the current state of our tool infrastructure is inadequate [10,58,59].

Usefulness of the Proposed Technology

The evaluation of a technology is based on its perceived EOU, which is closely connected to its perceived USF. This indicates that the process has been carefully planned and executed to provide ease of use, which is a crucial element in determining its overall effectiveness. Nevertheless, the moderate correlation between USF and actual USE suggests that although the technology is perceived as helpful, there might be other variables that influence its adoption. This may entail the requirement for more resilient implementation tactics, user enlightenment, or tackling specific obstacles that could hinder its utilization (see above). In general, according to the TAM results, the suggested process model is a feasible and efficient tool. However, its ultimate success will rely on resolving the recognized obstacles and guaranteeing that users feel assisted and self-assured in its utilization. The TAM study offers useful insights that can direct the subsequent development and improvement of the process model, guaranteeing that it fulfills user requirements and attains its desired results.

Contributions

Agile engineering contributes significantly to DT engineering by introducing a flexible, iterative approach that ensures stakeholder requirements and use cases are consistently addressed throughout the life cycle of the DT. The key contributions include the following:

- **Iterative Development**: Agile engineering emphasizes small, incremental development cycles, enabling continuous refinement and alignment of the DT with evolving project requirements. This is particularly valuable during the design and construction phases, where real-time adjustments are often necessary.

- **Stakeholder-Driven Process:** Agile engineering places stakeholders at the center of the development process. Frequent feedback loops ensure that the DT evolves in a way that directly reflects user needs and expectations, making it adaptable to diverse scenarios.
- **Handling Uncertainty and Complexity**: Construction projects often encounter unexpected changes, such as site-specific conditions or regulatory updates. Agile engineering's change-anticipatory nature allows the DT to incorporate these adjustments dynamically, avoiding rigid processes that might lead to delays or misalignments.
- **Focus on Rapid Value Delivery**: Agile methods encourage the identification of "quick wins"—high-priority use cases that deliver immediate value to stakeholders. This ensures that the DT generates benefits early in the project life cycle, boosting stakeholder confidence and project momentum.
- **Quality Assurance**: Agile frameworks integrate rigorous quality checks after each development cycle, ensuring that the DT consistently meets performance expectations and remains aligned with stakeholder goals.

In DT engineering, agile methods provide the flexibility and responsiveness needed to manage the evolving requirements of construction projects, ensuring that the DT remains relevant, useful, and aligned with real-world needs.

Change management plays a complementary role in digital twin (DT) engineering, providing a structured framework to manage the integration of diverse data sources and accommodate evolving project requirements. Its contributions include the following:

- **Systematic Information Integration:** Change management ensures that data from various sources (e.g., BIM models, sensor data, and stakeholder inputs) are incorporated into the DT systematically. This structured approach minimizes the risk of data inconsistencies and enhances the reliability of the DT.
- **Life Cycle Adaptability:** By establishing a process for recording, evaluating, and implementing changes, change management ensures that the DT remains relevant throughout its life cycle. This is crucial as the DT transitions from the design phase to construction and ultimately to operation.
- **Minimizing Risk:** Change management frameworks reduce the risks associated with integrating dynamic and heterogeneous data by formalizing procedures for assessing and mitigating potential impacts of changes.
- **Enhanced Collaboration:** Clear change management procedures foster transparency and improve communication among stakeholders. By documenting change requests and decisions, all parties stay informed and aligned, reducing organizational friction.
- **Support for Complex, Multi-Stakeholder Projects:** Construction projects often involve a wide range of stakeholders with differing priorities. Change management enables the reconciliation of these priorities by providing a structured process for evaluating and implementing changes in a balanced manner.
- **Alignment with Agile Engineering:** The change-driven nature of the process naturally complements agile engineering's iterative approach. Together, they create a seamless system where changes can be integrated continuously without disrupting the project timeline.
- **Enabling Real-Time Updates**: Change management supports the DT's ability to reflect real-world conditions by ensuring that updates—such as those stemming from as-built data or operational feedback—are incorporated systematically.
- **Enhancing Decision-Making:** Change management in DT engineering enables comprehensive data analysis and the simulation of various scenarios. These insights support well-informed decision-making and the implementation of automated processes to ensure optimal execution across all life cycle phases of an asset.

When combined, agile engineering and change management form a robust framework for DT engineering. Agile engineering provides the iterative, stakeholder-focused mechanism to develop and refine the DT, while change management offers the structured processes to handle complexity, mitigate risks, and ensure the DT evolves seamlessly over time. This synergy ensures that the DT remains a dynamic, reliable representation of the physical asset, capable of adapting to the diverse and shifting demands of construction engineering.

6.4. Contributions to ISO 19650-1

ISO 19650-1 specifies, among other things, how information must be transmitted between parties to support the decision-making of the respective appointing parties. Figure 11 depicts the pertinent diagram from ISO 19650. Due to the fact that the change management process considers information discipline by discipline, it serves as the foundation for the information exchange process outlined in ISO 19650-1. For instance, a stakeholder's decision can result in a change request, which then initiates the described change management process. Since change requests can occur at all ISO 19650-1 figure levels, the change management process can be applied between them freely, as depicted in Figure 12. In addition, it illustrates that the information delivery processes outlined in ISO 19650-1, which are influenced by numerous changes, are supported by the change management processes, which are in turn influenced by information generation.

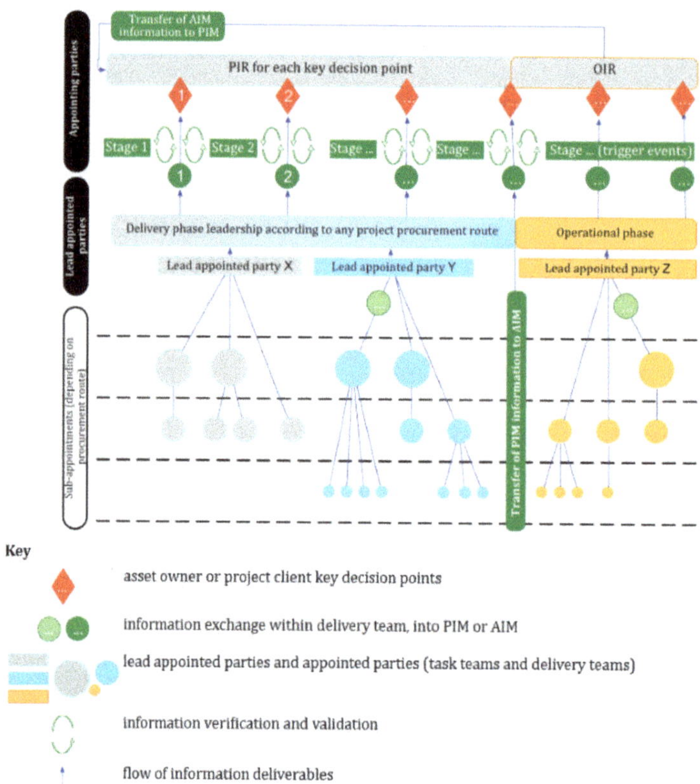

Figure 11. Illustration of an information delivery process according to ISO 19650-1.

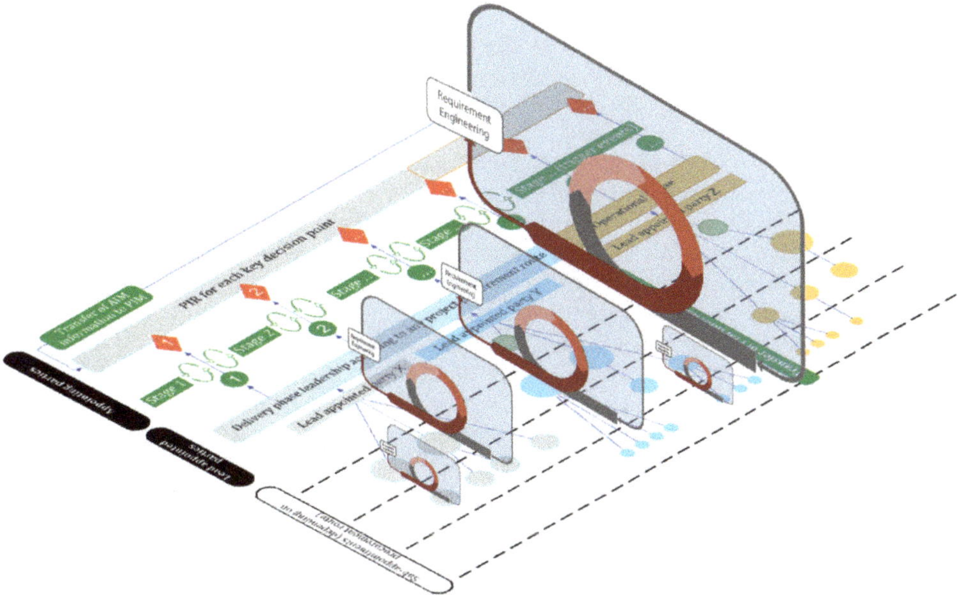

Figure 12. Change management process aligned with information delivery process according to ISO 19650-1.

6.5. Related Work and Discussion

It is not a novel concept to utilize information technology and software engineering to enhance established processes in the construction industry [8,60]. Fangxioa et al. [60] already investigated the idea of integrating change management with BIM. However, their proposal addresses the early design and planning phases as they pertain to the integration of changes into the BIM model. In contrast, we seek to address all phases of the building's life cycle. A comparable argument applies to the work of Kosicki et al. [8], which proposes a novel change process inspired by DevOps [61]. Like Fangxioa et al., Kosicki et al. only address the early design and planning phases with their Design Ops concept to enhance modeling collaboration. Again, our work aims to address all phases of the building's life cycle, not just the initial phases of planning and design. Moreover, our proposal emerged as an interdisciplinary effort within interdisciplinary projects, with civil engineers representing the stakeholders and computer scientists as the process management and digital twin specialists. We argue that it is this combination that renders our proposal meaningful and feasible.

The concept of the construction digital twin as presented in our article is not unfamiliar. Boje et al. [31] already introduced the concept in their recent work, in which they attempt to identify current deficiencies in BIM that impede the development of the CDT along with suggestions for achieving the construction of the CDT. In contrast to their work, which is rooted at the technological level, our work is rooted at the process level through the introduction of an agile, change-driven process for engineering the CDT. Importantly, our work promotes a bottom-up process for implementing BIM and, consequently, for constructing the CDT along the phases of a building's life cycle. Specifically, we elicited essential requirements based on the building life cycle phases that must be met for the successful construction of the CDT. Current manifestations of DTs in AECO follow a more ad hoc approach to delivering specific use cases [39,62–67]. We contend that both these requirements and an accompanying process are necessary. Our work aims to establish a generic, purely requirements-driven process that enables the targeting of diverse stakeholder needs and use cases. This is exemplified by the application of IT change management as the cornerstone of our agile process, as described in Section 4. In addition, because it is influenced by agile engineering, our proposed process includes quality metrics that enable continuous evaluation of both processes and final products. Our definitions of these metrics are, to the best of our knowledge, novel in construction engineering.

Afzal et al. [68] discuss the rapid evolution and application of a DT within the AECO sector, identifying five key components critical for its development: technologies, maturity levels, data layers, enablers, and functionalities. This highlights the growing importance of DTs in enhancing decision-making processes, optimizing operations, and improving the life cycle management of built assets. Our work aligns with their ideas in that technological readiness is a key factor for succeeding in successfully building a DT. In addition, the proposed maturity levels of Afzal et al. substantially align with a phase-based understanding of maturity in that given the actual project phase (design, construction, and operation) the DT matures. Yet, contrary to use, Afzal et al. neglect the actual engineering aspect of the DT, which for now poses the biggest challenges. Reja et al. [69] outline the objectives and implementation challenges of DTs in construction project management, framed within the PMBOK guidelines. This emphasizes the necessity of integrating geometric and non-geometric data to enhance decision-making and operational efficiency but identifies significant challenges related to data integration, interoperability, and the current state of DT technology. The work of Reja et al. thus underpins our thoughts and ideas, as well as our results in that most barriers are located at the technological layer. Apart from that, Reja et al., like Afzal et al. [68], also do not address the actual engineering aspect of the DT along a project's life cycle. In light of Afzal et al. [68] and Reja et al. [69], our work not only investigates challenges and opportunities, and relevant requirements for engineering DTs in construction engineering but in addition provides a novel process model with the aim to facilitate building DTs in construction engineering by outlining a roadmap and guidance on how to incorporate changes along the complete building life cycle.

Our previous evaluation of our proposed procedure indicates its viability for construction engineering. Importantly, the agile nature of our process ensures that the necessary requirements are specified for the subsequent application of changes to building models, the actual building, and the CDT. In turn, the change-driven nature of our process ensures that changes are evaluated prior to application, as well as after application, to ensure that requirements are met (cf., Figure 6). Our proposed quality metrics also permit evaluation of the process's successful application.

The proposed process provides not only the framework for engineering the CDT but also a proposal for implementing BIM in a bottom-up manner. Current BIM implementations are traditionally top-down, resulting in enormous, barely comprehensible, and practically impossible process models. This is exemplified when aligning our proposed process model with ISO 19650-1, the de facto standard governing the organization and digitization of information regarding buildings and civil engineering works, including BIM. We assert that our process model can provide the missing building block regarding the generation of information. Despite specifying the type and structure of information to be made available and processed between and during the various phases of the building's life cycle, ISO 19650-1 omits the crucial step of information generation. We are unaware of any other process that addresses the issue of information generation within the context of ISO 19650-1. We therefore claim that our work is paramount in offering practitioners a concise and efficient process model to implement the ISO 19650-1 standard for information delivery in modern BIM-based construction projects.

In summary, our contribution provides a skeleton process model for implementing BIM from the bottom up, as well as guidelines for iteratively conceiving the CDT. Inspired by agile engineering and IT change management, our process not only builds on well-established practices but also permits the immediate definition of quality criteria to evaluate the successful applicability of our proposed process model. We contend that the combination of all three—agile engineering, IT change management, and process quality metrics—provides a fertile environment for successfully implementing BIM and delivering the CDT. Importantly, the gestation of the DT using a combination of agile engineering and IT change management eventually delivers a platform for unified change management, one of the top-priority digital solution areas that are currently lacking appropriate tool support [15].

6.6. Threats to Validity

Naturally, threats to the validity of our approach exist. In the following, we discuss major threats to validity and how we mitigated those following Yin's guidelines [70].

6.6.1. Construct Validity

Construct validity refers to the appropriateness of the claimed experimental measures and the correspondence between theory and observations. We utilized the TAM for our results. We did not engage in critical reflections concerning the quality of the TAM except for assessing its validity for the case at hand, which we assessed successfully. Under the circumstance that none of the participants in our study had any prior experience with agile or change-driven engineering, results are not skewed by such a bias. For the time being, we believe that no reflections are necessary; however, once our proposal moves to a productive stage, reflections on its appropriateness are inevitable.

6.6.2. Internal Validity

Internal validity is utilized to create a cause-and-effect relationship between a treatment and an outcome in determining if the results support the claims, cf. our design challenge, as stated in Section 1. Our findings demonstrate that a flexible, change-driven strategy permits prompt responses to difficulties in the construction process. However, we have only addressed a preliminary evaluation of our proposal in terms of its perceived use thus motivating a need for a continuing empirical evaluation of our proposal in productive use to obtain stronger evidence for our claims. To counteract this risk, we examine our idea in the previously described projects BIM2BEM [71] and TIM [72].

6.6.3. External Validity

External validity refers to the applicability and applicability of a study's results to other contexts. We recognize that our method was only evaluated in a what-if environment, i.e., what if the process would be used. To mitigate this threat, it is necessary to apply larger, more realistic scenarios to empirically validate our current findings. Currently, it is not possible to conduct a comparative analysis with other proposals, except for those previously discussed in the context of related work, because none exist. However, based on our current evaluation, there is no reason to believe that our process cannot be successfully implemented in an actual construction environment.

6.7. Limitations

While this work addresses critical aspects of digital twin engineering, several limitations must be acknowledged. First, the scope of this study does not delve deeply into low-level technical implementation details, such as specific hardware configurations or software integration protocols. Instead, the focus has been on establishing a high-level framework and methodology, leaving finer-grained issues for subsequent research.

Additionally, considerations such as data privacy, security, and ownership are recognized as essential but are not comprehensively addressed in this work. These aspects are highly context-dependent and require tailored approaches that align with specific regulatory and organizational requirements. The handling of sensitive construction data or stakeholder information will likely necessitate a more detailed examination of privacy-preserving methods and robust data governance frameworks.

From an organizational perspective, implementing digital twins effectively requires alignment across multiple stakeholders, including construction firms, technology providers, and regulators. However, this study does not deeply explore the organizational dynamics, such as decision-making processes, change management, and stakeholder collaboration, that are critical for successful deployment. These challenges, including resistance to change or differing priorities among stakeholders, remain outside the scope of this work.

Moreover, the effective implementation of a digital twin necessitates the comprehensive digitization of construction and operational processes in general. This transformation involves converting traditional paper-based or manual workflows into digital processes. It requires the adoption of new technologies to achieve these digital processes and providing employee training to ensure their effective use. While this aspect is also not the primary focus of this paper, the presented framework establishes a strong foundation to address these challenges in future work.

Lastly, the proposed framework assumes a level of interoperability and standardization in data formats and communication protocols that may not yet be fully realized across diverse systems and projects. Addressing these organizational and technical gaps will be essential to validate and refine the framework in real-world applications.

7. Conclusions

In the construction industry, it is commonly assumed that BIM usage coincides with DT usage. In the context of Figure 1, however, the methods employed are primarily digital models or digital shadows. In AECO, it is initially necessary to raise awareness of the respective terms, whereas, in IT, a common understanding already exists. As a result of the increased use of digital methods and tools in the construction industry, including the introduction of BIM, more connections and interactions are emerging between the two disciplines. Thus, commonalities in the approaches become clearer and synergies can be utilized effectively in construction projects. This is evident in change management, whereas IT follows a considerably more systematic approach. Nonetheless, the fundamental processes are nearly identical.

This is the starting point for an important aspect of this article, which is the implementation of IT change management in the construction industry. This necessitates an even more systematic processing of changes, which ultimately includes more design process developments than is already typical in the BIM process. In the end, this would result in an improvement in efficiency and quality, and it would pursue a holistic approach. Critically, it should be noted that the creative problem-solving process in engineering and architecture is still at the forefront and that both DT and BIM must be viewed as tools.

The ultimate objective should be to achieve a DT by applying the described methods and processes in the most automated (BIM) design process possible. The advantages of such an approach would be extensive, and the new possibilities would improve results in every phase of the product's life cycle as a result of a significantly higher information level and quality. BIM in the design process can already be viewed as a DT, it must be noted. However, future possibilities cannot be predicted with absolute certainty at this time.

We argue that a focus on IT is advantageous. In its early days, software engineering struggled to successfully execute large-scale projects and therefore sought inspiration from the well-established construction discipline; this can be viewed as the birth of the waterfall model as it is used in the information technology industry. Experts in software engineering realized in the late 1990s, however, that such plan-based approaches fail to scale and anticipate change, resulting in the birth of agile. We argue that modern construction engineering should look to IT and adopt the prevalent working styles there, such as agile engineering and change management. Our proposal outlines the initial phase of a transformational change within AECO.

Despite the growing emphasis in construction projects on IT technical aspects, possibilities, and benefits, human and social factors must not be overlooked. Parallel to the technical solutions, it is crucial to work on the effects of established processes in the construction industry and the acceptance of stakeholders. As future work, we will conduct a comprehensive empirical evaluation of our proposal in the context of BIM2BEMFlow and TIM to assess its impact on established processes and stakeholders' acceptance.

7.1. Limitations

We recognize that our process is not the silver bullet for successfully implementing the CDT. Specific to our proposed process model, we identify two potential challenges.

7.1.1. Technical Challenges

Currently, a combination of open and closed BIM is the most common way to practice BIM. This results in immediate, unavoidable media disruptions at the level of information exchange. Evidently, this also affects our proposed procedure, as it ultimately relies on the assumptions of open formats and tools that permit simple aggregation, integration, and manipulation of data. However, we argue that to successfully implement BIM and move towards open BIM, it is necessary to fully realize BIM's potential. On a technical level, this necessitates potentially novel, open collaboration platforms that permit both static model management and evolution based on open, common formats, such as semantic web technologies [73] and dynamic data integration from simulations in early design and planning phases, as well as the actual building during construction and operation [58,59,74]. Such a platform comprises a central repository, e.g., a database-backed versioning system for tracking the evolution of modeling artifacts over time, a data warehouse for persisting, e.g., sensor readings, and integration for BIM issues, which act as the basis for a change request, i.e., a reported issue triggers the creation of an RFC. In terms of internal data representation, the IFC is the format of choice because of its open nature and readiness to integrate with different trades as well as BIM issues [75,76].

7.1.2. Organizational Challenges

Implementing our proposed process necessitates significant organizational transformations across design offices, construction companies, and facility management teams. Such transformations often require stakeholders to shift away from established practices, leading to resistance and hesitation in adopting new methodologies. Organizational challenges in adopting DTs are well documented and encompass a range of barriers, including low levels of knowledge, limited technology acceptance, unclear value propositions, and the need for cross-disciplinary collaboration [77].

For example, a systematic review identified critical barriers to the application of digital technologies in construction health and safety, including technical issues, training and knowledge gaps, implementation challenges, data analysis limitations, and system efficiency problems [78]. Similarly, another study identified thirty-seven barriers to using digital technologies to implement circular economy practices in the construction industry, categorized into areas such as organizational, infrastructure, regulatory, and technological challenges [79]. These findings illustrate the global nature of these challenges, transcending specific regional or organizational contexts.

To address these challenges, our proposed process provides a structured framework for eliciting transformational requirements, evaluating organizational changes, and assessing the successful implementation of these transformations. The framework emphasizes stakeholder engagement, iterative feedback, and clear value propositions, which are critical to fostering acceptance and ensuring success. By aligning with Kotter's principles for leading organizational change [80–83], our approach facilitates the smooth integration of digital twin technologies into established workflows, making the transformation more manageable and sustainable.

Author Contributions: Conceptualization, P.Z.; methodology, P.Z., A.J., L.S., H.E. and G.F.; writing—original draft preparation, P.Z., L.S. and H.E.; writing—review and editing, P.Z., A.J., L.S., H.E., G.F. and M.F.; visualization, P.Z., H.E. and L.S.; supervision, P.Z.; funding acquisition, M.F. and G.F. All authors have read and agreed to the published version of the manuscript.

Funding: The research leading to these results has received funding from FFG projects BIM2BEM-Flow [72] and Tunnel Information Modeling [73].

Data Availability Statement: Dataset available on request from the authors.

Conflicts of Interest: The authors declare no conflict of interest.

References

1. Gozde, B. Digital Twin Research in the AECO-FM Industry. *J. Build. Eng.* **2021**, *40*, 102730.
2. Begić, H.; Galić, M. A Systematic Review of Construction 4.0 in the Context of the BIM 4.0 Premise. *Buildings* **2021**, *11*, 337. [CrossRef]
3. Tang, S.; Sheldon, D.R.; Eastman, C.M.; Pishdad-Bozorgi, P.; Xinghua, G. A review of building information modeling (BIM) and the internet of things (IoT) devices integration: Present status and future trends. *Autom. Constr.* **2019**, *101*, 127–139. [CrossRef]
4. Farwick, M.; Schweda, C.M.; Breu, R.; Hanschke, I. A situational method for semi-automated Enterprise Architecture Documentation. *Softw. Syst. Model.* **2016**, *15*, 397–426. [CrossRef]
5. Breu, R. Ten Principles for Living Models—A Manifesto of Change-Driven Software Engineering. In Proceedings of the 2010 International Conference on Complex, Intelligent and Software Intensive Systems, Krakow, Poland, 15–18 February 2010.
6. Beck, K.; Beedle, M. Manifesto for Agile Software Development. 2001. Available online: http://agilemanifesto.org (accessed on 4 October 2022).
7. Chow, T.; Cao, D.-B. A survey study of critical success factors in agile software projects. *J. Syst. Softw.* **2008**, *81*, 961–971. [CrossRef]
8. Kosicki, M.; Tsiliakos, M.; ElAshry, K.; Borgstrom, O.; Rod, A.; Tarabishy, S.; Nguyen, C.; Davis, A.; Tsigkari, M. Towards DesignOps Design Development, Delivery and Operations for the AECO Industry. In *Towards Radical Regeneration*; Springer International Publishing: Cham, Switzerland, 2022.
9. Sakikhales, M.H.; Stravoravdis, S. Using agile project management and BIM for improved building performance. In *Building Information Modelling, Building Performance, Design and Smart Construction*; Springer: Berlin/Heidelberg, Germany, 2017; pp. 65–78.
10. Zech, P.; Jäger, A.; Fröch, G.; Pfluger, R.; Breu, R. Agile, continuous building energy modeling and simulation. *Simulation* **2024**, 00375497241251852. [CrossRef]
11. Ning, G.; Singh, V.; Taylor, C.; London, K.; Brankovic, L. Building Information Modelling: An Issue of Adoption and Change Management. In Proceedings of the ICAN Conference 2007, Sydney, Australia, 9–12 July 2007.
12. Davis, C.W. *Agile Metrics in Action: Measuring and Enhancing the Performance of Agile Teams*; Manning Publications: New York, NY, USA, 2015.
13. Succar, B.; Sher, W.; Williams, A. Measuring BIM performance: Five metrics. *Archit. Eng. Des. Manag.* **2012**, *8*, 120–142. [CrossRef]
14. Fred, D.D.; Bagozzi, R.P.; Warshaw, P.R. User Acceptance of Computer Technology: A Comparison of Two Theoretical Models. *Manag. Sci.* **1989**, *35*, 982–1003.
15. Yilmaz, G.; Salter, L.; McFarlane, D.; Schönfuß, B. Low-cost (Shoestring) digital solution areas for enabling digitalisation in construction SMEs. *Comput. Ind.* **2023**, *150*, 103941. [CrossRef]
16. Hevner, R.; March, S.T.; Park, J.; Ram, S. Design Science in Information Systems Research. *MIS Q.* **2004**, *28*, 75–105. [CrossRef]

17. Wieringa, R.J. *Design Science Methodology for Information Systems and Software Engineering*; Springer: Berlin/Heidelberg, Germany, 2014.
18. Radhakisan, B.; Gill, H. Cyber-physical systems. *Impact Control. Technol.* **2011**, *12*, 161–166.
19. Wolf, W. Cyber-physical systems. *Computer* **2009**, *42*, 88–89. [CrossRef]
20. Chi-Sheng, S.; Jyun-Jhe, C.; Reijers, N.; Tei-Wei, K. Designing CPS/IoT applications for smart buildings and cities. *IET Cyber-Phys. Syst. Theory Appl.* **2016**, *1*, 3–12.
21. Ragunathan, R.; Insup, L.; Liu, S.; Stankovic, J. Cyber-physical systems: The next computing revolution. In Proceedings of the 47th Design Automation Conference, New York, NY, USA, 13–18 June 2010.
22. Borrmann, A.; König, M.; Koch, C.; Beetz, J. *Building Information Modeling: Technology Foundations and Industry Practice*; Springer: Berlin/Heidelberg, Germany, 2018.
23. Azhar, S. Building Information Modeling (BIM): Trends, Benefits, Risks, and Challenges for the AEC Industry. *Leadersh. Manag. Eng.* **2011**, *11*, 241–252. [CrossRef]
24. Galler, R.; Huemer, C.; Bednar, T.; Huymajer, M.; Wenighofer, R.; Paskaleva, G.; Steiner, B.; Melnyk, O. Aktuelle Forschung im Bereich der Digitalisierung des konventionellen Tunnelbaus. *BHM Berg Hüttenmännische Monatshefte* **2023**, *168*, 601–607. [CrossRef]
25. *ISO 19650-1:2018*; International Organization for Standardization Organization and Digitization of Information About Buildings and Civil Engineering Works, Including Building Information Modelling (BIM)—Information Management Using Building Information Modelling—Part 1: Concepts and Principles. ISO: Geneva, Switzerland, 2018. Available online: https://www.iso.org/ (accessed on 23 November 2024).
26. Grieves, M.; Vickers, J. Digital twin: Mitigating unpredictable, undesirable emergent behavior in complex systems. In *Transdisciplinary Perspectives on Complex Systems*; Springer: Berlin/Heidelberg, Germany, 2017; pp. 85–113.
27. Kritzinger, W.; Karner, M.; Traar, G.; Henjes, J.; Sihn, W. Digital Twin in manufacturing: A categorical literature review and classification. *IFAC-Pap.* **2018**, *51*, 1016–1022. [CrossRef]
28. Singh, M.; Fuenmayer, E.; Hinchy, E.P.; Qiao, Y.; Murray, N.; Devine, D.; Twin, D. Digital Twin: Origin to Future. *Appl. Syst. Innov.* **2021**, *4*, 36. [CrossRef]
29. Flora, M.; Weiser, T.; Zech, P.; Fontana, A.; Ruepp, A.; Bergmeister, K. Added value in mechanized tunnelling by intelligent systems. *Geomech. Tunn.* **2021**, *14*, 522–599.
30. Fuller; Fan, Z.; Day, C.; Barlow, C.; Twin, D. Challenges and Open Research. *IEEE Access* **2020**, *8*, 108952–108971. [CrossRef]
31. Boje; Guerriero, A.; Kubicki, S.; Rezgui, Y. Towards a semantic Construction Digital Twin: Directions for future research. *Autom. Constr.* **2020**, *114*, 103179. [CrossRef]
32. Balaji, S.; Murugaiyan, M.S. Waterfall vs. V-Model vs. Agile: A comparative study on SDLC. *Int. J. Inf. Technol. Bus. Manag.* **2012**, *2*, 26–30.
33. Andrei, B.-A.; Casu-Pop, A.-C.; Gheorghe, S.-C.; Boiangiu, C.-A. A study on using waterfall and agile methods in software project management. *J. Inf. Syst. Oper. Manag.* **2019**, *13*, 125–135.
34. Schwaber, K.; Sutherland, J.; Alliance, S. The scrum guide. *Scrum Alliance* **2011**, *21*, 1–38.
35. Dybå, T.; Dingsøyr, T. Empirical studies of agile software development: A systematic review. *Inf. Softw. Technol.* **2008**, *50*, 833–859. [CrossRef]
36. Office of Government Commerce. *ITIL Version 3 Service Transition*; The Stationary Office: London, UK, 2007.
37. Architekten-Verein, Ö.I.-U. *BIM-Anwendungsfälle Öffentlicher Auftraggeber*; ÖIAV-Resort "Öffentliche Auftraggeber": Vienna, Austria, 2023.
38. Siemens. Digital Tunnel: Schneller Eröffnet. Sicherer Betrieben. 2024. Available online: https://www.siemens.com/de/de/produkte/automatisierung/produkte-fuer-spezifische-anforderungen/tunnelautomatisierung.html (accessed on 9 September 2024).
39. Deng, M.; Menassa, C.C.; Kamat, V.R. From BIM to digital twins: A systematic review of the evolution of intelligent building representations in the AEC-FM industry. *J. Inf. Technol. Constr.* **2021**, *26*, 58–83. [CrossRef]
40. Chu, J.; Varaskin, S.; Klotz, U.; Mengé, P. Construction Processes. In Proceedings of the 17th International Conference on Soil Mechanics and Geotechnical Engineering, Alexandria, Egypt, 5–9 October 2009.
41. Bernd-Holger, S. Cyber-physical Systems Engineering. In *Engineering Trustworthy Software Systems*; Springer: Berlin/Heidelberg, Germany, 2016; pp. 256–289.
42. Gilb, T.; Finzi, S. *Principles of Software Engineering Management*; Addison-Wesley Reading: Boston, MA, USA, 1988.
43. Samireh, J.; Wohlin, C. Global software engineering and agile practices: A systematic review. *J. Softw.* **2012**, *24*, 643–659.
44. Hazzan, O.; Dubinsky, Y. *Agile Software Engineering*; Springer Science & Business Media: Berlin/Heidelberg, Germany, 2009.
45. Rumane, R. *Quality Management in Construction Projects*; CRC Press: Boca Raton, FL, USA, 2017.
46. Borrmann, M.; König, C. *Koch and Beetz Jakob, Building Information Modeling*; Springer Fachmedien Wiesbaden GmbH: Wiesbaden, Germany, 2021.

47. Sillitti, A.; Succi, G. Source Code Repositories and Agile Methods. In Proceedings of the XP 2005: Extreme Programming and Agile Processes in Software Engineering, Sheffield, UK, 18–23 June 2005.
48. Nikola, M.; Granic, A. Technology acceptance model: A literature review from 1986 to 2013. *Univers. Access Inf. Soc.* **2015**, *14*, 81–95.
49. Riemenscheider, C.K.; Hardgrave, B. Explaining software development tool use with the technology acceptance model. *J. Comput. Inf. Syst.* **2001**, *41*, 1–8.
50. Hair, J.F., Jr.; Hult, G.T.M.; Ringle, C.R.; Sarstedt, M. *A Primer on Partial Least Squares Structural Equation Modeling (PLS-SEM)*; Sage Publications: London, UK, 2021.
51. Hair, J.F., Jr.; Hult, G.T.M.; Ringle, C.M.; Sarstedt, M.; Danks, N.P.; Ray, S. *Partial Least Squares Structural Equation Modeling (PLS-SEM) Using R: A Workbook*; Springer Nature: Berlin/Heidelberg, Germany, 2021.
52. Latan, H.; Noonan, R.; Matthews, L. Partial least squares path modeling. In *Partial Least Squares Path Modeling: Basic Concepts, Methodological Issues and Applications*; Springer: Berlin/Heidelberg, Germany, 2017.
53. Ray, S.; Danks, N.; Calero-Valdez, A. SEMinR: Domain-Specific Language for Building, Estimating, and Visualizing Structural Equation Models in R. 2021. Available online: https://ssrn.com/abstract=3900621 (accessed on 21 January 2025).
54. Hair, J.; Alamer, A. Partial least squares structural equation modeling (PLS-SEM) in second language and education research: Guidelines using an applied example. *Res. Methods Appl. Linguist.* **2022**, *1*, 100027. [CrossRef]
55. Nitzl; Roldan, J.L.; Cepeda, G. Mediation analysis in partial least squares path modeling: Helping researchers discuss more sophisticated models. *Ind. Manag. Data Syst.* **2016**, *116*, 1849–1864. [CrossRef]
56. Zhao, X.; Lynch, J.G., Jr.; Chen, Q. Reconsidering Baron and Kenny: Myths and truths about mediation analysis. *J. Consum. Res.* **2010**, *37*, 197–206. [CrossRef]
57. Preacher, K.J.; Hayes, A.F. Asymptotic and resampling strategies for assessing and comparing indirect effects in multiple mediator models. *Behav. Res. Methods* **2008**, *40*, 879–891. [CrossRef] [PubMed]
58. Zech, P.; Fröch, G.; Breu, R. A Requirements Study on Model Repositories for Digital Twins in Construction Engineering. In Proceedings of the International Conference on Cooperative Information Systems, Gröningen, The Netherlands, 30 October–3 November 2023.
59. Zech, P.; Pobitzer, P.; Fröch, G.; Breu, R. A Proposal for a Models-meet-Data Repository For Digital Twins in Construction Engineering. In Proceedings of the 2024 IEEE 21st International Conference on Software Architecture Companion (ICSA-C), Hyderabad, India, 4–8 June 2024.
60. Liu, F.; Jallow, A.K.; Anumba, C.J.; Wu, D. A Framework for Integrating Change Management with Building Information Modeling. *Comput. Civ. Build. Eng.* **2014**, *2014*, 439–446.
61. Ebert; Gallardo, G.; Hernantes, J.; Serrano, N. DevOps. *IEEE Softw.* **2016**, *33*, 94–100. [CrossRef]
62. Qiuchen, L.; Xiang, X.; Parlikad, A.K.; Schooling, J.M. Digital twin-enabled anomaly detection for built asset monitoring in operation and maintenance. *Autom. Constr.* **2020**, *118*, 103277.
63. Shahzad, M.; Shafiq, M.T.; Douglas, D.; Kassem, M. Digital Twins in Built Environments: An Investigation of the Characteristics, Applications, and Challenges. *Buildings* **2022**, *12*, 120. [CrossRef]
64. Broo, G.; Schooling, J. Digital twins in infrastructure: Definitions, current practices, challenges and strategies. *Int. J. Constr. Manag.* **2021**, *23*, 1254–1263. [CrossRef]
65. Donkers, A.J.; Yang, D.; de Vries, B.; Baken, N.H. Real-time building performance monitoring using semantic digital twins. in LDAC 2021 Linked Data in Architecture and Construction. In Proceedings of the 9th Linked Data in Architecture and Construction Workshop, Luxembourg, 11–13 October 2021.
66. Gang, Y.; Wang, Y.; Mao, Z.; Hu, M.; Sugumaran, V.; Wang, K.Y. A digital twin-based decision analysis framework for operation and maintenance of tunnels. *Tunn. Undergr. Space Technol.* **2021**, *116*, 104125.
67. Marc, W.; Markus, M.-W.; Herbrand, M.; Ullerich, C. The concept of digital twin to revolutionise infrastructure maintenance: The pilot project smartBRIDGE Hamburg. In Proceedings of the 27th ITS World Congress, Hamburg, Germany, 11–15 October 2021.
68. Afzal, M.; Man-Li, R.Y.; Shoaib, M.; Ayyub, M.F.; Tagliabue, L.C.; Bilal, M.; Ghafoor, H.; Manta, O. Delving into the Digital Twin Developments and Applications in the Construction Industry: A PRISMA Approach. *Sustainability* **2024**, *15*, 16436. [CrossRef]
69. Reja, V.K.; Pradeep, M.S.; Varghese, K. Digital Twins for Construction Project Management (DT CPM): Applications and Future Research Directions. *J. Inst. Eng. (India) Ser. A* **2024**, *105*, 793–807. [CrossRef]
70. Yin, R.K. *Case Study Research Design and Methods*; Sage: London, UK, 2014.
71. BIM2BEM-Flow. 2021. Available online: https://projekte.ffg.at/projekt/4396767 (accessed on 30 September 2022).
72. TIM. Tunnel Information Modelling. 2021. Available online: https://projekte.ffg.at/projekt/3368110 (accessed on 30 September 2022).
73. Pauwels, P.; Zhang, S.; Lee, Y.-C. Semantic web technologies in AEC industry: A literature overview. *Autom. Constr.* **2017**, *73*, 145–165. [CrossRef]

74. Zech, P.; Nardin, C.; Ristov, S.; Flora, M.; Breu, R. Digital-Twins-as-a-Service in Construction Engineering. In Proceedings of the 2024 IEEE 20th International Conference on Automation Science and Engineering, Bari, Italy, 28 August–1 September 2024.
75. Zech; Zech, P.; Goldin, E.; Hammes, S.; Geisler-Moroder, D.; Pfluger, R.; Breu, R. Model-Based Auto-Commissioning of Building Control Systems. In Proceedings of the 26th International Conference on Enterprise Information Systems (ICEIS 2024), Angers, France, 28–30 April 2024.
76. Zech, P.; Plörer, D.; Pfluger, R.; Breu, R. Scalable Building Energy Efficiency Balancing. In Proceedings of the 2024 Annual Modeling and Simulation Conference (ANNSIM), Washington, DC, USA, 20–23 May 2024.
77. De-Graft, J.O.; Perera, S.; Osei-Kyei, R.; Rashidi, M.; Bamdad, K.; Famakinwa, T. Barriers to the Adoption of Digital Twin in the Construction Industry: A Literature Review. *Informatics* **2023**, *10*, 14. [CrossRef]
78. Daniel, I.; Oshodi, O.S.; Nwankwo, N.; Emuze, F.A.; Chinyio, E. Barriers to the Application of Digital Technologies in Construction Health and Safety: A Systematic Review. *Buildings* **2024**, *14*, 2386. [CrossRef]
79. Thirumal, S.; Udawatta, N.; Karunasena, G.; Al-Ameri, R. Barriers to Adopting Digital Technologies to Implement Circular Economy Practices in the Construction Industry: A Systematic Literature Review. *Sustainability* **2024**, *16*, 3185. [CrossRef]
80. Slaman, Y.; Broten, N. *An Analysis of John P. Kotter's Leading Change*; Macat Library: London, UK, 2017.
81. Gustavsson, T. Benefits of agile project management in a non-software development context: A literature review. In Proceedings of the Fifth International Scientific Conference on Project Management in the Baltic Countries, Riga, Latvia, 14–15 April 2016; University of Latvia: Riga, Latvia, 2016.
82. Sheetal, S.; Sarkar, D.; Gupta, D. Agile processes and methodologies: A conceptual study. *Int. J. Comput. Sci. Eng.* **2012**, *4*, 892.
83. Khajavi, S.H.; Motlagh, N.H.; Jaribion, A.; Werner, L.C.; Holmström, J. Digital Twin: Vision, Benefits, Boundaries, and Creation for buildings. *IEEE Access* **2019**, *7*, 147406–147419. [CrossRef]

buildings

MDPI

Article

Dynamic Multi-Model Container Framework for Cloud-Based Distributed Digital Twins (dDTws)

Nidhal Al-Sadoon [1,*], Raimar J. Scherer [1] and Christoph F. Strnadl [2]

[1] Institute of Construction Informatics, TU Dresden, 01069 Dresden, Germany; raimar.scherer@tu-dresden.de
[2] Gaia-X AISBL, CTO Office, 1210 Brussels, Belgium; christoph.strnadl@gaia-x.eu
* Correspondence: nidhal.al_sadoon@tu-dresden.de

Abstract: The increasing complexity of data management in the Architecture, Engineering, and Construction (AEC) industry, driven by the adoption of distributed digital twins (dDTws) and cloud-based solutions, presents challenges in interoperability, data sovereignty, and scalability. Existing Building Information Modeling (BIM) and Common Data Environment (CDE) frameworks often fall short in addressing these issues due to their reliance on centralized and proprietary systems. This paper introduces a novel framework that transforms the Information Container for Linked Document Delivery (ICDD) into a dynamic, graph-based architecture. Unlike conventional file-based ICDD implementations, this approach enables fine-grained, semantically rich linking and querying across distributed models while maintaining data sovereignty and version control. The framework is designed to enhance real-time collaboration, ensure secure and sovereign data management, and improve interoperability across diverse project stakeholders. The framework leverages graph databases, semantic web technologies, and ISO standards such as ISO 21597 to facilitate seamless data exchange, automated linking, and advanced version control. Key functionalities include federated data storage, compliance with local and international regulations, and support for multidisciplinary workflows in large-scale AEC projects. To demonstrate the feasibility of the proposed framework, a simplified use case scenario is implemented and analyzed. By addressing critical challenges and enabling seamless integration of emerging technologies such as digital twins, this study advances the state of the art in data management for the AEC industry, providing a robust foundation for future innovations.

Keywords: distributed digital twins; data sovereignty; graph-based framework; interoperability; Architecture, Engineering, and Construction (AEC); semantic web technologies; ISO 21597; data management

1. Introduction

The rapid digital transformation in the Architecture, Engineering, and Construction (AEC) sector has introduced complex data management challenges that necessitate innovative approaches to handle the vast, multidisciplinary data generated across a project's lifecycle. The advent of digital twins in the Architecture, Engineering, and Construction industry has transformed construction project management, enabling real-time data monitoring, analysis, and optimization. However, with this shift towards data-driven methodologies, there is a growing emphasis on construction data management and data sovereignty, as stakeholders increasingly require secure and interoperable data frameworks that protect proprietary and sensitive information. Ensuring data sovereignty—where each entity retains control over its data assets—presents both technical and regulatory challenges. These challenges are exacerbated in cloud-based environments where distributed digital twins (dDTws) are integrated across diverse disciplines, raising concerns around secure data sharing, access control, and version management [1,2].

The construction industry's increasing adoption of advanced digital technologies like Building Information Modeling (BIM), Digital Twins (DTws), and cloud-based platforms has significantly enhanced project collaboration and lifecycle data integration. However, ongoing challenges around interoperability and data sovereignty continue to pose significant obstacles to these systems. While these tools enhance data sharing and operational efficiency, they remain constrained by significant challenges related to interoperability and data sovereignty. The lack of universal standards across BIM software and platforms hinders seamless data exchanges, leading to inefficiencies and potential data silos [3]. Furthermore, cloud-based systems, though critical for scalability and collaboration, raise concerns over data ownership and control, as proprietary data may be stored across multiple jurisdictions, potentially breaching local regulatory requirements [4,5]. Addressing these limitations is pivotal to realizing the full potential of digital transformation in the AEC industry while ensuring secure and sovereign data management practices.

Building upon the foundational multimodel methodology introduced by Fuchs, this research presents a graph-based dynamic multimodel container framework for distributed digital twins. Unlike conventional file-based multimodel containers, the proposed framework leverages graph databases to enhance scalability, facilitate real-time collaboration, and uphold data ownership principles. By embedding data access control mechanisms, this model provides stakeholders with greater control over their data assets, advancing a decentralized approach to construction data management. This research addresses critical challenges in data management for cloud-based distributed digital twins (dDTws) in the Architecture, Engineering, and Construction (AEC) industry. Specifically, it focuses on the integration of graph-based dynamic multimodel container frameworks to enhance data interoperability, sovereignty, and scalability. To achieve these objectives, this study formulates key research questions aimed at addressing gaps in existing frameworks and exploring innovative solutions for real-time collaboration:

RQ 1: How can a graph-based dynamic multimodel container framework enhance interoperability in cloud-based distributed digital twins (dDTws) for the AEC industry?

RQ 2: How can the proposed framework ensure data sovereignty in distributed digital twin environments while complying with international and local data regulations?

RQ 3: How can the integration of technologies like digital twins, semantic web, and graph-based databases improve real-time collaboration across diverse stakeholders in construction projects?

This paper is structured as follows: Section 2 presents a comprehensive literature review, outlining the state of the art in data management, interoperability, and data sovereignty in cloud-based distributed digital twins (dDTws) within the AEC industry. Section 3 introduces the proposed graph-based dynamic multimodel container framework, detailing its architecture, components, and functionalities. Section 4 discusses the research methodology employed to validate the framework, including case studies and performance benchmarks. Section 5 presents the results and analysis, highlighting the framework's impact on interoperability, scalability, and data sovereignty. Finally, Section 6 concludes the study by summarizing the findings, discussing implications for the industry, and identifying directions for future research.

2. Background

2.1. Foundations of Construction Data Management

In the Architecture, Engineering, and Construction (AEC) industry, the surge in digital tools such as Building Information Modeling (BIM) and digital twins has fundamentally transformed data generation, accessibility, and usage. BIM serves as a comprehensive digital representation of a building's physical and functional characteristics, facilitating collaboration among stakeholders and enhancing decision-making processes. Digital twins extend this concept by creating dynamic, real-time digital replicas of physical assets, enabling continuous monitoring and optimization of building performance. The integration of these technologies results in the generation of vast amounts of data, encompassing design specifications, construction processes, and operational parameters. This influx of data necessitates advanced frameworks for effective management, including data integration, interoperability, storage, processing, security, and privacy. This evolution supports sophisticated project management techniques but also brings complex data challenges that necessitate advanced management frameworks to handle the extensive data generated throughout a project's lifecycle [6–8].

Koutamanis [9] highlighted that the integration of these technologies requires advanced data processing, storage, and management solutions to handle diverse data types and formats, ranging from real-time sensor data to historical building information. This integration challenge is central to data complexity in AEC. A systematic review highlights the development of emerging technologies facilitating the evolution of BIM to digital twins in the built environment, emphasizing the need for effective data management strategies to leverage these advancements [10,11]. Omrany et al. [12] emphasized that effective data management can address issues such as data silos, redundant data storage, and security vulnerabilities by centralizing data access and enforcing standardized protocols. Such frameworks are crucial for supporting collaborative workflows, minimizing errors, and maintaining data consistency across the lifecycle.

The proliferation of data in AEC projects introduces challenges related to data interoperability, integration, and security. Managing large datasets across various project phases and ensuring seamless data sharing between stakeholders' demand advanced data management frameworks. In modern AEC projects, data management has become essential for harnessing the potential of BIM and digital twins. As data volume and complexity continue to grow, robust frameworks are necessary to ensure effective data integration, accessibility, and security. Implementing these frameworks can enable the AEC industry to leverage digital transformation fully, optimizing project performance and achieving better outcomes throughout the building lifecycle.

2.2. Interoperability Challenges in Existing BIM and CDE Solutions

Interoperability has been a persistent challenge in the Architecture, Engineering, and Construction (AEC) industry, as project stakeholders increasingly rely on digital tools to manage complex projects. With the rise of Building Information Modeling (BIM), digital twins, and other collaborative technologies, the need for seamless data exchange has intensified. However, the lack of standardized protocols across software platforms hinders effective communication and data sharing, resulting in inefficiencies, data duplication, and project delays [13,14].

BIM is widely adopted as a digital tool for modeling and managing construction data. However, the interoperability challenges between BIM tools primarily stem from the fragmentation of software ecosystems and their reliance on proprietary file formats. These interoperability gaps manifest in various forms. For example, inefficiencies arise when project stakeholders must manually merge design files from different disciplines, introducing delays and potential errors. Data silos are prevalent as actors rely on isolated authoring tools with limited cross-communication, leading to fragmentation. Additionally, exporting models often results in information loss—such as missing metadata or relational context—due to incompatible data schemas or software limitations. While open standards like the Industry Foundation Classes (IFC) and BIM Collaboration Format (BCF) are widely promoted, their adoption is inconsistent, leading to incomplete data transfers or loss of semantic information during model exchange [15]. For example, the IFC schema often struggles to capture project-specific data attributes, which causes difficulties in transferring complex BIM models between tools [16]. Common Data Environments (CDEs), on the other hand, provide a centralized platform for managing project information, enabling real-time collaboration. However, interoperability issues arise when integrating heterogeneous data sources such as BIM models, documents, and schedules. The absence of standardized CDE interfaces and data exchange protocols restricts cross-platform compatibility, resulting in data silos and inefficiencies [17].

Research has extensively highlighted these interoperability issues. For instance, Lu et al. [18] discuss the challenges of integrating BIM and digital twins, emphasizing the need for standardized data formats to facilitate effective communication among stakeholders. Similarly, Alonso et al. [19] highlight the interoperability challenges in the AEC industry, noting that the lack of standardized protocols leads to data silos and inefficiencies. Furthermore, Tulubas and Arditi [20] examine the impact of digital transformation on the AEC industry, identifying interoperability as a critical factor affecting the successful implementation of BIM and digital twins. Existing BIM systems primarily rely on file-based data exchanges, such as those using Industry Foundation Classes (IFC). However, IFC-based workflows often fail to capture the full range of project-specific data attributes, leading to information loss and misinterpretation during transfers [21].

To address these limitations, recent developments focus on linked data and multimodel approaches. The Information Container for Linked Document Delivery (ICDD), introduced under ISO 21597 [22], offers a potential solution by enabling the structuring and linking of heterogeneous data within a container model. However, its practical application is limited by the lack of seamless integration with existing CDEs and the absence of automated validation mechanisms for linked data [23]. Unlike traditional federated CDEs that mainly centralize access to static models, the proposed framework supports dynamic and versioned multimodel management. It further introduces semantic linking across heterogeneous models and aligns with the needs of distributed digital twin environments, enabling greater flexibility, scalability, and real-time model synchronization across multiple stakeholders. Nevertheless, while ICDD improves structured data exchange, it remains constrained by its file-based nature and dependency on manual validation processes. Additionally, the file-based nature of ICDD constrains real-time collaboration, as updates must often be manually reconciled across different stakeholders.

2.3. *Shared Data Environments and Cloud-Based Solutions*

The Architecture, Engineering, and Construction (AEC) industry has embraced shared data environments (SDEs) and cloud-based solutions to address the inherent complexity of project collaboration and data management. Shared data environments (SDEs) are centralized or distributed platforms designed to collect, manage, and share project data among various stakeholders throughout a project's lifecycle. They aim to provide a "single source of truth", where data are accessible, reliable, and up-to-date. Building Information Modeling (BIM) tools, often integrated with SDEs, enable stakeholders to visualize, simulate, and coordinate project components effectively [24]. Standards such as the BIM Collaboration Format (BCF) and Industry Foundation Classes (IFC) have been developed to facilitate data exchange, although their adoption and implementation remain inconsistent across regions and organizations [25]. These technologies have transformed traditional workflows, enabling better coordination and integration across stakeholders. However, challenges such as interoperability, data ownership, and scalability remain. While SDEs enhance project coordination, their centralized nature often leads to challenges related to data control and access rights. Proprietary solutions provided by leading BIM vendors, such as Autodesk and Bentley Systems, often lock users into specific ecosystems, which hinders interoperability [26].

Cloud-based solutions have become integral to modern SDEs, offering scalability, flexibility, and remote access to data. They enable real-time collaboration, reduce IT infrastructure costs, and provide enhanced data security through advanced encryption and access control mechanisms [27]. These solutions are particularly valuable for distributed teams, as they allow seamless interaction and data sharing regardless of geographical location. However, cloud-based systems introduce challenges related to data sovereignty and regulatory compliance. For instance, sensitive project data stored in international servers may fall under foreign jurisdiction, raising concerns about intellectual property rights and adherence to local laws [25,26]. Moreover, the reliance on cloud service providers can create dependency risks, where disruptions or changes in service agreements may significantly impact project workflows.

Researchers and practitioners are exploring federated platforms to address the limitations of centralized SDEs and cloud solutions. These platforms distribute data across multiple systems while maintaining interoperability through standardized protocols and governance frameworks. Federated solutions ensure that stakeholders retain sovereignty over their data while enabling collaboration through regulated data-sharing agreements [26]. Governance models, such as data cooperatives, have been proposed to provide a trust-based framework for shared data environments. These cooperatives establish shared ownership and decision-making processes among stakeholders, ensuring that data use aligns with collective goals while safeguarding individual interests [27].

2.4. Data Sovereignty in Cloud-Based AEC Environments

In the Architecture, Engineering, and Construction (AEC) industry, the shift towards cloud-based systems has revolutionized data sharing, collaboration, and project management. However, these advances have also raised significant concerns regarding data sovereignty—the ability of stakeholders to retain control and ownership over their data while ensuring compliance with local regulatory frameworks. Cloud computing inherently involves the storage of data across multiple jurisdictions, which can lead to conflicts between local data protection laws and global cloud services. For example, the General Data Protection Regulation (GDPR) in Europe imposes strict restrictions on the cross-border transfer of data, potentially clashing with the global infrastructure of major cloud providers like AWS or Microsoft Azure [28]. In the context of AEC, Turk et al. [29] highlighted that construction projects involve a dynamic network of partners, forming a "virtual organization" that changes throughout the project lifecycle. This dynamic nature complicates security management as partners may simultaneously collaborate on different projects with varying security requirements and potentially conflicting interests. The lack of clear jurisdictional boundaries can create vulnerabilities and legal risks.

One promising approach to addressing data sovereignty concerns is the use of federated cloud systems. These systems enable stakeholders to share and manage resources while retaining local control over data storage and compliance [30]. Federated cloud environments align with the principles of data sovereignty by distributing data across nodes managed by different organizations, ensuring that sensitive information remains within its regulatory jurisdiction [31]. Jaskula et al. [32] propose a federated CDE using blockchain to integrate multiple CDE solutions and provide a single source of truth for project data, aiming to address limitations of centralized BIM implementations. They argue that blockchain's decentralization, data immutability, and intellectual property protection can potentially solve some of the sovereignty challenges [33].

The integration of federated data platforms with semantic web technologies is another emerging trend in the AEC industry. Werbrouck [16] highlighted that these technologies provide machine-readable data structures, allowing stakeholders to enforce data sovereignty rules dynamically. Additionally, organizations can leverage access control mechanisms and metadata validation to ensure that only authorized entities can access sensitive information. From an organizational perspective, clear governance frameworks are crucial. Implementing contractual agreements that outline data ownership, usage rights, and compliance responsibilities can mitigate disputes and enhance trust among project participants [30]. Ensuring data sovereignty in cloud-based environments also entails addressing security and privacy concerns. Sacks et al. [34] propose a Cloud BIM (CBIM) paradigm that leverages semantic web technologies to integrate federated data platforms and address the limitations of current BIM practices, particularly in collaborative multidisciplinary design. The integration of federated data platforms with semantic web technologies holds significant potential for transforming BIM practices and creating a more intelligent and interconnected data ecosystem for the AEC industry.

Weber [28] advocates for data governance frameworks like Gaia-X, emphasizing the importance of data sovereignty in cloud-based AEC environments. She highlights that Gaia-X, a European project for federated and secure data infrastructure, supports decentralized infrastructure solutions. It emphasizes transparency, data security, data protection, interoperability, and scalability in its services, reflecting values aligned with data sovereignty. She advocates for data governance frameworks like Gaia-X, emphasizing the importance of data sovereignty in cloud-based AEC environments. By enabling data analysis across decentralized datasets while preserving local privacy, such frameworks offer practical solutions for AEC projects involving multiple stakeholders and jurisdictions.

2.5. *Advancing Construction with Semantic Web Technologies*

To overcome the challenges of fragmented data exchange in distributed environments, it is necessary to move beyond static multimodel containers and adopt more flexible data structures. This shift aligns with the broader push for dynamic, service-oriented infrastructures in the AEC sector. As Godager [35] aptly observed, "existing BIM formats can meet future requirements, where the potential in the construction industry to fully utilize semantic web technology is difficult with today's BIM standards" This vision reinforces the rationale for a distributed, graph-based multimodel container framework that adapts to varying stakeholder needs and project configurations.

To facilitate information exchange in the architecture, engineering, construction, and operation (AECO) sector, several international standards have been agreed upon. The Industry Foundation Classes (IFC) was the first standard developed by buildingSMART International [36]. In a "conventional" building information modelling (BIM) model, IFC is primarily used to represent the building design. However, most of the existing BIM authoring tools also support the export of building models as an IFC file. To capture the design details of the building, IFC contains a sophisticated schema. The second standard is the ISO 19650 series that standardizes information management covering the whole life cycle of an asset under construction using BIM. It is a business process standard that defines requirements for organizing operations information in construction processes. The standard defines a procedure for the appointing party to specify requirements for information delivery and management [34]. The series provides specifications for the execution of BIM-based construction projects. As a single source of truth, the common data environment (CDE) is defined according to ISO 19650 for information delivery aspects. The CDE is the cornerstone of transition in the processing of building data by facilitating the structuring information and data exchange processes in the course of a project between different stakeholders and providing tools for cloud-based collaboration [37]. Using centralized data storage within a CDE, the risk of data redundancy is reduced and timely access to up-to-date data is ensured. Last but not least, ISO 21597 "Information Container for Linked Document Delivery (ICDD)" specifies ontologies for the representation of interlinked datasets as a single source of information of federated data models and documents that could be used for the exchange of static state of project content between projects parties and also for archiving and documentation purposes.

On the other hand, technologies like digital twins and graph-based containers enhance multi-discipline overarching collaboration. In the course of a project's lifecycle, digital twins serve as a powerful platform for sharing information, fostering collaboration, and enabling informed decisions. It enables real-time sharing of project data, by providing a virtual replica of the physical asset or project and allowing team members from different domains to visualize and interact with the project in a shared virtual environment [38]. As Esser et al. [39] highlight, the iterative nature of AEC projects demands robust version control and change-tracking mechanisms, which are inadequately supported by current file-based data exchange solutions. This reinforces the need for a more dynamic, graph-based multimodel container capable of supporting fine-grained, temporal data management. The adoption of graph-based containers facilitates real-time data interchange and collaboration among stakeholders in the construction industry, resulting in improved project outcomes and heightened efficiency. The advantages are evident as this technology enables seamless communication, immediate progress updates, and early detection of potential issues before they escalate, and ultimately expedites decision-making processes. Considering the numerous parties involved in construction projects—ranging from architects to contractors—it can be daunting to ensure everyone is well informed about developments at each stage. Graph-based containers alleviate these challenges by furnishing a centralized platform where all stakeholders can access pertinent information promptly and without confusion or delay. By doing so, they empower better teamwork coordination leading to overall success while minimizing errors arising from miscommunication or inadequate access to up-to-date plans and documents.

Manipulating these standards made the multi-disciplinary collaboration between teams in a construction project possible. Currently, many collaborative platforms are used to share information in projects. By enabling a continuous flow of information and file updates, these collaborative platforms are seen as an overarching solution to improve collaboration. In a literature review published by Lindholm et al. [38], it is found that merging multiple approaches and leveraging their respective capabilities, such as knowledge graphs, common data environments, and digital twins, could support an integrated, automated system. By utilizing these platforms, all project actors can effectively communicate and collaborate, which results in improved collaboration performance, enhanced interoperability, continuous integration, advanced information retrieval, and streamlined workflows.

3. Approach

In response to the limitations outlined above, this paper introduces a dynamic multimodel container framework. This framework is specifically designed to enable flexible, semantic linking of heterogeneous data sources while preserving model sovereignty and enabling scalable management. The proposed framework constitutes a core component of the iECO project (2022). The project, amongst others, aims at developing a Gaia-X-based decentralized platform for a distributed digital twin and supporting collaboration in the construction industry [40]. In this chapter, we will demonstrate the framework architecture and explain the selection of each component, namely; graph database, dynamic multimodel container (DMMC), and distributed digital twins (dDTws).

3.1. File-Based vs. Graph-Based Multimodel Approach

The Multimodel (MM) approach firstly was developed in the Mefisto project [41] to represent linked building model data. A common basis of the approach is the connection of separate elementary models, in their original state, using ID-based links [42]. The links describe n-array relations between (two or more) individual elements of different models using an XML/XSD representation in separate link models and, together with the elementary models are saved in the MM container (MMC). When the approach was standardized as an Information Container for Linked Document Delivery (ICDD), the links were created and saved in RDF files, and the whole container—including the file with the link model—was compressed as a ZIP archive file with the extension '.icdd', as shown in Figure 1 (on the left). This modular but file-based architecture stores metadata and linksets across multiple RDF/XML documents (e.g., index.rdf, linkset.rdf, model-a.rdf). In contrast, the right side illustrates the proposed graph-based alternative, where the same entities and relationships are natively modeled as nodes and edges in a property graph database (e.g., Neo4j). This enables efficient querying, dynamic updates, and seamless navigation across interconnected models, improving interoperability and scalability for distributed Digital Twin environments. Even though using a file- or document-based database to store RDF data offers advantages such as flexibility and scalability, it is not suitable when dealing with the semantic complexity of multidisciplinary data, maintaining consistent cross-file references, and supporting dynamic, real-time updates across distributed systems.

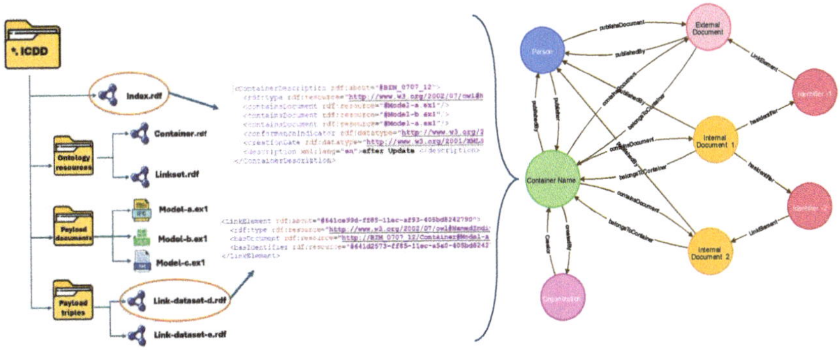

Figure 1. File-based ICDD (**left**) and graph-based multimodel container based on ICDD schema (**right**).

In that respect, however, multiple types of databases need to be considered when it comes to storing RDF triples. The most common choice for storing RDF triples is a relational database. It provides a structured way to store data and allows for efficient retrieval. However, due to its rigid table-based schema, it becomes difficult to represent complex and evolving RDF data structures that do not fit neatly into predefined categories. This mismatch leads to challenges when modeling semantic relationships and dynamically linked entities. Moreover, as the dataset grows, relational databases—especially if not optimized for the application domain—struggle with scalability because complex queries often require numerous joins across large tables, which significantly increases query latency and impacts overall performance [43].

On the other hand, graph databases are schema-free. They store and query RDF data in a more natural way, making it efficient for handling large amounts of interconnected data. They use a graph structure with nodes, edges, and properties (of nodes and edges) to represent and store data. Buron et al. [44] state that the use of graph databases is particularly beneficial for storing RDF triples as it aligns with the nature of the semantic web. By organizing data into easily navigable graphs, queries can be executed quickly without sacrificing accuracy or scalability. However, scalability may depend on the underlying graph database implementation, graph complexity, and deployment strategy, and should be evaluated carefully when applied to large-scale, dense digital twin networks. As such, graph databases are therefore essential when dealing with dynamic and interconnected data sets that require fast and accurate retrieval methods. Moreover, artificial intelligence (AI) technologies can benefit from knowledge graphs, because they provide a reliable semantic for knowledge-driven data storage. They enable semantic linking across sub-graphs, and provide an added layer of information. Knowledge graphs are also a good substitute for exact geometry, as they contain spatial relationships required for machine learning AI tools [37].

3.2. Dynamic Multimodel Container (DMMC)

The Multimodel Engine (MME) was developed firstly by Al-Sadoon et. al. [45] based on the standardized schema of the ICDD to implement functions as specified in ISO 21597, namely: create a container, add (internal and external) document(s), and create links between the added documents and between elements inside them. Then, dynamic functions were added turning it into a Dynamic Multimodel Engine (DMME) to allow for efficient collaboration among parties in a construction project and to provide more valuable services for overarching interdisciplinary decision-making; these functions are:

- Add dynamic values: this function was developed to enable the allocation of multiple dynamic values to elements in the building model, thereby enabling the consideration of dynamically changeable building elements' status at simulation runtime where the dynamic values contribute to real-time interoperability of interlinked simulation components and modules. This is crucial for achieving more reliable and precise simulation outcomes, especially in emergency events [46];
- Automation of document versioning and links update: To expand the workability of the ICDD and enhance its usefulness beyond pure data exchange, dynamic functions were developed. These include automatic document versioning whenever a new document is uploaded into the container and accordingly links of the linked elements contained in the newly added file will be automatically updated. As such, they ensure that the Multimodel container is capable of automatically managing document versions and updating linksets to maintain consistency and validity [47].

However, the DMMC created by this engine was file-based as well and used compressed ZIP files. The document itself is saved in the Payload documents folder, and the created links are saved as RDF files in the Payload triples folder as explained in Section 3.1.

In the file-based multimodel container, the container metadata, namely: container name, organization, names of internal document(s), and URLs, where external documents can be accessed, were saved in the so-called index file. Created links are saved as RDF triplets in a so-called linkset files. However, in our new approach here, we re-enacted the engine as a graph database-based engine using the graph database management system Neo4j, in which the created container and all its content are saved in a graph database instead of a file-based database. In the Neo4j-based implementation of the graph-based

DMME, key nodes include Container, Internal Document, External Document, Document Version, Access Control, Identifier, and Organization. These are linked by relationships such as ContainsDocument, version_Document, hasIdentifier, AllowAccess, and CreatedBy as shown in Figure 2. For example, versioning is handled through version_Document edges connecting multiple versions of a file, while AllowAccess links enforce access policies between Access Control nodes and documents. This graph structure enables flexible, low-latency queries that are essential for cross-referencing documents, tracking provenance, and enforcing fine-grained data governance across disciplines.

Figure 2. The graph-based DMME.

3.3. *Access Controlled Dynamic Mulimodel Container (DMMC)*

Data governance according to the Data Governance Act of the EU (DGA) needs management of the access rights of the data in the DMMC. This access right information should show a sufficient granularity and should be part of the meta-information of the DMMC. Therefore, we propose to restrict the access rights to complete documents and models of the DMMC, because each of these documents does have a unique author and hence an Intellectual Property right (IPR). As a sufficient granularity we propose to add to the DMMC an additional entity namely; **Access Control**. The entity has three properties: *Access Allowed, Access Allowed Partially*, and *Access Not Allowed.* This entity could be added at the document level, to define accessibility when creating links at the document level. Moreover, it could be added at the elements level to facilitate linking at the elements level. In this case, the value of **Access Control**, at the document level, shall be *Access Allowed* when all document elements could be shared for linking or *Access Allowed Partially* when some elements are allowed to be linked. To model partial access, the Access Control node is linked via *AllowAccess* relationships to specific Document Version or Identifier nodes, rather than entire documents. This enables element-level access control, where users or agents can retrieve only permissible model elements or document sections, supporting granular data sovereignty while maintaining an auditable model.

The framework proposed here is developed based on the architectural design used within the iECO project [48], and is based on Gaia-X Principles [49,50]. The platform architecture was designed to enhance IT-based data sharing and collaboration in the AEC and operations sector through a generic IT architecture for decentralized digital twins aiming at increasing the efficiency of the entire building life cycle while simultaneously satisfying heterogeneity and decentralization requirements and maintaining the sovereignty of all participants. Strnadl et al. [51] defined the major elements of the dDTw architecture and the associated logical data flow between these components. The proposed distributed digital twin (dDTw) architecture consists of the following layers as shown in Figure 3, respectively:

- Gaia-X Federation Catalog domain (light green-yellowish color in Figure 3);
- dDTw services domain (darker green);
- Policy and trust management domain based on distributed ledger technology (DLT) (dark and light purple).

Here in our research, the focus will be on developing a framework for the dDTw services domain, defining the entities and logical data flow, whereas the other layers are currently out of our research scope. Therefore, data flows from/to the Gaia-X Federation Catalog and policy and trust management domains are eliminated from Figure 3.

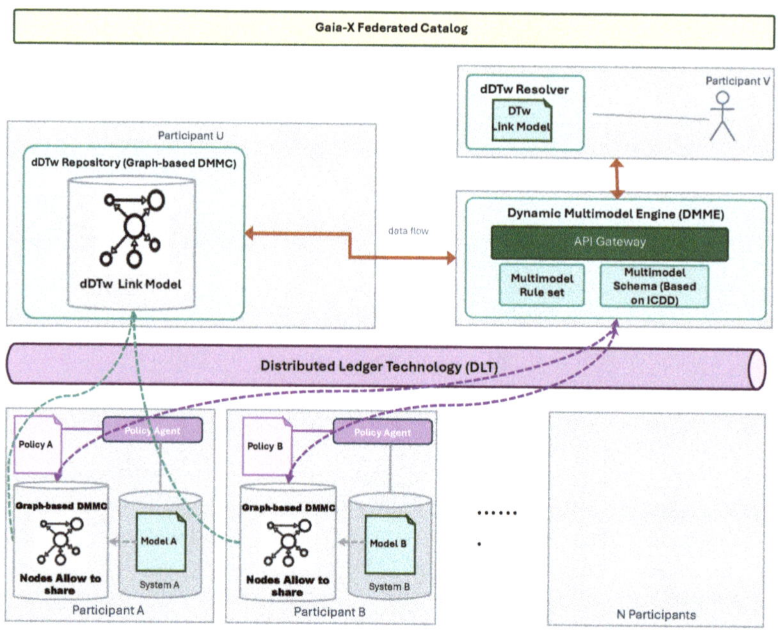

Figure 3. The architecture of the distributed digital twin (dDTw) illustrating the integration of the Gaia-X Federation Catalog, the dDTw services domain, and the Policy and Trust Management layer.

At the core of the dDTw concept, which is focused on data management, the dDTw Repository only stores the Link Model, i.e., the overarching model of a digital twin linking all its constituting sub-models and the relations between individual elements of entities of any sub-model. All actual data (e.g., the many different BIM models for the various professions, internet of things (IoT) data relating to different devices of a building) are stored at facilities nominated by the participants alone (e.g., they may store data on premise in their own computing center or nominate another trusted party, even a hyperscaler or another trusted cloud provider, to store these data sets). This allows all participants who create and expose data to maintain ultimate sovereignty over these data; otherwise (viz., if all data need to be stored at a central facility), the configuration will be equivalent to another common data environment (CDE).

Taking that into consideration, the core components of our graph-based dynamic multimodel framework architecture illustrating the data flow and the roles of core components across distinct layers are as follows. The framework is centered on the dDTw services domain, structured into two logical layers: a dDTw domain model layer and a dDTw core services layer. In the dDTw domain model layer, each participant creates a graph-based Dynamic Multimodel Container (DMMC) hosting their own domain models (e.g., Models A and B) and defining the value of *Access Control* for the model itself and each element thereof. In addition, for each domain model, policies shall determine who is allowed to retrieve the various sub-models of the distributed DTw, whereas, the dDTw core services layer contains the central Dynamic Multimodel Engine (DMME) that governs schema and rule sets based on ISO 21597, and manages link models through a DMMC-based repository. Data flow from individual participants' systems through policy-enforced access (shown in purple dashed arrows) into the shared link model is managed by Participant U. This supports a sovereign, interoperable exchange of multimodel data. The distributed ledger technology (DLT) facilitates decentralized trust between participants, while the Gaia-X Federated Catalog provides federated service descriptions.

4. Framework Verification

To verify the proposed framework, a use case is utilized here. Referring to Figure 3, firstly, domain models are created by systems in dDTw domain models layer. In our use case, we propose that the building model BeyerBau_Arch.ifc is created in system A. The architectural model comprises 1446 IFC elements representing architectural components. Participant A then creates the Graph-based Dynamic Multimodel Container, adds the building model as an Internal document to the container and assigns the *Access Allowed Partially* property at the document level, and assigns the *Access Allowed* property for the building's columns elements only (IFC column). In system B, the Project schedule file BeyerBau_schedule.xlsx is created. The Excel file includes 19 activities with planned start and end dates. Participant B then creates the Graph-based Dynamic Multimodel Container for system B, adds the schedule file as an Internal document to the container, and assigns the *Access Allowed* property at the document level; accordingly, all its elements are allowed to be shared.

Participant U on the dDTw service layer creates the Graph-based Dynamic Multimodel Container for the dDTw repository. For our current use case, Participant U firstly retrieves the elements that had the property *Access Allowed* from both domain models; Participant A and Participant B then create links between these elements. Figure 4 shows the query to retrieve the Identifiers, Descriptions, and URIs for the elements that have the property *Access Allowed*, from the building model BeyerBau_Arch.ifc. Moreover, the same query is performed on the BeyerBau_schedule.xlsx. Then, as an example, Participant U creates links between the columns from IFC file and their related schedule from the Excel file and saves the links, which contain the elements' URIs, as an external document in the Container. As such, the Container in the dDTw service layer contains only links that reference the sharable individuals in the dDTw(s). Finally, to prove the capability of accessing and processing the linked data, an API call is performed on the linked model using the elements' URIs to retrieve the data of the linked elements from the distributed digital twins. This API functionality is demonstrated using the linkage between an IFC file (BeyerBau_Arch.ifc) and an Excel schedule file (BeyerBau_schedule.xlsx). Figure 5 illustrates how the dynamic multimodel API enables cross-domain querying. The GET requests return JSON-formatted metadata for a 3D IFC model and its associated schedule, semantically linked through graph-based identifiers and properties.

Figure 4. Retrieving the elements with property *Access Allowed* from System A.

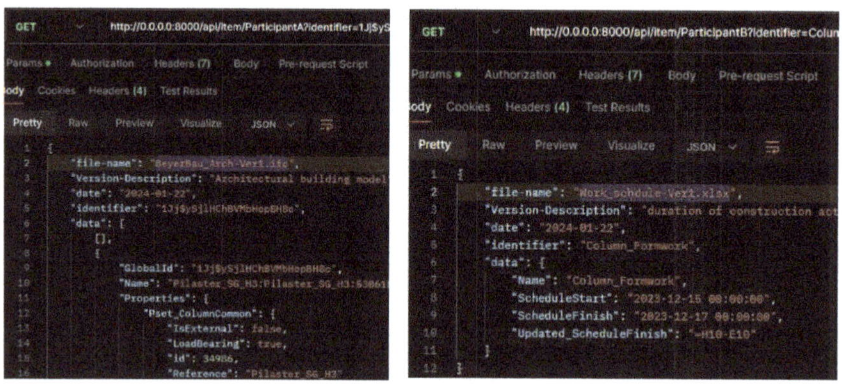

Figure 5. API implementation to retrieve the data of the linked elements.

To evaluate practical feasibility, we assessed the response time required to execute a semantic query for retrieving linked schedule elements associated with a given IFC component. As shown in Figure 4, the round-trip API response time was approximately 83 ms, demonstrating the efficiency of the graph-based linking framework in retrieving data across distributed sources.

5. Discussion

The proposed graph-based dynamic multimodel container framework significantly enhances interoperability in distributed digital twin (dDTw) environments for the AEC industry. By replacing the traditional file-based multimodel approach with a graph-based architecture, the framework overcomes limitations associated with siloed data exchanges and semantic inconsistencies (responding to the first component of RQ 1). The verification demonstrates that this approach supports seamless integration across diverse domains and platforms, as evidenced by the ability to link and retrieve heterogeneous data from distributed sources in real time (addressing the second component of RQ 1 regarding real-time data retrieval and platform independence). This improvement directly addresses Research Question 1, showcasing how the graph-based approach supports effective data exchange and collaborative workflows.

The framework's design emphasizes data sovereignty by embedding access control mechanisms within the multimodel container. Through granular access rights at both the document and element levels, stakeholders maintain control over their data while ensuring compliance with international and local regulations. These features were validated using the proposed use case, where participants could manage access rights dynamically and restrict sensitive data as needed. This capability aligns with Research Question 2 by demonstrating that the framework not only facilitates interoperability but also ensures trust and sovereignty in data sharing (corresponding to the twofold focus of RQ 2: control over access and legal/regulatory compliance).

The proposed framework significantly enhances collaboration in distributed digital twin (dDTw) environments by providing a centralized yet dynamic platform for real-time data sharing and interaction. By leveraging graph-based multimodel containers, the framework enables seamless linking of heterogeneous data sets, facilitating efficient communication and coordination among multidisciplinary teams. This capability addresses a critical need in the Architecture, Engineering, and Construction (AEC) industry, where effective collaboration among stakeholders is essential for project success. The integration of technologies such as dynamic linking, automated versioning, and semantic enrichment facilitates that all project participants have access to consistent, up-to-date information, reducing misunderstandings and errors. This improvement directly aligns with Research Question 3 (RQ 3), which seeks to explore how the framework fosters real-time collaboration across diverse domains.

While the proposed framework demonstrates significant advancements in interoperability and data sovereignty, its scalability remains a topic requiring further investigation. Graph databases, such as Neo4j, offer structural advantages over traditional relational databases when handling highly interconnected data. Unlike relational databases—which rely on join operations that become increasingly expensive as data grow—graph databases utilize index-free adjacency, allowing traversal queries to execute in near-constant time regardless of data size or relationship complexity. This makes them particularly suitable for dynamic, semantically linked data across multiple domains in the AEC industry. However, we acknowledge that performance in real-world applications depends not only on query efficiency but also on how the system handles growing datasets, distributed deployments, and concurrent queries. The framework's verification was conducted using a simplified use case involving only two data sources. While this scenario illustrates the feasibility of integrating heterogeneous data sets in a controlled environment, it does not fully capture the complexities and performance demands of large-scale, multidisciplinary AEC projects. Conducting extensive performance testing under diverse scenarios to identify and resolve potential bottlenecks. Moreover, potential adoption barriers must be considered. The AEC industry's traditionally cautious approach to new technologies may pose challenges, requiring targeted awareness initiatives, training programs, and clear demonstration of the benefits to various project stakeholders.

6. Conclusions and Future Work

This study presents a graph-based dynamic multimodel container framework designed to address key challenges in data management for distributed digital twins (dDTws) in the Architecture, Engineering, and Construction (AEC) industry. The framework demonstrates significant potential in enhancing interoperability, ensuring data sovereignty, and facilitating real-time collaboration among stakeholders. By leveraging graph databases, semantic web technologies, and standardized approaches such as ISO 21597, the proposed solution provides a robust platform for integrating and managing heterogeneous data sources in cloud-based environments. Validation through use cases highlights the framework's effectiveness in linking diverse datasets and improving collaborative workflows, though scalability requires further exploration.

Future work will focus on enhancing the framework's usability and accessibility by integrating a chat-based user interface to facilitate the creation of semantic links between data sources. This feature aims to simplify interaction with the system, allowing end users to perform advanced query functions without requiring expertise in query languages. By providing a user-friendly interface, the framework will enable a broader range of stakeholders to engage with and benefit from its functionalities, further democratizing access to sophisticated data management tools. Additionally, comprehensive testing with larger and more complex datasets will be conducted to refine the framework's scalability and optimize its performance in real-world AEC applications. While our framework demonstrated effective integration at the prototype level, future work will explore scalability enhancements, particularly in performance benchmarking in large-scale distributed deployments.

These developments will ensure that the proposed framework evolves into a comprehensive and scalable solution, fostering innovation and efficiency in the management of distributed digital twin environments.

Author Contributions: N.A.-S.: Conceptualization, methodology, and writing—original draft. R.J.S.: Supervision, writing—review and editing. C.F.S.: writing—review and editing. All authors have read and agreed to the published version of the manuscript.

Funding: This research was funded by Federal Ministry for Economic Affairs and Climate Action.

Data Availability Statement: Data are contained within the article.

Conflicts of Interest: Author Christoph F. Strnadl was employed by the company Gaia-X AISBL, CTO Office. The remaining authors declare that the research was conducted in the absence of any commercial or financial relationships that could be construed as a potential conflict of interest.

References

1. Haße, H.; van der Valk, H.; Weißenberg, N.; Otto, B. Shared digital twins: Data sovereignty in logistics networks. In *Data Science and Innovation in Supply Chain Management: How Data Transforms the Value Chain. Proceedings of the Hamburg International Conference of Logistics (HICL)*; epubli GmbH: Berlin, Germany, 2020; Volume 29, pp. 763–795.
2. von Scherenberg, F.; Hellmeier, M.; Otto, B. Data sovereignty in information systems. *Electron. Mark.* **2024**, *34*, 15. [CrossRef]
3. Chen, H.M.; Chang, K.C.; Lin, T.H. A cloud-based system framework for performing online viewing, storage, and analysis on big data of massive BIMs. *Autom. Constr.* **2016**, *71*, 34–48. [CrossRef]
4. Soni, P.K.; Dhurwe, H. Challenges and Open Issues in Cloud Computing Services. In *Advanced Computing Techniques for Optimization in Cloud*; Chapman and Hall/CRC: Boca Raton, FL, USA, 2024; pp. 19–37.
5. Gade, K.R. Data Governance in the Cloud: Challenges and Opportunities. *MZ Comput. J.* **2023**, *4*.
6. Radzi, A.R.; Azmi, N.F.; Kamaruzzaman, S.N.; Rahman, R.A.; Papadonikolaki, E. Relationship between digital twin and building information modeling: A systematic review and future directions. *Constr. Innov.* **2024**, *24*, 811–829. [CrossRef]
7. Sacks, R.; Brilakis, I.; Pikas, E.; Xie, H.S.; Girolami, M. Construction with digital twin information systems. *Data-Centric Eng.* **2020**, *1*, e14. [CrossRef]
8. Afzal, M.; Li, R.Y.M.; Shoaib, M.; Ayyub, M.F.; Tagliabue, L.C.; Bilal, M.; Ghafoor, H.; Manta, O. Delving into the Digital Twin Developments and Applications in the Construction Industry: A PRISMA Approach. *Sustainability* **2023**, *15*, 16436. [CrossRef]
9. Koutamanis, A. From Building Information Modelling to Digital Twins: Digital Representation for a Circular Economy. In *A Circular Built Environment in the Digital Age*; Springer International Publishing: Cham, Switzerland, 2024; pp. 3–20.
10. Deng, M.; Menassa, C.C.; Kamat, V.R. From BIM to digital twins: A systematic review of the evolution of intelligent building representations in the AEC-FM industry. *J. Inf. Technol. Constr.* **2021**, *26*, 58–83. [CrossRef]

11. Nguyen, T.D.; Adhikari, S. The role of bim in integrating digital twin in building construction: A literature review. *Sustainability* **2023**, *15*, 10462. [CrossRef]
12. Omrany, H.; Al-Obaidi, K.M.; Husain, A.; Ghaffarianhoseini, A. Digital twins in the construction industry: A comprehensive review of current implementations, enabling technologies, and future directions. *Sustainability* **2023**, *15*, 10908. [CrossRef]
13. Lombardi, A. Interoperability Challenges. Exploring Trends, Patterns, Practices and Possible Futures for Enhanced Collaboration and Efficiency in the AEC Industry. In *Coding Architecture: Designing Toolkits, Workflows, Industry*; Springer Nature: Cham, Switzerland, 2023; pp. 49–72.
14. Jaafar, K.; Awais, M. Navigating the Digital Landscape: Challenges of BIM and Digital Twin Adaptation. In *Transforming Industry using Digital Twin Technology*; Springer Nature: Cham, Switzerland, 2024; pp. 297–323.
15. Pauwels, P.; Zhang, S.; Lee, Y.C. Semantic web technologies in AEC industry: A literature overview. *Autom. Constr.* **2017**, *73*, 145–165. [CrossRef]
16. Werbrouck, J. The Web as a Common Data Environment: Management of Federated Multi-Models. Ph.D. Thesis, Department of Electronics and Information Systems Faculty of Engineering and Architecture, Ghent University, Ghent, Belgium, 2024.
17. Senthilvel, M.; Oraskari, J.; Beetz, J. Common data environments for the information container for linked document delivery. In Proceedings of the 8th Linked Data in Architecture and Construction Workshop, Dublin, Ireland, 17–19 June 2020; pp. 132–145.
18. Lu, Q.; Xie, X.; Heaton, J.; Parlikad, A.K.; Schooling, J. From BIM towards digital twin: Strategy and future development for smart asset management. In *International Workshop on Service Orientation in Holonic and Multi-Agent Manufacturing*; Springer International Publishing: Cham, Switzerland, 2019; pp. 392–404.
19. Alonso, R.; Borras, M.; Koppelaar, R.H.; Lodigiani, A.; Loscos, E.; Yöntem, E. SPHERE: BIM digital twin platform. *Proceedings* **2019**, *60*, 9.
20. Tulubas Gokuc, Y.; Arditi, D. Adoption of BIM in architectural design firms. *Archit. Sci. Rev.* **2017**, *60*, 483–492. [CrossRef]
21. Pauwels, P.; Poveda-Villalón, M.; Sicilia, Á.; Euzenat, J. Semantic technologies and interoperability in the built environment. *Semant. Web* **2018**, *9*, 731–734. [CrossRef]
22. *ISO 21597-1:2020*; Information Container for Linked Document Delivery—Exchange Specification—Part 1: Container. International Organization for Standardization: Geneva, Switzerland, 2020.
23. Hagedorn, P. Semantic Validation of Information Containers for Reliable BIM Information Exchange. Ph.D. Thesis, Ruhr-Universität Bochum, Bochum, Germany, 2024.
24. Xiao, F.; Fan, C. Building information modeling and building automation systems data integration and big data analytics for building energy management. In *Research Companion to Building Information Modeling*; Edward Elgar Publishing: Cheltenham, UK, 2022; pp. 525–549.
25. Onungwa, I.; Olugu-Uduma, N.; Shelden, D.R. Cloud BIM technology as a means of collaboration and project integration in smart cities. *Sage Open* **2021**, *11*, 21582440211033250. [CrossRef]
26. Bühler, M.M.; Nübel, K.; Jelinek, T.; Riechert, D.; Bauer, T.; Schmid, T.; Schneider, M. Data cooperatives as a catalyst for collaboration, data sharing and the digital transformation of the construction sector. *Buildings* **2023**, *13*, 442. [CrossRef]
27. Nübel, K.; Bühler, M.M.; Jelinek, T. Federated digital platforms: Value chain integration for sustainable infrastructure planning and delivery. *Sustainability* **2021**, *13*, 8996. [CrossRef]
28. Weber, B. (Ed.) *Data Governance: Nachhaltige Geschäftsmodelle und Technologien im Europäischen Rechtsrahmen*; Springer: Berlin/Heidelberg, Germany, 2023.
29. Turk, Ž.; Sonkor, M.S.; Klinc, R. Cybersecurity assessment of BIM/CDE design environment using cyber assessment framework. *J. Civ. Eng. Manag.* **2022**, *28*, 349–364. [CrossRef]
30. Liaqat, M.; Chang, V.; Gani, A.; Ab Hamid, S.H.; Toseef, M.; Shoaib, U.; Ali, R.L. Federated cloud resource management: Review and discussion. *J. Netw. Comput. Appl.* **2017**, *77*, 87–105. [CrossRef]
31. Wu, C.; Wu, F.; Qi, T.; Wang, Y.; Yang, Y.; Huang, Y.; Xie, X. Game of Privacy: Towards Better Federated Platform Collaboration under Privacy Restriction. *arXiv* **2022**, arXiv:2202.05139.
32. Jaskula, K.; Perera, S.; Nanayakkarawasam, S.; Papadonikolaki, D.E.; Rovas, D. Blockchain-Based Common Data Environments: Prototype and Validation Through User Study. 2024. Available online: https://papers.ssrn.com/sol3/papers.cfm?abstract_id=4713471 (accessed on 30 November 2024).
33. Parn, E.A.; Edwards, D. Cyber threats confronting the digital built environment: Common data environment vulnerabilities and block chain deterrence. *Eng. Constr. Archit. Manag.* **2019**, *26*, 245–266. [CrossRef]
34. Sacks, R.; Wang, Z.; Ouyang, B.; Utkucu, D.; Chen, S. Toward artificially intelligent cloud-based building information modelling for collaborative multidisciplinary design. *Adv. Eng. Inform.* **2022**, *53*, 101711. [CrossRef]
35. Godager, B.A. Critical review of the integration of bim to semantic web technology. *Int. Arch. Photogramm. Remote Sens. Spat. Inf. Sci.* **2018**, *42*, 303–308.

36. *ISO 19650-1: 2018*; Organization and Digitization of Information About Buildings and Civil Engineering Works, Including Building Information Modelling (BIM)-Information Management Using Building Information Modelling Part 1. ISO: Geneva, Switzerland, 2018.
37. Attaran, M.; Celik, B.G. Digital Twin: Benefits, use cases, challenges, and opportunities. *Decis. Anal. J.* **2023**, *6*, 100165. [CrossRef]
38. Lindholm, J.; Johansson, P.; Yitmen, I. Collaborative digital platform for integrated design and production planning and control: A literature review. In Proceedings of the 2023 European Conference on Computing in Construction and the 40th International CIB W78 Conference, Heraklion, Crete, Greece, 10–12 July 2023; European Council on Computing in Construction: Porto, Portugal, 2023; Volume 4, pp. 877–884.
39. Esser, S.; Vilgertshofer, S.; Borrmann, A. Version control for asynchronous BIM collaboration: Model merging through graph analysis and transformation. *Autom. Constr.* **2023**, *155*, 105063. [CrossRef]
40. Gaia-X. Gaia-X: A Federated Secure Data Infrastructure. 2021. Available online: https://www.gaia-x.eu/ (accessed on 20 November 2024).
41. Scherer, R. MEFISTO: Eine Modell-, Informations-und Wissensplattform für das Bauwesen; Tagungsband 2. Mefisto Kongress, 13 Oktober 2011. Inst. für Bauinformatik: Dresden, Germany. Available online: https://baublog.file1.wcms.tu-dresden.de/2011/09/08/2-mefisto-kongress/ (accessed on 10 November 2024).
42. Fuchs, S.; Kadolsky, M.; Scherer, R.J. Formal description of a generic multi-model. In Proceedings of the 2011 IEEE 20th International Workshops on Enabling Technologies: Infrastructure for Collaborative Enterprises, Paris, France, 27–29 June 2011; IEEE: Piscataway, NJ, USA, 2011; pp. 205–210.
43. Alocci, D.; Mariethoz, J.; Horlacher, O.; Bolleman, J.T.; Campbell, M.P.; Lisacek, F. Property graph vs RDF triple store: A comparison on glycan substructure search. *PLoS ONE* **2015**, *10*, e0144578. [CrossRef] [PubMed]
44. Buron, M.; Goasdoué, F.; Manolescu, I.; Merabti, T.; Mugnier, M.L. Revisiting RDF storage layouts for efficient query answering. In Proceedings of the SSWS 2020-13th International Workshop on Scalable Semantic Web Knowledge Base Systems, Athens, Greece, 2 November 2020.
45. Al-Sadoon, N.; Scherer, R.J. IFC semantic extension for dynamic fire safety evacuation simulation. In Proceedings of the CIB W78 Conference, Luxembourg, 11–15 October 2021; pp. 11–15.
46. Al-Sadoon, N.; Katranuschkov, P.; Scherer, R.J. Extending ICDD implementation to a dynamic multimodel framework. In *ECPPM 2022-eWork and eBusiness in Architecture, Engineering and Construction 2022*; CRC Press: Boca Raton, FL, USA, 2023; pp. 115–122.
47. Al-Sadoon, N.N.; Scherer, R.; Menzel, K. From static to dynamic information containers. In *EC3 Conference 2023*; European Council on Computing in Construction: Porto, Portugal, 2023; Volume 4, pp. 320–326.
48. iECO 2022. iECO Project. Available online: https://ieco-gaiax.de/ (accessed on 25 September 2024).
49. Gaia-X. Gaia-X Architecture Document 22.10. 2022. Available online: https://docs.gaia-x.eu/technical-committee/architecture-document/22.10/ (accessed on 1 October 2024).
50. Strnadl, C.F. Gaia-X Technical Implementation Architecture. Version v1.10. A Version 2.00 is Forthcoming. 2023. Available online: https://ieco-gaiax.de/technische-gaia-x-architektur/ (accessed on 10 November 2024).
51. Strnadl, C.F.; Katranuschkov, P.; Menzel, K.; Sethi, M.; Kenklies, B.; Weber, B. Gaia-X-based decentralized platform architecture for a distributed digital twin in the AECO sector. *J. Inf. Technol. Constr. (ITcon)* **2024**, *in press*.

buildings

MDPI

Article

Integrating PC Splitting Design and Construction Organization Through Multi-Agent Simulation for Prefabricated Buildings

Yi Shen [1], Jing Wang [2,*] and Guan-Hang Jin [1]

1 Shanghai Jianke Engineering Consulting Co., Ltd., Shanghai 200032, China; vasahi@163.com (Y.S.); jinguanhang@jkec.com.cn (G.-H.J.)
2 School of Management, Shanghai University of Engineering Science, Shanghai 201620, China
* Correspondence: wangjingme@sues.edu.cn

Abstract: Prefabricated building projects represent industrialized and intelligent construction through factory production, standardized design, and mechanized assembly. This study presents a multi-agent simulation approach to model the prefabricated construction process, allowing for the concurrent optimization of the prefabricated component (PC) splitting design and the construction organization plan through iterative simulation. (1) Employing a questionnaire survey, it identifies critical factors affecting schedule and cost from a design–construction coordination perspective. (2) Based on these findings, an agent-based model was developed incorporating PC installation, crane operations, and storage yard spatial constraints, along with interaction rules governing these agents. (3) Data interoperability was achieved among Revit, NetLogo3D and Navisworks. This integrated environment offers project managers digital management of design and construction plans, simulation support, and visualization tools. Simulation results confirm that a hybrid resource allocation strategy utilizing both tower cranes and mobile cranes enhances resource leveling, accelerates schedule performance, and improves cost efficiency.

Keywords: prefabricated building; multi-agent simulation; PC splitting design; construction organization; BIM-5D

1. Introduction

1.1. Background

By the end of 2020, the cumulative floor area of prefabricated buildings mandated at the land conveyance stage in Shanghai totaled approximately 150 million square meters. In 2020, newly started prefabricated construction comprised approximately 91.7% of the total above-ground floor area of all new building projects in Shanghai [1]. Prefabricated construction significantly shortens project timelines by enabling factory production of components to occur concurrently with on-site foundation work. This parallel process, coupled with rapid on-site assembly, reduces overall duration by up to 30%. Furthermore, it drastically cuts labor needs by shifting skilled work to controlled factory settings, minimizing on-site manpower and enhancing safety, thus alleviating reliance on scarce skilled labor. Despite numerous advantages, prefabricated construction is often perceived as less cost-effective compared to conventional cast-in-place construction. One of the main reasons for this perception is the lack of coordination among various distinct operations, such as production, transportation, and on-site assembly of prefabricated components [2].

https://doi.org/10.3390/buildings15203773

1.2. Problem Statement

Buildings where part or all of the components are prefabricated in a factory, then transported to the construction site and assembled through reliable connections, are called prefabricated buildings. The precast components are composed of structural elements like prefabricated beams, slabs, columns, and walls, as well as larger prefabricated units like stairs, balconies, air conditioning panels, integrated bathrooms, and integrated kitchens. The prefabricated construction process typically begins with an architectural design institute producing building drawings. Subsequently, the factory splits the components and units in the design drawings based on constraints related to production, construction, and transportation, ensuring they are producible, transportable, and constructible. Finally, the construction unit assembles the prefabricated components and units provided by the factory on-site, ensuring the completed building meets the design requirements. Therefore, reducing deviations within the closed-loop collaboration formed by design, production, and construction is a crucial issue for enhancing the quality of prefabricated construction.

1.3. Research Objectives

The prefabricated construction process places higher demands on data sharing and collaboration among design, production, and construction parties. Envision a smart project management system capable of digitally storing design drawings from the design team and production drawings from the factory, while simulating the entire assembly and construction process for the builders. If the simulation reveals component processing errors that fail to meet construction constraints, feedback can be promptly provided to the factory. When the simulation flags progress or cost performance below expectations, the design, production, and construction teams must synchronize their efforts to optimize their plans. Thus, intelligent engineering project management serves as the key link connecting standardized design, industrialized production, and prefabricated construction. By simulating the prefabricated construction process and resource allocation scenarios, potential issues surface early and can be addressed proactively. Digitally and intelligently coordinating management across design, production, and construction stakeholders from the owner's perspective represents an essential embodiment of China's construction industry modernization.

2. Literature Review

2.1. Multi-Agent Simulation Technology in Construction Project Management

The applications of multi-agent systems (MAS) are considered to be among the most promising paradigms for detailed investigations and reliable problem-solving methods, and MAS applications make it possible for researchers and practitioners to better understand complex systems [3]. With its unique capacity to simulate dynamic, bottom-up interactions, the MAS provides innovative solutions to numerous challenges in construction project management practice [4].

The MAS can simulate the complete construction supply chain, from precast manufacturing to on-site installation. By modeling supply chain participants (e.g., modeling suppliers, transporters) and prefabricated modules as agents, project managers can assess logistics strategies to decrease delays, reduce costs, and refine just-in-time delivery systems [5]. Through agent-based modeling, it can simulate the construction environment to determine the relationship between crew size and unit duration changes [6]. The MAS is developed to orchestrate the sequence of inter-group construction activities, addressing factors such as site congestion, worker movements, and material consumption [7]. The MAS can additionally study the general emergence of results through the adjustment of agent attributes and serves as a reliable tool to predict the impact of construction measures for on-site managers [8]. The multi-agent-based simulation system can help managers to test and quantify the impact of different construction strategies so as to choose the most effective one to execute [9].

The building information modeling (BIM) and agent-based modeling (ABM) integration method highlighted benefits to construction projects, reduced construction costs, and enhanced productivity [10]. The integration of reinforcement learning and agent-based simulation approaches can be used to optimize project duration under resource constraints and support construction practitioners in project planning decision-making [11]. The integration of expert knowledge with sophisticated simulation tools offers significant value, providing managers with a powerful resource to navigate project complexities, enhance strategic planning, and ultimately improve the likelihood of successful project execution and completion [12].

Multi-Agent Systems (MAS) decompose a system into a large number of 'agents' with diverse attributes and behavioral rules. This approach naturally simulates the interactions and adaptations between individuals, thereby effectively demonstrating macroscopic emergent behavior in a bottom-up manner. In contrast, traditional macro-level models like System Dynamics typically rely on averages or assumed aggregation rules for top-down modeling, making it difficult to capture the complex emergent phenomena arising from individual heterogeneity and local interactions.

Regarding the simulation mechanism, MAS is more flexible, as it can adopt either event-driven or time-stepped approaches, with its core focus being the modeling of synchronous or asynchronous interactions among agents. Discrete Event Simulation (DES), on the other hand, strictly adheres to an event-triggered clock advancement mechanism and is more suitable for scenarios centered around discrete processes, such as queuing systems.

Appropriate multi-agent decision-making can effectively coordinate and integrate the needs or expectations of all stakeholders, which can reduce conflicts, improve the success probability of the project, maximize the overall returns on interest, and contribute to the project's sustainability [13]. On the other hand, The MAS can model the ripple effects of a design change, simulating its impact on various agents (e.g., designers, contractors, suppliers) and processes. This capability enables a more comprehensive assessment of potential cost and schedule implications prior to formal change approval.

2.2. Digital Solutions for Prefabricated Building Projects

Modular construction requires detailed and comprehensive planning, high initial costs, and navigating transportation and design constraints [14]. Integrated statistical and mathematical techniques (including distribution fitting) were utilized to develop a predictive model that computes the associated cost savings and growth [15]. The digitalized workflow can significantly reduce task duration, improve project cost assessment and evaluate the financial feasibility of semi-automation in off-site construction projects [16].

Considering the interaction between resource allocation conditions and other uncertain factors, the construction time is mainly affected by the supply of materials and weather conditions, while the familiarity level of work affects the construction time and cost [17]. The performance of precast construction is highly dependent on the effectiveness of production planning for the precast components. The multi-agent-based precast production planning model synchronizes production scheduling with resource allocation [18]. The hybrid approach that combines MAS with deep learning provides scenario-based estimations of CO_2 emissions, costs, and schedule performance for Modular-integrated construction (MIC) [19].

Recently, the construction industry has benefited from the increased application of smart construction led by the core technologies of the fourth industrial revolution, such as modular construction, BIM, AI, and AR/VR, which enhance productivity and work efficiency.

2.3. The Methods of Multi-Tower Crane Operation Management

The growing adoption of off-site construction methods has increased the critical role of cranes within the construction sector. By integrating 3D site modeling, BIM, and crane simulations within the Unity game engine, the Construction Digital Twin (CDT) overcomes the limitations of conventional 2D-based planning by providing a three-dimensional representation of site conditions [20]. The onsite crane operation management includes BIM-based multi-crane lift animation, scheduling and cost analyses, motion controlling in the BIM environment, safety monitoring and clash detection, and spatiotemporal site analyses [21]. Effective crane management is imperative to ensure that construction projects are completed on time, within budget, and with a high degree of safety [22].

Multiple tower crane layout planning (MTCLP) is a complex combinatorial problem controlled by a number of variables, such as site configuration, building layout, material storage positions, and workload [23]. The collaborative planning for stacking and installation of prefabricated building components (CPSIP) aims to minimize construction duration by preventing collisions among tower cranes operating simultaneously in overlapping areas [24]. The agent-based simulation (ABS) model has the superiority of quantitatively assessing the effect of conflict on the overall time and costs of tower crane operations. It is capable of simulating tower crane operations and interactions between different agents of the model [25]. The ABM applies a dynamic supply selection system and tests numerous scenarios to ensure the most efficient linkage between tasks, cranes, and supply locations [26]. By clarifying the transfer relationship between the component material supply point, the component initial positioning point, and the tower crane optional positioning point, as well as the cooperative relationship between each positioning point and the tower crane operation, the tower crane positioning optimization model is used to automatically calculate and generate the best positioning layout method of the tower crane on the project site [27].

In project management, progress, cost, and safety are regarded as primary objectives. There has been extensive research on the MTCLP problem, most of which, however, adopts the perspective of construction planning. Relatively less attention has been paid to the influence of design schemes, particularly prefabricated component splitting schemes, on MTCLP.

3. Methods

While prefabricated buildings can be categorized by structural materials (concrete, steel, timber, hybrid) and functional use (residential, commercial, mixed-use), this research specifically investigates projects involving prefabricated concrete residential buildings. As shown in Figure 1, a hybrid online and offline questionnaire was administered to practitioners in the prefabricated construction industry to identify key factors influencing the interaction between PC splitting designs and construction organization plans. The empirical data gathered, combined with a comprehensive literature review, served as the foundation for developing the multi-agent simulation (MAS) model, which represents the prefabricated construction process and its internal interactions. The validity of the MAS model was then assessed through a case study using the NetLogo 3D platform. Finally, data interoperability among Revit, NetLogo 3D, and Navisworks was achieved, enabling the implementation of BIM 5D in engineering practice.

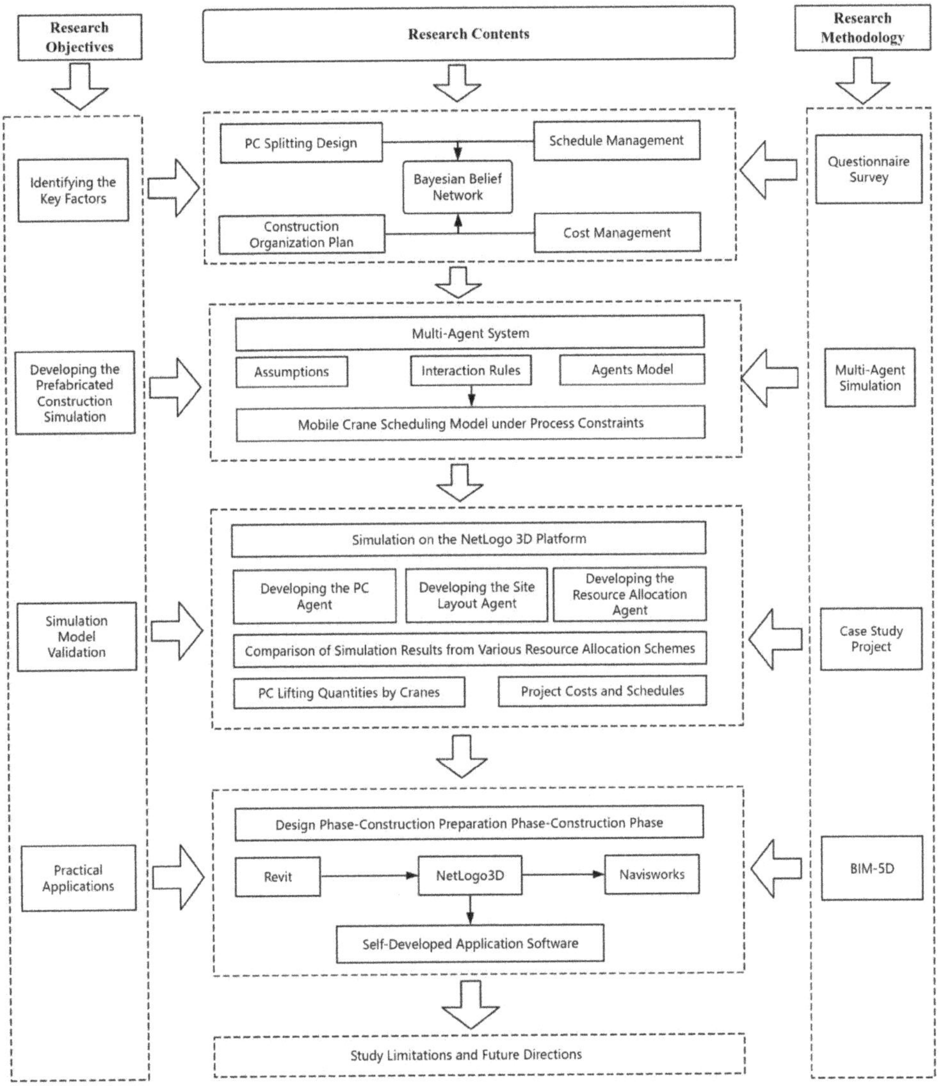

Figure 1. Research Roadmap.

3.1. Questionnaire Survey

The questionnaire was distributed to 75 industry practitioners in Shanghai, yielding 60 valid responses and an 80% response rate (respondent details are provided in Table 1). This study investigates the interplay between PC splitting designs and construction organization plans from a project management perspective, utilizing a Bayesian Belief Network (BBN) model. As a foundational step, a structural relationship diagram of the influencing factors was developed (see Figure 2).

Data analysis of the survey results yielded the following conclusions: (1) In designing PC splitting plans, horizontal components (e.g., slabs and stairs) should be split preferentially; (2) The most highly utilized resources on construction sites are installation labor, lifting equipment, and storage yard space; (3) The most critical factor affecting construction organization management is the number of prefabricated component types, indicating that greater variety significantly increases project management complexity.

Table 1. Demographic Profile of Survey Respondent.

Demographic Profile	Category	Number of Respondents	Percentage
Work Experience	Below 5 years	27	45%
	5–10 years	18	30%
	Over 10 years	15	25%
Work Role	Design	6	10%
	Production	3	5%
	Construction	15	25%
	Consulting	21	35%
	Supervision	6	10%
	Client	9	15%

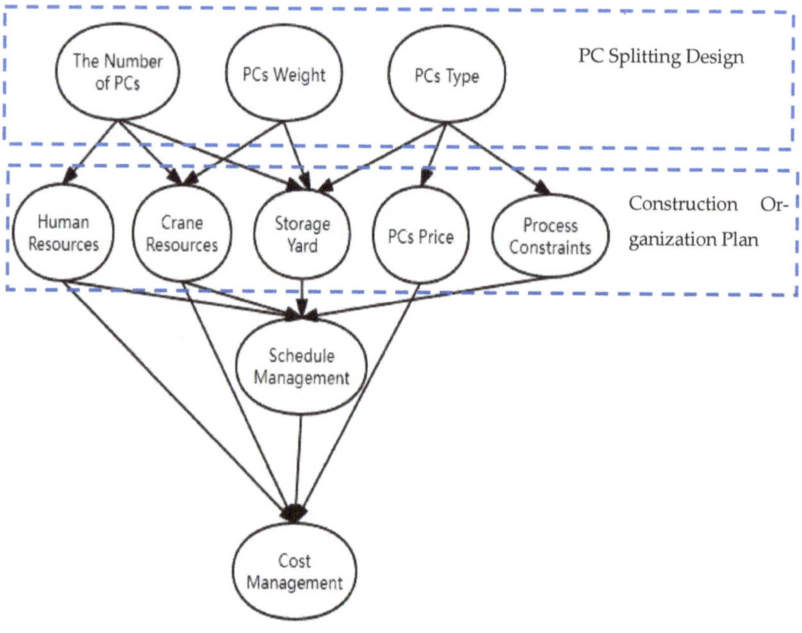

Figure 2. The Structural Relationship Diagram of the Influencing Factors.

3.2. Developing the Prefabricated Construction Simulation

3.2.1. Assumptions

The simulation process for prefabricated construction is simplified into the following steps: (1) PCs arrive at the site and are stored in the stacking area, subject to space constraints; (2) Cranes (e.g., tower cranes or mobile cranes) transport the PCs from the stacking area to their designated installation positions; (3) Once all components on the current floor are installed, a waiting period is imposed until the cast-in-place concrete attains the required design strength, after which assembly of the subsequent floor may proceed; (4) The assembly task is deemed complete when no further components arrive and no components remain in the stacking area.

The analysis focuses solely on internal site constraints affecting the prefabricated construction process, with external supply factors excluded for the time being. Based on the simulation process, the following assumptions are adopted: (1) The PC plant is assumed to possess sufficient materials and machinery, ensuring timely responses to delivery demands; (2) Each crane operation is assumed to carry only one PC, with direct installation and no secondary handling; (3) In accordance with on-site construction requirements, PC lifting and installation are permitted only after the completion of foundation works and certain main structural works. Thus, it is assumed that these sub-projects are finished and all necessary preparatory work is in place prior to simulation initiation.

3.2.2. Interaction Rules

1. PC Assembly Rules

First, determine the floor where the PC is located based on the Z-value range of its installation elevation, with those on lower floors taking precedence over those on higher floors. Then, determine the installation sequence for PCs on the same floor, where vertical components take precedence over horizontal components. Finally, for PCs on the same floor with the same attributes, the installation sequence is determined based on the set priority value, where a smaller value indicates a higher priority. The entire process of PC installation includes arrival on site, hoisting, and assembly into the designated position.

2. Multi-Tower Crane Avoidance Rules

The following avoidance rules are established for the multi-crane construction scenario:

(1) Lower cranes yield to higher cranes: Higher cranes are typically positioned in central locations and handle more intensive workloads. Lower cranes must evaluate the movement patterns of higher cranes prior to operation.
(2) Later-arriving cranes yield to earlier-arriving cranes: In overlapping work zones, cranes entering the area subsequently must yield to those that arrived earlier.
(3) Moving cranes yield to stationary cranes: Mobile cranes must yield to any stationary crane within shared operational zones.
(4) Unloaded cranes yield to loaded cranes: During simultaneous operations, unloaded cranes must yield right-of-way to loaded cranes.
(5) Guest cranes yield to host cranes: Cranes entering another crane's designated primary work zone must yield to the host crane operating in that zone.
(6) Synchronized operations: All cranes must coordinate lifting and lowering operations according to specified timeframes.

3. Crane Operation Rules

Tower cranes initially process PCs assigned to their designated building units. They select the highest-priority task from the pending queue and execute tasks sequentially until completion. When a crane serves more than one building unit, PCs from different building units may be handled by various cranes, necessitating collision checks based on each crane's horizontal coordinates and maximum boom length. Each tower crane is constrained to serve a maximum of two building units.

Mobile cranes are automatically allocated to building units with the slowest assembly progress. Both mobile and tower cranes can operate simultaneously on the same building and floor, with no collision detection modeled between these heterogeneous crane types. To mitigate collision risks, a maximum of two mobile cranes is permitted to operate concurrently on a building unit.

4. Site Layout Rules

Storage areas are constrained to tower crane working ranges to avoid double-handling and cross-interference. PCs are zoned by installation sequence, specs, type, and building.

The maximum storage yard volume must be less than the cumulative total volume of PCs arriving per day. If this condition is satisfied, the storage layout agent imposes no constraints on the assembly construction simulation process; otherwise, constraints are applied. These constraints can be alleviated through two methods: modifying the site layout to expand the storage volume or increasing the waiting time for new PC arrivals to allow space release.

3.2.3. Multi-Agent Model

Workspace, project duration, allocation of workforce, materials and machinery are the critical resources for construction projects. Project managers need to expend time and effort reviewing, comprehending, and coordinating these resources [28]. Based on questionnaire surveys and literature analysis, the agents involved in prefabricated construction and their interaction processes are constructed from a project management perspective. As shown in Figure 3, once the main agent receives a PC assembly task issued by the PC agent, it activates the site layout agent, and the resource agent allocates resources from its resource pool.

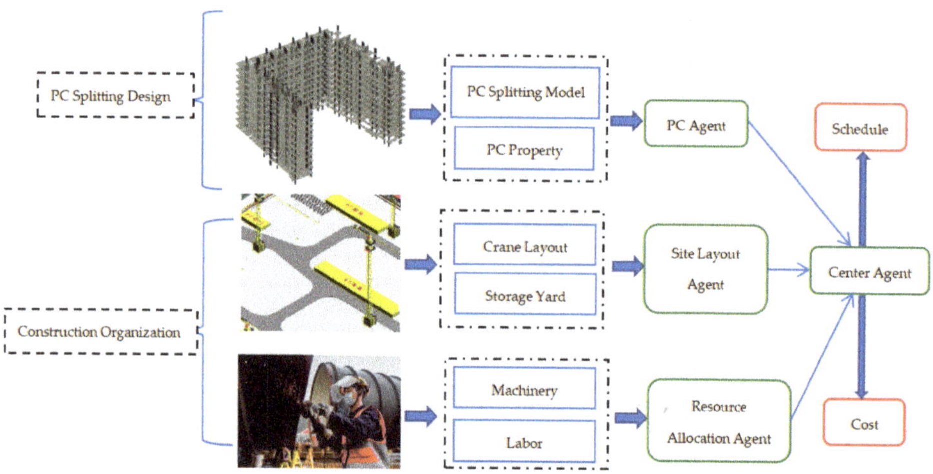

Figure 3. Multi-Agent Simulation Architecture for Prefabricated Construction.

Different prefabricated building BIM models correspond to different PC splitting designs, while different site layout BIM models and resource allocations correspond to different construction organization plans. When the same PC splitting design is simulated with different construction organization plans, an optimal construction organization plan can be identified through comparative analysis. Conversely, an optimal PC splitting design can be obtained by applying different PC splitting plans under the same construction organization plan.

The simulation process is constructed based on the agents and interaction rules:

(1) The PC Agent is composed of the PC Splitting Model Agent and the PC Property Agent. The list of PCs pending assembly is generated based on PC assembly rules.

(2) The Site Layout Agent consists of the Crane Layout Agent and the Storage Yard Agent. The Crane Layout Agent undertakes assembly tasks initiated by the PC Agent based on crane avoidance and operational rules. The Storage Yard Agent continuously monitors whether the storage capacity limit is reached according to the site layout rules and promptly reports to the Main Agent if the limit is exceeded.

(3) The Resource Allocation Agent, composed of the Mechanical Equipment Agent and the Workforce Agent, is activated by the PC Agent. A higher task load triggers greater deployment of mechanical equipment, which in turn requires increased allocation of labor.
(4) The Center Agent acts as a play maker or a control room that interacts with other agents and directs the process. When simulation results (e.g., schedule or cost) deviate from preset values, the Center Agent will adjust the resource allocation plan and relaunch the simulation.

As illustrated in Figure 4, the PC Agent automatically generates an initial PC list, initiates PC assembly tasks based on the floor, orientation attributes, and installation priority values of the PCs, and simultaneously activates the Resource Allocation Agent and the Site Layout Agent. The Resource Allocation Agent releases machinery resources, which in turn automatically allocate labor resources and calculate the direct cost incurred upon the completion of each assembly task. Concurrently, the Site Layout Agent continuously evaluates whether the available storage space can accommodate the daily concentrated delivery of PCs by monitoring real-time spatial volume. The system determines whether to initiate a work pause for cast-in-place concrete to attain its design strength by detecting a change in floor level, which is indicated by a difference in the Z-coordinates between successive assembly tasks. Once the list is exhausted, the direct costs from all assembly tasks are aggregated to compute the total project duration and total cost. These outcomes are then evaluated against predefined benchmarks. If the results are unsatisfactory, modifications are implemented either to the PC splitting design—prompting the PC Agent to regenerate the list—or to the construction organization plan—leading the Resource Allocation Agent to re-allocate resources.

3.2.4. Mobile Crane Scheduling Model Under Process Constraints

A buffer of mobile cranes is reserved to enhance scheduling flexibility, ensuring construction progress remains unaffected by transportation constraints.

$$m = [\sum_{i=1}^{n} q_i/\partial Q] + 1 \tag{1}$$

In Equation (1), m represents the total number of mobile cranes participating in transportation simultaneously, Q denotes the standard load capacity, q_i represents the load capacity of the i-th transportation task, and [] denotes the integer function. The parameter values ∂ lie within the interval (0, 1). Typically, as the number of resource constraints increases, the number of mobile cranes involved in transportation also increases, leading to a smaller parameter value ∂.

A single construction process may be split into multiple transportation tasks, multiple construction processes may be merged into a single transportation task, there may be a one-to-one correspondence between processes and tasks, or certain construction processes may have no associated transportation tasks. Suppose the time window for transportation task i is $[ET_i, LT_i]$. If transportation task 1 is not subject to process constraints, its time window spans the entire duration of the transportation plan. If transportation task 2 is simultaneously constrained by processes B, C, and D, its time window is defined as $ET_2 = \min\{ET_B, ET_C, ET_D\}$, $LT_2 = \max\{LT_B, LT_C, LT_D\}$. If both transportation task 3 and task 4 are constrained by process E, their time windows are set to $ET_3 = ET_4 = ET_E$, $LT_3 = LT_4 = LT_E$.

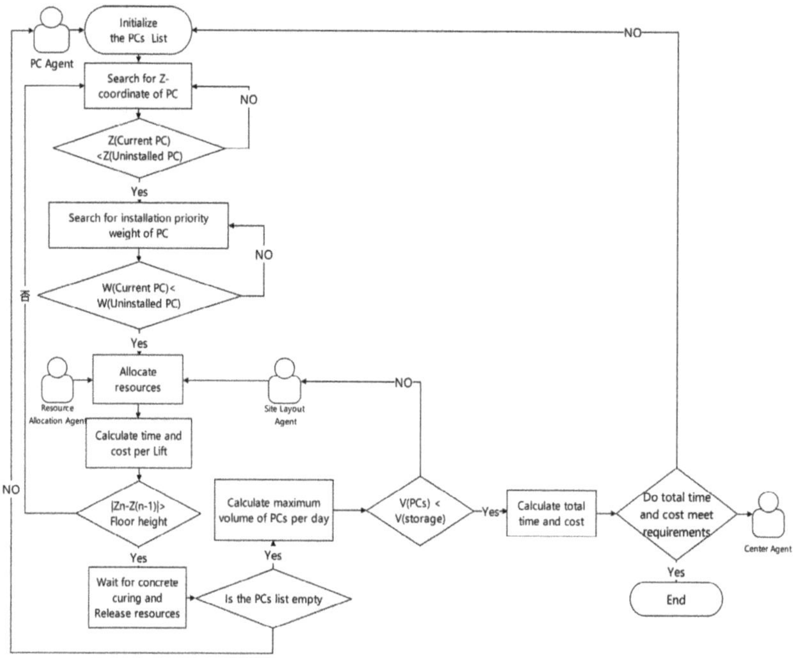

Figure 4. Multi-Agent Simulation Process for Prefabricated Construction.

If the earliest start time of transportation task i is earlier than the earliest start time within the corresponding construction process, meaning mobile cranes arrive at the construction site prematurely, it may occupy limited on-site resources and disrupt construction activities. If the latest finish time of transportation task i is later than the latest finish time within the corresponding construction process, it will inevitably delay the construction progress. Therefore, soft time constraints are adopted, with distinct penalty costs $P(t)$ assigned for both early and late arrivals, as specified in Equation (2). The a is the penalty coefficient for excessively early initiation of transportation activities, while the b is the penalty coefficient for excessively late completion.

$$P(t) = \begin{cases} a(ET_i - t),\ t < ET_i \\ 0,\ ET_i \le t \le LT_i \\ b(t - LT_i),\ t > LT_i \end{cases} \tag{2}$$

The objective of process-constrained scheduling is to optimally deploy mobile cranes in coordination with the construction schedule, ensuring their operation within the time windows defined by the construction process constraints.

$$\begin{gathered} minC_L = \sum_{i=0}^{n} (m_i c_k t_{ik} + P(t_i)), k = 1,2...m \\ s.t. \\ m_i = \begin{cases} q_{ik}/Q_k, m_i \in \mathbb{Z} \\ [q_{ik}/Q_k] + 1, m_i \notin \mathbb{Z} \end{cases} \\ q_{ik} \le Q_k \\ t_i = \max(t_{i_1}, t_{i_2}...t_{i_{m_i}}) \\ ET_i \le t_i \le LT_i \end{gathered} \tag{3}$$

In Equation (3), C_L represents the total transportation cost, c_k denotes the daily cost generated by mobile crane k, t_{ik} indicates the time during which mobile crane k is occupied by transportation task i, m_i is the number of mobile cranes k allocated to transportation task i, t_i signifies the duration of transportation task i, q_{ik} and Q_k represent the actual load transported by mobile crane k in task i and the standard load capacity of mobile crane k, respectively.

Therefore, the load transported by each mobile crane per task must not exceed its standard load capacity, and the duration of each transportation task must be constrained by both the maximum transport time of the corresponding crane and the time window of its associated construction process. When these constraints are satisfied, the crane scheduling scheme achieves the minimal total transportation cost, indicating that the crane allocation and transport time have been optimized under construction process constraints.

3.3. Selecting the Simulation Method

NetLogo 3D 7.0.0 is a multi-agent programmable modeling software that can be used to study the interaction between multiple heterogeneous agents and the phenomenon of their interaction over time [4]. As shown in Figure 5, based on the multi-agent simulation structure and interaction protocol for prefabricated construction, the simulation test was conducted on the NetLogo 3D 7.0.0 platform using case data from a prefabricated building project.

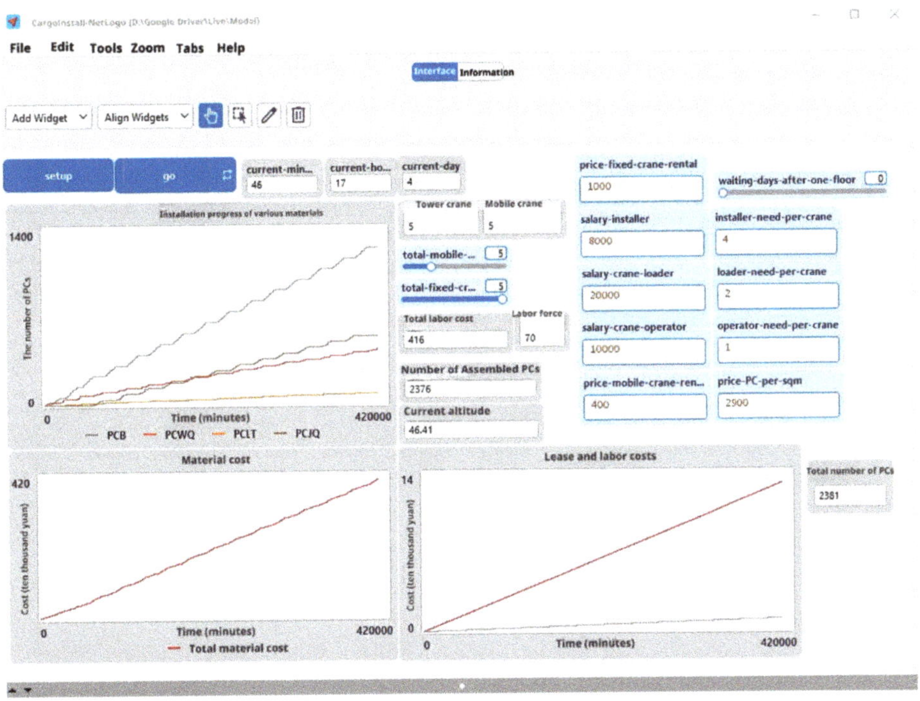

Figure 5. User Interface of NetLogo 3D 7.0.0 for Multi-Agent Simulation Testing in Prefabricated Construction.

4. Case Study Project

A case study of a prefabricated building project, shown in Figure 6, was conducted to implement and validate the proposed multi-agent simulation model. The project site comprises eight prefabricated building units (designated #1 to #8) with heights between 13 and 18 stories and a total area of 77,961.81 square meters.

Figure 6. BIM Model of the Prefabricated Building Cluster for the Case Project.

4.1. Developing the PC Agent

4.1.1. Developing the PC Splitting Model Agent

The PC Splitting Agent delineates which PCs are present after splitting and their respective installation positions. Consequently, as summarized in Table 2, key attributes—including PC family name, unique ID, dimensional properties, volume, and three-dimensional coordinates—were extracted from the project's BIM dataset using a dedicated plugin for Revit 2018. The case study project involved a total of 14,249 PCs. Owing to the extensive volume of data, Table 2 presents only a representative subset. In this context, the length, width, and height of the PCs refer to the volumetric dimensions in the BIM model. Detailed graphical explanations are provided in Appendix A.

Table 2. The Case Data of PC Splitting Model Agent.

Family Name	PC Unit ID	Length (m)	Width (m)	Height (m)	Volume (m^3)	Coordinate X (m)	Coordinate Y (m)	Coordinate Z (m)
PCJQ-01	010-01-003-0001	1.950	0.250	2.602	1.261	119.885	233.310	10.490
PCQ-01	010-01-002-0001	1.250	0.200	2.110	0.203	118.435	233.710	4.490
PCB-01	010-01-001-0001	3.095	1.270	0.060	0.239	123.070	233.900	4.265
PCLT-01	010-01-004-0001	3.080	1.245	0.180	0.842	117.195	226.830	2.770
……								

4.1.2. Developing the PC Property Agent

The PC Property Agent captures key installation attributes including orientation, priority, time, and material cost. As shown in Table 3, the priority value (where 1 indicates the highest priority) defines the recommended installation sequence within the same floor. As the Project Manager enters this data, various construction projects can adapt their parameters with flexibility.

Table 3. The Case Data of PC Property Agent.

Family Type *	Vertical/Horizontal	Installation Priority Weight	Installation Operation Time (Per PC)	PC Material Cost (Per Cubic Meter)
PCJQ	Vertical	1	30 min	¥4647
PCQ	Vertical	2	35 min	¥4414
PCB	Horizontal	3	35 min	¥4292
PCLT	Vertical	4	35 min	¥4051

* Family types refer to the structural types of PCs, such as PCJQ for precast shear walls, PCQ for precast walls, PCB for precast slabs, and PCLT for precast staircases.

4.2. Developing the Site Layout Agent

4.2.1. Developing the Crane Layout Agent

As shown in Table 4, the maximum boom length of the tower crane, 3D positional data, and rotation angle are also extracted from the BIM site layout model using a Revit 2018 software plugin. However, the codes corresponding to the prefabricated buildings for different tower cranes are input by the Project Manager.

Table 4. The Case Data of Crane Layout Agent.

Tower Crane ID	Max Boom Length * (m)	Coordinate X (m)	Coordinate Y (m)	Coordinate Z (m)	Rotation Angle	Corresponding Building ID
C1	50	33.295	11.911	0.000	76.5	7#
C2	50	106.232	−8.827	0.000	346.2	8#
C3	50	124.486	39.609	0.000	346.2	6#
C4	50	56.595	74.867	0.000	346.2	5#
C5	50	116.537	93.193	0.000	346.2	4#
C6	50	121.809	139.953	0.000	356.1	3#
C7	50	61.992	135.092	0.000	346.2	2#
C8	50	49.565	212.552	0.000	346.2	1#

* When multiple tower cranes operate at the same height, the maximum boom length is a critical parameter for determining whether a collision may occur between the tower cranes.

4.2.2. Developing the Storage Yard Agent

As shown in Table 5, the storage yard type, 3D positional data, and area are also extracted from the BIM site layout model using a Revit 2018 software plugin. And the maximum stacking height is entered by the Project Manager.

Table 5. The Case Data of Storage Yard Agent.

Yard ID	Yard Type	Coordinate X (m)	Coordinate Y (m)	Coordinate Z (m)	Yard Area (m^2)	Yard Height Limit (m)
S1	PC	44.234	238.589	−1.950	426.92	4
S2	PC	124.225	238.788	−1.950	211.71	4
S3	PC	95.904	188.420	−1.950	635.12	4
S4	PC	180.919	162.914	−1.950	211.71	4
S5	PC	214.912	244.844	−1.950	211.71	4
S6	PC	8.176	192.013	−1.950	142.10	4
S7	PC	78.019	106.955	−1.950	211.71	4
S8	PC	42.361	66.443	−1.950	211.71	4
S9	PC	42.746	35.028	−1.950	211.71	4
S10	PC	96.833	9.415	−1.950	211.71	4
S11	PC	111.364	35.028	−1.950	379.75	4
S12	PC	101.459	66.398	−1.950	419.66	4
S13	PC	194.536	67.691	−1.950	379.75	4
S14	PC	189.029	35.255	−1.950	378.95	4

4.3. Developing the Resource Allocation Agent

The data for Resource Allocation Agents are all entered by the Project Manager.

4.3.1. Developing the Machinery Resource Agent

As illustrated in Table 6, the mechanical equipment used in the case project comprises tower cranes, mobile cranes, and grouting machines. The machinery Agent includes the machinery model, type, operational parameters, mobilization cost, and rental cost. Mobilization cost encompasses one-time expenses such as installation, dismantling, and other associated activities.

Table 6. The Case Data of Machinery Resource Agent.

Machinery Model	Machinery Type	Operational Parameters	Mobilization Cost	Rental Cost (Per Equipment Shift *)
QTZ250	tower crane	Preparation time: 10 min/operation Lowering speed: 40 m/min Lifting speed: 20 m/min	¥125,000	¥1444.89
QY50B	Mobile Crane	Preparation time: 8 min/operation Lowering speed: 30 m/min Lifting speed: 15 m/min	¥250,000	¥1191.33
NL-415	Grouting Machine	None	¥0	¥30.9

* An 8 h operation of a single machine is defined as one equipment shift.

4.3.2. Developing the Labor Resource Agent

Labor resources are allocated based on the quantity of equipment mobilized by the Machinery Resource Agent. As shown in Table 7, the Labor Resource Agent is configured by trade type and its corresponding labor costs.

Table 7. The Case Data of Labor Resource Agent.

Trade Type	Labor Cost (Per Man-Day *)	Number of Workers Allocated Per Machine
PC Worker	¥265	Tower Crane: 1 Mobile Crane: 1
Surveyor	¥218	Tower Crane: 2
Rigger	¥500	Tower Crane: 1 Mobile Crane: 1
Helper	¥218	Tower Crane: 1 Mobile Crane: 1 Grouting Machine: 4

* An 8 h work period by one worker is defined as one man-day.

5. Results and Discussion

5.1. Simulation Results from Various Resource Allocation Schemes

Resource allocation is a critical component of construction planning. For this case project, three distinct resource allocation schemes were devised based on its scale. These schemes adhered to the typical principle that the number of tower cranes does not exceed the number of building units, and mobile cranes do not outnumber tower cranes. Consequently, a comprehensive data analysis was conducted on the simulation results derived from each scheme.

(1) Scheme 1 (4C0M): The first scheme deploys 4 tower cranes, each with the capacity to serve two building units simultaneously. This scheme involves no mobile cranes and is hereafter referred to as the 4C0M scheme.
(2) Scheme 2 (4C2M): The second scheme also utilizes 4 tower cranes (each serving two units), which are supplemented by 2 mobile cranes. This is denoted as the 4C2M scheme.
(3) Scheme 3 (8C2M): The third scheme entails the use of 8 tower cranes, with each crane dedicated to a single building unit, in conjunction with 2 mobile cranes. This is abbreviated as the 8C2M scheme.

5.1.1. Simulation Results Under the 4C0M Resource Allocation Scheme

When the 4C0M resource allocation scheme was applied to the construction simulation of the case project, the direct total cost was RMB 53,312,240 and the project duration was 305 days, as shown in the simulation results in Table 8.

Table 8. Simulation Results under the 4C0M Resource Allocation Scheme for the Case Project.

Building Unit ID	Start Date	End Date	Direct Cost	Crane ID	PC Units Hoisted
1#	1 December 2024	22 July 2025	¥7,846,820	C1	2092
2#	1 December 2024	2 October 2025	¥12,650,060	C2	2956
3#	1 December 2024	16 April 2025	¥3,456,630	C3	1078
4#	1 December 2024	22 April 2025	¥4,950,630	C0	1472
5#	10 December 2024	20 August 2025	¥8,540,120	C1	2417
6#	8 December 2024	23 May 2025	¥460,772	C2	1324
7#	6 December 2024	1 May 2025	¥4,148,790	C3	1147
8#	8 December 2024	1 July 2025	¥7,111,470	C0	1763
Total	The project duration: 305 days		¥53,312,240	4C0M	14,249

Simulation data reveals that Tower Crane C3 prematurely withdrew from lifting operations and remained idle during the later phase, while Tower Crane C2 was the last to complete its lifting tasks. Since Building Unit 2# associated with Crane C2 contained the largest quantity of PCs, its assembly duration was the longest, consequently exerting the most significant impact on the overall project timeline. In accordance with multi-agent interaction rules, mobile cranes are programmed to automatically detect and assist the tower crane experiencing the highest workload pressure. Thus, subsequent simulation tests will incorporate two mobile cranes to mitigate the imbalance in tower crane resource utilization.

5.1.2. Simulation Results Under the 4C2M Resource Allocation Scheme

When the 4C2M resource allocation scheme was applied to the construction simulation of the case project, the direct total cost reached RMB 59,723,560 and the project duration was 181 days, as detailed in the simulation results presented in Table 9.

The introduction of two mobile cranes in this simulation test series resulted in a significant reduction in the total project duration. Considering the substantial volume of lifting operations required for the assembly of the case project and the need to facilitate on-site construction management, the most conventional resource allocation scheme will be adopted, which assigns one tower crane per building unit. Consequently, four additional tower cranes will be included in the third simulation test series.

Table 9. Simulation Results under the 4C2M Resource Allocation Scheme for the Case Project.

Building Unit ID	Start Date	End Date	Direct Cost	Crane ID	PC Units Hoisted
1#	1 December 2024	27 May 2025	¥11,097,810	C1 M0 M1	1392 439 261
2#	1 December 2024	6 May 2025	¥11,911,350	C2 M0 M1	1307 802 847
3#	1 December 2024	11 April 2025	¥3,894,440	C3 M0 M1	1073 2 3
4#	1 December 2024	6 May 2025	¥5,557,370	C0 M0 M1	1297 83 92
5#	3 December 2024	6 May 2025	¥8,844,580	C1 M0 M1	1308 578 531
6#	3 December 2024	15 May 2025	¥5,418,280	C2 M0 M1	1291 17 16
7#	6 December 2024	1 May 2025	¥4,622,270	C3	1147
8#	8 December 2024	31 May 2025	¥8,377,460	C0 M0 M1	1390 186 187
Total	The project duration: 181 days		¥59,723,560	4C2M	14,249

5.1.3. Simulation Results Under the 8C2M Resource Allocation Scheme

The application of the 8C2M resource allocation scheme to the case project simulation yielded a direct total cost of RMB 70,971,360 and a project duration of 168 days, as shown in Table 10. Notably, despite the substantial cost increase resulting from the addition of four tower cranes, the corresponding reduction in project duration was marginal.

Table 10. Simulation Results under the 8C2M Resource Allocation Scheme for the Case Project.

Building Unit ID	Start Date	End Date	Direct Cost	Crane ID	PC Units Hoisted
1#	1 December 2024	18 May 2025	¥10,827,630	C1 M0 M1	1373 311 408
2#	1 December 2024	18 May 2025	¥15,047,220	C2 M0 M1	1433 797 726
3#	1 December 2024	16 April 2025	¥5,048,880	C3	1078
4#	1 December 2024	17 May 2025	¥7,142,030	C4 M0 M1	1415 28 29

Table 10. *Cont.*

Building Unit ID	Start Date	End Date	Direct Cost	Crane ID	PC Units Hoisted
5#	1 December 2024	18 May 2025	¥11,436,920	C5 M0 M1	1484 448 485
6#	1 December 2024	14 May 2025	¥6,586,830	C6 M0 M1	1311 6 7
7#	1 December 2024	25 April 2025	¥5,656,560	C7	1147
8#	1 December 2024	18 May 2025	¥9,225,290	C0 M0 M1	1367 229 167
Total	The project duration: 168 days		¥70,971,360	8C2M	14,249

5.2. Comparison of Simulation Results from Various Resource Allocation Schemes

Typically, multiple tower cranes are deployed and removed from the site simultaneously. Uneven utilization of tower crane resources can lead to idleness and consequent resource waste. As illustrated in Figure 7, a comparative analysis of PC assembly volumes per crane across the three simulation scenarios demonstrates that collaboration between mobile cranes and tower cranes results in more balanced PC lifting distributions and significantly reduced idle time among tower cranes.

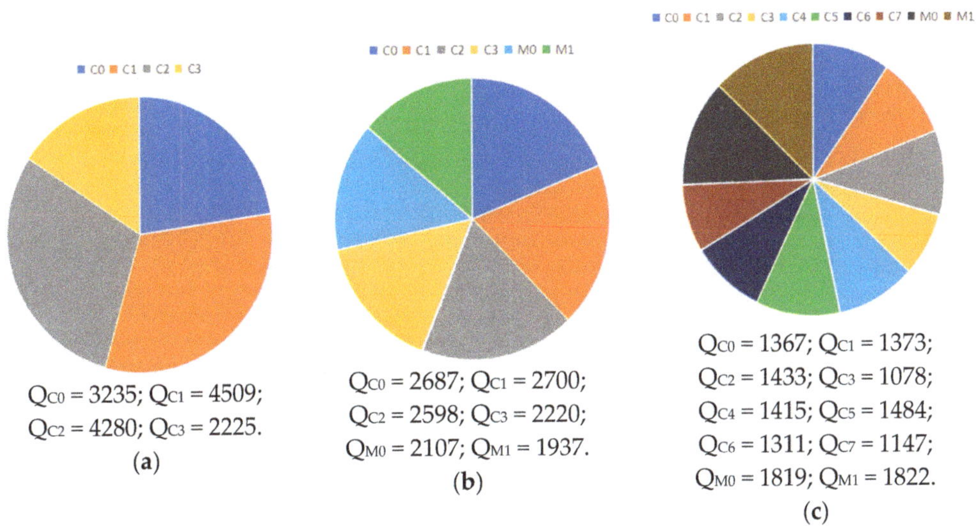

Figure 7. Comparison of PC Lifting Quantities by Cranes under Different Resource Allocation Schemes. (**a**) PC Lifting Quantities by Cranes in the 4C0M Resource Allocation Scheme; (**b**) PC Lifting Quantities by Cranes in the 4C2M Resource Allocation Scheme; (**c**) PC Lifting Quantities by Cranes in the 8C2M Resource Allocation Scheme.

A Gantt chart illustrating the project schedule was developed from simulation results of the three resource allocation schemes. As demonstrated in Figure 8, increasingly balanced resource allocation corresponds to higher synchronization of construction progress among individual building units.

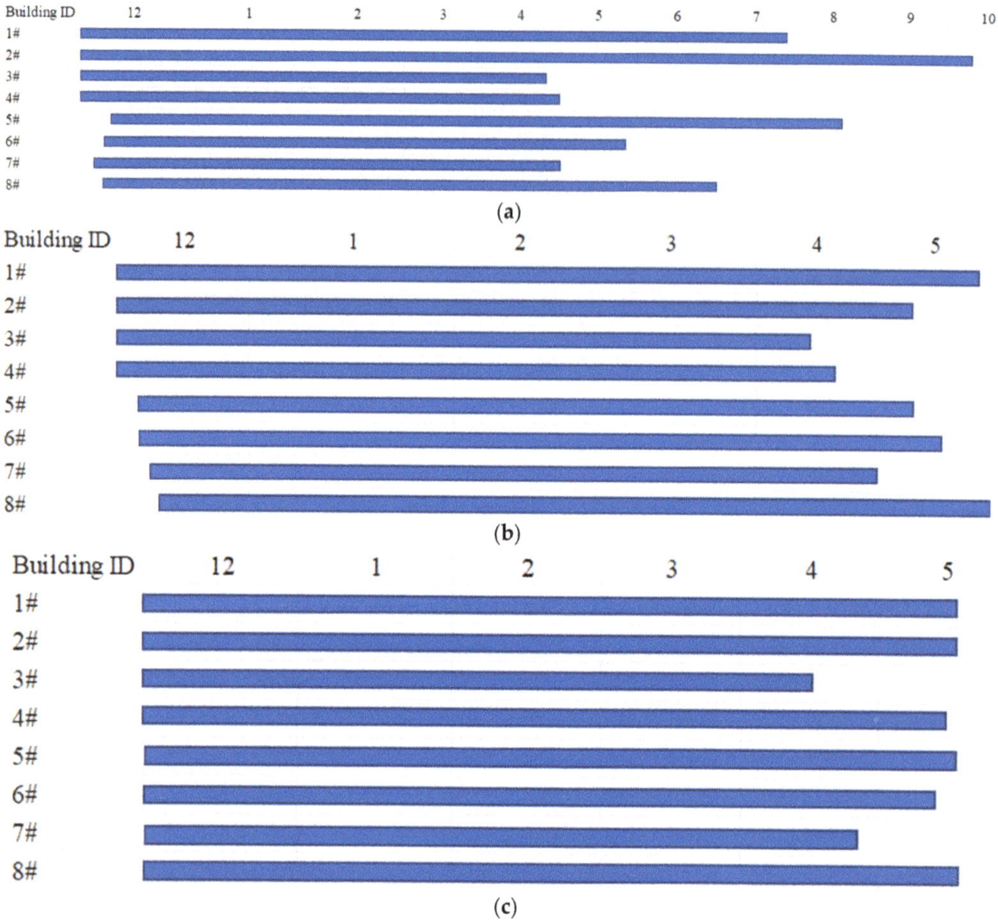

Figure 8. Comparison of Project Schedules under Different Resource Allocation Schemes. (**a**) Project Schedule Gantt Chart in the 4C0M Resource Allocation Scheme; (**b**) Project Schedule Gantt Chart in the 4C2M Resource Allocation Scheme; (**c**) Project Schedule Gantt Chart in the 8C2M Resource Allocation Scheme.

The case study, utilizing the same prefabricated building project and PC splitting design, compares three resource configurations: 4C0M (¥53,312,240; 305 days), 4C2M (¥59,723,560; 181 days), and 8C2M (¥70,971,360; 168 days). Comparing 4C0M and 4C2M shows that adding two mobile cranes increased cost by 12.03% but cut duration by 40.66%. In contrast, adding four tower cranes (4C2M vs. 8C2M) resulted in a further 18.83% cost increase for only a marginal 7.18% reduction in duration. Consequently, as shown in Figure 9, the 4C2M scheme demonstrates superior economic efficiency by achieving significant time savings at a relatively moderate cost.

Reducing the project duration often requires additional resource allocation, which consequently increases construction costs. The simulations can be used to identify the point at which the cost of an additional mobile crane outweighs the benefit of a shorter duration. As shown in Table 11, a comparison of the resource allocation schemes (4C1M, 4C2M, 4C3M) against the 4C0M baseline demonstrates that the 4C1M scheme is the most economically efficient. This is due to the higher operating cost of mobile cranes compared to tower cranes. Therefore, the optimal strategy is not to maximize their number, but to deploy them in a way that effectively complements the tower cranes and addresses temporary shortfalls in lifting capacity.

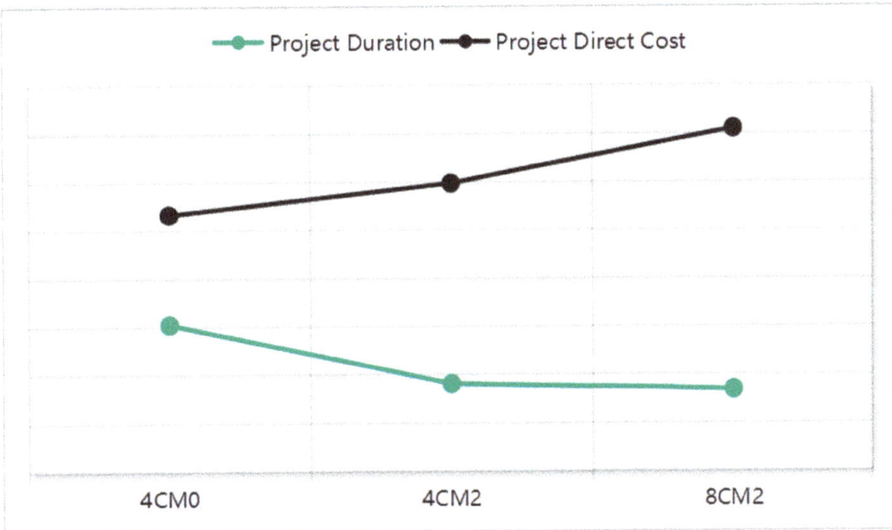

Figure 9. Comparison of Project Duration and Cost under Different Resource Allocation Schemes.

Table 11. Data Analysis on the Marginal Effect of Mobile Cranes.

Resource Allocation Scheme	The Project Direct Cost	The Project Duration	Cost Increase	Schedule Reduction
4CM0	¥53,312,240	305 days	/	/
4CM1	¥55,142,440	193 days	3.43%	36.72%
4CM2	¥59,723,560	181 days	12.03%	40.66%
4CM3	¥62,286,190	155 days	16.83%	49.18%

5.3. BIM-5D Visualization of Simulation Results

Navisworks, developed by Autodesk, is a professional 3D model review software primarily used for data integration, clash detection, and visual simulation in BIM projects. To comply with the data import specifications of Navisworks 2018, simulation results are exported in CSV format. As illustrated in Figure 10, the data pertaining to building units, tower cranes, and site layout are exported via a plug-in of Revit 2018, after which the project manager supplements the resource allocation data. The aforementioned data are imported into NetLogo 3D 7.0.0 to perform construction process simulation. The resulting simulation data are then imported into Navisworks 2018 to generate the BIM-5D animated visualization. To ensure the interoperability of BIM models, Revit and Navisworks must be on the same version. However, any version of Revit can interface with any version of NetLogo3D, provided its database data can be exported.

This interoperability facilitates rapid dynamic visualization of planned schedules and direct costs, which enables more efficient 5D BIM (integrating 3D models, time, and cost) management for prefabricated construction projects on site.

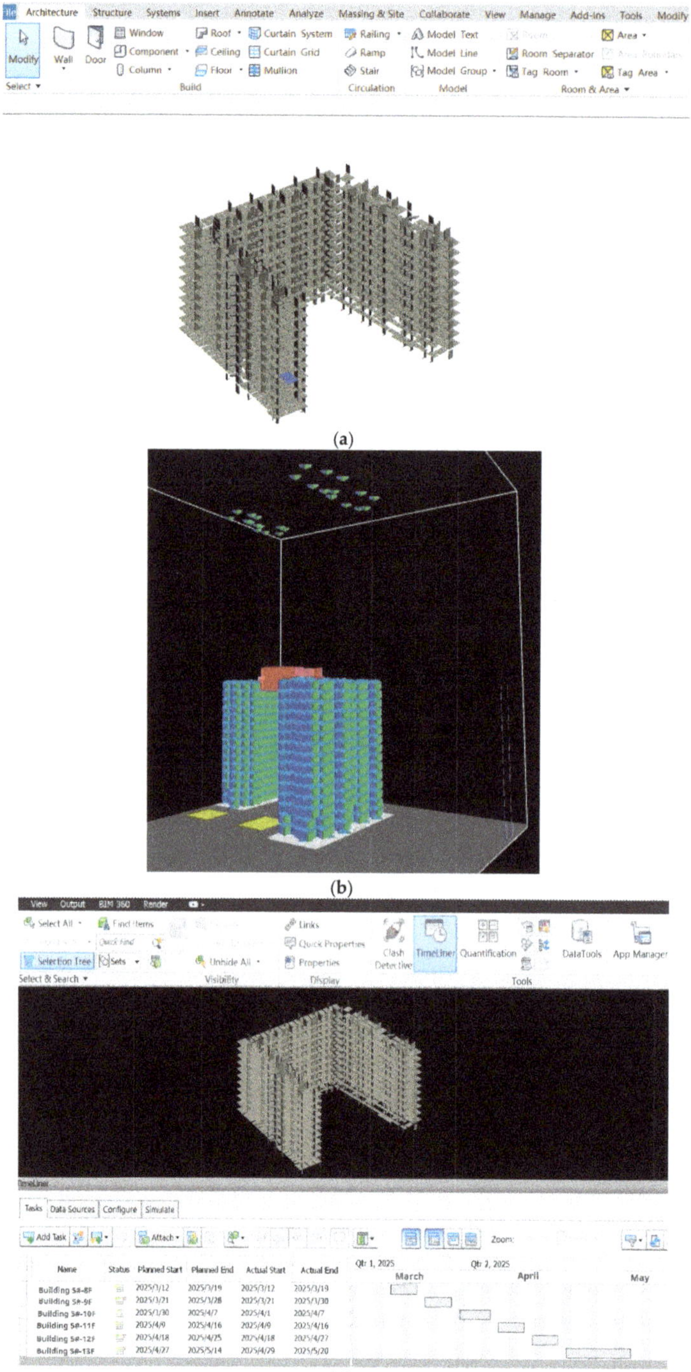

Figure 10. Revit 2018, NetLogo3D 7.0.0 and Navisworks 2018 Interfaces for Prefabricated Construction. (**a**) Revit 2018 3D Model Display; (**b**) NetLogo 3D 7.0.0 Simulation Output; (**c**) Navisworks 2018 BIM 5D Presentation.

This study has several limitations. First, it specifically investigated prefabricated concrete residential buildings in Shanghai. Consequently, the findings may not be directly generalizable to other regions or construction types. Second, the simulation model operated under simplifying assumptions, such as uninterrupted material supply. While this facilitated a clearer analysis of internal site logistics, these assumptions may not fully capture real-world uncertainties, potentially affecting the accuracy of resource utilization estimates.

6. Conclusions

This study establishes integrated data linkages between the PC splitting plan from the detailed design phase and the construction organization plan from the construction preparation phase to develop a multi-agent simulation model with associated interaction rules. The approach enables granular simulation of the prefabricated construction process by modeling the hoisting and transportation of each individual PC. By decomposing the complexity of prefabricated construction into agent-based elements and reassembling them through rule-based interactions, the method offers a simplified yet systematic representation of the construction workflow. Finally, case projects were simulated using NetLogo 3D 7.0.0, with output results subsequently imported into Navisworks 2018 for BIM-5D visualization applications.

Furthermore, the paper makes two key algorithmic contributions. First, it introduces a novel backward calculation approach to tackle storage yard space constraints, a limitation often overlooked in existing studies. This method determines the maximum daily volume of PCs that can be delivered to the site, thereby optimizing the balance between storage capacity and on-site resource allocation. Second, the paper develops a mobile crane scheduling model that explicitly incorporates process constraints. This model enhances crane operational efficiency, which is critical for accelerating project timelines.

In the case study, with four tower cranes, introducing a single mobile crane (the 4C1M scheme) increased costs by a mere 3.43% over the 4C0M scheme, while reducing project duration by 36.72%. These results indicate that an optimal crane configuration can yield significant economic benefits. In contrast, with two mobile cranes, doubling the tower cranes to eight (the 8C2M scheme) increased costs by 18.83% for a limited duration reduction of only 7.18%. This comparison clearly demonstrates that adding mobile cranes is a far more cost-effective strategy for reducing duration than adding tower cranes. Despite this lower cost-effectiveness, the 8C2M scheme offers compensatory operational simplicity, as the one-to-one pairing of cranes to building units streamlines on-site coordination.

6.1. Practical Applications

The NetLogo 3D 7.0.0 platform was employed for simulation tasks, as it is better suited for single-building analyses, whereas its performance for building clusters is significantly slower. For the management aspects of the project, the full-process management software for prefabricated construction was independently developed within the Visual Studio 2022 development environment, utilizing SQL Server 2022 as the database management tool. Users can import agent data into the software interface, input parameters such as the project start date, expected project completion duration, expected project investment cost, and the maximum number of buildings served by each tower crane, then initiate the simulation by clicking the "Start Simulation" button. After approximately three minutes of processing, the simulation results are displayed on the interface, with an option to download more detailed data. The output primarily includes the start time, end time, and direct costs for each PC assembly task, floor level, building and project. Direct costs comprise expenses for PC materials, equipment usage and labor. The software has been tested during both the design and construction phases of two large-scale projects. Test results demonstrate that both the accuracy and computational speed of the simulation meet the requirements for practical application in real-world prefabricated construction projects.

A distinctive strength of this research lies in its close alignment with practical project management requirements, emphasizing both seamless multi-platform data integration and adaptability to diverse application scenarios. (1) During the design phase, the BIM model of the PC splitting design (provided by the detailing unit) is loaded and simulated under standardized construction organization plans. This process allows for the rapid screening of different design options against contractual cost and schedule targets. (2) During the construction preparation phase, with the PC splitting design finalized, the contractor's construction organization plan is simulated and analyzed for deviations from contracted cost and schedule. This process facilitates plan optimization and enables construction execution supported by BIM-5D simulations. (3) During the construction phase, the project's status is monitored by comparing simulation data with actual progress to identify schedule and cost deviations. By establishing deviation thresholds, the system provides early warnings to facilitate proactive control.

6.2. Recommendations for Future Research

The data collection for this study was initially confined to Shanghai, which limits the generalizability of the findings. To address this, applying the proposed methodology to diverse geographic regions is a crucial direction for future work. Furthermore, while the current research focused on residential buildings, the framework shows significant promise for adaptation to other project types, such as infrastructure projects (e.g., bridges and tunnels) and industrial facilities. Future studies should validate its efficacy in these contexts.

The perspective of prefabricated construction management will gradually extend from "project management" to "whole-life asset management." The comprehensive digital assets (including BIM models and construction process data) accumulated during the construction phase can be seamlessly delivered to the operation and maintenance phase, supporting smart facility operations, space management, and energy consumption analysis. This approach maximizes asset value, demonstrating that prefabricated construction is not only a transformation in building methodology but also a cornerstone for future smart cities and digital asset management.

Author Contributions: Conceptualization, Y.S. and J.W.; methodology, Y.S., J.W. and G.-H.J.; software, J.W. and G.-H.J.; validation, Y.S., J.W. and G.-H.J.; investigation, J.W. and G.-H.J.; resources, Y.S. and J.W.; data curation, J.W. and G.-H.J.; writing—original draft preparation, J.W. and G.-H.J.; writing—review and editing, Y.S. and J.W.; visualization, J.W.; supervision, Y.S.; project administration, Y.S. and G.-H.J.; funding acquisition, Y.S. All authors have read and agreed to the published version of the manuscript.

Funding: This research was funded by Scientific Research and Innovation Projects of Shanghai Jianke Consulting Group Co., Ltd., grant number KY10000249.2023003.

Data Availability Statement: Data are contained within the article.

Conflicts of Interest: Authors Yi Shen and Guan-Hang Jin were employed by the company Shanghai Jianke Engineering Consulting Co., Ltd. The remaining author declares that the research was conducted in the absence of any commercial or financial relationships that could be construed as a potential conflict of interest.

Appendix A

The main types of PCs comprise load-bearing walls, non-load-bearing exterior envelopes, slabs, stairs, columns, beams, and interior finishing components. In contrast, the case study project incorporates only the first four types, whose volumetric dimensions are detailed in Appendix A.

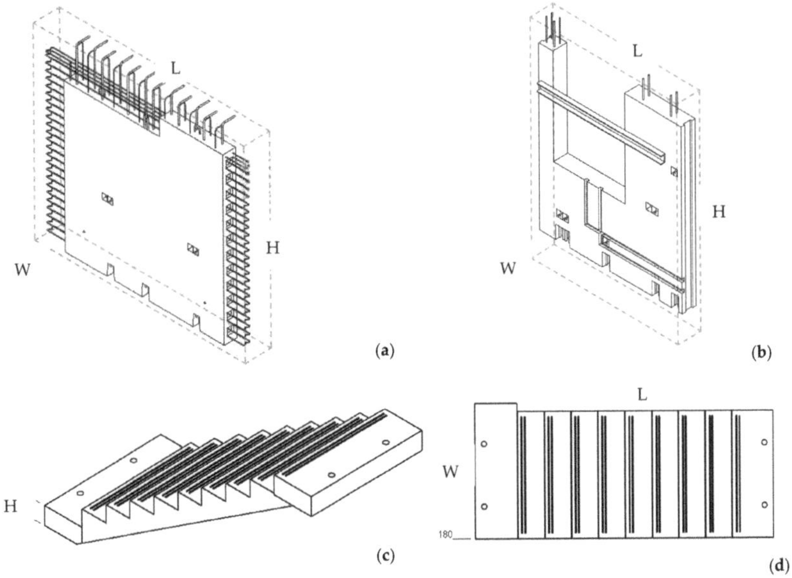

Figure A1. Dimension Callouts for PC BIM Model. (**a**) Shear Wall or Slab Dimension Callout; (**b**) Non-Load-Bearing Wall Dimension Callout; (**c**) Stair Dimension Callout; (**d**) Dimension Callout on Stair Plan.

References

1. "14th Five-Year" Plan for Prefabricated Buildings in Shanghai. Available online: https://zjw.sh.gov.cn/ghjh/20211109/f5ed3fe865b447b7b064fc695cae1351.html (accessed on 3 November 2021).
2. Yin, J.; Huang, R.; Sun, H.; Cai, S. Multi-Objective Optimization for Coordinated Production and Transportation in Prefabricated Construction with on-Site Lifting Requirements. *Comput. Ind. Eng.* **2024**, *189*, 110017. [CrossRef]
3. Xiang, L.; Tan, Y.; Shen, G.; Jin, X. Applications of Multi-Agent Systems from the Perspective of Construction Management: A Literature Review. *Eng. Constr. Archit. Manag.* **2022**, *29*, 3288–3310. [CrossRef]
4. Feng, J.; Liu, B.; Tang, J.; Wang, Q. The Emergence of the Contractor's Innovation Capability at Project Level: An Agent-Based Modeling Approach. *Buildings* **2023**, *13*, 2941. [CrossRef]
5. Attajer, A.; Mecheri, B. Multi-Agent Simulation Approach for Modular Integrated Construction Supply Chain. *Appl. Sci.* **2024**, *14*, 5286. [CrossRef]
6. Zhang, C.; Zhang, F.; Yin, S.; Fu, Y.; Liu, J.; Duan, P. Study on the Optimization of Duration for Repetitive Projects Considering Spatial Interference Effects in Operations. *J. Asian Archit. Build. Eng.* **2025**, 1–26. [CrossRef]
7. Jiang, S.; Yang, B.; Liu, B. Precast Components On-Site Construction Planning and Scheduling Method Based on a Novel Deep Learning Integrated Multi-Agent System. *J. Build. Eng.* **2025**, *102*, 111907. [CrossRef]
8. Liu, B.; Yang, B.; Zhang, B.; Dong, M.; Jiang, S.; Xiao, J. Spatio-Temporal Deduction of Floor Construction Based on the Agent Modeling of Construction Actors. *Autom. Constr.* **2022**, *142*, 104487. [CrossRef]
9. Liu, B.D.; Yang, B.; Han, Y.; Xiao, J.Z.; Dong, M.S. Establishment and Application of Multi-Agent Simulation System Based on On-Site Construction Performers. In Proceedings of the 17th East Asian-Pacific Conference on Structural Engineering and Construction, 2022, EASEC-17, Singapore, 14 March 2023. [CrossRef]
10. Kim, K.; Faust, K.M.; Leite, F. Simulation Modeling Efforts in the Construction Industry: Integrated Application of BIM and Agent-Based Modeling. In Proceedings of the Computing in Civil Engineering 2023, Corvallis, OR, USA, 25 January 2024. [CrossRef]
11. Kedir, N.S.; Somi, S.; Fayek, A.R.; Nguyen, P.H.D. Hybridization of Reinforcement Learning and Agent-Based Modeling to Optimize Construction Planning and Scheduling. *Autom. Constr.* **2022**, *142*, 104498. [CrossRef]

12. Pourrahimian, E.; Salhab, D.; Hamzeh, F.; AbouRizk, S. A Decision Support System for Evaluating Construction Project Recovery Plans. *Can. J. Civ. Eng.* **2025**, *52*, 1336–1354. [CrossRef]
13. Hu, Y.; Wu, L.; Li, N.; Zhao, T. Multi-Agent Decision-Making in Construction Engineering and Management: A Systematic Review. *Sustainability* **2024**, *16*, 7132. [CrossRef]
14. Zohourian, M.; Pamidimukkala, A.; Kermanshachi, S.; Almaskati, D. Modular Construction: A Comprehensive Review. *Buildings* **2025**, *15*, 2020. [CrossRef]
15. Abdul Nabi, M.; El-adaway, I.H. Risk-based approach to predict the cost performance of modularization in construction projects. *J. Constr. Eng. Manag.* **2021**, *147*, 04021133. [CrossRef]
16. Mehdipoor, A.; Iordanova, I.; Al-Hussein, M. Enhancing the Manufacturing Process in Light-Gauge Steel Off-Site Construction Using Semiautomation. *J. Constr. Eng. Manag.* **2025**, *151*, 04025055. [CrossRef]
17. Yuan, Z.; Man, Q.; Guan, Z.; Yi, C.; Zheng, M.; Chang, Y.; Li, H.X. Simulation and Optimization of Prefabricated Building Construction Considering Multiple Objectives and Uncertain Factors. *J. Build. Eng.* **2024**, *86*, 108830. [CrossRef]
18. Wang, Z.; Hu, H.; Gong, J.; Ma, X. Synchronizing Production Scheduling with Resources Allocation for Precast Components in a Multi-Agent System Environment. *J. Manuf. Syst.* **2018**, *49*, 131–142. [CrossRef]
19. Attajer, A.; Mecheri, B.; Hadbi, I.; Amoo, S.N.; Bouchnita, A. Sustainable Supply Chain Strategies for Modular-Integrated Construction Using a Hybrid Multi-Agent-Deep Learning Approach. *Sustainability* **2025**, *17*, 5434. [CrossRef]
20. Jang, D.-H.; Roh, G.-T.; Jeon, C.-H. Simulation-Based Optimization of Crane Lifting Position and Capacity Using a Construction Digital Twin for Prefabricated Bridge Deck Assembly. *Buildings* **2025**, *15*, 475. [CrossRef]
21. Tak, A.N.; Taghaddos, H.; Mousaei, A.; Bolourani, A.; Hermann, U. BIM-Based 4D Mobile Crane Simulation and Onsite Operation Management. *Autom. Constr.* **2021**, *128*, 103766. [CrossRef]
22. Khodabandelu, A.; Park, J.; Arteaga, C. Improving Multitower Crane Layout Planning by Leveraging Operational Flexibility Related to Motion Paths. *J. Manag. Eng.* **2023**, *39*, 04023035. [CrossRef]
23. Huang, C.; Wang, Z.K.; Li, B.; Wang, C.; Xu, L.S.; Jiang, K.; Liu, M.; Guo, C.X.; Zhao, X.F.; Yang, H. Discretized Cell Modeling for Optimal Layout of Multiple Tower Cranes. *J. Constr. Eng. Manag.* **2023**, *149*, 04023068. [CrossRef]
24. Zhang, W.; Zhang, H.; Yu, L. Collaborative Planning for Stacking and Installation of Prefabricated Building Components Regarding Crane-Collision Avoidance. *J. Constr. Eng. Manag.* **2023**, *149*, 04023029. [CrossRef]
25. Younes, A.; Marzouk, M. Tower Cranes Layout Planning Using Agent-Based Simulation Considering Activity Conflicts. *Autom. Constr.* **2018**, *93*, 348–360. [CrossRef]
26. Khodabandelu, A.; Park, J.; Arteaga, C. Crane Operation Planning in Overlapping Areas Through Dynamic Supply Selection. *Autom. Constr.* **2020**, *117*, 103253. [CrossRef]
27. Liu, C.; Zhang, F.; Han, X.; Ye, H.; Shi, Z.; Zhang, J.; Wang, T.; She, J.; Zhang, T. Intelligent Optimization of Tower Crane Location and Layout Based on Firefly Algorithm. *Comput. Intell. Neurosci.* **2022**, *2022*, 6810649. [CrossRef] [PubMed]
28. He, C.; Liu, M.; Zhang, Y.; Wang, Z.; Hsiang, S.M.; Chen, G.; Li, W.; Dai, G. Space–Time–Workforce Visualization and Conditional Capacity Synthesis in Uncertainty. *J. Manag. Eng.* **2023**, *39*, 15. [CrossRef]

buildings

MDPI

Article

Energy-Efficient Multi-Objective Scheduling for Modern Construction Projects with Dynamic Resource Constraints

Mudassar Rauf * and Jabir Mumtaz *

College of Mechanical and Electrical Engineering, Wenzhou University, Wenzhou 325035, China
* Correspondence: mudassarrauf16@gmail.com (M.R.); jabirmumtaz@wzu.edu.cn (J.M.)

Abstract

The rapidly evolving business landscape, driven by stringent energy conservation policies, compels construction firms to adopt energy-efficient project-centric structures, particularly in modern construction projects. These firms face a complex, multi-mode, resource-constrained, multi-project scheduling problem characterized by dynamic project arrivals and multiple resource constraints, including global, local, and non-renewable capacities. This environment pressures managers to simultaneously optimize the conflicting objectives of minimizing total project duration and total energy consumption. To address this challenge, we propose a novel multi-objective Smart Raccoon Family Optimization (SRFO) algorithm. The SRFO, a hybrid evolutionary approach, is designed to enhance global exploration and local exploitation. Its performance is boosted by integrating a non-dominated sorting mechanism, a dedicated energy-efficient search strategy, and enhanced genetic operators. The SRFO simultaneously optimizes two conflicting objectives: minimizing the total project duration and total energy consumption. This approach effectively integrates the unique constraint of off-site component production and on-site assembly within an intelligent scheduling framework. Empirical validation across benchmark problems and a real-world case study is conducted, comparing the SRFO with existing multi-objective approaches, such as NSGA-III, MOABC, and MOSMO. Performance is assessed using convergence and distribution metrics, augmented by TOPSIS-based multi-criteria decision-making. Results conclusively demonstrate that the proposed SRFO significantly outperforms existing approaches and offers a robust, high-quality solution for project management in energy-constrained environments.

Keywords: modern construction projects; multi-objective optimization; energy-efficient scheduling; resource-constrained; swarm intelligence; management decision-making

1. Introduction

The modern construction sector is a major energy consumer and a significant contributor to carbon emissions, leading to environmental issues, such as the greenhouse effect [1]. Governments worldwide are implementing policies to promote energy-saving measures in large-scale constructions to address these concerns. For instance, China aims to achieve carbon neutrality by 2060, prompting specific policies to control energy consumption and emissions across all future projects [2]. Global attention is shifting towards energy-aware scheduling and green manufacturing. This is particularly critical in the construction sector, which involves a complex, distributed supply chain of off-site component production and on-site assembly. Improving energy efficiency is essential for sustainable development [3,4]. The rapidly evolving business landscape, driven by stringent energy conservation policies, compels construction firms to adopt energy-efficient project-centric structures, particularly in modern construction projects.

In addition to energy efficiency, firms are under increasing pressure to reduce project construction costs and improve delivery times. Planning and scheduling are essential for projects that involve assigning start or finish times to tasks under various constraints [5]. In real life, project managers face tremendous pressure to complete a project with limited resources. Only considering precedence constraints and activity duration is an irrational assumption, as projects require resources ranging from budget to human resources and raw materials to equipment [6]. Therefore, integrating resource constraints into project scheduling yields resource-constrained project scheduling (RCPS) problems [7]. In contrast to fundamental RCPS problems, which typically assume a single project and a single execution mode, over 90% of industrial projects are managed concurrently within multi-project environments [8,9]. The concurrent execution of multiple projects can significantly influence a firm's efficiency, offering advantages such as reduced project durations, enhanced resource allocation, and lower management expenses, but it also increases scheduling complexity [10,11]. In a multi-project environment, multiple projects must compete to capture available resources. Furthermore, activities can often be executed in a variety of modes, each with specific resource requirements and differing durations [12]. Integrating multi-project execution and execution mode selection within the RCPSP framework defines the multi-mode resource constraint multi-project scheduling (MRCMPS) problem [13].

Consequently, to remain competitive in the rapidly evolving business landscape, construction firms are now forced to operate within a complex, multi-mode, resource-constrained, multi-project scheduling problem characterized by dynamic project arrivals and multiple resource constraints, including global renewable, local renewable, and non-renewable resource capacities. This demanding environment pressures managers to simultaneously optimize the conflicting objectives of minimizing total project duration and total energy consumption. Determining the optimal schedule under these circumstances presents a substantial challenge for managers. Therefore, advanced energy-saving techniques are urgently needed to reduce energy consumption and emissions in the construction industry and to achieve sustainable development.

To overcome the challenges of integrating complex resource constraints and conflicting energy objectives, this work proposes a novel multi-objective smart raccoon family optimization (SRFO) algorithm. The SRFO is a hybrid evolutionary approach designed to enhance global exploration and local exploitation by integrating a non-dominated sorting mechanism, a dedicated energy-efficient search strategy, and enhanced genetic operators. The core contributions of this study, aimed at addressing the research gap in energy-efficient scheduling for modern construction projects, are summarized as follows:

- To develop a comprehensive mathematical model for the MRCMPS that simultaneously optimizes two conflicting criteria: minimizing total project duration and minimizing total energy consumption;
- To develop a novel SRFO algorithm, enhanced with non-dominated sorting, an energy-efficient search operator (ESO), and a smart repair procedure (SRP) to ensure efficient exploration and feasible solutions across trade-off objectives;
- To rigorously compare the proposed SRFO against established multi-objective metaheuristics (NSGA-III, MOABC, and MOSMO) using comprehensive benchmark problems and a real-world construction case study.

The remainder of this work is structured as follows: Section 2 presents a literature review and research gap analysis. Section 3 provides a detailed description of the problem and the mathematical model. Section 4 features an in-depth presentation of the proposed

https://doi.org/10.3390/buildings16020392

SRFO. Section 5 delves into computational experiments and the examination of their results. Finally, Sections 6 and 7 provide discussion, conclusions, and directions for future research.

2. Literature Review

2.1. Multi-Mode Resource-Constrained Multi-Project Scheduling

Researchers have developed objective functions and optimization techniques to address this complexity and identify the most efficient project plan and schedule. The foundational MRCMPS problem, which addresses multiple projects competing for various resources and execution modes, has been investigated through several lenses, primarily focusing on time and cost metrics. Tseng et al. [14] studied MRCMPS problems with renewable and non-renewable resources, while accounting for due dates and resource availability levels. Asta et al. [8] investigated the MRCMPS problems with global, local renewable, and non-renewable resources, with the main objective being the minimization of project duration, and makespan as a secondary objective for tie-breaking. Besikci et al. [9] modeled MRCMPS problems as a resource portfolio problem for budgeting, considering only local renewable and non-renewable resources.

Various approaches are used to optimize objective functions in MRCMPS problems. Kucuksayacigil et al. [15] focused on minimizing makespan and maximizing net present value using NSGA-II. Geiger [16] developed a variable-neighborhood search-based method to optimize delay and makespan. Ripon et al. [17] considered a hierarchical optimization approach to minimize project duration. Kannimuthu et al. [18] proposed a probabilistic global search algorithm to minimize multiple trade-off objectives. Xu et al. [19] extended the MRCMPS problem to a fuzzy random environment for a large-scale hydropower construction project and considered only renewable and non-renewable resources, with the objectives of optimizing project duration and quality. Song et al. [20] investigated MRCMPS specifically for modern construction, studying renewable and non-renewable resources to minimize project duration and cost. Javanmard et al. [21] developed a hybrid algorithm based on GA, PSO, and cuckoo search for the MRCMPS problem, while considering time-of-use energy usage. Silva et al. [22] proposed an ant colony optimization (ACO) algorithm for the MRCPS problem with the aim of minimizing energy consumption. Ahmeti et al. [23] investigated the MRCMPSP with renewable and non-renewable constraints and proposed a hybrid constraint programming approach to minimize project delay. Davari et al. [24] proposed a mixed-integer programming model for MRCMPS problems that considers renewable and non-renewable constraints to minimize the makespan, net present value, and resource consumption.

2.2. Multi-Objective Optimization Approaches

The literature shows that although many studies optimize a single objective, organizations are increasingly interested in finding the optimal solution to two or more conflicting objectives. Various techniques are employed to address multi-objective optimization challenges, including the weighted-sum method, Pareto solutions, and multi-criteria decision-making methods [25,26]. Issa and Tu [27] and Gomez et al. [28] reviewed multi-objective optimization techniques for the RCMPS problems. Although exact methods give optimal solutions, they consume more computational resources, limiting their use for large and complex problems [27]. Consequently, metaheuristics such as genetic algorithms (GA) [29] and artificial bee colony (ABC) [30] are among the most frequently used methods for solving project scheduling problems. The non-dominated sorting concept is particularly prevalent among researchers in this domain. For instance, NSGA-II has been widely applied. Kucuksayacigil et al. [31] presented NSGA-II for RCMPS problems with a backward-forward pass procedure. In another research, Kucuksayacigil et al. [15] developed a hybrid

 https://doi.org/10.3390/buildings16020392

NSGA-II to optimize net present value and makespan simultaneously. Lafmejani et al. [32] presented NSGA-II for MRCPSP to maximize cost and project duration simultaneously. Tirkolaee et al. [33] developed the NSGA-II to reduce the net present value while maximizing the project duration. Zheng et al. [34] recommended an NSGA-II-based algorithm to optimize the makespan and robustness measure for the RCMPSP. Afshar et al. [35] presented a multi-objective GA for MRCMPS problems. Wang et al. [36] presented a hybrid GA for a multi-objective RCMPS problem with doubly constrained resources on the critical chain. Besides GA, several researchers investigated the ABC algorithm's performance on project scheduling problems and proved that the ABC provides better results than the particle swarm optimization algorithm [37–43].

Swarm intelligence optimization algorithms mimic collective behavior in nature to efficiently solve complex optimization problems, offering adaptability, scalability, and robustness in dynamic environments [44]. The raccoon optimization algorithm (ROA) is a recently developed swarm intelligence optimization algorithm developed by Koohi et al. [45]. The ROA is designed to balance the exploitation and exploration effects to achieve optimal results for continuous problems, based on raccoons' foraging behavior. Rauf et al. [46] proposed a raccoon family optimization algorithm (RFOA) for MRCMPSP to improve the performance of basic ROA by introducing a family of raccoons where each member is accountable for the optimal solution. Song et al. [20] enhanced the RFOA's performance by integrating niche genetics and solving the bilevel project scheduling problem. While the RFOA is simple and efficient at quickly finding near-optimal solutions, its primary limitation is its tendency to get trapped in local optima. Several researchers emphasize that integrating problem-specific knowledge is critical for enhancing algorithm performance [47–49]. Therefore, to overcome the limitations of RFOA, a novel SRFO algorithm is developed. The SRFO integrates modified genetic operators (crossover and mutation), an energy-efficient smart search operator, and a smart repair procedure to augment exploration/exploitation and verify constraint compliance. A non-dominated sorting mechanism is also introduced to enhance the efficiency of solving multi-objective problems.

2.3. Research Gap

A review of the state of the art reveals a substantial focus on traditional project objectives such as completion time, cost, net present value, and quality, within the MRCMPS literature. However, the critical objective of minimizing total energy consumption, a necessity driven by global environmental policies, especially in energy-intensive modern construction, remains significantly underdeveloped. For instance, Song et al. [20] investigated the MRCMPS for prefabricated buildings, aiming to minimize project duration and cost, but they did not specifically target energy efficiency. Other existing studies, such as those by Silva et al. [22] and Javanmard et al. [21], have considered energy consumption, but their models typically do not integrate dynamic project arrivals and often frame the problem as a single-objective optimization problem. The inherent inverse relationship between project duration and energy consumption, where speeding up construction often necessitates greater resource intensity and thus higher energy use, creates a critical conflict that single-objective or cost-focused models cannot effectively resolve.

As shown in Table 1, the literature, therefore, lacks a dedicated multi-objective optimization framework capable of simultaneously and efficiently balancing the conflicting objectives of minimizing project duration and minimizing energy consumption. The critical research gap addressed by this work is the absence of a robust metaheuristic designed for this highly constrained environment, which is characterized by the following:

- Simultaneous minimization of project duration and total energy consumption;

https://doi.org/10.3390/buildings16020392

- Management of three distinct resource types (global renewable, local renewable, and non-renewable);
- Handling dynamic project arrivals and multi-mode execution selection.

Table 1. Literature summary of the current multi-objective MRCMPS problem.

Reference	Objectives				Dynamic		Optimization Algorithms
	Completion Time	Energy Consumption	Project Cost	Other	Yes	No	
Asta et al. [8]	√	-	-	√	√	-	Monte Carlo, Hyper-heuristic
Beşikci et al. [9]	-	-	√	-	-	√	GA
Kucuksayacigil et al. [15]	√	-	√	-	-	√	Hybrid NSGA-II
Silva et al. [22]	-	√	-	-	-	√	ACO
Javanmard et al. [21]	-	√	-	√	-	√	Hybrid GA
Geiger [16]	√	-	-	-	√	-	Variable Neighborhood Search
Xu et al. [19]	√	-	-	√	-	√	Hybrid PSO
Song et al. [20]	√	-	√	-	-	√	Niche Genetic-RFOA
Davari et al. [24]	√	-	√	-	-	√	Mixed Integer Programming
Tirkolaee et al. [33]	√	-	√	-	-	√	NSGA-II
Rauf et al. [46]	-	-	√	-	-	√	RFOA
This study	√	√	-	-	√	-	Smart Raccoon family optimization

Addressing this complex, multi-layered gap requires a robust metaheuristic tailored with problem-specific knowledge, such as the proposed SRFO algorithm. The SRFO is specifically engineered for this bi-objective, constrained problem by integrating a non-dominated sorting mechanism to manage the conflicting time/energy trade-off and by incorporating problem-specific enhancements, such as the ESO and SRP, to efficiently generate and maintain feasible, high-quality solutions amidst strict resource and precedence constraints.

3. Problem Description

The problem under investigation focuses on modern construction projects, which inherently involve multiple projects and multi-mode activities spanning off-site manufacturing, delivery, and on-site assembly. This integrated process requires the consideration of project activities that can be executed in several modes. The projects are broken down into major parts using a work breakdown structure to divide the project into manageable activities. The precedence relationships among these activities are captured in a project network. Each activity can also be carried out in various ways, each with its own resource requirements and processing times. A visual representation of the concurrent scheduling of multiple projects, incorporating various execution modes and the limitations imposed by resource availability, is presented in Figure 1. As demonstrated, some concurrently scheduled activities cannot start because of resource constraints, while others must wait for their predecessor activities to finish. The multi-project scheduling problem becomes much more complex because of these factors.

First, projects are selected based on their arrival dates, and each activity is assigned an execution mode according to the non-renewable resources' availability. Next, start and finish times are allocated to activities based on the resources' availability and precedence constraints. Two critical performance measures in this context are project completion duration and project energy consumption. These represent conflicting objectives: minimizing one may increase the other, requiring a trade-off. Optimizing the project scheduling problem under these circumstances involves simultaneously minimizing total project completion duration and energy consumption. The complexity of construction scheduling stems from resource constraints, precedence relationships, and the absolute requirement that on-site assembly activities can only begin after the required components arrive on time. The model operates under the assumption that resource capacities, task-specific

https://doi.org/10.3390/buildings16020392

resource demands, and the durations of activities across different modes are both fixed and deterministic. Additionally, the framework allows for the concurrent execution of various projects, provided that resource limits are respected and individual project release schedules are followed. The notations assumed for the mathematical modeling of the current problem are defined in Abbreviations.

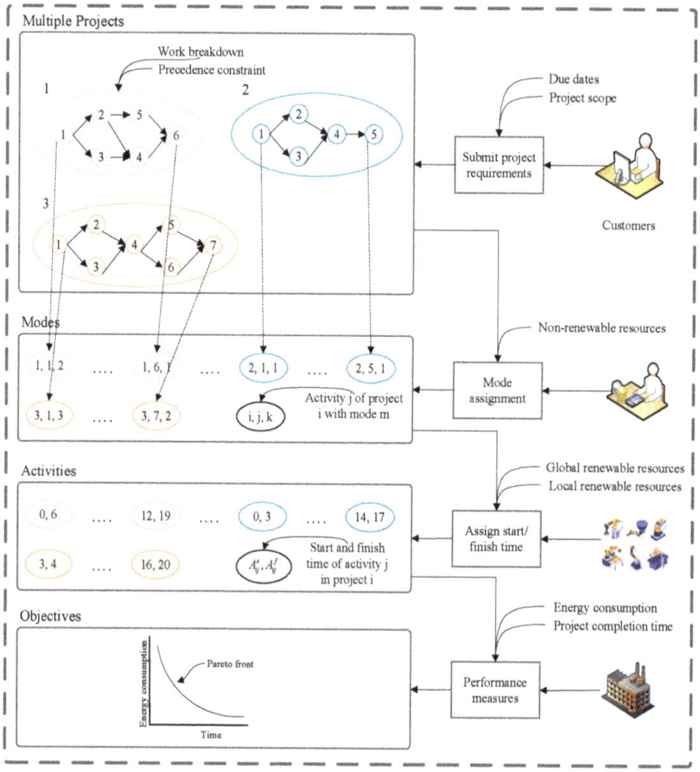

Figure 1. Illustrative framework for the multi-criteria scheduling of project portfolios under multi-mode execution and resource limitations.

Subject to:

$$f_1 = \sum_{i=1}^{I} TEC_i \tag{1}$$

$$f_2 = \max(FT_i)\ \forall i \tag{2}$$

$$TEC_i = \sum_{j=1}^{J} \sum_{m=1}^{M} EC_{ijm}.X_{ijm}.Y_{ijt}\ \forall t \tag{3}$$

$$X_{ijm} = \begin{cases} 1 & \text{if } j^{\text{th}}\text{activity of } i^{\text{th}}\text{project is executed in } m^{\text{th}} \text{ mode} \\ 0 & \text{otherwise} \end{cases} \tag{4}$$

$$Y_{ijt} = \begin{cases} 1 & \text{if } j^{\text{th}} \text{ activity} i^{\text{th}} \text{ project is executed at time t} \\ 0 & \text{otherwise} \end{cases} \tag{5}$$

$$FT_i = max(A_{ij}^{f})\ \forall j \tag{6}$$

https://doi.org/10.3390/buildings16020392

$$A_{ij}^{f} = A_{ij}^{s} + \sum_{m=1}^{M} A_{ijm}^{d} . X_{ijm} \tag{7}$$

$$\sum_{j=1}^{J} \sum_{m=1}^{M} R_{ijmk}^{nr} . X_{ijm} \leq TR_{ik}^{nr} \ \forall \{i = 1, 2, \ldots, I\} \tag{8}$$

$$\sum_{i=1}^{I} \sum_{j=1}^{J} \sum_{m=1}^{M} R_{ijmg}^{gr} . X_{ijm} . Y_{ijt} \ \leq TR_{g}^{gr} \ \forall \{t = 0, 1, 2, \ldots, HP\} \tag{9}$$

$$\sum_{j=1}^{J} \sum_{m=1}^{M} R_{ijml}^{lr} . X_{ijm} . Y_{ijt} \ \leq TR_{l}^{lr} \ \forall t \tag{10}$$

$$\sum_{m=1}^{M} X_{ijm} = 1 \tag{11}$$

$$ST_1 = 0 \tag{12}$$

$$ST_i \geq RD_i \tag{13}$$

$$A_{ij\prime}^{s} \geq max\left(A_{ij}^{f}\right) \ \forall (j, j\prime) \ \in \ \mathrm{Pd}_i \tag{14}$$

$$\sum_{t=0}^{HP} Y_{ijt} = 1 \ \forall \{j = 1, 2, \ldots, J\} \tag{15}$$

Equations (1) and (2) indicate the objective functions used to minimize the total energy consumption and total project time, respectively. Equation (3) calculates the project's (i) total energy consumption. Here, EC_{ijm} represents the total energy consumed by the specific equipment and processes required to complete activity (j) in project (i) using execution mode (m) over its entire duration. Equation (4) is the decision variable with a value of 1 if the activity (j) of the project (i) is executed in the mode (m); otherwise, its value is 0. Equation (5) is a decision variable with a value of 1 if the activity (j) of the project (i) is performed at a time (t); otherwise, it is 0. According to Equation (6), the conclusion of project i is defined by the completion of its final task, representing the maximum finish time among all constituent activities. The precise finish time for an individual task j within project i is determined using Equation (7). Equation (8) enforces the non-renewable resource constraint, mandating that the cumulative use of resource k stays within the total permissible budget. The availability of shared global renewable resources at any specific time t is protected by Equation (9), preventing over-allocation across the project portfolio. Similarly, Equation (10) restricts the usage of site-specific local renewable resources to ensure they do not exceed project-dependent capacities at time t. Equation (11) stipulates that a single execution mode must be selected for each activity, and this selection remains fixed throughout the task's duration. The temporal baseline is established by Equation (12), which sets the start of the primary project to zero. Equation (13) ensures that no project commences prior to its designated release time. Structural logic is maintained by Equation (14), which prevents a successor activity j′ from starting until its predecessor j has concluded. Finally, Equation (15) guarantees that each activity j is assigned to the schedule exactly once.

The mathematical model developed in this section precisely captures the complex constraints inherent in energy-efficient modern construction projects, including precedence relationships, multi-mode execution selection, and simultaneous consumption constraints for three distinct resource types (local renewable, global renewable, and non-renewable). Given the NP-hard nature of the MRCMPS problem and the bi-objective nature of minimizing both time and energy, an exact solution method is computationally infeasible for large instances. The following section introduces the proposed metaheuristic optimization ap-

https://doi.org/10.3390/buildings16020392

proach, the SRFO algorithm, specifically designed to navigate this combinatorial challenge and generate high-quality Pareto-optimal solutions efficiently.

4. Proposed Optimization Approach

This section provides a detailed description of the proposed SRFO algorithm for solving the resource-constrained multi-project scheduling problem with various execution modes and project arrivals. The foraging behavior of raccoons inspires the standard RFO algorithm. Unlike traditional evolutionary algorithms such as GAs, the RFO algorithm comprises several subgroups, endowing it with multi-group collaborative optimization. The original RFO algorithm is designed for single-objective optimization problems. However, the current problem falls into discrete multi-objective optimization problems. Therefore, the Pareto concept, smart repair procedure (SRP), energy-efficient local search, and crossover operation are incorporated into the original RFO algorithm. The structure of the proposed SRFO is organized into three distinct stages: the initialization phase, global optimization, and local optimization. A detailed visual guide to this multi-objective framework is provided in the flowchart presented in Figure 2.

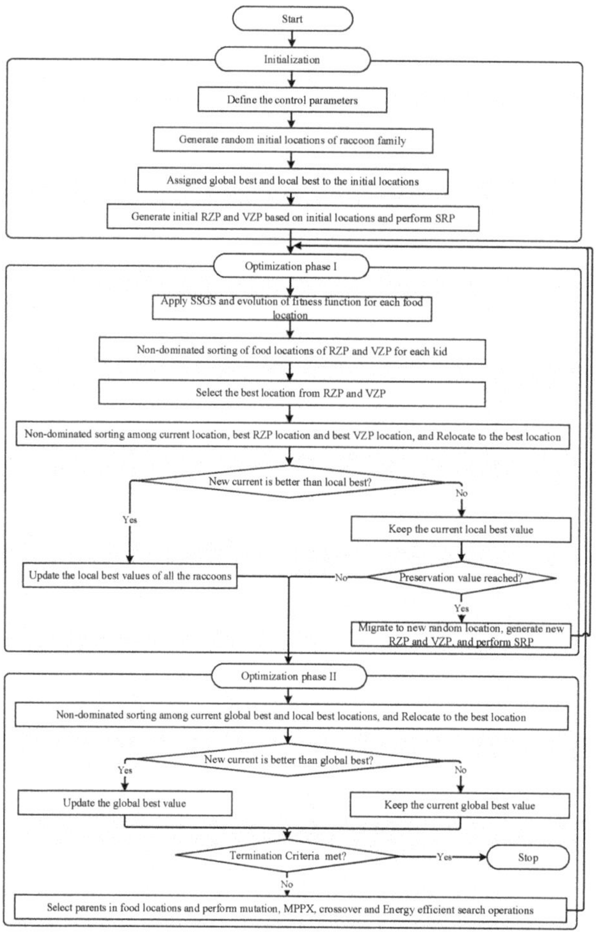

Figure 2. Flowchart of the multi-objective smart raccoon family optimization (SRFO) algorithm.

https://doi.org/10.3390/buildings16020392

Given the nature of the current multi-project scheduling challenge, the problem is defined within a discrete optimization framework. Because the environment involves distinct variables such as project selection, activities ordering, and mode assignment, the SRFO utilizes a specific food representation to navigate this discrete solution space. The current multi-project scheduling problem is discrete and includes multiple trade-off objectives. As illustrated in Figure 3, the search space is mapped through a specific food location encoding scheme. This representation is composed of three distinct vectors that sequentially define the sequence of projects, the order of activities, and the assigned execution modes. The serial schedule generation scheme (SSGS) is employed for decoding purposes, as proposed by Asta et al. [8]. The SSGS translates the precedence-feasible task sequence (S′) and the selected mode vector (M) into a concrete schedule by following a stage-by-stage allocation logic while dynamically managing the renewable resource constraints. At each stage $n = 1, \ldots, J$, the algorithm selects the next activity from the sequence S′ and determines its earliest possible start time $\left(A^{s}_{ij}\right)$ such that:

1. The activity starts only after all its predecessor activities have finished;
2. The required units of global and local renewable resources (R^{lr}_{ijml}, R^{gr}_{ijml}) for the selected mode are available for the entire duration of the activity without exceeding the total global and local renewable resource capacities (TR^{lr}_{il} and TR^{gr}_{g}).

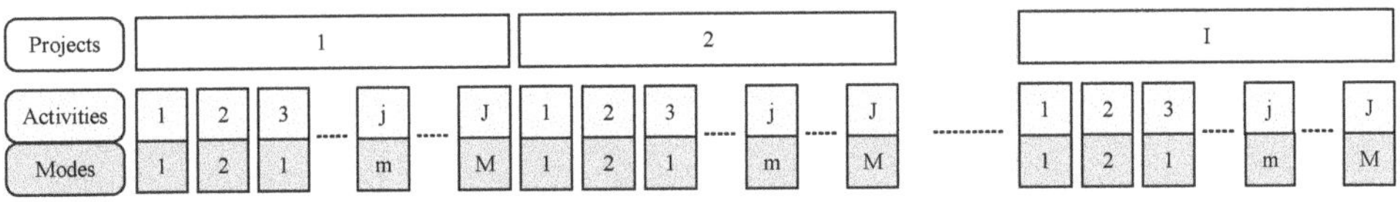

Figure 3. Encoding scheme for candidate solution representation within the raccoon foraging space.

If a resource conflict occurs (i.e., the demand exceeds the available capacity), the activity is delayed to the earliest time slot where the resource requirements can be satisfied. This ensures that the generated schedule is not only theoretically optimal in terms of time and energy but also practically executable within the fixed resource limits of the construction site.

4.1. Initialization

The first stage of the proposed SRFO is the initialization phase. The initialization phase is divided into four steps: define parameters, generate initial location, assign global and local best, and generate population.

Step 1: The process commences with the specification of all necessary algorithmic control parameters.
Step 2: The initial positions of the raccoon family are established by distributing them randomly across the feasible solution space. This preliminary setup is designated as the zero-th iteration of the search process.
Step 3: In the third step, the mother raccoon and the kids' current random locations are set to global and local optimum, respectively.
Step 4: During the final initialization phase, the starting population is established. The algorithm uses reachable zone populations (RZP) and visible zone populations (VZP). Because the multi-project scheduling environment is discrete and governed by complex resource and precedence dependencies, some candidate food locations in this initial set may not initially be feasible. Therefore, a novel SRP is developed to check the food location's feasibility and repair it. The steps to implement SRP are presented in the pseudo-code Algorithm 1 below.

 https://doi.org/10.3390/buildings16020392

Algorithm 1: Steps of Smart Repair Procedure (SRP)

```
Input: Set of Projects 𝓘, Task Sequences {S_i}_{i∈𝓘}, Mode Vectors {M_i}_{i∈𝓘}, Predecessors 𝓟𝓓_{ij}, NRR
       Capacities TR^{nr}_{ik}, Requirements R^{nr}_{ijmk}, Durations A^d_{ijm}
Output: Feasible Sequences {S'_i}, Feasible Mode Vectors {M'_i}
foreach project i ∈ 𝓘 do
    Precedence Feasibility Repair
    S'_i ← ∅;
    𝓐_i ← {j ∈ Tasks(i) | 𝓟𝓓_{ij} = ∅} ;                         // Init Available Set
    n ← 1;
    J_i ← Total activities in project i;
    while n ≤ J_i do
        Scan input sequence S_i from left to right;
        Find first activity j* ∈ S_i such that j* ∈ 𝓐_i;
        Append j* to S'_i;
        𝓐_i ← 𝓐_i \ {j*};
        foreach successor s of j* in project i do
            if 𝓟𝓓_{is} ⊆ S'_i then
                𝓐_i ← 𝓐_i ∪ {s};
            end
        end
        n ← n + 1;
    end
    Non-renewable capacity repair
    M'_i ← M_i;
    foreach non-renewable resource k do
        Calculate current usage U_{ik} = Σ_{j=1}^{J_i} R^{nr}_{i,j,M'_i[j],k};
        while U_{ik} > TR^{nr}_{ik} do
            Identify set 𝓙_{red} of activities in project i with alternative modes requiring less resource k;
            BestAct ← null, MinRatio ← ∞;
            foreach activity j ∈ 𝓙_{red} do
                Let m_{curr} be current mode, m_{low} be alternative mode;
                ΔTime ← A^d_{ijm_{low}} − A^d_{ijm_{curr}};
                ΔRes ← R^{nr}_{ijm_{curr}k} − R^{nr}_{ijm_{low}k};
                Ratio_j ← ΔTime/ΔRes;
                if Ratio_j < MinRatio then
                    MinRatio ← Ratio_j;
                    BestAct ← j;
                    BestMode ← m_{low};
                end
            end
            M'_i[BestAct] ← BestMode;
            U_{ik} ← U_{ik} − ΔRes_{best};
        end
    end
end
return ({S'_i}, {M'_i});
```

4.2. Optimization Phase I

The most crucial parts of this algorithm are the optimization phases. These optimization stages are executed systematically throughout every evolutionary cycle, denoted as $i, i \in \{0, 1, \ldots, NI\}$. The first optimization phase is known as the local optimization phase. The local optimization phase involves three sequential procedures: assessing solution fitness alongside non-dominated sorting, moving the raccoon toward the optimal position, and initiating the migration process.

Step 1: The initial step involves assessing the fitness values for every potential food location, which represent the set of candidate solutions. Each food location consists of two different types of foods due to the current problem's bi-objective nature. Therefore, each kid's non-dominated sorting of RZP and VZP food locations is performed. This sorting divides food locations into various fronts comprising non-dominated solutions. The Pareto front, which is ranked first, is considered the best front, and the food locations in the first-ranked Pareto front are considered the best. The step-by-step sorting process for food locations is given in Figure 4. Here, the x-axis and y-axis are the two trade-off objectives (completion time, TEC).

https://doi.org/10.3390/buildings16020392

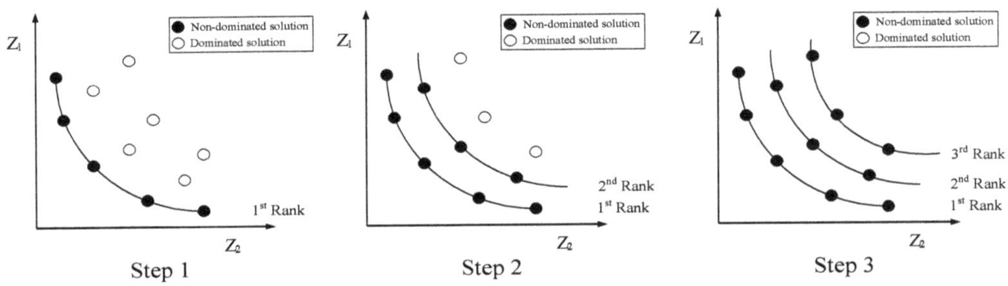

Figure 4. Step-by-step sorting process of food locations.

Step 2: The algorithm identifies the top-tier Pareto front by evaluating the fitness of the current position, the highest-performing value within the RZP (R_{ki}^{best}), and the leading value from VZP (V_{ki}^{best}). Based on this evaluation, the kid raccoon transitions toward the most favorable positions within the primary Pareto front. Following this shift, a new round of non-dominated sorting is conducted between the updated current coordinates and the existing local optimum $loc_{k(i-1)}$. The resulting premier Pareto front is archived and designated as the new local optimum L_k^{opt}. To prepare for the global optimization stage, the kid raccoons transmit their revised current locations and local optima to the group leader.
Step 3: To mitigate the risk of stalling at local optima and to circumvent premature convergence, the group leader's decision-making process is guided by a preservation parameter n_{pres} and a migration factor (MF). Initially, n_{pres} is assigned a value of zero. If a raccoon's location remains stagnant, this counter increments by one; conversely, any change in position resets n_{pres} back to zero. Once the stagnation counter n_{pres} reaches the threshold defined by the MF, the group leader mandates a migration phase. During migration, the kid raccoon is displaced from its current search area and relocated to a randomized position entirely outside its previous RZP and VZP zones. Following the successful relocation of the raccoon, the n_{pres} counter is reset to zero to restart the monitoring process.

4.3. Optimization Phase II

During the global optimization stage, the group leader aggregates data regarding the most favorable local food positions identified by the kids to refine its own coordinates. This step, which constitutes the second optimization phase, focuses on leveraging the collective search efforts to improve the overall global position. This phase consists of three significant steps: relocation to the global optimum location, termination criteria check, and population generation.

Step 1: The group leader assesses her existing position g_{i-1} against the local optimal coordinates L_k^{opt} identified by the kids through non-dominated sorting and the subsequent ranking of Pareto fronts. The leader then transitions to a new location g_i corresponding to a position on the top-ranked Pareto front. Following this movement, a secondary non-dominated sorting is executed, comparing the new current position g_i with the existing global optimum G_{opt}. The resulting first-ranked Pareto front from this comparison is then designated as the updated global optimum value G_{opt}.
Step 2: In this step, the termination criteria are checked. If the termination criteria are met, the algorithm terminates; otherwise, a new population is generated.
Step 3: At this step, a new population is generated. To expand the search within the reachable (RZP) and visible (VZP) zones, genetic mechanisms, specifically crossover and mutation, are utilized to produce additional candidate solutions, as depicted in Figure 5. Moreover, a novel energy-efficient search operator (ESO) has been developed to minimize energy consumption. To enhance the search process, genetic operators are utilized to

 https://doi.org/10.3390/buildings16020392

broaden the local exploration area, whereas the ESO is designed for rapid identification of optimal solutions. Given that the problem structure is organized into three distinct tiers, encompassing projects, activities, and execution modes, these search mechanisms are executed across multiple levels. Specifically, the ESO is implemented at the third level, focusing on mode assignment to allocate both renewable and non-renewable resources to various project tasks. Further, the modified precedence-preserving crossover (MPPX) and swap mutation genetic operators are applied to activities and multiple projects to generate the following food locations. The steps for the ESO are given below in pseudo-code Algorithm 2. The coordinated local and global search procedures are executed iteratively for a total of NI cycles, continuing until the predefined stopping conditions are satisfied. This repetitive cycle ensures that the algorithm thoroughly explores the solution space and refines candidate schedules through successive generations. The hybrid design of the SRFO, which integrates non-dominated sorting with problem-specific knowledge (such as the ESO and SRP), provides a robust and efficient mechanism for exploring the solution space and exploiting high-quality, energy-efficient schedules. The computational performance and superior efficacy of the proposed SRFO algorithm, along with a detailed comparison against established metaheuristics, are validated through extensive experimentation in the subsequent section.

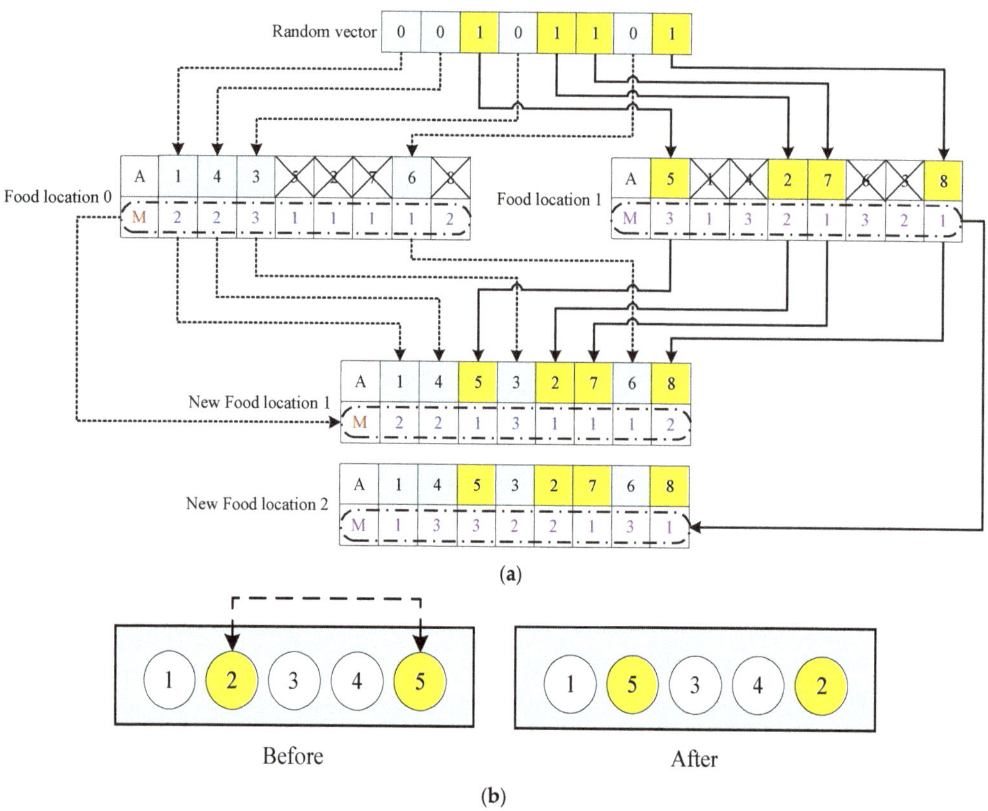

Figure 5. (**a**) MPPX crossover operation and (**b**) swap mutation operation.

https://doi.org/10.3390/buildings16020392

Algorithm 2: Steps for Energy-efficient Search Operator (ESO)

```
Input: Current Solution X = {{S_i}, {M_i}}_{i∈I}, Energy Parameters EC_ijm, NRR Capacities TR^nr_ik,
       Requirements R^nr_ijmk
Output: Energy-Optimized Solution X'
X' ← X;
foreach project i ∈ I do
    Select a random activity j from project i;
    Identify current mode m_curr = M'_ij;
    Find set of candidate modes M_better = {m' | EC_ijm' < EC_ijm_curr};
    if M_better ≠ ∅ then
        Select a random mode m' ∈ M_better;
        // Non-Renewable Resource Feasibility
        Calculate new NRR usage U'_ik assuming mode m' for task j;
        IsNRRFeasible ← (∀k, U'_ik ≤ TR^nr_ik);
        if IsNRRFeasible then
            // Accept the energy-saving mode
            M'_i[j] ← m';
        end
        else
            // Reject and retain current mode
            M'_i[j] ← m_curr;
        end
    end
end
return X';
```

5. Computational Experiments and Results

In this section, we outline the experimental setup and the application of the Taguchi method for optimizing the parameters of the SRFO, NSGA-III [34], MOABC [50], and MOSMO [1] algorithms. Performance evaluation is conducted using adapted MISTA [51] benchmark problems. These benchmarks were constructed by merging single-project data from the J10, J20, and J30 PSPLIB sets to form multi-mode, multi-project networks. Specifically, the computational experiments used four instances for each of the three size categories (small, medium, and large), yielding a total of 12 benchmark problems for comprehensive validation. To address the absence of energy-related data in the original benchmarks, we adopted the data assignment approach established by Yue et al. [1]. Additional model parameters were generated using a uniform distribution within a specified range $[\alpha, \beta]$. Finally, the effectiveness of the SRFO is benchmarked against the aforementioned algorithms using a comprehensive suite of metrics covering convergence, solution distribution, and multi-criteria decision-making (MCDM).

5.1. Parameter Tuning

Appropriate parameter selection significantly affects the performance of algorithms. The performance of metaheuristic algorithms is highly sensitive to their parameter settings. Consequently, precise selection and calibration are required to achieve optimal outcomes for specific problem instances. To analyze the influence of five key SRFO parameters, specifically the number of kids (k), the migration factor (f), the mutation rate (m), the crossover rate (c), and the greedy search operator (g), this study employs the Taguchi method in conjunction with orthogonal arrays. Each of these five parameters was evaluated across three distinct levels [$k \in \{3, 5, 10\}$,$f \in \{50, 100, 150\}$,$m \in \{0.1, 0.2, 0.3\}$, $g \in \{0.1, 0.3, 0.6\}$, $c \in \{0.3, 0.5, 0.7\}$]. Given this configuration, an L27 (35) orthogonal array was implemented, necessitating a total of 27 experimental trials per test case. To ensure data reliability, each trial was executed ten times, with the results for both objective functions (Z_1, Z_2) meticulously documented. The variation in experimental responses was analyzed by converting raw data into signal-to-noise (S/N) ratios. Although S/N ratios are

https://doi.org/10.3390/buildings16020392

generally categorized into three types, namely, "nominal-is-best," "larger-the-better," and "smaller-the-better". The "smaller-the-better" criterion was adopted here. This selection aligns with the minimization nature of our objective functions and established literature in the field [52].

For the design of the experiment and Taguchi analysis, a MINITAB^{TM} 18 is used. A visual observation-based method is used to identify the effects of parameter of algorithms. S/N ratios for both objective functions are given in Figure 6, which shows the impact of the objective functions' parameters. It can be seen from Figure 6 that the number of kids (k) and greedy search operator (g) performed best at level 1, mutation (m) at level 2, and crossover (c) at level 3 for both objectives. However, that is not the case for the migration factor (f). The migration factor (f) performed best at level 1 and worst at level 2 for the first objective, while it performed worst at level 1 and best at level 3 for the second objective. Since the migration factor (f) performed best for the second objective and medium for the first objective at level 3, level 3 is selected. For a fair comparison, the parameters of the other compared algorithms are also fine-tuned using the Taguchi method. The parameters' combination of algorithms is given in Table 2.

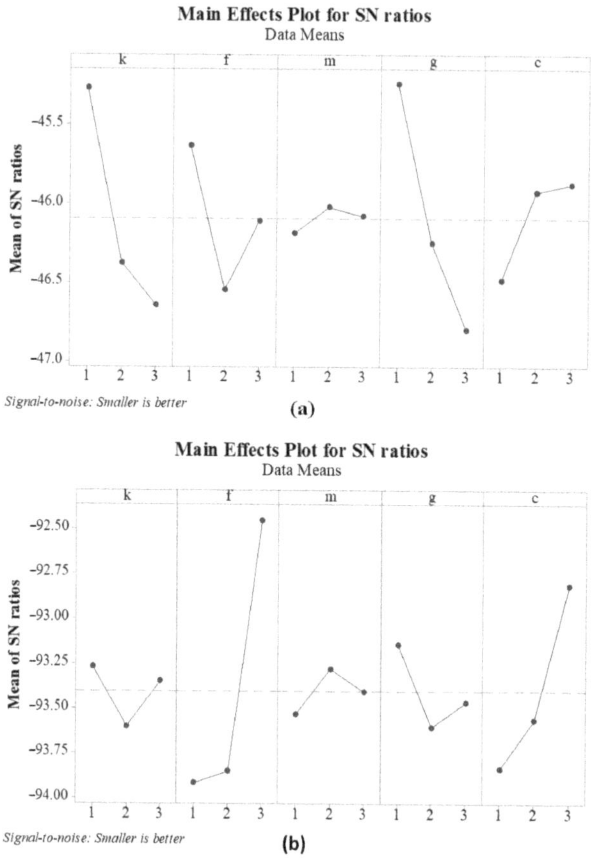

Figure 6. Effect of parameters on the objective functions. (**a**) Parameters' effect on objective function 1. (**b**) Parameters' effect on objective function 2.

https://doi.org/10.3390/buildings16020392

Table 2. Parameters' combination of algorithms.

Algorithms and Parameters	Value
Smart raccoon family optimization (SRFO)	
Number of kids (*K*)	3
Migration factor (*MF*)	150
Mutation rate (*m*)	0.2
Crossover rate (*c*)	0.7
Greedy search operator rate (*g*)	0.1
Reachable zone population (RZP)	60
Visible zone population (VZP)	240
Non-dominated sorting genetic algorithm (NSGA-III)	
Population size (*PS*)	300
Mutation rate (*m*)	0.1
Crossover rate (*c*)	0.7
Multi-objective artificial bee colony (MOABC)	
Number of food sources (*NS*)	300
Number of neighborhoods (*NN*)	10
Limit cycle (*LC*)	150
Multi-objective spider monkey optimization (MOSMO)	
Swarm count (SC)	20
Food source population	300
Maximum number of groups	10
Loop count (LC)	100

5.2. Analysis of Results

In this phase of the study, the benchmark instances previously described are processed using the proposed SRFO, along with MOABC, NSGA-III, and MOSMO. The primary objective is to evaluate and contrast the computational effectiveness of the SRFO against these established metaheuristic frameworks. The literature shows that several algorithms are effective for solving project scheduling problems. However, the performance of the proposed SRFO algorithm is compared with that of the MOSMO, NGGA-III, and MOABC algorithms. As mentioned above, the proposed SRFO and other algorithms are implemented in MATLABTM R2020b and run on a system with a Core i7-10710U processor at 1.10 GHz and 16.00 GB of memory. For a fair comparison, the parameters of all algorithms are also fine-tuned using the Taguchi method. Each algorithm is run independently, with its encoding and decoding, initial population, constraints, and fitness function kept identical to avoid their effects on the algorithms' performance. All algorithms are run 10 times per case to obtain reliable data, and the mean value across runs is recorded.

It is essential to compare the performance of one algorithm with that of the others using performance indicators. In a multi-objective optimization problem, we have to deal with multiple conflicting objectives, whereas in single-objective optimization problems, we care only about minimizing or maximizing one objective. Therefore, comparing the performance of algorithms in multi-objective optimization problems is not straightforward and requires additional steps. For this purpose, various researchers have suggested different performance indicators/metrics. These metrics can be classified as convergence and distribution metrics [53]. Besides these metrics, the researchers have also used the technique for order of preference by similarity to ideal solution (TOPSIS), a multi-criteria decision-making technique (MCDM) to compare algorithms' performance on multi-objective optimization problems [26]. Most researchers have used two or more performance metrics to compare algorithms' performance on multi-objective optimization problems. Therefore, to make a fair and comprehensive comparison, convergence, distribution, and one MCDM metric

 https://doi.org/10.3390/buildings16020392

(TOPSIS) are selected as performance indicators to compare the algorithm's performance for multi-objective optimization problems.

5.2.1. Comparison Based on Objective Functions and Computational Time

Table 3 presents a comparison of the proposed SRFO algorithm with competitors (MOABC, NSGA-III, and MOSMO) based on raw objective function values and computational efficiency across small, medium, and large problem instances. The values reported for project completion time and TEC are the mean and standard deviation (Std) obtained from 10 independent runs on each instance. Since both objectives are minimization objectives, the lower values are better.

Table 3. Mean values of performance indicators based on convergence metrics.

Algorithms	CPU Time (s)		Time (Days)		TEC (Units)	
	Mean	Std	Mean	Std	Mean	Std
I = 2, J = 40, M = 3						
SRFO	15.34	**0.54**	**26.40**	**1.97**	**5172.28**	**154.14**
MOABC	16.35	0.55	31.75	2.75	5718.98	366.65
NSGA-III	17.29	0.68	26.50	2.87	5389.70	212.19
MOSMO	**13.24**	0.94	27.02	2.96	5346.14	193.59
I = 5, J = 100, M = 3						
SRFO	59.24	**2.20**	**67.12**	**9.67**	**14,658.77**	**473.54**
MOABC	63.96	2.38	81.67	14.11	15,840.42	996.83
NSGA-III	72.72	2.54	84.67	16.94	15,045.50	710.22
MOSMO	**55.84**	2.47	73.00	10.02	15,108.30	655.88
I = 10, J = 200, M = 3						
SRFO	**180.91**	**6.66**	**228.25**	**8.96**	**29,392.50**	**1143.84**
MOABC	161.6	7.02	263.78	11.17	33,473.44	1411.47
NSGA-III	214.39	7.05	257.75	21.32	32,610.55	1955.92
MOSMO	199.36	11.87	249.89	12.06	32,210.26	1019.67

The results in Table 3 demonstrate that SRFO consistently achieves the best trade-off, recording the lowest mean values for both Time and TEC across all three problem sizes. For the large-scale problem, SRFO achieves a mean duration of 228.25 days and a TEC of 29,392.50, significantly outperforming the next-closest competitor. Furthermore, the standard deviation (Std) values for SRFO's objective functions are consistently lower than those of the competing algorithms, especially for the larger instances. This indicates that SRFO exhibits superior robustness and stability, consistently generating high-quality solutions with less variability than the general-purpose metaheuristics.

The table also reports the mean and standard deviation of CPU Time (seconds), addressing computational feasibility. In the medium instance, the SRFO runs in an average of 59.24 s, demonstrating that, while MOSMO is marginally faster (55.84 s), the computational effort of SRFO remains highly competitive, especially given its verified superiority in solution quality and stability. This efficiency is critical for its practical application as a decision-support tool.

5.2.2. Comparison Based on Convergence Metrics

Convergence metrics relate to the quality and number of solutions an algorithm produces; the closer the solutions are to the true Pareto front, the better the algorithm. In convergence metrics, researchers have used the quality metric (QM) [32,50], the inverted generational distance (IGD) [50,53–55], and a number of Pareto solutions (NPS) [32,53]. The performance of the proposed SRFO is compared with that of MOABC and NSGA-III based on QM, IGD, and NPS. A smaller IGD value indicates better convergence toward

 https://doi.org/10.3390/buildings16020392

the true Pareto front, a higher NPS indicates a greater number of non-dominated solutions discovered, and a higher QM score indicates a higher percentage of solutions that remain non-dominated when compared against the sets of all other competing algorithms. A comparison of algorithms based on these performance indicators is given in Table 4. Table 4 shows that the proposed SRFO provides better results, with the lowest IGD and the highest NPS and QM values across all instances.

Table 4. Performance indicators based on convergence metrics.

Algorithms	IGD	NPS	QM (A, *)
	I = 2, J = 40, M = 3		
SRFO	**42.13**	**0.29**	**0.63**
MOABC	290.03	0.19	0.35
NSGA-III	143.86	0.24	0.38
MOSMO	93.79	0.29	0.38
	I = 5, J = 100, M = 3		
SRFO	**74.21**	**0.47**	**0.73**
MOABC	329.66	0.17	0.26
NSGA-III	113.52	0.17	0.26
MOSMO	110.97	0.19	0.29
	I = 10, J = 200, M = 3		
SRFO	**630.11**	**0.39**	**0.66**
MOABC	2342.34	0.22	0.36
NSGA-III	1551.18	0.20	0.33
MOSMO	1237.77	0.20	0.33

5.2.3. Comparison Based on Distribution and MCDM Metrics

The distribution metrics measure the evenness of solutions' distribution; the more even it is, the better the trade-offs between conflicting objectives are. In distribution metrics, researchers have used the spacing metric (SM) [33,52,53,56] and the diversity metric (DM) [32,33,53]. The smaller the SM value, the better the distribution, while a larger DM value means the algorithm's solutions cover a larger solution space. A comparison of algorithms based on these performance indicators is given in Table 5. From the average SM and DM values, the solution obtained from the proposed SRFO shows a better distribution across all test cases than those of other algorithms.

Table 5. Performance indicators based on distribution and MCDM metrics.

Algorithms	SM	DM	TOPSIS
	I = 2, J = 40, M = 3		
SRFO	**67.83**	**52.07**	**1.00**
MOABC	119.15	51.66	0.10
NSGA-III	92.12	51.77	0.83
MOSMO	81.23	49.10	0.79
	I = 5, J = 100, M = 3		
SRFO	**41.61**	**145.44**	**1.00**
MOABC	192.22	112.73	0.11
NSGA-III	480.78	96.89	0.27
MOSMO	102.52	98.85	0.55
	I = 10, J = 200, M = 3		
SRFO	**194.72**	**223.09**	**1.00**
MOABC	376.11	177.44	0.23
NSGA-III	572.41	134.57	0.29
MOSMO	294.59	138.53	0.37

https://doi.org/10.3390/buildings16020392

The technique for order of preference by similarity to an ideal solution (TOPSIS) is an MCDM method. It is commonly used to select the best alternative based on different trade-off criteria. However, it can be adapted to compare the performance of different algorithms for multi-objective optimization problems due to its high flexibility and simplicity. The steps for performing the TOPSIS are adopted from Rauf et al. [26]. The proposed SRFO is compared with the NSGA-III, MOABC, and MOSMO algorithms using TOPSIS's steps, and the results are shown in Table 5. The average value shows that the proposed SRFO achieves a better trade-off between objectives than other algorithms.

5.2.4. Pareto Fronts (PFs)

The proposed SRFO's performance is compared with NSGA-III, MOABC, and MOSMO on Pareto front-based comparisons. Pareto fronts obtained by these algorithms for small-, medium-, and large-size problems are illustrated in Figure 7. Since both objectives (time and cost) need to be minimized, a Pareto front closer to the origin is better. As shown in Figure 7, the Pareto fronts obtained by the proposed SRFO are closer to the origin. The proposed SRFO leverages ESO, genetic operators, and non-dominated sorting mechanisms to enhance exploration and exploitation. Further, the addition of SRP in the proposed SRFO increases efficiency. Therefore, it can be concluded that the proposed SRFO outperformed the other algorithms based on the Pareto fronts.

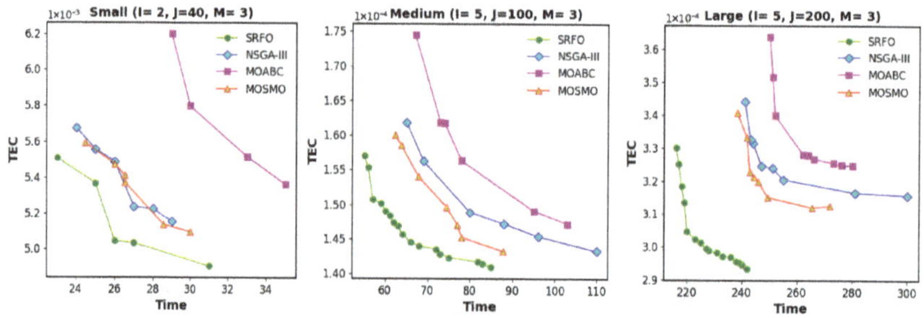

Figure 7. Pareto fronts obtained by algorithms for various size problems.

5.2.5. Statistical Analysis

To rigorously validate the observed performance differences in the mean values, a nonparametric statistical analysis was conducted using the Wilcoxon signed-rank test. This test is appropriate for comparing the performance of two related algorithms across multiple problem instances. The test assesses whether the differences between the paired observations (SRFO vs. Competitor) come from a distribution with a non-zero median. The threshold for statistical significance was set at $\alpha = 0.05$.

The Wilcoxon test was performed pairwise, comparing the ranks of the proposed SRFO algorithm against its three competitors: MOABC, NSGA-III, and MOSMO. The results, summarized in Table 6, confirm the robust superiority of SRFO across most of the critical convergence and multi-criteria decision-making metrics. For the key metrics IGD and QM, the SRFO consistently ranked first in all pairwise comparisons against MOABC, NSGA-III, and MOSMO. The p-values for the comparisons against MOSMO and the other algorithms were 0.1250, suggesting the differences are statistically significant at a $\alpha = 0.1$ confidence level. SRFO ranks highest on every problem for these key metrics, providing strong empirical evidence of its superior convergence capability. Similarly, the SRFO demonstrated superior performance in the TOPSIS metric ($p = 0.1250$).

https://doi.org/10.3390/buildings16020392

Table 6. Wilcoxon signed-rank pairwise comparison test results (p-values).

Metric	SRFO vs. MOABC (p-Value)	SRFO vs. MOSMO (p-Value)	SRFO vs. NSGA-III (p-Value)	Winner Rank
		Convergence Metrics		
IGD	0.1250	0.1250	0.1250	SRFO
QM	0.1250	0.1250	0.1250	SRFO
NPS	0.1250	0.2500	0.1250	SRFO
		Distribution & MCDM Metrics		
TOPSIS	0.1250	0.1250	0.1250	SRFO
SM	0.3750	0.3750	0.3750	-
DM	0.2500	0.1250	0.2500	SRFO

The SRFO also performed favourably against MOSMO in the DM (p = 0.1250) and NPS (p = 0.2500). The differences between SRFO and all competitors were not statistically significant for the SM (p = 0.3750), indicating all algorithms produced solutions with a statistically similar level of distribution uniformity. Overall, the statistical analysis confirms that the enhanced operators within SRFO lead to statistically superior solution convergence and quality compared to the established metaheuristics.

5.3. An Illustrative Example Case Study

Project-based companies must simultaneously execute several projects with limited resources to meet deadlines. In the real world, project managers are pressured to finish a project with limited resources. Budget, human resources, raw materials, and equipment are all examples of these resources. The current project scheduling problem for multiple projects with different release dates and execution modes is based on an advanced planning and scheduling (APS) system for a well-known construction component manufacturing company. This scenario involves scheduling the production and delivery pipeline for four distinct modern construction projects (or major component groups) that compete for shared factory (global) and project-specific (local) resources. The proposed SRFO is used to help the construction component manufacturer formulate a detailed, energy-efficient production and logistics plan, ensuring timely component supply to multiple assembly sites. The goal is to provide the managers with optimum solutions for the trade-off objective.

This case study models the complexities of simultaneous scheduling for four distinct modern construction projects ($i = 4$), which compete for shared factory-level (global) and project-specific (local) resources. The case study is meticulously structured to reflect a high-fidelity construction environment, comprising 78 distinct activities ($j = 78$), each of which can be executed via one of three available modes ($m = 3$). The precedence network is defined by 120 finish-to-start constraints given in Figure 8. This complex scheduling environment is governed by three distinct resource types: eight categories of global renewable resources, including shared factory equipment and labor teams, with capacities ranging from 1 to 3 units; two project-specific local renewable resources, such as cranes; and two types of non-renewable resources, representing budget and raw material limits. To maintain technical rigor and account for real-world manufacturing variability, the parameter ranges for activity durations (A^{d}_{ijm}) and average power consumption rates (P_{ijm}) were derived directly from actual production logs. The available capacities of global, local, and non-renewable resources are given in Table 7.

The proposed SRFO is implemented to solve the case problem with the fine-tuned parameters. Pareto points obtained from the proposed SRFO, NSGA-III, MOABC, and MOSMO algorithms are shown in Figure 9. As shown in Figure 9, the Pareto front obtained by the proposed SRFO is closer to the origin than those of the other algorithms. The proposed SRFO algorithm facilitates a comprehensive sensitivity analysis by generating a

https://doi.org/10.3390/buildings16020392

well-distributed Pareto front. This allows project managers to evaluate the "cost" of time in terms of energy, and vice versa. For the current case study, we identified three characteristic selection points (A, B, and C) to represent different managerial priorities. Pareto Point A has a minimum project duration (2380) and maximum energy consumption (24,852.5). In contrast, Point B has the minimum energy consumption (23,341.8) and the maximum project duration (3834). Point C (2436, 24,396.1) is obtained by implementing TOPSIS with equal weights.

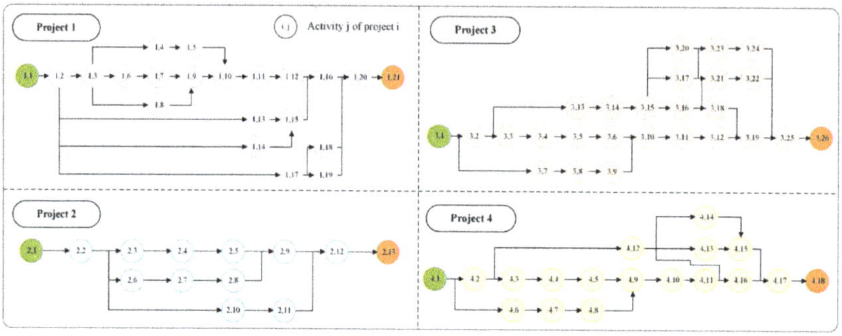

Figure 8. Precedence diagrams of the projects.

Table 7. Capacity limits for shared global renewable, project-specific local renewable, and non-renewable resource categories.

Sr.	Resource Types	Capacity	Type of Resources
1	GR1	3	Global
2	GR2	3	Global
3	GR3	3	Global
4	GR4	2	Global
5	GR5	2	Global
6	GR6	3	Global
7	GR7	1	Global
8	GR8	2	Global
9	LR1	Project dependent	Local
10	LR2	Project dependent	Local
11	NR1	Project dependent	Non-renewable
12	NR2	Project dependent	Non-renewable

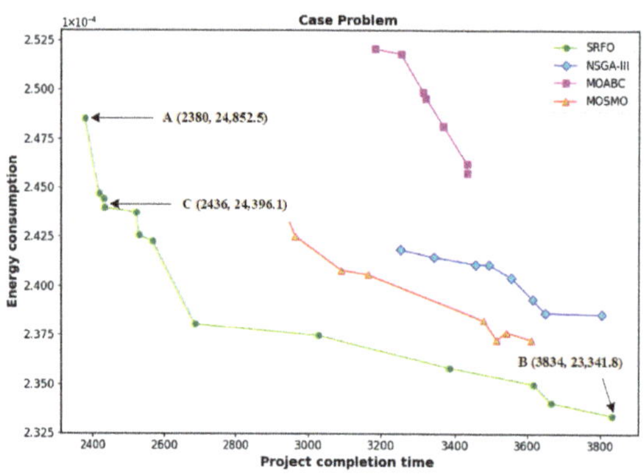

Figure 9. Pareto fronts for case study problem.

https://doi.org/10.3390/buildings16020392

To evaluate the performance gain of the proposed SRFO, a baseline schedule was established using the serial schedule generation scheme (SSGS) with a standard earliest-start-time priority rule. This baseline represents a traditional scheduling approach that prioritizes completion time under resource constraints but lacks multi-objective optimization for energy efficiency. As shown in Table 8, the Baseline Point resulted in a project duration of 2650 days and a total energy consumption (TEC) of 27,140.5 units. The sensitivity analysis provides critical insights into the dynamics between the conflicting objectives. Regarding the sensitivity to time reduction, transitioning from the Baseline Point to Point A (Time-Critical) reduces the total project duration by 10.2%, dropping from 2650 to 2380 days. However, this acceleration necessitates the selection of more resource-intensive execution modes, which is directly reflected in an increase in total energy consumption. When evaluating sensitivity to energy conservation, moving from Point A to the balanced Point C shows that a minor increase in duration of 2.3% yields a significant energy saving of 1.8%. Conversely, achieving the maximum possible energy savings at Point B requires the project duration to extend by 61% compared to the time-critical point, indicating that energy efficiency within this specific project network is highly sensitive to completion speed. Ultimately, the analysis of performance gain over the baseline confirms that the SRFO-Balanced (Point C) is Pareto-superior to the traditional Baseline Point. It simultaneously reduces project duration by 8.1% and energy consumption by 10.1% relative to standard industrial heuristics, validating the technical efficacy of the proposed optimization approach.

Table 8. Comparison of representative Pareto optimal solutions and baseline.

Selection Point	Strategy	Duration (Days)	TEC (Energy Units)
Baseline Point	Standard Heuristic	2650	27,140.5
Point A	Time-Critical	2380	24,852.5
Point B	Energy-Saving	3834	23,341.8
Point C	Balanced (TOPSIS)	2436	24,396.1

The results confirm that the SRFO successfully integrates the construction constraint, where on-site assembly is gated by the arrival of construction components, into an optimized timeline. By utilizing the ESO and SRP, the algorithm produces schedules that are not only theoretically optimal but also practically feasible under strict resource and precedence limitations.

6. Discussion

The experimental results presented in Section 5 unequivocally demonstrate the superior performance of the proposed SRFO algorithm compared to established multi-objective algorithms, including NSGA-III, MOABC, and MOSMO, across diverse problem sizes and metrics. This superior performance is directly attributed to the specialized components integrated into the SRFO framework, which effectively address the multi-layered constraints of the energy-efficient MRCMPS problem.

Statistical validation through the Wilcoxon signed-rank test confirms that SRFO consistently outperforms its counterparts in key convergence and multi-criteria decision-making metrics. Specifically, the significantly lower IGD values and superior QM and NPS scores confirm that the SRFO population converges faster toward the true Pareto front and identifies a higher density of non-dominated solutions. This enhanced convergence is largely driven by the integration of the non-dominated sorting mechanism, which efficiently manages the trade-off between project duration and energy consumption during the evolutionary process.

https://doi.org/10.3390/buildings16020392

Furthermore, the results observed for the SM and DM indicate that SRFO generates solutions that are not only closer to the optimal front but also more uniformly distributed across the feasible space. This uniform distribution is a direct consequence of the enhanced global exploration capability enabled by the RFO base algorithm and the integration of the MPPX and swap mutation genetic operators. Adding the ESO at the mode assignment level ensures the local exploitation phase effectively biases the search toward energy-minimizing modes while maintaining resource feasibility.

The real-world case study and subsequent sensitivity analysis best illustrate the practical relevance of the SRFO. The generated Pareto front provides project managers with a robust decision-support tool by quantifying the trade-offs between duration and energy. Sensitivity analysis revealed that the SRFO-Balanced solution (Point C) is superior to traditional industry heuristics, simultaneously reducing project duration by 8.1% and energy consumption by 10.1% compared to a standard baseline established by standard heuristics. Managers can choose Point A (duration: 2380) for time-critical needs or Point B (TEC: 23,341.8) for maximum energy conservation, while Point C (2436, 24,396.1) offers a balanced compromise. The ability of SRFO to provide high-quality, robust schedules while maintaining competitive computational efficiency confirms its viability for scientific management in energy-constrained construction environments

7. Conclusions and Future Work

This research provides both a practical algorithmic framework and critical insights into sustainable, intelligent construction project scheduling, offering significant implications for industries prioritizing energy efficiency and dynamic resource allocation. We have addressed the complex challenges of MRCMPS, characterized by varying project release dates and multiple resource constraints. By integrating project scheduling with mode assignment, we developed a comprehensive solution framework that effectively balances two conflicting objectives: minimizing total project duration and total energy consumption, which is particularly relevant to low-carbon strategies in the modern construction sector. The inclusion of realistic constraints, such as global, local, and non-renewable resource capacities, alongside mandatory component supply limits, enhances the practical applicability of this approach to modern construction project management. To solve this complex combinatorial optimization problem, we proposed a novel multi-objective SRFO algorithm. The SRFO integrates several advanced features, including a non-dominated sorting mechanism to handle multiple objectives, specialized genetic operators (MPPX and swap mutation) for solution refinement, and a problem-specific ESO for rapid local exploitation. To ensure peak performance, the algorithm's parameters were meticulously fine-tuned using the Taguchi method.

Extensive experimental validation across both benchmark problems and a real-world case study demonstrated the SRFO's superior capabilities. The algorithm was rigorously compared against established approaches, including NSGA-III, MOABC, and MOSMO, using a comprehensive set of evaluation metrics. Three convergence metrics (QM, IGD, NPS), two distribution metrics (SM, DM), TOPSIS-based multi-criteria decision-making, and the Wilcoxon signed-rank test consistently confirmed the SRFO's advantages in solution quality, convergence speed, and Pareto front distribution. Specifically, the case study results highlighted the algorithm's effectiveness, showing that the SRFO-Balanced solution achieved 8.1% reductions in project time and 10.1% in energy consumption compared to traditional industry heuristics. These results underscore the effectiveness of the SRFO in generating high-quality, feasible schedules while respecting complex resource constraints.

From a practical standpoint, this research provides project managers with a robust decision-support tool for scheduling complex project portfolios under stringent energy

https://doi.org/10.3390/buildings16020392

constraints. Future studies could enhance the model's practicality by incorporating real-world uncertainties, such as fuzzy activity durations, resource transfer time and cost considerations, and integrating various real-life constraints to develop a hyper-heuristic approach, all of which are key challenges in intelligent construction. These advancements would further strengthen the connection between theoretical optimization and practical project management challenges.

Author Contributions: Conceptualization, M.R.; Methodology, M.R.; Software, M.R.; Validation, M.R.; Data curation, J.M.; Writing—original draft, M.R.; Writing—review & editing, J.M.; Visualization, M.R. and J.M.; Supervision, J.M.; Project administration, J.M.; Funding acquisition, J.M. All authors have read and agreed to the published version of the manuscript.

Funding: This work has been supported by the Basic Scientific Research Project of Wenzhou City (G20240020, G2023036).

Data Availability Statement: Data will be made available on request.

Conflicts of Interest: No potential conflicts of interest were reported by the author(s).

Abbreviations

Indices	
i	Projects, $1 \leq i \leq I$
j	Activities, $1 \leq j \leq J$
m	Modes, $1 \leq m \leq M$
l	Local renewable resources, $1 \leq l \leq LR$
g	Global renewable resources, $1 \leq g \leq GR$
k	Non-renewable resources, $1 \leq k \leq K$
t	Time, $1 \leq t \leq HP$
Parameters and variables	
HP	A finite planning horizon
A^{d}_{ijm}	Estimated completion duration of the activity j belonging to project i when performed using execution mode m
Pd_i	Set of all the predecessors of activities in the project i
TR^{lr}_{il}	Total local renewable resource l available for the project i
TR^{gr}_{g}	Total global renewable resource g
TR^{nr}_{ik}	Total non-renewable resource $k$available for the project$i$
R^{lr}_{ijml}	Quantity of local renewable resource l consumed by task j within project i when operating under mode m
R^{gr}_{ijmg}	Quantity of global renewable resource g consumed by task j within project i when operating under mode m
R^{nr}_{ijmk}	Quantity of non-renewable resource k consumed by task j within project i when operating under mode m
RD_i	Release time of the project i
EC_{ijm}	Energy consumption of mode m of activity j within project i
A^{s}_{ij}	Start time of the activity j within project i
A^{f}_{ij}	Finish time of the activity j within project i
ST_i	Start time of the project i
FT_i	Finish time of the project i
TC_i	Total cost of the project i

 https://doi.org/10.3390/buildings16020392

References

1. Yue, L.; Wang, H.; Mumtaz, J.; Rauf, M.; Li, Z. Energy-efficient scheduling of a two-stage flexible printed circuit board flow shop using a hybrid Pareto spider monkey optimisation algorithm. *J. Ind. Inf. Integr.* **2023**, *31*, 100412. [CrossRef]
2. Gao, K.; Huang, Y.; Sadollah, A.; Wang, L. A review of energy-efficient scheduling in intelligent production systems. *Complex Intell. Syst.* **2020**, *6*, 237–249. [CrossRef]
3. Yuan, Y.; Ye, S.; Lin, L.; Gen, M. Multi-objective multi-mode resource-constrained project scheduling with fuzzy activity durations in prefabricated building construction. *Comput. Ind. Eng.* **2021**, *158*, 107316. [CrossRef]
4. Xin, X.; Jiang, Q.; Li, C.; Li, S.; Chen, K. Permutation flow shop energy-efficient scheduling with a position-based learning effect. *Int. J. Prod. Res.* **2023**, *61*, 382–409. [CrossRef]
5. Pellerin, R.; Perrier, N. A review of methods, techniques and tools for project planning and control. *Int. J. Prod. Res.* **2019**, *57*, 2160–2178. [CrossRef]
6. Xie, L.; Chen, Y.; Chang, R. Scheduling Optimization of Prefabricated Construction Projects by Genetic Algorithm. *Appl. Sci.* **2021**, *11*, 5531. [CrossRef]
7. Kannimuthu, M.; Ekambaram, P.; Raphael, B.; Kuppuswamy, A. Resource unconstrained and constrained project scheduling problems and practices in a multiproject environment. *Adv. Civ. Eng.* **2018**, *2018*, 9579273. [CrossRef]
8. Asta, S.; Karapetyan, D.; Kheiri, A.; Özcan, E.; Parkes, A.J. Combining monte-carlo and hyper-heuristic methods for the multi-mode resource-constrained multi-project scheduling problem. *Inf. Sci.* **2016**, *373*, 476–498. [CrossRef]
9. Beşikci, U.; Bilge, Ü.; Ulusoy, G. Multi-mode resource constrained multi-project scheduling and resource portfolio problem. *Eur. J. Oper. Res.* **2015**, *240*, 22–31. [CrossRef]
10. Xin, S.; Su, Q.; Wang, Q.; Wang, Q. Optimization of Resource-Constrained Multi-Project Scheduling Problem Based on the Genetic Algorithm. In Proceedings of the 2018 15th International Conference on Service Systems and Service Management (ICSSSM), Hangzhou, China, 21–22 July 2018.
11. Li, F.; Xu, Z. A multi-agent system for distributed multi-project scheduling with two-stage decomposition. *PLoS ONE* **2018**, *13*, e0205445. [CrossRef] [PubMed]
12. Afshar Nadjafi, B. A solution procedure for preemptive multi-mode project scheduling problem with mode changeability to resumption. *Appl. Comput. Inform.* **2018**, *14*, 192–201. [CrossRef]
13. Lova, A.; Maroto, C.; Tormos, P. A multicriteria heuristic method to improve resource allocation in multiproject scheduling. *Eur. J. Oper. Res.* **2000**, *127*, 408–424. [CrossRef]
14. Tseng, C.-C. Two heuristic algorithms for a multi-mode resource-constrained multi-project scheduling problem. *J. Sci. Eng. Technol.* **2008**, *4*, 63–74.
15. Küçüksayacıgil, F.; Ulusoy, G. Hybrid genetic algorithm for bi-objective resource-constrained project scheduling. *Front. Eng. Manag.* **2018**, *7*, 426–446. [CrossRef]
16. Geiger, M.J. A multi-threaded local search algorithm and computer implementation for the multi-mode, resource-constrained multi-project scheduling problem. *Eur. J. Oper. Res.* **2017**, *256*, 729–741. [CrossRef]
17. Chakrabortty, R.K.; Abbasi, A.; Ryan, M. Multi-mode resource-constrained project scheduling using modified variable neighborhood search heuristic. *Int. Trans. Oper. Res.* **2020**, *27*, 138–167. [CrossRef]
18. Kannimuthu, M.; Raphael, B.; Ekambaram, P.; Kuppuswamy, A.; Management, A. Comparing optimization modeling approaches for the multi-mode resource-constrained multi-project scheduling problem. *Eng. Constr.* **2019**, *27*, 893–916. [CrossRef]
19. Xu, J.; Feng, C. Multimode resource-constrained multiple project scheduling problem under fuzzy random environment and its application to a large scale hydropower construction project. *Sci. World J.* **2014**, *2014*, 463692. [CrossRef] [PubMed]
20. Song, Y.; Wang, J.; Lu, J.; Si, X. Research on collaborative scheduling of multiple projects of prefabricated building based on the niche genetic-raccoon family optimization algorithm. *Alex. Eng. J.* **2023**, *64*, 1015–1033. [CrossRef]
21. Javanmard, S.; Afshar-Nadjafi, B.; Taghi Akhavan Niaki, S. A bi-objective model for scheduling of multiple projects under multi-skilled workforce for distributed load energy usage. *Oper. Res.* **2022**, *22*, 2245–2280. [CrossRef]
22. da Silva, A.R.V. Techniques to Solve a Multi-Mode Resource Constrained Project Scheduling Problem with Energy Saving. Master's Thesis, Federal Fluminense University, Niterói, Brazil, 2017.
23. Ahmeti, A.; Musliu, N. Hybridizing constraint programming and meta-heuristics for multi-mode resource-constrained multiple projects scheduling problem. In Proceedings of the 13th international conference on the practice and theory of automated timetabling-patat, Leuven, Belgium, 24–27 August 2021.
24. Davari Ardakani, H.; Dehghani, A. Multi-objective Optimization of Multi-mode Resource-constrained Project Selection and Scheduling Problem Considering Resource Leveling and Time-varying Resource Usage. *Int. J. Supply Oper. Manag.* **2022**, *9*, 34–55. [CrossRef]
25. Rauf, M.; Sarfraz, S.; Shehab, E.; Javeed, S.; Jahanzaib, M. Multi-objective optimization for models sequencing in mixed-model assembly lines. In Proceedings of the Advances in Transdisciplinary Engineering, Singapore, 10–14 July 2017.

 https://doi.org/10.3390/buildings16020392

26. Rauf, M.; Guan, Z.; Sarfraz, S.; Mumtaz, J.; Shehab, E.; Jahanzaib, M.; Hanif, M. A smart algorithm for multi-criteria optimization of model sequencing problem in assembly lines. *Robot. Comput.-Integr. Manuf.* **2020**, *61*, 101844. [CrossRef]
27. Issa, S.; Tu, Y. A survey in the resource-constrained project and multi-project scheduling problems. *J. Proj. Manag.* **2020**, *5*, 117–138. [CrossRef]
28. Gómez Sánchez, M.; Lalla-Ruiz, E.; Fernández Gil, A.; Castro, C.; Voß, S. Resource-constrained multi-project scheduling problem: A survey. *Eur. J. Oper. Res.* **2023**, *309*, 958–976. [CrossRef]
29. Rauf, M.; Mumtaz, J.; Adeel, R.; Minhas, K.A.; Usman, M. An Efficient Q-Learning-Based Multi-Objective Intelligent Hybrid Genetic Algorithm for Mixed-Model Assembly Line Efficiency. *Symmetry* **2025**, *17*, 811. [CrossRef]
30. Ji, Z.; Mumtaz, J.; Ke, K. Using SABC algorithm for scheduling unrelated parallel batch processing machines considering deterioration effects and variable maintenance. *Eng. Proc.* **2024**, *75*, 20.
31. Küçüksayacigil, F.; Ulusoy, G. A genetic algorithm application for multi-objective multi-project resource constrained project scheduling problem. In Proceedings of the 15th Workshop of the EURO Working Group, Istanbul, Turkey, 10–13 June 2014.
32. Nemati-Lafmejani, R.; Davari-Ardakani, H.; Najafzad, H. Multi-mode resource constrained project scheduling and contractor selection: Mathematical formulation and metaheuristic algorithms. *Appl. Soft Comput.* **2019**, *81*, 105533. [CrossRef]
33. Tirkolaee, E.B.; Goli, A.; Hematian, M.; Sangaiah, A.K.; Han, T. Multi-objective multi-mode resource constrained project scheduling problem using Pareto-based algorithms. *Computing* **2019**, *101*, 547–570. [CrossRef]
34. Zheng, Z.; Shumin, L.; Ze, G.; Yueni, Z. Resource-constraint multi-project scheduling with priorities and uncertain activity durations. *Int. J. Comput. Intell. Syst.* **2013**, *6*, 530–547. [CrossRef]
35. Afshar, M.R.; Shahhosseini, V.; Sebt, M.H. A Genetic Algorithm with a New Local Search Method for Solving the Multimode Resource-constrained Project Scheduling Problem. *Int. J. Constr. Manag.* **2022**, *22*, 357–365. [CrossRef]
36. Wang, W.-X.; Wang, X.; Ge, X.-L.; Deng, L. Multi-objective optimization model for multi-project scheduling on critical chain. *Adv. Eng. Softw.* **2014**, *68*, 33–39. [CrossRef]
37. Tahooneh, A.; Ziarati, K. Using Artificial Bee Colony to Solve Stochastic Resource Constrained Project Scheduling Problem. In *Advances in Swarm Intelligence*; Springer: Berlin/Heidelberg, Germany, 2011.
38. Akbari, R.; Zeighami, V.; Ziarati, K. Artificial bee colony for resource constrained project scheduling problem. *Int. J. Ind. Eng. Comput.* **2011**, *2*, 45–60. [CrossRef]
39. Shi, Y.-j.; Qu, F.Z.; Chen, W.; Li, B. An Artificial Bee Colony with Random Key for Resource-Constrained Project Scheduling. In *International Conference on Life System Modeling and Simulation*; Springer: Berlin/Heidelberg, Germany, 2010.
40. Nouri, N.; Krichen, S.; Ladhari, T.; Fatimah, P. A discrete artificial bee colony algorithm for resource-constrained project scheduling problem. In Proceedings of the 5th International Conference on Modeling, Simulation and Applied Optimization (ICMSAO), Hammamet, Tunisia, 28–30 April 2013.
41. Jia, Q.; Guo, Y. Hybridization of ABC and PSO algorithms for improved solutions of RCPSP. *J. Chin. Inst. Eng.* **2016**, *39*, 727–734. [CrossRef]
42. Ziarati, K.; Akbari, R.; Zeighami, V. On the performance of bee algorithms for resource-constrained project scheduling problem. *Appl. Soft Comput.* **2011**, *11*, 3720–3733. [CrossRef]
43. Chen, A.H.-L.; Liang, Y.-C.; Padilla, J.D. An entropy-based upper bound methodology for robust predictive multi-mode RCPSP schedules. *Entropy* **2014**, *16*, 5032–5067. [CrossRef]
44. Mumtaz, J.; Minhas, K.A.; Rauf, M.; Yue, L.; Chen, Y. Solving line balancing and AGV scheduling problems for intelligent decisions using a Genetic-Artificial bee colony algorithm. *Comput. Ind. Eng.* **2024**, *189*, 109976. [CrossRef]
45. Koohi, S.Z.; Hamid, N.A.W.A.; Othman, M.; Ibragimov, G. Raccoon Optimization Algorithm. *IEEE Access* **2019**, *7*, 5383–5399. [CrossRef]
46. Rauf, M.; Guan, Z.; Yue, L.; Guo, Z.; Mumtaz, J.; Ullah, S. Integrated planning and scheduling of multiple manufacturing projects under resource constraints using raccoon family optimization algorithm. *IEEE Access* **2020**, *8*, 151279–151295. [CrossRef]
47. Geng, Y.-D.; Li, J.-Q. A knowledge-driven multiobjective algorithm for distributed hybrid flowshop with group and carryover setup in glass manufacturing systems. *Comput. Ind. Eng.* **2023**, *181*, 109325. [CrossRef]
48. Wang, J.-J.; Wang, L. A knowledge-based cooperative algorithm for energy-efficient scheduling of distributed flow-shop. *IEEE Trans. Syst. Man Cybern. Syst.* **2018**, *50*, 1805–1819.
49. Luo, C.; Gong, W.; Lu, C. Knowledge-driven two-stage memetic algorithm for energy-efficient flexible job shop scheduling with machine breakdowns. *Expert Syst. Appl.* **2024**, *235*, 121149. [CrossRef]
50. Yue, L.; Guan, Z.; Zhang, L.; Ullah, S.; Cui, Y. Multi objective lotsizing and scheduling with material constraints in flexible parallel lines using a Pareto based guided artificial bee colony algorithm. *Comput. Ind. Eng.* **2019**, *128*, 659–680. [CrossRef]
51. Wauters, T.; Kinable, J.; Smet, P.; Vancroonenburg, W.; Berghe, G.V.; Verstichel, J. The multi-mode resource-constrained multi-project scheduling problem. *J. Sched.* **2016**, *19*, 271–283. [CrossRef]
52. Ding, L.; Guan, Z.; Luo, D.; Rauf, M.; Fang, W. An Adaptive Search Algorithm for Multiplicity Dynamic Flexible Job Shop Scheduling with New Order Arrivals. *Symmetry* **2024**, *16*, 641. [CrossRef]

 https://doi.org/10.3390/buildings16020392

53. Tavana, M.; Abtahi, A.-R.; Khalili-Damghani, K. A new multi-objective multi-mode model for solving preemptive time–cost–quality trade-off project scheduling problems. *Expert Syst. Appl.* **2014**, *41*, 1830–1846. [CrossRef]
54. Saif, U.; Guan, Z.; Zhang, L.; Mirza, J.; Lei, Y. Hybrid Pareto artificial bee colony algorithm for assembly line balancing with task time variations. *Int. J. Comput. Integr. Manuf.* **2017**, *30*, 255–270. [CrossRef]
55. Saif, U.; Guan, Z.; Liu, W.; Zhang, C.; Wang, B. Pareto based artificial bee colony algorithm for multi objective single model assembly line balancing with uncertain task times. *Comput. Ind. Eng.* **2014**, *76*, 1–15. [CrossRef]
56. Zhang, R.; Chang, P.-C.; Song, S.; Wu, C. A multi-objective artificial bee colony algorithm for parallel batch-processing machine scheduling in fabric dyeing processes. *Knowl.-Based Syst.* **2017**, *116*, 114–129. [CrossRef]

 https://doi.org/10.3390/buildings16020392

buildings

MDPI

Article

Internal and External Landscape Features of 18 Parks in Hangzhou, China That Cool the Park and the Surrounding Urban Areas: Strategies for Other Cities

Tao Ma [1], Mengxin Yang [2,*], Shaojie Zhang [3], Xiaofan Jiang [1] and Wenbin Nie [2]

1 College of Life and Environment Sciences, Huangshan University, Huangshan 242700, China; 107070@hsu.edu.cn (T.M.); 107081@hsu.edu.cn (X.J.)
2 College of Landscape Architecture, Zhejiang Agriculture and Forestry University, Hangzhou 311300, China; niewenbin@zafu.edu.cn
3 School of Architecture & Urban Planning, Anhui Jianzhu University, Hefei 230601, China; shaojiezhang@ahjzu.edu.cn
* Correspondence: ymxzbl123@163.com

Abstract

As one of China's "New Four Furnaces", the city of Hangzhou faces significant heat challenges exacerbated by rapid urbanization. Urban parks offer effective nature-based solutions, but optimizing their multi-dimensional cooling performance—encompassing cooling area (PCA), efficiency (PCE), intensity (PCI), and gradient (PCG)—remains a key challenge. This study quantitatively analyzed the internal and external landscape features of 18 parks in Hangzhou, revealing that park cooling performance is not simply a case of "bigger is better." We found that parks with more complex shapes and irregular boundaries exhibited higher cooling efficiency per unit area (PCE) compared to larger parks with smooth, simple shapes, though sometimes at the expense of peak PCI. Furthermore, the surrounding built environment is critical: high building density within a 300 m buffer zone was found to significantly impede the spatial extent of the cooling effect (PCA). Based on these findings, we propose that to effectively mitigate urban heat, cities should (1) shift focus away from creating large, isolated parks with smooth boundaries; (2) prioritize a network of smaller, morphologically diverse parks with irregular edges that extend into the community; and (3) enhance each park's cooling reach through strategies like green streets and tree-lined paths. These approaches offer tangible, actionable guidance for designing high-performance cooling green infrastructure in dense urban environments.

Keywords: urban heat island effect; urban parks; cooling effect; landscape pattern; influencing factors

1. Introduction

Urbanization constitutes a systematic evolutionary process characterized by interconnected demographic, economic, spatial, and socio-cultural transformations [1]. A defining contemporary trend is the accelerating concentration of global population and socio-economic activities within cities, fundamentally altering the equilibrium between the built and natural environments [2]. Statistical data reveal that the global urbanization rate rose from 43.4% in 1991 to 55.7% in 2019, with projections indicating a rise to 68% by 2050 [3]. This process is particularly rapid in developing nations, exemplified by China, driving dramatic urban spatial expansion and inducing profound transformations in urban landscape patterns. Concurrently, global climate change, manifested predominantly

https://doi.org/10.3390/buildings16030630

through rising mean temperatures and an increased frequency of extreme weather events, poses a substantial and escalating threat to public health [4].

The combined pressures of urbanization and global climate change are exacerbating urban thermal environmental issues. On one hand, the widespread conversion of natural surfaces to impervious materials enhances the land surface's absorption and storage of solar radiation and its emission of longwave radiation. This directly elevates surface temperatures and disrupts the urban thermal balance [5,6]. On the other hand, urban expansion and intensification of development, driven by the needs of growing populations and industries, have increased greenhouse gas emissions. This has already contributed to a rise in the global average temperature of approximately 1.1 °C [7]. High energy consumption and thermal accumulation in cities further impair public health and quality of life [8]. The interaction of these processes accelerates ecological degradation, manifested notably in the urban heat island (UHI) effect and persistent heatwaves [9]. Addressing these challenges urgently requires collaborative efforts between policymakers and researchers to develop systematic solutions.

In response to the severe urban thermal environment, diverse mitigation strategies have been proposed by both academia and practitioners. These encompass (1) utilizing blue-green infrastructure to reduce ambient urban temperatures through its cooling effects [10,11]; (2) optimizing urban morphology to enhance ventilation [12]; and (3) applying high-albedo construction materials [13]. Among these approaches, harnessing the cooling effects of blue-green infrastructure is widely acknowledged as one of the most effective strategies, consistent with sustainable development goals [14]. Beyond thermal mitigation, urban blue-green infrastructure delivers critical ecosystem services, including microclimate regulation, carbon sequestration, air purification, water conservation, and biodiversity protection [15]. Moreover, it holistically enhances residents' health and well-being, as well as urban livability, by fostering physical activity, improving environmental quality, generating economic benefits, and strengthening social cohesion [16].

Urban parks, as representative blue-green infrastructure, effectively mitigate local temperatures, enhance human thermal comfort, and reduce heat-related health risks through mechanisms such as canopy shading, increased surface albedo, and vegetation transpiration [17–19]. Evidence suggests that park visits can substantially alleviate heat stress symptoms and support human adaptation to a warming climate [20]. Given these benefits, urban parks are increasingly recognized as a sustainable, nature-based solution with strong potential for cooling, offering a functional response to urban heat challenges [21,22]. As public demand grows for ecologically livable environments, the cooling services delivered by urban parks have gained significant societal attention [23]. There is a pressing need for rationally planned urban spaces that enable equitable and efficient access to public resources, thereby minimizing health risks and social tensions associated with uneven distribution of environmental amenities [24]. Consequently, a systematic investigation into the factors influencing the cooling performance of urban parks is essential for optimizing their thermal mitigation effects. Therefore, this study aims to address the following key research questions: (1) How can the multi-dimensional cooling performance of urban parks—encompassing their cooling area, efficiency, intensity, and gradient—be comprehensively quantified? (2) What are the key internal and external landscape characteristics that drive these cooling performance indicators, and what complex trade-offs exist among them? (3) Based on these findings, what targeted optimization strategies can be proposed to enhance the cooling benefits of urban parks in high-density urban environments?

This study investigated 18 urban parks in the Hangzhou metropolitan area. Utilizing Landsat 8 OLI_TIRS remote sensing imagery and Gaode satellite data, it integrated remote sensing and geographic information system (GIS) technologies to assess the rel-

https://doi.org/10.3390/buildings16030630

ative importance (weight) of diverse factors affecting park cooling effects. The research primarily involved four key components: (1) retrieving land surface temperature (LST) and quantifying park cooling indicators; (2) quantifying the internal and external landscape characteristics of the parks; (3) analyzing the influence of these landscape characteristics on park cooling effects; and (4) proposing targeted optimization strategies based on the analytical findings.

2. Materials and Methods

2.1. Regional Overview

The study area is located in Hangzhou City, southeastern China (29°11′–30°33′ N, 118°21′–120°30′ E). Characterized by a subtropical monsoon climate, the region experiences hot and humid summers, with extreme high temperatures reaching 39.8–42.9 °C. Consequently, Hangzhou is classified as one of China's "New Four Furnaces" and faces significant urban heat challenges. To enhance the representativeness of the study and minimize thermal interference from suburban areas, the research scope was confined to Hangzhou's core urban zone. This zone was delineated based on four central districts—Shangcheng, Gongshu, Xihu, and Binjiang—as specified in the Hangzhou Territorial Space Master Plan (2021–2035) [25] (Figure 1). Within this defined area, 18 urban parks were selected as study sites (Table 1). The spatial boundary of each park was digitized using data sourced from the AutoNavi Map (AMap) platform (version 16.09.0; AutoNavi Software Co., Ltd., Beijing, China) [26] and mapped within the ArcGIS 10.8 software environment. To ensure a consistent meteorological background for a robust cross-sectional comparison of the parks, a single, cloud-free Landsat 8 image from a representative high-temperature day (27 September 2021) was selected for analysis.

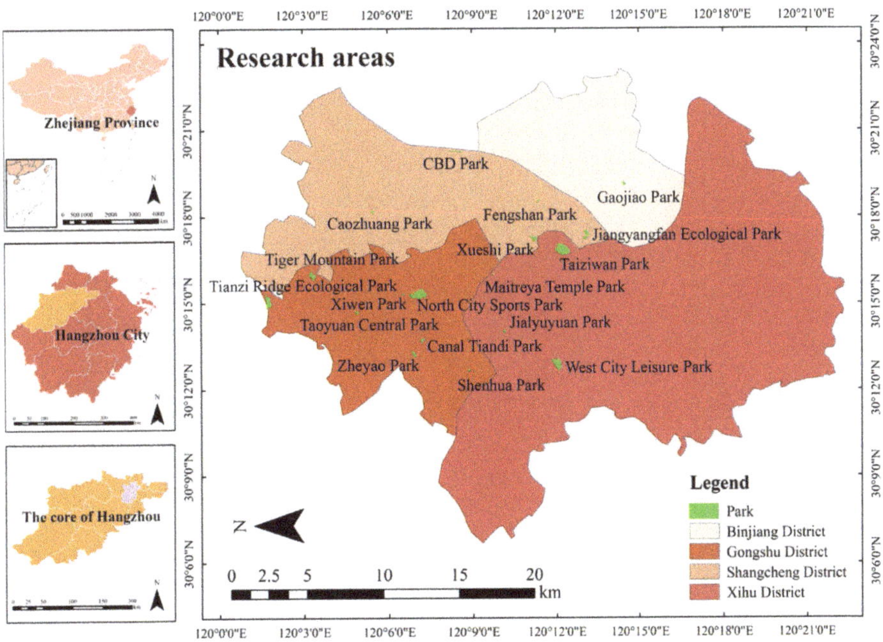

Figure 1. The location of the research areas.

 https://doi.org/10.3390/buildings16030630

Table 1. The attributes of 18 urban parks.

Serial Number	English Name	Area/Hectares (Area/Acres)	Serial Number	English Name	Area/Hectares (Area/Acres)
1	Fengshan Park	1.66 (4.11)	10	Tiger Mountain Park	11.57 (28.60)
2	CBD Park	2.84 (7.02)	11	Tianzi Ridge Ecological Park	18.49 (45.69)
3	Caozhuang Park	2.47 (6.10)	12	Gaojiao Park	3.00 (7.41)
4	Shenhua Park	1.45 (3.58)	13	Xueshi Park	7.97 (19.69)
5	North City Sports Park	41.59 (102.77)	14	Taiziwan Park	42.21 (104.30)
6	Xiwen Park	1.01 (2.50)	15	Jiangyangfan Ecological Park	10.75 (26.56)
7	Canal Tiandi Park	4.46 (11.02)	16	West City Leisure Park	25.37 (62.69)
8	Zheyao Park	5.27 (13.02)	17	Mituosi Park	1.04 (2.57)
9	Taoyuan Central Park	3.17 (7.83)	18	Jialvyuan Park	2.55 (6.30)

2.2. Research Methods

2.2.1. Land Surface Temperature Retrieval

Urban parks provide a measurable cooling effect, offering a vital ecosystem service that can mitigate climate change impacts and support sustainable urban development. Given the logistical challenges and high costs associated with collecting in situ air temperature measurements, land surface temperature (LST) data serve as a practical and efficient proxy for evaluating urban park cooling performance [27]. Accordingly, this study employed LST data to characterize the cooling effects of urban parks. To capture these effects under pronounced thermal conditions, we selected study dates characterized by high daily air temperatures and obtained the corresponding LST imagery for analysis.

This study utilized land surface temperature (LST) data derived from satellite imagery with a spatial resolution of 30 m. LST was selected as a robust proxy for near-surface air temperature due to the infeasibility of acquiring high-density, city-wide air temperature data and the strong spatial correlation between the two variables established in the previous literature. Hangzhou, situated within a subtropical monsoon climate zone and frequently influenced by tropical cyclones, experiences a scarcity of cloud-free days during summer. Consequently, most summertime satellite imagery of the region fails to meet the stringent quality requirements for research. To acquire more representative and reliable LST data, a clear day in September was selected for analysis. This approach not only aligns with the local climatic characteristics but also ensures the scientific validity of the data for subsequent analysis. The specific LST images employed were obtained from Landsat 8 OLI_TIRS satellite data (Path 119, Row 39) for 21 September 2021, sourced from the Geospatial Data Cloud platform [28]. Meteorological records for that date indicate an average temperature of 27 °C, a maximum temperature of 33 °C, a cloud cover of 0.62%, and no precipitation (0 mm). Furthermore, no typhoon activity was recorded, suggesting minimal influence from large-scale ocean–atmosphere circulation patterns on the local climatic conditions during the data acquisition period.

This study applied the radiative transfer equation to calculate land surface thermal radiation intensity. This was achieved by subtracting atmospheric effects from the radiation received by the sensor. Subsequently, land surface temperature (LST) was estimated based on this calculated intensity [29,30]. To account for phenological characteristics, the Normalized Difference Vegetation Index (NDVI) was calculated using surface reflectance data derived from Landsat imagery of the study area (Formula (1)). Furthermore, vegetation coverage (P_V) was derived from the NDVI values and was then used to estimate land surface emissivity (Formula (2)).

$$NDVI = \frac{Band_{NIR} - Band_{RED}}{Band_{NIR} + Band_{RED}} \quad (1)$$

https://doi.org/10.3390/buildings16030630

Here, $Band_{NIR}$ and $Band_{RED}$ represent the near-infrared band and the red band of Landsat imagery, respectively. In this study, NDVI data corresponding to the image acquisition dates were utilized to estimate the time required to reach the maximum rate of NDVI change.

$$P_v = \left(\frac{NDVI - NDVI_{bare}}{NDVI_{veg} - NDVI_{bare}}\right)^2. \quad (2)$$

"$NDVI_{veg}$" and "$NDVI_{bare}$" represent the normalized difference vegetation index values for fully vegetated and completely bare soil surfaces, respectively. Subsequently, based on the vegetation coverage (P_v), the land surface emissivity (ε) was estimated using Formula (3) [31]. This provided fundamental data for subsequent processing steps.

$$\varepsilon = 0.985P_v + 0.960(1 - P_v) + \frac{0.06P_v\,(1 - P_v)}{0.004P_v} + 0.986 \quad (3)$$

Subsequently, ENVI 5.6 (L3Harris Geospatial, Boulder, CO, USA), a commercial software package for geospatial imagery analysis, was employed for subsequent modeling and analysis [32]. Land surface temperature (LST) was retrieved using the radiative transfer equation via the software's built-in FLAASH module, thereby deriving blackbody radiation data corresponding to LST (Formula (4)).

$$D_t = [L_] - L\uparrow - \tau(1 - \varepsilon)L\downarrow]/\tau\varepsilon \quad (4)$$

In Formula (4), D_t (unit: $W \cdot m^{-2} \cdot sr^{-1} \cdot \mu m^{-1}$) represents blackbody radiation. $L\downarrow$ (unit: $W \cdot m^{-2} \cdot sr^{-1} \cdot \mu m^{-1}$) and $L\uparrow$ (unit: $W \cdot m^{-2} \cdot sr^{-1} \cdot \mu m^{-1}$) represent downwelling radiance and upwelling radiance values, respectively. "τ" denotes atmospheric transmittance. The values of $L\downarrow$, τ and $L\uparrow$ can be obtained by using the Atmospheric Correction Parameter Calculator [33], entering the geographical location of the target city and the observation time to retrieve the corresponding data. Then, through Planck's Law (Formula (5)), retrieve and determine the Land Surface Temperature (LST) of the study area.

$$T_s = \frac{K_2}{\ln(K_1/D_t(T_s) + 1)} \quad (5)$$

Here, T_s represents the surface temperature value in Kelvin. To convert it to degrees Celsius, 273.15 is subtracted. K_1 and K_2 denote the calibration constants for the Landsat data [34]. The surface temperature data obtained in this study demonstrated strong temporal continuity and spatial heterogeneity. This provided a solid foundation for building a stable and reliable model of urban cooling spaces. By applying the radiative transfer method procedures described above, we acquired the surface temperature vector map necessary for this research. This dataset supported subsequent quantitative assessments of urban park cooling effects, analysis of influencing factors, and related quantitative studies. Consequently, it supplied essential data support for optimizing urban park cooling effects and resource allocation. The retrieved Landsat 8 surface temperature data for the study area are shown in Figure 2.

https://doi.org/10.3390/buildings16030630

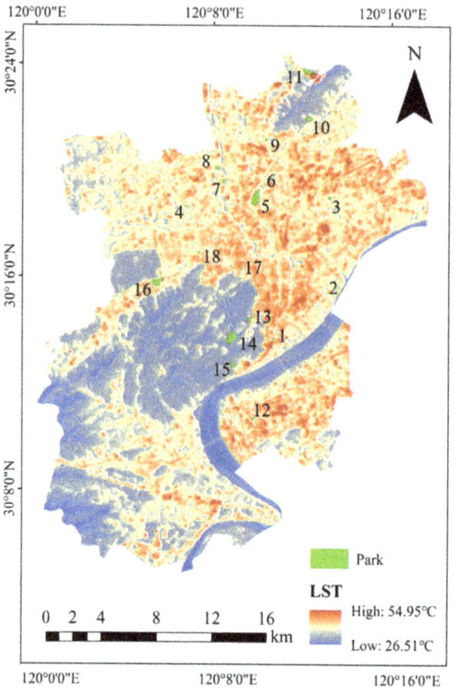

Figure 2. Spatial distribution pattern of LST (The park numbers in the image are consistent with those in Table 1).

2.2.2. Quantification of Park Cooling Indicators

Building on prior studies, this research adopted perspectives of maximization and accumulation. Four key indicators—Park Cooling Area (PCA), Park Cooling Efficiency (PCE), Park Cooling Intensity (PCI), and Park Cooling Gradient (PCG)—were employed to comprehensively quantify and evaluate the cooling effects of urban parks within the Hangzhou metropolitan area. This approach provides a theoretical foundation for subsequent investigations into the relationships between influencing factors and urban park cooling performance. The specific metrics are defined as follows: (1) Park Cooling Area (PCA) is defined as the maximum buffer area within which the park's cooling effect is detectable [35], directly representing its spatial extent of influence. (2) Park Cooling Efficiency (PCE) is defined as the ratio of the maximum cooling range (S_{max}) to the park area (S_{park}) [36], reflecting the cooling benefit per unit area. (3) Park Cooling Intensity (PCI) is quantified as the difference between the initial inflection point temperature and the average park temperature [37]; this metric captures residents' intuitive perception of cooling, where higher values correspond to a more pronounced thermal sensation. (4) Park Cooling Gradient (PCG) is defined as the average cooling intensity per unit distance, calculated by dividing PCI by the park's maximum cooling distance [38]. This indicator characterizes the park's overall cooling rate and capacity.

The quantification of the aforementioned indicators is contingent upon the precise determination of the park cooling distance. This distance is defined as the point on the temperature profile where a notable inflection or stabilization occurs [39], corresponding to the maximum spatial extent of the cooling effect (Figure 3). Through the fitting of land surface temperature (LST) data from urban parks in Hangzhou, this study empirically confirmed the existence of a maximum effective cooling distance, thus providing a basis for further

https://doi.org/10.3390/buildings16030630

analysis. The methodological procedures were as follows. First, informed by prior studies suggesting a maximum cooling distance of approximately 900 m [40,41] and consistent with the 30 m resolution of the satellite imagery employed, a series of 30 contiguous buffers, each 30 m in width, was generated outward from each park boundary. Subsequently, the average LST for each buffer zone was calculated and plotted to construct corresponding LST profile graphs. It should be noted that the analysis specifically targeted the cooling impact of parks on adjacent built-up land within these buffers. The temperature profiles were modeled using a third-order polynomial function, T(x) (Formula (6)), where the x-axis denotes the distance from the park boundary and the y-axis denotes the LST value. This approach establishes a functional relationship between LST and distance from the park edge [42].

$$T = ax^3 + bx^2 + cx \tag{6}$$

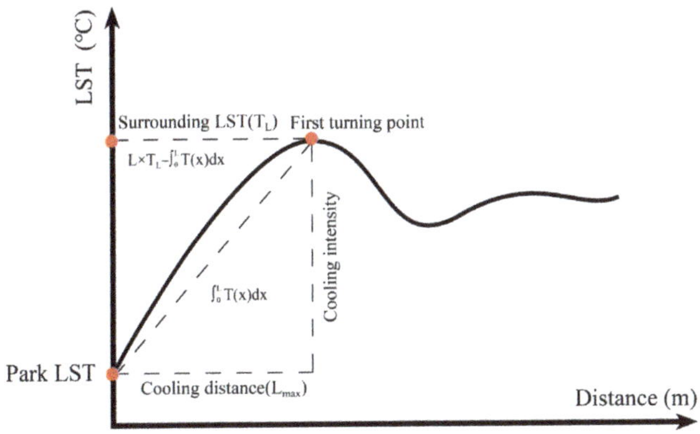

Figure 3. Visualization of LST change curve of park cooling process.

As the distance from the park boundary increased, the land surface temperature initially exhibited a rising trend, but the slope of the curve gradually flattened until it approached zero. The point where the curve's slope was zero was defined as the first inflection point, denoted as "x_1". The distance from the park boundary to "x_1" was defined as the maximum cooling range, indicating that within this buffer zone, the land surface temperature showed an initial declining trend as the distance from the park increased [43]. The park's cooling distance is denoted by "L", while "L_{max}" refers to the maximum distance at which the cooling effect can be observed. This derivative-based approach was chosen for its objectivity, as it identifies the point where the park's influence statistically dissipates without relying on arbitrary temperature thresholds. Subsequently, based on the magnitude of the urban park cooling distance, the park's cooling effect was quantified using four indicators: cooling area, cooling efficiency, cooling intensity, and cooling gradient. This quantification was conducted to analyze the park cooling effect from the perspectives of maximization and accumulation.

2.2.3. Quantifying the Internal and External Landscape Features of Parks

Research indicates that both internal and external landscape characteristics significantly influence the cooling effect of urban parks [44]. Accordingly, this study selected nine landscape characteristics—both within and surrounding the parks—to analyze their impact on urban park cooling (Table 2). These comprised internal characteristics (park area, park perimeter, park shape complexity, proportion of green space, and proportion of water body within the park) and external characteristics (road network density, building

https://doi.org/10.3390/buildings16030630

density, proportion of green space, and proportion of water bodies within a 300 m buffer zone around each park). This buffer size was chosen based on its common use and validated effectiveness in previous park cooling studies for capturing neighborhood-scale influences [45]. The selection aimed to (1) evaluate how these factors relate to four quantitative cooling indicators (PCA, PCE, PCI, and PCG), (2) explore the mechanisms underlying park cooling formation, (3) identify planning and design strategies that can effectively enhance cooling performance, and (4) improve the practical applicability of cooling effect assessments. Shape complexity was quantified using the Landscape Shape Index (LSI), calculated as follows (Formula (7)):

$$\mathrm{LSI} = \frac{\mathrm{P}}{2\sqrt{\pi \times \mathrm{S_{park}}}} \tag{7}$$

Table 2. The influencing factors on the park cooling effect.

Category	Sub-Category	Influencing Factors	Definition
Internal	Park Geometry	Park—Shape—area	The area of urban parks
		Park—Shape—circumference	The circumference of the urban park
		Park—Complex in shape	The complexity of the shapes of urban parks
	Park Composition	Park—water body—proportion	The proportion of water bodies in urban parks
		Park—green space—proportion	The proportion of vegetation in urban parks
External	Surrounding Environment (300 m Buffer)	Buffer zone—Road—density	The road network density within the 300 m buffer zone of the urban park
		Buffer zone—Building—density	The building density within the 300 m buffer zone of the urban park
		Buffer zone—Green space—proportion	The proportion of vegetation within the 300 m buffer zone of the urban park
		Buffer zone—Water body—proportion	The proportion of water bodies within the 300 m buffer zone of urban parks

Here, P denotes the park perimeter, and S_{park} represents the park area. A higher LSI value indicates a more irregular park shape [46], signifying a greater degree of shape complexity [47].

To further investigate the relationships between urban park cooling indicators and their potential influencing factors, this study employed Pearson correlation analysis to identify significant positive or negative correlations. Initially, based on a land cover vector map (https://www.tianditu.gov.cn/), vector data for water bodies, vegetation, roads, and buildings within the core urban area of Hangzhou (encompassing Shangcheng, Gongshu, Binjiang, and Xihu Districts) were extracted and clipped using ArcGIS (version 10.8.1; Esri Inc., Redlands, CA, USA) [48]. This procedure generated the following dataset for each of the 18 urban parks for subsequent analysis: internal water body area, internal green space area, road length within a 300 m buffer, building area within a 300 m buffer, green space area within a 300 m buffer, and water body area within a 300 m buffer. The selection of a 300 m buffer for analysis was based on two considerations. First, it aligns with the 30 m spatial resolution of the land surface temperature (LST) satellite imagery, ensuring consistency and scientific rigor in the data analysis. Second, factors within this approximate range exert a relatively strong influence on park cooling effects, with their impact attenuating as distance from the park increases. The results of the Pearson correlation analysis revealed that the

https://doi.org/10.3390/buildings16030630

internal and external landscape characteristics of the studied urban parks exhibited varying degrees and directions of influence on the different cooling indicators, with several factors demonstrating a statistically significant impact on the parks' cooling effect. Given the inherent mathematical correlation among park area, perimeter, and LSI, we performed this correlation analysis as an exploratory step. In the subsequent discussion, these metrics were not treated as fully independent drivers; rather, their effects were interpreted collectively as indicators of park 'scale' and 'shape complexity'.

3. Result

3.1. Results of Park Cooling Effect Indicators

This study employed four cooling indicators to quantify and assess the cooling effects of urban parks. Analysis revealed significant variations in these indicators across the 18 studied parks. As summarized in Table 3, the mean values for Park Cooling Area (PCA), Park Cooling Efficiency (PCE), Park Cooling Intensity (PCI), and Park Cooling Gradient (PCG) were 207.01 hectares, 58.61, 0.018, and 0.64 °C, respectively. The observed ranges were 46.40–526.23 hectares for PCA, 3.21–273.22 for PCE, 0.005–0.032 for PCI (it is important to note that PCI is a dimensionless ratio representing the total accumulated thermal load reduction—e.g., a PCI of 0.02 signifies a 2% reduction—not a direct temperature difference), and 0.15–1.17 °C for PCG. Following normalization to a scale of 0.1–0.9, the calculated variances were 0.059 (PCE), 0.080 (PCG), 0.095 (PCA), and 0.084 (PCI). These results suggest that the four indicators exhibited comparable levels of dispersion and variability.

Table 3. The indicator data of park cooling effect.

Serial Number	Park Name	Park Cooling Area (PCA) (ha(Acres))	Park Cooling Efficiency (PCE)	Park Cooling Intensity (PCI)	Park Cooling Gradient (PCG)
1	Fengshan Park	64.1631 (158.5512)	38.5950	0.0123	0.4704
2	CBD Park	297.9927 (736.3347)	105.0941	0.0229	0.7754
3	CaoZhuang Park	274.6435 (678.6534)	111.2687	0.0315	1.1688
4	Shenhua Park	396.8403 (980.6094)	273.2233	0.0147	0.5219
5	Chengbei Sports Park	433.3634 (1070.8643)	10.4209	0.0196	0.7257
6	Xiwen Park	138.3300 (341.8228)	137.1998	0.0274	1.0031
7	Canal heaven and earth park	73.4091 (181.4011)	16.4494	0.0147	0.5189
8	Zheyao Park	328.0625 (810.6617)	62.2117	0.0244	0.8756
9	Taoyuan Central Park	270.9284 (669.4795)	85.5184	0.029	1.0584
10	Hushan Park	46.4007 (114.6593)	4.0088	0.0045	0.1504
11	Tianziling Ecological Park	91.4336 (225.9348)	4.9447	0.0103	0.3997
12	Higher Education Park	114.5708 (283.1118)	38.1991	0.0195	0.7399
13	Bachelor's Park	81.3710 (201.0700)	10.2158	0.007	0.2317
14	Prince Bay Park	337.8643 (834.8770)	8.0048	0.0179	0.5554
15	Jiangyangfan Ecological Park	526.2382 (1300.3551)	48.9365	0.0195	0.6405
16	Chengxi Leisure Park	81.4635 (201.3000)	3.2113	0.0045	0.1596
17	Mituo Temple Park	54.5149 (134.7088)	52.5218	0.0164	0.6248
18	Jialvyuan Park	114.5641 (283.0950)	44.8938	0.024	0.8795
Summary	Mean	212.5855 (525.3129)	64.1627	0.0172	0.6417
	Max	526.2382 (1300.3551)	273.2233	0.0315	1.1688
	Min	46.4007 (114.6593)	3.2113	0.0045	0.1504

This study utilized the K-means clustering method to classify the 18 urban parks according to the similarity of their cooling indicators. First, the four cooling indicators—Park Cooling Area (PCA), Park Cooling Efficiency (PCE), Park Cooling Intensity (PCI), and Park Cooling Gradient (PCG)—were normalized. Subsequently, the parks were grouped into distinct clusters based on comparable patterns of high or low values across these normalized indicators. The optimal number of clusters, determined to be five, was identified through a

https://doi.org/10.3390/buildings16030630

comprehensive approach incorporating the silhouette coefficient, elbow, and gap statistic methods [25]. The cluster analysis of the 18 parks (Figure 4) revealed spatial heterogeneity and structural characteristics in their cooling functions. Conducting landscape structure analysis on parks with varying emphases in cooling effects supports the optimization of blue-green infrastructure development in urban parks, with the objective of enhancing or even maximizing their cooling performance.

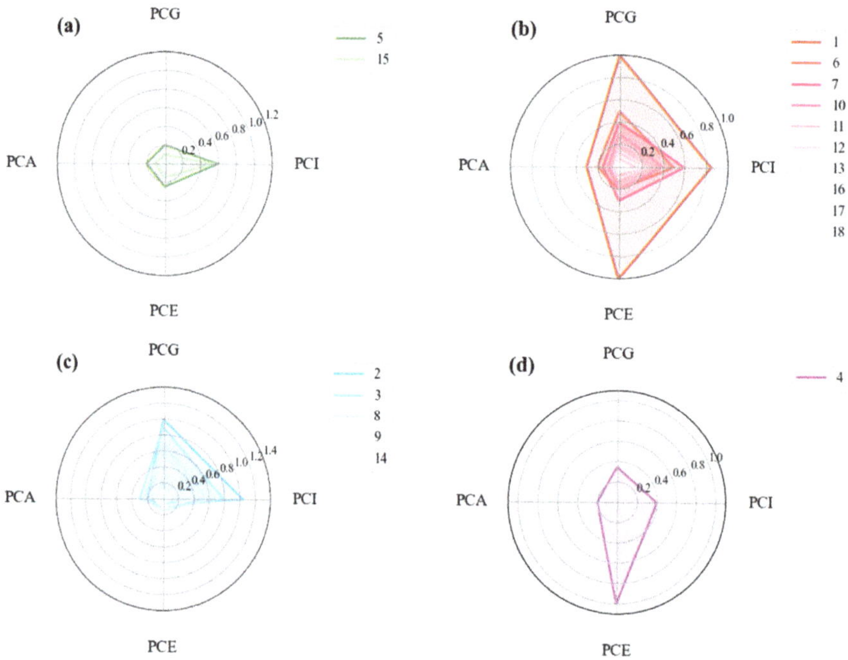

Figure 4. Radar charts illustrating the four distinct 'Cooling Bundle' profiles identified among the urban parks: (**a**) Type 1, (**b**) Type 2, (**c**) Type 3, and (**d**) Type 4. Park identification numbers in the legends correspond to those in Table 1.

Based on the cluster analysis of the cooling effects of 18 urban parks, it was found that all parks were assigned to four of the five statistically optimal clusters, with the fifth cluster, representing a uniformly low-performance profile, remaining empty. Consequently, their performance could be classified into four main types. The first type, represented by Chengbei Sports Park and Jiangyangfan Ecological Park, was dominated by Park Cooling Area (PCA) and Park Cooling Gradient (PCG). These parks are typically comprehensive parks with larger areas and substantial water bodies. The second type, which constituted the largest group and included ten parks such as Fengshan Park and Xiwen Park, excelled in PCG due to their superior blue-green infrastructure. The third type, represented by parks like CBD Park and Prince Bay Park, was characterized by relatively high PCG and Park Cooling Intensity (PCI), mostly comprising irregularly shaped parks with dense vegetation. The fourth type, represented by Shenhua Park, was dominated by Park Cooling Efficiency (PCE), manifesting as small parks with complex shapes but high cooling economic efficiency. It is noteworthy that all studied parks belonged to these four well-performing categories, in contrast to a hypothetical fifth category of parks that would perform poorly across all metrics due to sparse vegetation and limited water bodies. This cluster analysis not only revealed the significant spatial heterogeneity in the cooling effects of urban parks but also

https://doi.org/10.3390/buildings16030630

provided an important scientific basis for optimizing urban park planning and design to effectively mitigate the threats of urban heat island effects and heatwave events [49,50].

3.2. Results of Internal Landscape Characteristics in Parks

Internal landscape characteristics were quantified for the 18 parks using key metrics: area, perimeter, landscape shape index (LSI), and the proportions of water bodies and green space (Table 4). Analysis of these metrics revealed significant inter-park variations in scale, spatial morphology, and landscape composition.

Table 4. The data of internal landscape characteristics in parks.

Serial Number	Park Name	Area (m^2)	Circumference (m)	LSI	Proportion of Water Body	Proportion of Green Space
1	Fengshan Park	16,624.7000	657.6021	1.4400	0.1894	0.6028
2	CBD Park	28,354.8528	1798.8684	3.0174	0.0000	0.5523
3	Caozhuang Park	24,682.9006	680.0959	1.2206	0.1882	0.5656
4	Shenhua Park	14,524.3951	481.7073	1.1275	0.0000	0.7935
5	Chengbei Sports Park	415,861.5133	3445.7906	1.5079	0.1082	0.5377
6	Xiwen Park	10,082.3765	403.0615	1.1324	0.0000	0.5993
7	Canal heaven and earth park	44,627.1545	1118.8478	1.4940	0.0516	0.6621
8	Zheyao Park	52,733.2407	988.5577	1.2137	0.1700	0.6080
9	Taoyuan Central Park	31,680.7006	860.7569	1.3645	0.0097	0.6818
10	Hushan Park	115,748.3021	1441.2593	1.1947	0.3225	0.5469
11	Tianziling Ecological Park	184,911.3170	2457.5131	1.6111	0.0030	0.6476
12	Higher Education Park	29,993.0922	845.7932	1.3771	0.0711	0.6629
13	Bachelor's Park	79,652.3877	1277.6287	1.2773	0.0950	0.6633
14	Prince Bay Park	422,075.7609	2516.5824	1.0930	0.0479	0.8799
15	Jiangyangfan Ecological Park	107,534.8409	2129.0363	1.8313	0.0835	0.7941
16	Chengxi Leisure Park	253,679.6410	2281.8088	1.2776	0.0934	0.7239
17	Mita Temple Park	10,379.4862	449.2935	1.2451	0.0000	0.4206
18	Jialvyuan Park	25,518.9378	672.8126	1.1883	0.1168	0.6636

The study parks exhibited considerable variation in site area, reflecting the diversity of the research sample. Prince Bay Park and Chengbei Sports Park were the largest, with areas of 422,275.76 m^2 and 415,861.51 m^2, respectively. In contrast, Xiwen Park and Mituo Temple Park were notably smaller, each covering approximately 10,000 m^2. A positive correlation was observed between park perimeter and area. Chengbei Sports Park had the longest perimeter (3445.79 m), whereas Xiwen Park had the shortest (403.06 m). The Landscape Shape Index (LSI), which quantifies shape complexity and boundary irregularity, ranged from 1.09 to 3.02 across the parks. CBD Park exhibited the highest LSI value (3.02), significantly exceeding those of other parks, indicating the most tortuous boundary morphology and complex spatial geometry. Conversely, Prince Bay Park (LSI = 1.09) and Shenhua Park (LSI = 1.13) had values close to 1, suggesting relatively regular, smooth boundaries and simple shapes. Regarding landscape composition, green space constituted the dominant land cover in most parks. The green space ratio exceeded 40% in all samples, with a high mean coverage. Notably, Prince Bay Park had both the largest area and the highest green space ratio (87.99%), followed by Jiangyangfan Ecological Park (approximately 18.9%). In contrast, no substantial water bodies were present in CBD Park, Shenhua Park, Xiwen Park, or Mituo Temple Park (water proportion: 0%), a characteristic potentially related to their urban settings and functions. In summary, the 18 parks provided strong gradient variation in scale, morphological complexity, and habitat composition, thereby offering a robust dataset for subsequent analysis of the relationship between internal park landscape features and the cooling effect.

In summary, the 18 parks provide a strong gradient of variation in their internal characteristics. The park areas ranged from 1.01 ha to 42.21 ha, with a mean of 11.28

https://doi.org/10.3390/buildings16030630

ha. The proportion of green space was consistently high across all parks (Mean = 64.31%, Min = 42.06%), whereas the proportion of water bodies showed greater variability (Mean = 9.76%, ranging from 0% to 32.25%). This wide range and diversity in scale, morphology, and composition offered a robust dataset.

3.3. Results of External Landscape Features in Parks

Regarding the external buffer zone landscape characteristics of the 18 parks, road density and building density were selected to quantify the intensity of surrounding urban development, while the proportion of green space and the proportion of water bodies were selected to evaluate the condition of the external ecological matrix (Table 5).

Table 5. The data of park external environment.

Serial Number	Park Name	Road Density	Building Density	Green Space Ratio	Water Body Proportion
1	Fengshan Park	0.0483	0.1690	0.1812	0.0263
2	CBD Park	0.0304	0.0484	0.1897	0.4594
3	Caozhuang Park	0.0527	0.1187	0.2637	0.0336
4	Shenhua Park	0.0412	0.1187	0.2993	0.0194
5	Chengbei Sports Park	0.0607	0.1527	0.1830	0.1070
6	Xiwen Park	0.0732	0.2011	0.2120	0.2124
7	Canal heaven and earth park	0.0377	0.1531	0.2268	0.1759
8	Zheyao Park	0.0355	0.0788	0.1842	0.1151
9	Taoyuan Central Park	0.0246	0.0832	0.2500	0.0707
10	Hushan Park	0.0307	0.0804	0.4842	0.0544
11	Tianziling Ecological Park	0.0110	0.0577	0.1022	0.0070
12	Higher Education Park	0.0418	0.1853	0.2782	0.0313
13	Bachelor's Park	0.0296	0.1045	0.2544	0.3484
14	Prince Bay Park	0.0199	0.0453	0.7484	0.1698
15	Jiangyangfan Ecological Park	0.0155	0.0139	0.7644	0.0448
16	Chengxi Leisure Park	0.0394	0.1537	0.2463	0.0725
17	Mita Temple Park	0.0465	0.2269	0.1683	0.0000
18	Jialvyuan Park	0.0603	0.1962	0.2010	0.0624

Statistical analysis revealed significant spatial heterogeneity in the external environments of the studied parks. Concerning artificial construction elements, pronounced disparities were observed in surrounding road density and building density among parks, reflecting the diversity of their urban contexts. Road density served as an indicator not only of traffic accessibility but also of the degree of landscape fragmentation by impervious surfaces. The data indicated that the road densities around Xiwen Park, Chengbei Sports Park, and Jialvyuan Park all exceeded 0.06 km/km^2, with the highest value reaching 0.073 km/km^2, suggesting their locations within densely networked urban built-up areas. In contrast, Tianziling Ecological Park and Jiangyangfan Ecological Park exhibited markedly lower road densities (approximately 0.01–0.015 km/km^2), indicative of minimal anthropogenic disturbance. A comparable pattern was observed for building density. The vicinity of Mituo Temple Park exhibited the highest building density (22.69%), followed by Xiwen Park (20.11%) and Jialvyuan Park (19.62%). This spatial pattern confirms that these parks are embedded within high-density building clusters and represent typical community parks or urban core parks. Conversely, the building densities around Jiangyangfan Ecological Park and Prince Bay Park were merely 1.39% and 4.53%, respectively, denoting a more open spatial configuration in their immediate surroundings. External green spaces and water bodies constitute the ecological matrix facilitating material and energy exchange between the parks and their environs.

https://doi.org/10.3390/buildings16030630

The proportion of external green space varied considerably across the sampled parks. Jiangyangfan Ecological Park and Prince Bay Park exhibited the highest proportions, reaching 76.44% and 74.84%, respectively. These high values suggest strong ecological connectivity with adjacent scenic areas or natural hills. Conversely, Tianziling Ecological Park had the lowest external green space proportion (10.22%), while most other parks ranged between 18% and 30%. The proportion of external water bodies demonstrated even greater variability, largely determined by proximity to major urban water systems. CBD Park and Xueshi Park showed significantly higher external water body proportions (45.94% and 34.84%, respectively) than other samples, reflecting distinct waterfront characteristics. In contrast, Mituo Temple Park had no substantial water body in its vicinity (0%), and both Shenhua Park and Tianziling Ecological Park exhibited minimal external water body proportions (<2%). Overall, the external environments of the sampled parks covered a comprehensive spectrum from high-density built-up areas (e.g., Mituo Temple Park, Xiwen Park) to high-naturalness scenic zones (e.g., Jiangyangfan Ecological Park, Prince Bay Park). This environmental gradient provided an ideal basis for examining how external landscape characteristics serve as driving mechanisms influencing the internal ecological performance of parks.

3.4. Results of Factors Influencing the Cooling Effect of Parks

The cooling effect of urban parks was found to be influenced by multiple factors, with significant positive or negative correlations identified between specific park characteristics and the quantified cooling indicators (Table 6).

Table 6. Pearson correlation coefficients of the influenced factors and the park cooling indexes.

Indicator Category	Influencing Factors	Park Cooling Area (PCA)	Park Cooling Efficiency (PCE)	Park Cooling Intensity (PCI)	Park Cooling Gradient (PCG)
Internal park landscape	Park—Shape—area	0.298	−0.478 *	−0.274	−0.313
	Park—Shape—circumference	0.362	−0.517 *	−0.301	−0.343
	Park—Complex in shape	0.233	0.006	0.096	0.057
	Park—water body—proportion	−0.158	−0.341	−0.230	−0.215
	Park—green space—proportion	0.383	0.107	−0.103	−0.172
External park landscape	Buffer zone—Road—density	−0.167	0.271	0.344	0.400
	Buffer zone—Building—density	−0.517 *	0.073	0.046	0.131
	Buffer zone—Green space—proportion	0.458	−0.111	−0.077	−0.165
	Buffer zone—Water body—proportion	0.044	−0.011	0.053	−0.007

Note: * Significant at the 0.05 level (two-tailed).

The internal landscape characteristics of urban parks were found to exert complex influences on their cooling effects. First, while larger park area and perimeter significantly expanded the Park Cooling Area (PCA), they were associated with reduced Park Cooling Efficiency (PCE) and Park Cooling Intensity (PCI) per unit area, as well as a decreased Park Cooling Gradient (PCG). This indicates that unlimited expansion of park size is not optimal and suggests the existence of a threshold for maximizing cooling benefits [51]. Second, parks with more complex shapes exhibited higher PCE values but lower PCI and PCG values, implying that fragmented designs may enhance cooling efficiency per unit area at the expense of overall cooling intensity and gradient. Third, a higher proportion of green space within parks showed positive correlations with PCA and PCE but negative correlations with PCI and PCG. This suggests that increased vegetation coverage, while extending the cooling range and improving efficiency, may attenuate the peak cooling intensity. Finally, the proportion of water bodies within parks showed negative correlations with all cooling indicators. The mechanism underlying this apparent cooling suppression requires further investigation. Therefore, in park planning and design, it is essential to

https://doi.org/10.3390/buildings16030630

rationally determine park size, optimize vegetation configuration, and carefully consider water body design to balance cooling benefits with resource utilization efficiency.

The external landscape characteristics of parks also critically influenced their cooling effect. Specifically, a higher proportion of impervious surfaces (e.g., roads, buildings) within the 300 m buffer was associated with a greater temperature difference between the park internal and exterior, thus enhancing PCE, PCI, and PCG. However, excessively high building density impeded cold air diffusion, resulting in reduced PCA. In contrast, external green spaces and water bodies demonstrated a dual nature. First, they could generate a cumulative cooling effect when integrated with the park, significantly extending the cooling range (which was positively correlated with PCA). This synergy offers a potential optimization strategy for land-constrained cities. Second, by lowering the ambient temperature, they reduced the temperature difference between the park and its surroundings, thereby diminishing the park's relative cooling efficiency and intensity, as well as residents' perception of the cooling gradient (negatively correlated with PCE, PCI, and PCG) [52]. These findings indicate that the cooling performance of parks does not occur in isolation but emerges from close interaction with the surrounding environment. Therefore, to maximize cooling effectiveness, urban planning must shift from the conventional paradigm of creating large, isolated "nodes" with smooth boundaries towards a new approach that prioritizes morphologically complex, irregular green spaces that actively integrate with the wider urban matrix.

4. Discussion

4.1. Threshold of Cooling Efficiency in Urban Parks

To determine the Threshold Value of Efficiency (TVoE)—a term we define as the point of diminishing returns for park scale—this study employed logarithmic curves to fit the relationships between park area and park perimeter (Figure 5). The slope of the fitted curve indicated that the efficiency threshold for park area was 29.91 hectares. Specifically, when park area exceeded 29.91 hectares, the increase in Park Cooling Area (PCA) was less than the increase in park area. The efficiency threshold for park perimeter was 69.00 km. The trend of the fitted curve between PCA and perimeter suggested that when park size surpasses a certain range, further expansion in area is not associated with a significant increase in the cooling area. This indicates that, from the perspective of PCA, very large parks may be less cost-effective than smaller parks. In this study, the fitted curves between urban park cooling extent and park area/perimeter exhibited relatively low confidence levels. Therefore, while this 29.91-hectare threshold provides a valuable reference, it should be interpreted cautiously as an indicative benchmark rather than a definitive limit, reflecting the general trend of cooling benefits amidst the observed statistical variations. On one hand, this might be influenced by the quantity and attributes of the research samples; on the other hand, it might be because factors such as park shape complexity (e.g., Landscape Shape Index, LSI) and the spatial distribution of internal vegetation and water bodies appear to be more closely linked to the variation in cooling effect. Future research should conduct further quantitative analysis on the relationship between urban park cooling area and park area/perimeter to obtain more precise and compelling data, exploring the planning and layout principles for optimizing park cooling effects. This finding has transformative implications for urban park design, suggesting the need for a paradigm shift away from merely pursuing increases in area or perimeter. To maximize cooling cost-effectiveness, planning must prioritize morphological complexity over sheer size. This involves creating spatial models of a "compact core + edge infiltration" and designing parks with high perimeter-to-area ratios and elongated, penetrating configurations that increase the interface with the urban fabric for enhanced thermal exchange. Furthermore, as discussed in

https://doi.org/10.3390/buildings16030630

our strategies, these parks should be interconnected via linear green infrastructure, such as green streets and tree-lined paths, to extend their cooling services deep into the city. These principles provide a new, evidence-based pathway for mitigating the urban heat island effect and enhancing urban livability.

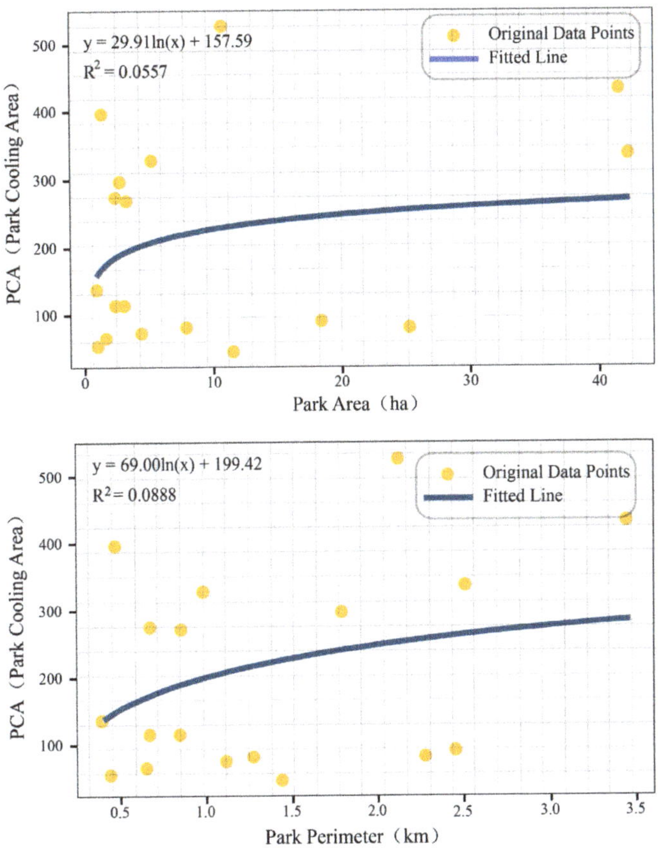

Figure 5. Relationship between the PCA and park areas well as park perimeter.

4.2. *Strategies for Optimizing Park Cooling Effects*

For all cities aiming to mitigate the urban heat island effect, our findings provide three clear directives for optimizing park cooling services: (1) regulating internal artificial constructions, (2) enhancing the ecological matrix, and (3) establishing a network of radiating green infrastructure. This approach aims to jointly mitigate the urban heat island (UHI) effect through spatial morphological adjustments and biological community structural improvements.

From the perspective of built environment management (Directive 1), it is necessary to address park boundary morphology and spatial geometric characteristics, the construction of buffers against high-density built-up areas, and the enhancement of blue-green infrastructure connectivity.

Regarding park boundary morphology and spatial geometric characteristics, the boundary fragmentation and high LSI values observed in some parks (e.g., CBD Park, LSI > 3.0) in Table 4 suggest that edge effects should be carefully considered in planning. Although complex boundaries facilitate the infiltration of cool air into the surroundings,

https://doi.org/10.3390/buildings16030630

they also intensify the intrusion of external heat flow [53]. Therefore, in optimizing the built environment, the integrity and compactness of the park's core area should be maintained. By constructing a spatial model of "compact core + edge infiltration," the stability of the internal cool island may be better supported while utilizing ventilation corridors to deliver cool air to surrounding high-density building areas (areas with building density > 20% in Table 5).

Regarding the construction of buffers against high-density built-up areas, some parks (e.g., Xiwen Park, Jialvyuan Park) were found to be surrounded by dense road networks (road density > 0.06) and building clusters, facing intense external thermal radiation stress. A multi-layered, three-dimensional protection system should be established at the park edges. This system would utilize vertical greening, sound-insulating and heat-insulating walls, or micro-topography treatments to mitigate heat conduction from the external hardscape environment [54,55]. Simultaneously, the construction intensity of internal artificial facilities should be controlled, the proportion of non-ecological hard paving should be strictly limited, and the application of permeable concrete and permeable bricks should be promoted to enhance the evaporative cooling potential of the surface.

Regarding the enhancement of blue-green infrastructure connectivity, considering the differences in water body and green space ratios shown in Table 5, built environment interventions should aim to mitigate the park isolation effect. For parks with high surrounding construction intensity and a lack of external water body support (e.g., Mituo Temple Park), linear landscapes such as green streets and tree-lined pedestrian paths should be constructed to physically connect them with city-scale wind corridors and the surrounding blue-green network, forming an integrated urban ventilation and cooling network.

From the perspective of optimizing ecological substrates (Directive 2), it is essential to integrate scientific principles, spatial planning, and social equity. Firstly, priority should be given to the use of native tree species (e.g., *Cinnamomum camphora*, *Ginkgo biloba*) combined with multi-layered configurations of trees, shrubs, and grasses. Spatial arrangements should be rationally designed based on functional zoning and pedestrian flow density; for instance, increasing tall canopy trees in high-activity areas to provide sufficient shading. Importantly, plant configuration must reflect social equity. In communities with pronounced heat island effects and low-income populations, high-transpiration and high-shading plants (e.g., *Platanus* spp., *Firmiana simplex*) should be prioritized, while small green spaces and water bodies can be incorporated to extend the coverage of cooling services. In summary, comprehensive approaches—such as strategic water layout, vertical greening, bamboo–grass combinations, and ecological corridor design—can significantly enhance the extent and quality of park cooling effects. These measures not only effectively mitigate heat but also balance ecological functions with landscape value, providing residents with a more comfortable and healthy urban environment, thereby contributing to improved urban livability and climate resilience.

Finally, regarding the establishment of a radiating green network (Directive 3), our findings highlight the necessity of extending cooling services beyond park boundaries through green-treed streets and tree-lined paths that radiate out from the parks. These linear green infrastructures act as thermal conduits, delivering cool air from the park core into the surrounding dense urban fabric. By prioritizing mature tree canopies and protected bike lanes along these corridors, cities can effectively cool areas that lack the space for even small pocket parks, thereby enhancing the overall thermal comfort and climate resilience of the entire city.

https://doi.org/10.3390/buildings16030630

4.3. Research Deficiencies and Prospects

Focusing on the park cooling effect, this study quantified the influencing factors of the cooling effect, thereby providing a scientific basis for enhancing the cooling effect of urban parks and for their rational planning. However, the current research still has certain shortcomings and limitations. First, the land surface temperature (LST) data acquired from the Landsat 8 OLI_TIRS satellite have limited spatial resolution, resulting in relatively low accuracy [56,57]. These resolution limitations may have a significant impact on the research findings; future studies should prioritize improving the spatial resolution of LST data. Furthermore, research on the diurnal variation in the park cooling effect is constrained by the detection and imaging time of satellite imagery, an aspect that could also be addressed and further optimized in future research. Additionally, it is important to acknowledge that our use of LST serves as a proxy for air temperature, and the 2D landscape metrics simplify the city's complex 3D morphology. Our correlation-based approach is also exploratory and does not establish causality. Therefore, the results presented throughout this discussion should be interpreted as observed associations that warrant further mechanistic investigation. Finally, future studies should also consider factors such as seasonality, regional characteristics, and vegetation, conducting comparative or more refined investigations to advance research on the park cooling effect. This would contribute to mitigating the ecological impacts of rapid urbanization and global climate change, promoting the equitable distribution of public social resources, and enhancing residents' physical and mental well-being and environmental livability.

5. Conclusions

This study employed Pearson correlation analysis to quantify the relationships between the cooling effect indicators of 18 urban parks in Hangzhou and their internal and external landscape characteristics. The aim was to explore the factors influencing park cooling effects, thereby providing a scientific basis for planning and design strategies to enhance urban ecological service resilience. The results revealed that all 18 parks exhibited significant cooling effects, with the cooling radiation distance extending several times beyond the park area. Furthermore, correlations between nine indicators—encompassing internal park landscape structure (park area, perimeter, green space ratio, water body ratio, shape complexity, and vegetation growth status) and the surrounding environment (building density, road network density, and green space ratio)—and the cooling effects were quantified. The analysis demonstrated that both internal park characteristics and external environmental factors significantly influenced the cooling effect. These findings provide a scientific basis for optimizing the cooling performance of urban parks. It is suggested that, within limited urban spaces, scientifically informed park planning and design can provide more equitable cooling services. This approach would help mitigate the threats posed by rapid urbanization and global climate change to residents' well-being and livelihoods, thereby contributing to more livable urban environments.

Specifically, to "scientifically inform park planning", our findings provide two clear directives for cities like Hangzhou. First, to enhance the performance of existing parks, planners must prioritize morphological complexity over sheer size, designing parks with irregular boundaries and optimizing internal vegetation to boost cooling efficiency. Second, to expand cooling services, the focus should be on developing a network of strategically placed, smaller-to-medium-sized parks, which our results suggest are more cost-effective, rather than concentrating resources on a few mega-parks. Adopting this dual strategy of optimizing quality and expanding quantity offers a tangible pathway for any city to better mitigate urban heat.

https://doi.org/10.3390/buildings16030630

Author Contributions: Methodology, T.M., M.Y. and W.N.; software, S.Z. and X.J.; validation, M.Y.; formal analysis, W.N.; investigation, S.Z.; resources, M.Y. and X.J.; data curation, S.Z.; writing—original draft preparation, T.M.; writing—review and editing, T.M.; visualization, X.J.; supervision, M.Y.; project administration, W.N. All authors have read and agreed to the published version of the manuscript.

Funding: This research received no external funding.

Data Availability Statement: The data that has been used is confidential.

Conflicts of Interest: The authors declare that they have no known competing financial interests or personal relationships that could have appeared to influence the work reported in this paper.

References

1. Acuto, M.; Parnell, S.; Seto, K.C. Building a global urban science. *Nat. Sustain.* **2018**, *1*, 2–4. [CrossRef]
2. Aram, F.; García, E.H.; Solgi, E.; Mansournia, S. Urban green space cooling effect in cities. *Heliyon* **2019**, *5*, e01339. [CrossRef]
3. Arias, P.; Bellouin, N.; Coppola, E.; Jones, R.; Krinner, G.; Marotzke, J.; Naik, V.; Palmer, M.; Plattner, G.-K.; Rogelj, J.; et al. Climate Change 2021: The Physical Science Basis. In *Contribution of Working Group I to the Sixth Assessment Report of the Intergovernmental Panel on Climate Change*; Technical Summary; Cambridge University Press: Cambridge, UK, 2021.
4. Chen, Y.; Yue, W.; La Rosa, D. Which communities have better accessibility to green space? An investigation into environmental inequality using big data. *Landsc. Urban Plan.* **2020**, *204*, 103919. [CrossRef]
5. Dong, J.; Peng, J.; He, X.; Corcoran, J.; Qiu, S.; Wang, X. Heatwave-induced human health risk assessment in megacities based on heat stress-social vulnerability-human exposure framework. *Landsc. Urban Plan.* **2020**, *203*, 103907. [CrossRef]
6. Du, C.; Jia, W.; Chen, M.; Yan, L.; Wang, K. How can urban parks be planned to maximize cooling effect in hot extremes? Linking maximum and accumulative perspectives. *J. Environ. Manag.* **2022**, *317*, 115346. [CrossRef]
7. Du, H.; Cai, W.; Xu, Y.; Wang, Z.; Wang, Y.; Cai, Y. Quantifying the cool island effects of urban green spaces using remote sensing Data. *Urban For. Urban Green.* **2017**, *27*, 24–31. [CrossRef]
8. Du, H.; Song, X.; Jiang, H.; Kan, Z.; Wang, Z.; Cai, Y. Research on the cooling island effects of water body: A case study of Shanghai, China. *Ecol. Indic.* **2016**, *67*, 31–38. [CrossRef]
9. Dymond, J.R.; Shepherd, J.D.; Law, R.; Martin, B.; Schindler, J.; Belliss, S. A cost-effective method for mapping land cover at national scale. *Sci. Remote Sens.* **2026**, *13*, 100376. [CrossRef]
10. Fang, W.; Cao, J.; Biswas, A.; Feng, Q.; Wang, Y. Impacts of coordinated development policies on urban heat islands in the Beijing-Tianjin-Hebei urban agglomeration, China. *Sustain. Cities Soc.* **2024**, *112*, 105614. [CrossRef]
11. Gao, J.; Zhang, L.; Meng, Q.; Hu, X.; Livesley, S.J. Multi-perspective evaluation framework of three-dimensional cooling and energy saving potential of urban parks based on numerical simulation. *Sustain. Cities Soc.* **2025**, *119*, 106109. [CrossRef]
12. Gu, Z.; Liu, Y.; Yuan, L.; Tan, M. A Review on the Methodology of Urban Park Cool Island Impact Mechanism Research. *Chin. Landsc. Archit.* **2016**, *32*, 113–115.
13. Guo, A.; Yue, W.; Yang, J.; Li, M.; Zhang, Z.; Xie, P.; Zhang, M.; Lu, Y.; He, T. Quantifying the cooling effect and benefits of urban parks: A case study of Hangzhou, China. *Sustain. Cities Soc.* **2024**, *113*, 105706. [CrossRef]
14. Hao, N.; Li, X.; Han, D.; Nie, W. Quantifying the Impact of Street Greening during Full-Leaf Seasons on Emotional Perception: Guidelines for Resident Well-Being. *Forests* **2024**, *15*, 119. [CrossRef]
15. Hu, N.; Wang, G.; Ma, Z.; Ren, Z.; Zhao, M.; Meng, J. The cooling effects of urban waterbodies and their driving forces in China. *Ecol. Indic.* **2023**, *156*, 111200. [CrossRef]
16. Imran, H.; Kala, J.; Ng, A.; Muthukumaran, S. Effectiveness of green and cool roofs in mitigating urban heat island effects during a heatwave event in the city of Melbourne in southeast Australia. *J. Clean. Prod.* **2018**, *197*, 393–405. [CrossRef]
17. Kabisch, N.; Frantzeskaki, N.; Pauleit, S.; Naumann, S.; Davis, M.; Artmann, M.; Haase, D.; Knapp, S.; Korn, H.; Stadler, J.; et al. Nature-based solutions to climate change mitigation and adaptation in urban areas: Perspectives on indicators, knowledge gaps, barriers, and opportunities for action. *Ecol. Soc.* **2016**, *21*, 39. [CrossRef]
18. Karlessi, T.; Santamouris, M.; Synnefa, A.; Assimakopoulos, D.; Didaskalopoulos, P.; Apostolakis, K. Development and testing of PCM doped cool colored coatings to mitigate urban heat island and cool buildings. *Build. Environ.* **2011**, *46*, 570–576. [CrossRef]
19. Kim, K.; Yi, C.; Lee, S. Impact of urban characteristics on cooling energy consumption before and after construction of an urban park: The case of Gyeongui line forest in Seoul. *Energy Build.* **2019**, *191*, 42–51. [CrossRef]
20. Lin, W.; Yu, T.; Chang, X.; Wu, W.; Zhang, Y. Calculating cooling extents of green parks using remote sensing: Method and test. *Landsc. Urban Plan.* **2015**, *134*, 66–75. [CrossRef]
21. Liu, H.; Huang, B.; Cheng, X.; Yin, M.; Shang, C.; Luo, Y.; He, B.-J. Sensing-based park cooling performance observation and assessment: A review. *Build. Environ.* **2023**, *245*, 110915. [CrossRef]

https://doi.org/10.3390/buildings16030630

22. Liu, R.; Zhang, X.; Wang, W.; Wang, Y.; Liu, H.; Ma, M.; Tang, G. Global-scale ERA5 product precipitation and temperature evaluation. *Ecol. Indic.* **2024**, *166*, 112481. [CrossRef]
23. Liu, Z.; Fu, L.; Wu, C.; Zhang, Z.; Zhang, Z.; Lin, X.; Li, X.; Hu, Y.; Ge, H. Spatialized importance of key factors affecting park cooling intensity based on the park scale. *Sustain. Cities Soc.* **2023**, *99*, 104952. [CrossRef]
24. Meng, Q.; Gao, J.; Zhang, L.; Hu, X.; Qian, J.; Jancsó, T. Coupled cooling effects between urban parks and surrounding building morphologies based on the microclimate evaluation framework integrating remote sensing data. *Sustain. Cities Soc.* **2024**, *102*, 105235. [CrossRef]
25. Mitraka, Z.; Chrysoulakis, N.; Kamarianakis, Y.; Partsinevelos, P.; Tsouchlaraki, A. Improving the estimation of urban surface emissivity based on sub-pixel classification of high resolution satellite imagery. *Remote Sens. Environ.* **2012**, *117*, 125–134. [CrossRef]
26. Naserikia, M.; Hart, M.A.; Nazarian, N.; Bechtel, B.; Lipson, M.; Nice, K.A. Land surface and air temperature dynamics: The role of urban form and seasonality. *Sci. Total Environ.* **2023**, *905*, 167306. [CrossRef]
27. United Nations, Department of Economic and Social Affairs. *World Urbanization Prospects: The 2018 Revision*; United Nations: New York, NY, USA, 2019; pp. 101–103.
28. Niclòs, R.; Puchades, J.; Coll, C.; Barberà, M.J.; Pérez-Planells, L.; Valiente, J.A.; Sánchez, J.M. Evaluation of Landsat-8 TIRS data recalibrations and land surface temperature split-window algorithms over a homogeneous crop area with different phenological land covers. *ISPRS J. Photogramm. Remote Sens.* **2021**, *174*, 237–253. [CrossRef]
29. Nie, W.; Yang, F.; Xu, B.; Bao, Z.; Shi, Y.; Liu, B.; Wu, R.; Lin, W. Spatiotemporal Evolution of Landscape Patterns and Their Driving Forces Under Optimal Granularity and the Extent at the County and the Environmental Functional Regional Scales. *Front. Ecol. Evol.* **2022**, *10*, 954232. [CrossRef]
30. Peng, J.; Dan, Y.; Qiao, R.; Liu, Y.; Dong, J.; Wu, J. How to quantify the cooling effect of urban parks? Linking maximum and accumulation perspectives. *Remote Sens. Environ.* **2021**, *252*, 112135. [CrossRef]
31. Peng, S.; Piao, S.; Ciais, P.; Friedlingstein, P.; Ottle, C.; Bréon, F.-M.; Nan, H.; Zhou, L.; Myneni, R.B. Surface urban heat island across 419 global big cities. *Environ. Sci. Technol.* **2012**, *46*, 696–703. [CrossRef] [PubMed]
32. Phuyal, P.; Kramer, I.M.; Kadel, I.; Wouters, E.; Magdeburg, A.; Groneberg, D.A.; Kuch, U.; Ahrens, B.; Dhimal, M.L.; Dhimal, M.; et al. On people's perceptions of climate change and its impacts in a hotspot of global warming. *PLoS ONE* **2025**, *20*, e0317786. [CrossRef] [PubMed]
33. Qiu, K.; Jia, B. The roles of landscape both inside the park and the surroundings in park cooling effect. *Sustain. Cities Soc.* **2020**, *52*, 101864. [CrossRef]
34. Ramanathan, V.; Head, P.; Eltahir, E.; Daigger, G.T.; Smith, C.E.; Yokohari, M.; Childs, P.; Ma, J.; Yu, K. Climate Design: Holistic Solution for Climate Resilience. *Landsc. Arch. Front.* **2025**, *13*, 87–97.
35. Ren, C.; Yang, R.; Cheng, C.; Xing, P.; Fang, X.; Zhang, S.; Wang, H.; Shi, Y.; Zhang, X.; Kwok, Y.T.; et al. Creating breathing cities by adopting urban ventilation assessment and wind corridor plan—The implementation in Chinese cities. *J. Wind Eng. Ind. Aerodyn.* **2018**, *182*, 170–188. [CrossRef]
36. Shi, M.; Chen, M.; Jia, W.; Du, C.; Wang, Y. Cooling effect and cooling accessibility of urban parks during hot summers in China's largest sustainability experiment. *Sustain. Cities Soc.* **2023**, *93*, 104519. [CrossRef]
37. Su, W.; Chang, Q. Nature-based Solutions for Urban Heat Mitigation and Implementation Path Thereof: A Case Study of Beijing. *Landsc. Archit.* **2022**, *29*, 26–32.
38. Sun, F.; Xiang, J.; Tao, Y.; Tong, C.; Che, Y. Mapping the social values for ecosystem services in urban green spaces: Integrating a visitor-employed photography method into SolVES. *Urban For. Urban Green.* **2019**, *38*, 105–113. [CrossRef]
39. Sun, R.; Chen, L. How can urban water bodies be designed for climate adaptation? *Landsc. Urban Plan.* **2012**, *105*, 27–33. [CrossRef]
40. Tang, B.; Lü, Y.; Wang, H. Identifying conservation priority areas of ecosystem services by simulating preference scenarios. *Ecol. Front.* **2025**, *45*, 1613–1624. [CrossRef]
41. Tian, H.; Qin, Y.; Li, Z.; Han, C.; Ding, Q.; Li, Q.; Ren, Q.; Dai, W.; Qin, H.; Chen, H.; et al. Changes of ecosystem services in Beijing and its multi-scale response to urbanization. *Acta Ecol. Sin.* **2025**, *45*, 2209–2224.
42. Tian, P.; Li, J.; Cao, L.; Pu, R.; Wang, Z.; Zhang, H.; Chen, H.; Gong, H. Assessing spatiotemporal characteristics of urban heat islands from the perspective of an urban expansion and green infrastructure. *Sustain. Cities Soc.* **2021**, *74*, 103208. [CrossRef]
43. Tong, Z.; Yang, J.; Liu, Y.; Zhang, Z.; Liu, S.; Lu, Y.; Pang, B.; An, R. Cooling and optimizing urban heat island based on a thermal knowledge-informed multi-type ant colony model. *Remote Sens. Environ.* **2024**, *306*, 114138. [CrossRef]
44. Wolch, J.R.; Byrne, J.; Newell, J.P. Urban green space, public health, and environmental justice: The challenge of making cities 'just green enough'. *Landsc. Urban Plan.* **2014**, *125*, 234–244. [CrossRef]
45. Xiao, Y.; Piao, Y.; Wei, W.; Pan, C.; Lee, D.; Zhao, B. A comprehensive framework of cooling effect-accessibility-urban development to assessing and planning park cooling services. *Sustain. Cities Soc.* **2023**, *98*, 104817. [CrossRef]

 https://doi.org/10.3390/buildings16030630

46. Huang, X.; Wang, X.; Li, J.; Zhang, M.; Chen, S.; Xu, B.; Nie, W. Multi-Scale Applicability Analysis of Three Ecological Network Construction Methods in Resilience Assessment. *Land Degrad. Dev.* **2025**, *36*, 1594–1613. [CrossRef]
47. Xu, H.; Shi, T.; Wang, M.; Fang, C.; Lin, Z. Predicting effect of forthcoming population growth–induced impervious surface increase on regional thermal environment: Xiong'an New Area, North China. *Build. Environ.* **2018**, *136*, 98–106. [CrossRef]
48. Xu, T.; Zhang, L.; Xie, H.Q.; Xu, L. The multifaceted effects of high-temperature exposure on human health in a changing climate. *Ecol. Front.* **2025**, *45*, 1874–1876. [CrossRef]
49. Yan, M.; Chen, L.; Leng, S.; Sun, R. Effects of local background climate on urban vegetation cooling and humidification: Variations and thresholds. *Urban For. Urban Green.* **2023**, *80*, 127840. [CrossRef]
50. Yang, M.; Nie, W.; Wu, R.; Yan, H.; Tian, S.; Wang, K.; Shi, L.; Cheng, X.; Ji, T.; Bao, Z. Towards more equitable cooling services of urban parks: Linking cooling effect, accessibility and attractiveness. *J. Environ. Manag.* **2024**, *370*, 122475. [CrossRef] [PubMed]
51. Yao, R.; Wang, L.; Huang, X.; Niu, Z.; Liu, F.; Wang, Q. Temporal trends of surface urban heat islands and associated determinants in major Chinese cities. *Sci. Total. Environ.* **2017**, *609*, 742–754. [CrossRef]
52. Yu, K. Climate Design for One Planet. *Landsc. Arch. Front.* **2024**, *12*, 4–7. [CrossRef]
53. Yu, Z.; Guo, X.; Jørgensen, G.; Vejre, H. How can urban green spaces be planned for climate adaptation in subtropical cities? *Ecol. Indic.* **2017**, *82*, 152–162. [CrossRef]
54. Yue, X.; Lin, J.; Yang, Y. Mitigation Role of Urban Green Space in Reducing Heat Island Effect—A Case Study of Central Urban Area of Baoding City. *Landsc. Archit.* **2018**, *25*, 66–70.
55. Zhang, N.; Zhen, W.; Shi, D.; Zhong, C.; Li, Y. Quantification and mapping of the cooling effect of urban parks on the temperate monsoon climate zone. *Sustain. Cities Soc.* **2024**, *101*, 105111. [CrossRef]
56. Zhang, Q.; Zhou, D.; Xu, D.; Rogora, A. Correlation between cooling effect of green space and surrounding urban spatial form: Evidence from 36 urban green spaces. *Build. Environ.* **2022**, *222*, 109375. [CrossRef]
57. Zhu, W.; Sun, J.; Yang, C.; Liu, M.; Xu, X.; Ji, C. How to Measure the Urban Park Cooling Island? A Perspective of Absolute and Relative Indicators Using Remote Sensing and Buffer Analysis. *Remote Sens.* **2021**, *13*, 3154. [CrossRef]

https://doi.org/10.3390/buildings16030630

MDPI AG
Grosspeteranlage 5
4052 Basel
Switzerland
Tel.: +41 61 683 77 34

Buildings Editorial Office
E-mail: buildings@mdpi.com
www.mdpi.com/journal/buildings

www.ingramcontent.com/pod-product-compliance
Lightning Source LLC
Chambersburg PA
CBHW061435210926
51850CB00008B/1521

* 9 7 8 3 7 2 5 8 7 0 8 2 0 *